"*The Church* is a gift to students, teachers, parishioners, pastors, and anyone else hoping to know more about how the Christian community has understood itself over the centuries. Cwiekowski wears his learning lightly, drawing on the very best of contemporary scholarship to tell an engaging story of both continuity and change in the church. All the qualities that marked his earlier bestseller *The Beginnings of the Church*—balance, clarity, substantive content, crisp prose—are on full display in this new volume, extending the lessons of history from the age of the apostles to the era of Pope Francis."

—Edward P. Hahnenberg
Author of *Theology for Ministry: An Introduction for Lay Ministers*

"The book *The Church: Theology in History* is an invaluable resource to help us reconnect with the historical dimension of the Church. Offering a unified narrative of the theological tradition as Church history is crucial, particularly today in an age of dissonant, ahistorical understandings of Christianity's past."

—Massimo Faggioli
Professor of Historical Theology
Villanova University

"Clear, calm, historically sensitive, and well-structured, Fr. Cwiekowski's book will be helpful for anyone—college students, candidates for ecclesial ministries, scholars, and general readers—interested in understanding better the Church in its historical journey and in its contemporary situation."

—Christopher J. Ruddy
Associate Professor of Historical and Systematic Theology
The Catholic University of America

Frederick J. Cwiekowski, PSS

The Church

Theology in History

**LITURGICAL PRESS
ACADEMIC**

Collegeville, Minnesota
www.litpress.org

Cover design by Monica Bokinskie. *Dream of Innocent III* by Giotto di Bondone.

Scripture texts in this work are taken from the *New Revised Standard Version Bible* © 1989, Division of Christian Education of the National Council of the Churches of Christ in the United States of America. Used by permission. All rights reserved.

Excerpts from documents of the Second Vatican Council are from *Vatican Council II: Constitutions, Decrees, Declarations; The Basic Sixteen Documents*, edited by Austin Flannery, OP, © 1996. Used with permission of Liturgical Press, Collegeville, Minnesota.

Excerpts from the English translation of *The Roman Missal* © 2010, International Commission on English in the Liturgy Corporation. All rights reserved.

From *The Collected Works of St. John of the Cross*, translated by Kieran Kavanaugh and Otilio Rodriguez Copyright © 1964, 1979, 1991 by Washington Province of Discalced Carmelites ICS Publications 2131 Lincoln Road, N.E. Washington, DC 20002-1199 U.S.A. www.icspublications.org

© 2018 by Order of Saint Benedict, Collegeville, Minnesota. All rights reserved. No part of this book may be reproduced in any form, by print, microfilm, microfiche, mechanical recording, photocopying, translation, or by any other means, known or yet unknown, for any purpose except brief quotations in reviews, without the previous written permission of Liturgical Press, Saint John's Abbey, PO Box 7500, Collegeville, Minnesota 56321-7500. Printed in the United States of America.

Library of Congress Cataloging-in-Publication Data

Names: Cwiekowski, Frederick J., author.
Title: The church : theology in history / Frederick J. Cwiekowski, P.S.S.
Description: Collegeville, Minnesota : Liturgical Press, 2018. | Includes bibliographical references and index.
Identifiers: LCCN 2018009686 (print) | LCCN 2017053403 (ebook) | ISBN 9780814644911 (ebook) | ISBN 9780814644683
Subjects: LCSH: Church—History of doctrines.
Classification: LCC BV598 (print) | LCC BV598 .C95 2018 (ebook) | DDC 262.009—dc23
LC record available at https://lccn.loc.gov/2018009686

*To my brother Bob,
to the memory of my sister Kathy,
and to my sister Judith*

Contents

Preface ix

Chapter 1 Beginnings: Jesus and His Disciples 1

Chapter 2 The First Christian Churches 30

Chapter 3 The Church: AD 70 to the End of the First Century—Part 1 64

Chapter 4 The Church: AD 70 to the End of the First Century—Part 2 93

Chapter 5 Christian Antiquity—Part 1: Second and Third Centuries 116

Chapter 6 Christian Antiquity—Part 2: Constantine to Gregory I and John Damascene 147

Chapter 7 Medieval Understandings of Church 180

Chapter 8 The Reformation Era and Early Modern Catholicism (1500–1800) 235

Chapter 9 Theologies of the Church: 1815 to the Eve of Vatican II 276

Chapter 10 The Second Vatican Council (1962–1965) 315

Chapter 11 From Vatican II to Pope Francis 344

Appendix 1 Contemporary Biblical Scholarship 383

Appendix 2 Our Understanding of Jesus 388

Index of Names 393

Index of Subjects 398

Preface

This book is born of two desires. The first: to share what I believe is the fascinating story of the various ways in which the church has been understood through the centuries. The second: to cast light on the spiritual riches often present in theological understandings of the church. This effort is intended for an educated readership, for those who wish to deepen their understanding of the church—where we are now, where we have come from, and what resources from the past might help us as we look to the future. It is also offered to those engaged in a formal study of the theology of the church, in senior years of college, perhaps, in seminaries, and in lay ministry and diaconate programs. I hope that it will enrich the lives of clergy, religious, and those contemplating life in the church. The book makes more readily accessible the good scholarly work that has been done on the theology of the church. The general readership may read the text as it stands and consult the notes only as interest leads them. Those engaged in formal study will find in the notes references for further academic pursuit of given topics.

Three assumptions have guided the preparation of the text. First, the experience of having done doctoral studies at the Catholic University of Louvain during the Second Vatican Council has given me an abiding appreciation for the value of studying the development of theology in its historical context. While true of all areas of theology, this is indispensable in understanding the theology of the church. Second, I am and want to be guided by Thomas Aquinas and Bonaventure, who taught that theology is not simply an intellectual endeavor but a participation in God's wisdom, leading to union with God. May this study of the lived and written efforts of others to express an understanding of church contribute to an embrace of the mystery of the church in God's plan. Third, the topic of the church is not of first importance in the study of our faith; that place belongs to the triune God and the incarnation of God's Son. But the topic of the church is vitally important because the church is the community invited to share the very life of God through the risen Lord and the presence of his Spirit. It is also called to keep alive the memory of Jesus and to pass on—sometimes it does this better than others—the Gospel of God he has given us. Though we have not always seen it this way, all the baptized have a responsibility for being church and contributing to its mission. This study aspires to provide resources for the people of God making its way in this twenty-first century.

The contents page indicates the areas of study included in this work. If the first six chapters seem disproportionate to the rest of the book, it is because they treat the church's historical roots in the ministry of Jesus and the first generations of the church, along with the singularly important and seminal insights regarding the church in the New Testament and in the worship and writings of the patristic period. Chapter 7, on the medieval period, is somewhat longer than others because of the length of the period. The developments dealt with in chapter 9 are crucial to appreciating the place of Vatican II in ecclesial self-understanding. While I write this largely from a Roman Catholic perspective, I hope the work may be of interest to members of other Christian churches with whom Catholic Christians share a common heritage of many centuries.

With gratitude, I acknowledge my indebtedness to those who have inspired my theological interest or have taught me so much about the theology of the church. I single out Eugene A. Walsh, PSS, during my final years of college seminary; Raymond E. Brown, PSS, teacher and later colleague over many years; and Canon Roger Aubert, my thesis director at the Catholic University of Louvain. I would mention also Monsignor Gérard Philips, also of the University of Louvain, the works of Yves Congar and Henri de Lubac, and the writings of Joseph A. Komonchak. I thank the Society of St. Sulpice, Province of the United States, for underwriting my post-seminary studies and the students and faculties of St. Mary's Seminary and University of Baltimore and of St. Patrick's Seminary and University of Menlo Park, California, at each of which I have taught for many years. I am grateful to the library staffs of both schools for their invaluable assistance in tracking down many of the resources I have used in this book. I thank Ronald D. Witherup, PSS, and James W. Lothamer, PSS, who have read the entire manuscript and have made helpful suggestions. The limitations of the final text I accept as my responsibility. Finally, I express gratitude to Dr. Margaret M. Turek and Dr. Michon M. Matthiesen for their encouragement and support throughout what has been a lengthy project, and to Hans Christoffersen, Stephanie Lancour, Colleen Stiller, Lauren L. Murphy, and Tara Durheim, who have very graciously guided this project for Liturgical Press.

CHAPTER ONE

Beginnings: Jesus and His Disciples

The story of the church's understanding of itself and its mission begins with Israel's coming to see itself as a people chosen by God, his "treasured possession out of all the peoples . . . a priestly kingdom and a holy nation" (Exod 19:5-6).[1] More immediately, the earliest community of Jesus' disciples after his resurrection has its beginnings in the disciples and followers who associated with Jesus during the course of his public ministry. Jesus and these earliest followers are frequently designated as the *Jesus movement*. The term must be used with caution: while some did leave their work and homes to follow Jesus, many who accepted his teaching did not; nor did they adopt a distinctive lifestyle. Importantly, all remained committed to their Jewish religious identity, even if they accepted Jesus' distinctive teachings on certain points. We must keep in mind too that the earliest gospel descriptions of Jesus' ministry see him focused on God and God's kingdom and only implicitly on Jesus himself.[2] This first chapter will focus on Jesus and his earliest followers as they are understood in contemporary biblical scholarship.[3]

---

[1] Unless otherwise noted, all scriptural quotations are from the New Revised Standard Version of the Bible, copyright 1989.

[2] Raymond E. Brown, "Early Church: Church in the New Testament," in *New Jerome Biblical Commentary* [henceforth NJBC], ed. Raymond E. Brown, Joseph A. Fitzmyer, and Roland E. Murphy (Englewood Cliffs, NJ: Prentice-Hall, 1990), art. 80, sec. 9.

[3] Of particular importance in this area is the work of University of Notre Dame biblical scholar John P. Meier, *A Marginal Jew: Rethinking the Historical Jesus*, 5 vols. (vols. 1–3, New York: Doubleday, 1991–2001; vols. 4–5, New Haven, CT: Yale University Press, 2015–2016), and that of British biblical scholar James D. G. Dunn, *Christianity in the Making*, vol. 1, *Jesus Remembered* (Grand Rapids, MI: Eerdmans, 2003).

Our principal sources of information about the earliest followers of Jesus are the four gospels. We appreciate much more now than we did in the past that these books were not intended to be strictly historical accounts. They were composed primarily as testimonies of faith, based on memories of Jesus passed on orally and then in writing by his disciples and the succeeding generation. Nevertheless, scholars are confident that we can know the basic contours of the early Jesus movement. Appendix 1 gives some background notes concerning the method of biblical interpretation used in this chapter and the next and in the studies from which they draw.

The Beginning: A People Chosen by God

Both historically and theologically a proper understanding of Jesus' followers and the early centuries of the post-resurrection church demands that we see them in the context of the Greco-Roman world and, more precisely, Jewish history and religious tradition.[4] A brief review of that history and tradition sets the stage for our study. Our story begins with the call to Abraham, thought to have occurred sometime in the period between about 2000 to 1750 BC. The book of Genesis tells us that God entered into a special relationship, a covenant, with Abraham and his wife Sarah, promising to give their progeny a special role in God's plan and to make of them a great nation (Gen 12:1-3; 17:1-7, 15-16). Abraham and Sarah's grandson Jacob, later called Israel, is said to be the father of twelve sons, the

---

The account given in this chapter and the next makes use of the historical-critical method, while recognizing that the "faith-view of the evangelists" is ultimately decisive in our understanding of the church. The quoted phrase is from the German exegete Rudolf Schnackenburg, cited by Joseph Ratzinger/Pope Benedict XVI, *Jesus of Nazareth: From the Baptism in the Jordan to the Transfiguration*, trans. Adrian J. Walker (New York: Doubleday, 2007), xiii.

[4] On the wider Greco-Roman background, see Diarmaid MacCulloch, *Christianity: The First Three Thousand Years* (New York: Viking, 2009), chap. 1; on Jewish historical and religious background, see Addison G. Wright, Roland Murphy, and Joseph A. Fitzmyer, "A History of Israel," in NJBC, art. 75, and Lawrence Boadt, *Reading the Old Testament: An Introduction*, rev. Richard Clifford and Daniel Harrington (New York: Paulist Press, 2012).

progenitors, it is supposed, of the twelve tribes of Israel, who later settled in what came to be known as the land of Israel. In the biblical story, one of Jacob's sons, Joseph, was instrumental in his kin's coming to Egypt. Generations later, the event of the exodus (ca. 1300 BC), in which the descendants of Israel, under Moses' leadership, were delivered from Egypt, is regarded as the privileged moment when God rescued them from bondage and made of them a covenant people and gave them the *Torah*, the Law. During the following period, from about 1250 to 1020 BC, the often-fractious Israelite tribes underwent a transition from a semi-nomadic existence to an agricultural economy and urban life.

A period of monarchy began when the tribal peoples, facing more complex issues of settled life and needing to defend themselves against powerful neighbors, clamored for a king. Under Saul, the first of Israel's kings (ca. 1020–1000 BC), the tribes maintained much of their authority. King David (1000–962 BC), to whom the prophet Nathan announced God's promise of a dynasty that would never end (2 Sam 7), and his son Solomon (961–922) united the tribes into a single nation, the Kingdom of Israel. The city of Jerusalem, strategically placed between the territory of the several tribes of the north and the two in the south, became the nation's capital and the site of the magnificent temple of Solomon, a new focal point of Israel's religious identity. The reigns of David and Solomon constitute the "golden age" of Israel's history. Israel's army kept enemies at bay, and economic prosperity allowed for the development of a bureaucracy that began keeping written records, among them, the earliest of the biblical writings.

Following Solomon's death, tribal tensions reasserted themselves and the nation became divided, a kingdom of Israel in the north and a kingdom of Judah in the south. When the powerful elites of either nation neglected their religious identity or their duties toward the poor and the lowly, prophets called the people to reaffirm their fidelity to the Lord and thus to their identity as God's chosen people. We see the oft-repeated message uttered through the prophets, "And you shall be my people, and I will be your God" (Jer 30:22). For the next several centuries, each nation struggled to hold its own against the surrounding nations and the mighty empires of Assyria and Babylon.

The northern kingdom of Israel fell to the Assyrians in 722 BC. In 587 BC the kingdom of Judah was overtaken by the Babylonians; both the city of Jerusalem and the temple were destroyed, and many Jews were taken to Babylon. Thus began the nearly fifty-year period of the exile and the beginning of the Diaspora ("dispersion"), when Jews were scattered throughout the Mediterranean world. In the crucible of this experience and in the effort to preserve their religious identity, Jewish scribes collected the oral and written traditions of their people and edited them in many of the books that now constitute the Old Testament.[5] On the eve of and during the exile itself prophets led Israel to look to the day when God would fulfill the promises of the past in ways more wondrous than the great events that first established Israel's identity and its relationship with the Lord God. It seems most likely that during this period, in the absence of the temple, the synagogue (which translates from the Greek as the "assembly") emerged to provide a place for prayer and meditation on the Word of God, the Torah.

After Babylon was conquered by the Persians in 538 BC, the Persian king Cyrus allowed Jews to return to Jerusalem and, with his assistance, to rebuild the temple, beginning what is now known as Second Temple Judaism. The rebuilt temple was a very modest one. The even greater task facing the returning exiles concerned ethnic identity and the restoration of Jewish religious life, the latter made especially difficult by differing interpretations of what was normative to Judaism. Also, from this time on the Jews were dominated by a succession of foreign powers: first the Persian conquerors of Babylon; then Alexander the Great in his conquest of Syria and Palestine in 333 BC; then the Ptolemaic pharaohs of Egypt (ca. 300–200 BC), followed by the Seleucids of Syria (200–164 BC). Respite from foreign domination came with the Maccabean revolt from 175 to 135 BC and Jewish Hasmonean Rule from then until the establishment of Roman power in Palestine in 63 BC. Roman rule extended over the province of

---

[5] Most of the books in what Christians call the Old Testament are the Hebrew Scriptures as well. Christian use of the term does not imply that these shared books have been replaced or made obsolete by the New Testament; they are no less the Word of God and are reverenced as such.

Palestine throughout the time of Jesus' ministry and the entire New Testament period.

Exilic and Postexilic Period: Second Temple Judaism

The Judaism that developed in the exilic and postexilic period, especially after the conquest by Alexander, took on a distinctive character. Three general traits are important. First, Israel's hope in a restored Davidic monarchy in the near future gave way to a hope for a distant future, at the end of time, when God would bring together the scattered tribes of Israel and inaugurate God's final saving action. On that *day of the Lord* there would be justice and peace, for Israel first and, through them, for all peoples. Looking to the fulfillment of God's promises at the end of time is technically referred to as an *eschatological* perspective (from the Greek *eschaton*, meaning "end time"). The hope for this end-time saving work of God became more pronounced as the burden imposed by foreign oppressors weighed more heavily on the Jewish people.

A second trait related to the shift in expectations concerning God's saving action. Where some lamented a lack of leadership, others looked to divinely appointed agents in the unfolding of God's plan. A scribal postscript to the book of Malachi, apparently written soon after the postexilic restoration of the temple but placed last among the books of the Hebrew prophets, looks to the return of the prophet Elijah before "the great and terrible day of the LORD comes" (Mal 4:5). Because Elijah had been taken to heaven (2 Kgs 2:11) it was thought that his return would be a harbinger of the day of the Lord, a day of judgment for those who opposed the Lord and a day of vindication for the just and the lowly. The book of Daniel, thought to be written in the period between 167 and 164 BC during intense Seleucid persecution, laments that there was in that day no ruler, prophet, or leader (Dan 3:38).[6] The last two of the noncanonical Psalms of Solomon, written in the first century BC, look to an earthly

---

[6] The NRSV considers the Prayer of Azariah, in which this verse is found, a deuterocanonial addition to the book of Daniel, so Dan 3:15. The Catholic Church regards the prayer as canonical, so Dan 3:38.

kingdom to be established before the consummation of the world and a divinely anointed leader (Messiah) with both political and spiritual power.

A third trait of the Judaism of this period is the development of *apocalyptic* (from Greek *apokalypsis,* meaning "unveiling" or "revelation"). Apocalyptic literature uses highly symbolic language to convey encouragement in the midst of foreign persecution. It predicts God's victory over evil and looks to a new order beyond the present when God will reign. The book of Daniel is a clear example of this type of writing. In the second half of the book, visions tell of beasts rising from the sea, symbol of chaos, and a human figure, "one like a son of man," coming from the heavens, to whom is given a kingship that will never by destroyed (Dan 7:1-14). The figure signifies the kingdom of "the holy ones of the Most High" (Dan 7:18). Apocalyptic imagery was popular in Jesus' day; he used it in some of his preaching.

British biblical scholar James D. G. Dunn identifies "four pillars" of Second Temple Judaism at the time of Jesus and of the New Testament church.[7] Three of these pillars were characteristic of historic Judaism: "belief in God, God's revelation of the Torah to Israel, and Israel as the people who lives by the Torah in obedience to God."[8] The fourth pillar was the Jerusalem temple, whose magnificent restoration was begun about 20 BC by Herod the Great (34–4 BC) and that became "the centre of Israel's national and religious life."[9]

Belief in God, the first pillar, took the form of a "highly self-conscious" monotheism as observant Jews faced the religious pluralism of the time.[10] The one true God of Jewish faith was identified as the God who was creator of all and sovereign ruler of all, the God who revealed himself when he brought Israel out of Egypt and

---

[7] James D. G. Dunn, *The Partings of the Ways between Christianity and Judaism and Their Significance for the Character of Christianity,* 2nd ed. (London: SCM Press, 2006), chap. 2, and *Jesus Remembered,* 286–92.

[8] *Encyclopedia Judaica* (1971–1972), 10:387, cited by Dunn, *Jesus Remembered,* 287.

[9] Dunn, *Partings of the Ways,* 42.

[10] Richard Bauckham, *God Crucified: Monotheism and Christology in the New Testament* (Grand Rapids, MI: Eerdmans, 1998), 1–22, at 6.

created a people as God's own. Within this context were three personifications—God's Wisdom, God's Word, and God's Spirit—all intrinsic to the divine identity, by which the one and only God related to the world and to history outside of himself.[11] This theological development would serve as the matrix of the very early Christian reflection, after Jesus' resurrection, on his identity within this monotheistic belief.

The Jerusalem temple, the fourth pillar, had political significance through the power of the high priests and the priestly families and economic importance in the revenue it generated through the temple tax, the daily sacrifices and offerings, and the pilgrim traffic. But most of all, "the Temple was the place where God had chosen to put his name, the focal point for the divine-human encounter and the sacrificial cult on which human well-being and salvation depended, a primary identity marker of Israel the covenant people."[12]

How Jesus and his followers related to these "four pillars" would be an important indication of how they saw themselves.

John the Baptist and Jesus' First Followers

We turn now to what we know about the self-understanding of the earliest followers of Jesus during his public ministry. This can be done only in tandem with what we know about that ministry. Looking at these earliest followers is preliminary to understanding how they saw themselves after the resurrection.

Our account begins with John the Baptist, both because of Jesus' own baptism at the hands of John and because the first disciples of Jesus were likely once disciples of John. John preached the imminent reign of God with its attendant judgment of Israel. He called people to a baptism of repentance and, perhaps as well, to a preparation for the intervention of God's final agent who would inaugurate the coming kingdom. Jesus' own baptism by John indicates his acceptance of John as a prophet. It may also indicate Jesus' resolve to engage in

---

[11] James D. G. Dunn, *Did the First Christians Worship Jesus? The New Testament Evidence* (Louisville, KY: Westminster John Knox Press, 2010), 116–29.

[12] Dunn, *Jesus Remembered*, 287.

John's ministry, perhaps, at least for a while, by initially becoming John's disciple.[13]

The Fourth Gospel tells us that the first disciples of Jesus emerged from the circle of disciples of the Baptist (John 1:35-45). Though the Synoptics say nothing of this, some scholars believe that in this instance the Gospel according to John is giving us the more accurate information. (The term "Synoptics," from the Greek, meaning "with one eye," refers to the Gospels according to Matthew, Mark, and Luke. When printed in parallel columns, one sees at a glance the many similarities between the three texts.) Specifically named are Andrew, his brother Simon, and Philip, all originally from Bethsaida, and Nathanael. Mention is also made of an unnamed disciple (John 1:40); some scholars suggest that this unnamed disciple is the "Beloved Disciple" of the Fourth Gospel and the leader, some years later, of the Johannine community.

Jesus' Kingdom Message for the People of Israel

As John the Baptist's preaching drew crowds to himself, so also did the preaching of Jesus. Jesus preserved the judgment theme of John but emphasized the good news that God was about to come in power to save and restore his sinful and scattered people. Mark 1:14b-15 is generally thought to represent the core of Jesus' preaching: "The time is fulfilled, and the kingdom of God has come near; repent, and believe in the good news." The four elements of the citation help us discern the self-understanding of Jesus' followers. That "the time is fulfilled" evokes the expectation, voiced by Israel's prophets, that the day would come at an end time or a "new age" when God would fulfill the divine promises of salvation for Israel and, through them, for all the nations of the earth. This is the eschatological perspective described above. Jesus boldly proclaimed that God's promises concerning this definitive offer of salvation were being fulfilled in him and in his ministry.

Second, the expression "kingdom of God" is a symbolic term: it points to God's effective presence forgiving, embracing, reconciling

---

[13] John P. Meier, *Marginal Jew: Rethinking the Historical Jesus*, vol. 2: *Mentor, Message, and Miracles* (New York: Doubleday, 1994), 123, 1041–42.

Israel and, ultimately, all of humankind. While the term is rarely used in the Old Testament, the notion of God's rule is prominent, especially in Isaiah and in the Psalms. The translation "kingdom of God" refers to the community or the situation where God's will prevails; "reign of God" refers to God's active and sovereign power. Jesus' use of the expression proclaims "the definitive coming of God . . . to bring the present state of things to an end and to establish his [God's] full and unimpeded rule over the world in general and Israel in particular."[14] The coming of the kingdom would also mean, in part, the advent of God's justice, the end of unjust suffering, rewards for those who remained faithful to God's ways, and sharing one day, even with non-Israelites, in the heavenly banquet promised by the prophets.

(No single image or story can adequately describe what is meant by the term the kingdom of God. Jesus used parables to convey insights into the meaning of God's sovereign and active rule and to invite his listeners to accept the gift and challenge of that rule in the varied circumstances of their lives. In what "field," for example, is God revealed and what does one need to sell in order to buy into that saving presence [Matt 13:44]? Is one willing to trust the good news that God's dealing with us is like a woman who searches for what is lost and rejoices when it is found [Luke 15:8-10]? Who is the Lazarus at one's door who needs to be noticed [Luke 16:19-31] or the victim of robbers who is one's neighbor in need [Luke 10:29-37]?)

Third: "The kingdom of God has *come near.*" The gospel evidence gives two indications regarding the presence of the kingdom. Some texts (e.g., Luke 11:20 and 17:21) clearly assert that the reign of God was being established in the deeds of Jesus' own ministry. Other texts point to a future yet imminent kingdom (e.g., Mark 14:25; Matt 6:10; and Luke 11:2). The two types of sayings suggest that the kingdom of God is the dynamic event of God's coming in power to rule his people Israel in the final days, an event whose "partial and preliminary realization" was taking place in Jesus and in his ministry and which "would soon be displayed in full force."[15]

---

[14] Ibid., 349.
[15] Ibid., 453.

Fourth: Jesus calls for a response that consists of repentance and belief. The word "repent" translates the Greek word *metanoiete* (from *meta*, "beyond," and *nous*, "mind"), a call "to go beyond the mind that they have, to see things in a new way" because of Jesus and his message. It calls for a change of one's life and a participation in the saving event unfolding through him, a "willingness to enter into the world opened up by the novelty of Jesus himself, to believe what has become a possibility in him."[16] The gospel texts tell us that Jesus' disciples had no little struggle as they tried to understand Jesus and accept his message.

Jesus' Followers Taught to Pray

Two elements related to Jesus' preaching about the coming kingdom became identifying characteristics of his companions. First, Jesus taught his disciples to pray the Lord's Prayer or the Our Father (Luke 11:2-4 and Matt 6:9-13). The original form of the prayer was likely an eschatological prayer for the coming of the kingdom; the form in the present gospel texts was adapted for the ordinary life of believers in the post-resurrection church. The address to God is likely the address Jesus himself used: *abbā* ("my own dear father"), now shared with his followers and evoking the image of a child acknowledging total dependence on a loving and powerful father. The first two petitions, in the Lucan form, may have had the sense of: "Father, reveal yourself in all your power and glory [= hallowed be your name] by coming to rule as king [= your kingdom come]."[17]

Originally, the three petitions in the second half of the prayer probably had a similar eschatological tone. "Give us this day our daily [*epiousios*] bread" may originally have meant "Give us today the bread we need [now] and our bread for the future [*epiousios*]." The rare Greek word in question may mean either "daily" or "future." The "bread for the future" would refer to the heavenly banquet, a favorite image of the coming kingdom (Isa 25:6; Matt 8:11; Luke

---

[16] Robert Barron, *The Priority of Christ: Toward a Postliberal Catholicism* (Grand Rapids, MI: Brazos Press, 2007), 165–66.

[17] Meier, *Marginal Jew*, 2:299.

13:29). If so, the petition prays that the kingdom come quickly. The second petition asks for forgiveness in the judgment that the divine king will make on the last day. The final petition asks that God not let the disciple fail in the final struggle with Satan, often mentioned in late Jewish apocalyptic as an event of the final times. When Jesus' prayer was used by his followers after the resurrection, its eschatological character diminished as the prayer came to be applied to ordinary life.[18]

Jesus' Followers Not to Fast

A prohibition against fasting, associated with the imminent coming of the kingdom, was a second identifying feature of Jesus' followers.[19] The prohibition ran counter to the voluntary fasting practiced by devout Jews in the century before Christ and during the first century AD. It also stood opposed to what seems to have been a practice inculcated by John the Baptist as a sign of repentance and part of prayer for deliverance from the coming judgment. Jesus said his disciples should not fast at all. He compared his followers to wedding guests enjoying the banquet at which the bridegroom is present (Mark 2:19-20). The Old Testament describes God metaphorically as the spouse of Israel (e.g., Isa 54:4-8; 62:4) and looks to the day when God will restore a marital relationship with his people (Hos 2:16-20). The prohibition against fasting is based on the supposition that the kingdom was in some sense already present in Jesus and in his ministry, bringing with it a joy that makes fasting incongruous. This is consistent with Jesus' welcoming tax collectors and sinners to his table (Mark 2:13-17; Matt 11:19; Luke 19:7) and his being accused of being "a glutton and a drunkard" (Matt 11:19). After Jesus' resurrection, as the early Christians came to realize that the end time was not to come quickly, the practice of fasting became widespread (Mark 2:19b-20).

---

[18] See the reflection on the Lord's Prayer in Benedict XVI, *Jesus of Nazareth*, chap. 5.
[19] Meier, *Marginal Jew*, 2:439–50.

12 *The Church*

Jesus' Followers and Torah

Jesus and his disciples lived in the context of Palestinian Judaism. Theirs was "a religion based on a covenant between its God and the *people* of Israel (not isolated individuals . . .), a religion that was lived and practiced by a visible community, a religion that preserved this community's identity and holiness as God's people by observing the clear boundaries of purity rules, a religion that insisted that commitment of the heart had to be embodied in commitment to right actions toward one's neighbors in the community, and a religion that embodied its people-centered consciousness by regular pilgrimages to the Jerusalem temple for communal worship."[20] The Law (*tora*, from which we get our English noun Torah) had a key role in shaping Jewish religious identity. The notion of law included several meanings: "instruction," "teaching," "direction," "directive," or "law," passed on in oral or written form.[21] The Law was variously interpreted by different sects or movements in Jesus' day, and so it was with Jesus. In some instances, for example, his prohibition of divorce and of oaths, his was a radical interpretation, revoking institutions that were seen as being permitted and even regulated by Mosaic Law. In his prohibition of divorce Jesus recalled God's original plan in Genesis and looked to its restoration in the dawning end time. The prohibition of oaths may be a sign of reverence for the all-truthful God and Jesus' refusal to have him called to witness the not always truthful statements of his creatures.[22] Jesus affirmed the sacred institution of the Sabbath but interpreted it in a benign and practical way for pious Jewish peasants, an alternative to those who advocated a rigorist approach characteristic of sectarian groups. He encouraged his followers to see the Sabbath as willed by God in the beginning to serve human need, now being restored through his ministry.[23] Jesus showed a lack of concern over matters of ritual impurity; his disciples followed him, convinced that as God's charismatic prophet of the

---

[20] John P. Meier, *Marginal Jew: Rethinking the Historical Jesus*, vol. 4: *Law and Love* (New York: Doubleday, 2009), 43–44.
[21] Ibid., 4:27.
[22] Ibid., 4: chaps. 32–33 and p. 654.
[23] Ibid., 4:293–97.

end time his word and example were authoritative.[24] There is no indication that Jesus ever challenged the ritual of circumcision.

Jesus' followers were confronted with his challenging teachings, sometimes very bluntly put: "what God has joined let no one separate," "swear not at all," "come follow me," "let the dead bury their dead," "whoever loses his life will save it," "you cannot serve God and Mammon."[25] Their following these demands was based on their belief that their lives were to reflect the final reign of God coming in Jesus. They accepted too, at Jesus' direction, that "the love of God and the love of neighbor [were] the *first* and *second* commandments of the Torah, superior to all others. Love—of God first and of [the] neighbor second, in that pointed order—[was] supreme in the Law."[26]

Jesuit biblical scholar Daniel Harrington identifies five characteristic elements in Jesus' teaching that, taken together, constituted the core values of the Jesus movement: the invitation to address God with startling intimacy and total trust as *abbā*; to see the heart of the Law in the commandments to love God and love neighbor, extending the latter even to the love of enemies (Matt 5:43-48); having a special concern for those who were suspect because of their occupation, social position, or behavior, a teaching forcibly taught by Jesus' own example; the need to embrace a radical ethic by avoiding the root causes of murder, adultery, divorce, or false oaths; and the need to accept God's prodigal forgiveness and to show a similar forgiveness to others.[27]

In addition to interpreting the Torah, Jesus also took on the role of a wisdom teacher. The beatitudes are a type of wisdom teaching. Other sayings bear a close resemblance to wisdom material, as, for example, the saying attributed to Jesus: "Come to me, all you that

---

[24] Ibid., 4: chap. 35, esp. 413–15.

[25] Translations from ibid., 4:550–51.

[26] Ibid., 4:575–76. In chap. 36, Meier deals with the love commandments of Jesus, in Mark 12:28-34, in the tradition common to Matt and Luke (5:44 and 6:27, respectively), and in John 15:12, 17.

[27] Daniel J. Harrington, *The Church according to the New Testament: What the Wisdom and Witness of Early Christianity Teach Us Today* (Chicago: Sheed & Ward, 2001), 5–6. See also "The Torah of the Messiah," in Pope Benedict XVI, *Jesus of Nazareth*, 99–127.

are weary and are carrying heavy burdens, and I will give you rest" (Matt 11:28; see Sir 24:19; 51:23). Jesus' parables and riddles also resonate with Israel's wisdom tradition.[28] Teaching his disciples and encouraging them to address God with bold intimacy (*abbā*) reminded them of God's Holy Wisdom inviting those who receive her to become friends of God (Wis 7:27).

Jesus' teaching did not focus primarily on himself; it focused on the coming rule of God and what that involved for Israel. Implicit in Jesus' words and deeds was the pivotal role he had in the unfolding of these events. Recalling, after the resurrection, the claims implicit in Jesus' words and deeds helps explain why the early Christian church transferred the emphasis of their preaching from the coming of the kingdom to Jesus himself.

Jesus' Meals: Signs of the Coming Kingdom

Jesus' meals with his disciples and with outcasts and sinners were yet another identifying feature of the Jesus movement. Where John the Baptist proclaimed God's coming primarily in terms of impending divine judgment, Jesus emphasized God's gracious and inclusive mercy and compassion. Concern for "the least, the last and the lost in his society"[29] was a fundamental feature of his ministry. Jesus' public meals with sinners and religious outcasts were meant to dramatize and initiate God's final offer of salvation to Israel. "They were, in the wide sense of the word, 'sacramental'—that is, concrete signs and means by which sinful human beings experienced God's love coming to them through Jesus."[30]

To those who criticized these meals as an affront to the Law, Jesus responded with parables about the caring love of God for those who were lost (Luke 15: parables of the lost sheep, the lost coin, and the

---

[28] Ben Witherington III, *The Jesus Quest: The Third Search for the Jew of Nazareth* (Downers Grove, IL: InterVarsity Press, 1995), chap. 7.

[29] Ibid., 188.

[30] John P. Meier, "The Eucharist at the Last Supper: Did It Happen?," *Theology Digest* 42 (Winter 1995): 338.

prodigal son). At times Jesus invoked the symbol of the end-time banquet (Luke 14:16-24 and parallels).

Jesus' Followers

Jesus' followers related to him in different ways. John Meier outlines three concentric circles among those who followed Jesus. He gives a strong caveat that we not oversimplify what we know from the limited available evidence and that, in all but the innermost circle of the Twelve, the boundaries between each group were not hard and fast. These considerations draw on Meier's work.[31]

An outermost circle of Jesus' followers consisted of crowds of the curious or miracle-seekers who listened to Jesus. Some of this group gave him a sympathetic, at times an enthusiastic, hearing, though most never committed themselves to him or to his message. Their numbers may have been one reason why Jesus set up an embryonic structure among those who did follow him. Many of those who belonged to this outer circle may have been among those who were tolerant of Jesus' disciples after the resurrection, even if they did not join them or accept what they thought were their eccentric beliefs.

A middle circle of followers consisted of those who were called *disciples*. The basic meaning of both the Greek word *mathētēs* and the Latin word *discipulus*, from which we get our English word "disciple," is "learner" or "student." While the term "disciple" was applied to any member of the Christian community after the resurrection, it had a very specific meaning during Jesus' ministry. Three characteristics identified a disciple: a specific call from Jesus to follow him, immediately and unreservedly; a willingness literally to leave family, home, and occupation and to accompany him, indefinitely, in his ministry of preaching and teaching; an acceptance of the possibility that this following would provoke hostility and opposition, most immediately from one's family, for obvious reasons, but also, as the opposition to Jesus grew, from religious authorities as well. It is in the context of growing opposition to him that Jesus most probably spoke of the

---

[31] John P. Meier, *Marginal Jew: Rethinking the Historical Jesus*, vol. 3: *Companions and Competitors* (New York: Doubleday, 2001), part 1.

need to lose one's life or to take up one's cross if one were to follow him (e.g., Mark 8:34-35 and parallels). These radical demands were imposed only on the select group who were his disciples. Women, if not by name, were included in this circle of disciples. In the table-fellowship that was so important a characteristic of Jesus' ministry, the tightly woven group of disciples was taught to be "radically open to others, even those 'outside the pale.' "[32]

Associated with this middle circle were others, deeply committed to Jesus, who did not leave their homes and families to follow him and who evidently were not asked to do so. These faithful people, not usually called followers and never called disciples, supported him with food and lodging and money when his ministry brought him to their towns or villages. Among this group are the familiar names of Martha and Mary, Lazarus, and Zacchaeus; no doubt there were many others (Mark 14:3-9, 12-16; Luke 10:38-42; John 12:1-8).

The Twelve

The innermost circle of disciples was the special group of the Twelve. There are four lists of this group in the New Testament: Mark 3:14-19; Matthew 10:2-3; Luke 6:14-16; and Acts 1:13-14. The discrepancies of the names in the final third of these lists can be explained by the supposition that while the memory of the Twelve remained in the tradition when the gospels and Acts were written, the memory of the names had become unclear.

Some of the Twelve, we saw, seem to have originally been disciples of John the Baptist. Some were fishermen. One was a tax collector. Another was known as a "zealot," quite probably signifying his zealous attitude concerning the Law. The Greek *kananaios* in Matthew and Mark may be a transcription of the Aramaic word for "zealous"; most scholars do not think the militaristic Zealot party existed much before the 60s. The gospel portrayal of the Twelve as frequently missing the point of Jesus' teaching is likely historical since the tradition was preserved in gospels written when the Twelve were venerated in the memory of the community.

---

[32] Ibid., 3:73.

Several reasons support the idea that the Twelve were identified as such during Jesus' ministry. It seems very unlikely that the early church would create the notion of a twelve and then include among them one who betrayed him. The election of Matthias (Acts 1:15-26) to replace Judas shows a concern to have the Twelve intact in the early days of the post-resurrection community. Scholars believe that Paul's mention of those who saw the risen Christ (1 Cor 15:3-8) comes from a pre-Pauline formula that implies the Twelve were a distinct group at the time of the resurrection appearances. We know too that the desert community at Qumran, also looking forward to the dawn of God's end time, had a symbolic group of twelve representing the twelve patriarchs of Israel.

Jesus' selection of the Twelve was a symbolic action initiating the fulfillment of Jewish hopes, expressed in the words of the prophets, in postexilic writing, and in Hebrew wisdom, that one day the scattered tribes of Israel would be gathered anew in the Promised Land. In the face of the sad history of divisions and successive dispersions of the Jewish people, the Jewish sage Ben Sira (ca. 180 BC) spoke for many when he prayed that the "God of all" would "give new signs and work other wonders," that he would "hasten the day" when he would "gather all the tribes of Jacob, and give them their inheritance, as at the beginning" (Sir 36:1-16). Only in Matthew 19:28 and Luke 22:28-30 does Jesus speak of the purpose of the Twelve. Meier expresses the sense of the Matthean text as follows: "You [that is, you Twelve who symbolize and embody the eschatological Israel right now] will sit on twelve thrones judging the twelve tribes of Israel [when the kingdom fully comes and the twelve tribes are restored]."[33] This saying and the absence of any directive concerning the founding of a new community separate from Israel are decisive indications that Jesus saw his mission in terms of renewing Israel from within, in view of the advent of God's final salvation. That the Twelve are men comes from their symbolic role representing the twelve patriarchs at Israel's beginning. Jesus is not part of the Twelve; he stands above them.

---

[33] Ibid., 3:153–54.

While scholars dispute the point, Jesus may have given a limited mission to the Twelve to their fellow Israelites, as a further step in the direction of gathering the scattered people of Israel (Mark 6:7-13; Matt 10:5-6).

A study of the Twelve in the New Testament shows the significance of keeping in mind the *three stages* in the development of the gospel tradition (see appendix 1). The narrative in Mark 3:14 states simply that "he [Jesus] appointed twelve, whom he also named apostles [a phrase missing in several ancient texts], to be with him, and to be sent out to proclaim the message." These are the words of the evangelist (stage 3). As such, they give a different reason for the selection of the Twelve than we see in the words attributed to Jesus (reflecting stage 1) in Matthew and Luke (from the "sayings source," the "Q" material unknown to Mark but common to Matthew and Luke).

The fact that the saying of Jesus is quoted late in Matthew and Luke does not mean it came from late in Jesus' ministry. With few exceptions, the arrangement of the material in each gospel is the work of the evangelist. The editors of the gospels (stage 3) organized the stories and sayings (stages 1 and 2) they had at their disposal to meet the needs of the communities for which they were writing and to articulate the theological viewpoint they wished to communicate.

Peter in the Ministry of Jesus

Peter had a prominent role among the Twelve. All four gospels (e.g., Mark 1:36; 8:29; Matt 15:15; 18:21; Luke 12:41; John 6:68) attest to Peter's role as spokesman and/or leader of the Twelve or of the disciples in general. One of the most famous Petrine passages is Peter's confession of faith at Caesarea Philippi and his being granted the "keys to the kingdom" (Matt 16:13-20). Neither Mark nor Luke mention the saying about the power of the keys, even though Luke's book of Acts gives a prominent a place to Peter. Such an omission suggests that the Matthean passage may bear a good deal of post-resurrection editing that reflects Peter's unquestionably significant role in the early decades of the church rather than historical memories from the ministry of Jesus. More of this in the following chapters.

Even allowing for the development of some of the Petrine texts in the post-resurrection oral tradition and editing by the gospel writers, clearly Peter was a key figure among Jesus' disciples and among the Twelve during Jesus' ministry. Peter is the most frequently mentioned disciple in the gospels. Jesus himself probably gave Simon the name Peter, from the Aramaic word for "rock," though originally the name may have been a nickname ("Rocky"), referring to some aspect of Simon's personality.[34] Peter most probably made some type of confession of faith in Jesus, even if that confession was not an adequate one, as the Matthean passage in its entirety indicates (Matt 16:13-23). The important place Peter had among the disciples during Jesus' ministry would continue in the prominent role he had in the early church.

Women Followers of Jesus

Biblical evidence clearly points to the inclusion of women among the followers of Jesus. It is reasonable to suppose that women were among the group gathered around Jesus in the scene in Mark 3:31-35. Here, Jesus contrasts his mother and brothers who stand outside asking for him with those gathered around him who, if they do the will of God, are "brother and sister and mother" to him. Luke speaks of women healed by Jesus who accompanied him and the Twelve and of the many who assisted them with their resources (Luke 8:1-3). Mark 15:40-41 (par.) tells of "many women" who accompanied Jesus to Jerusalem. They and others who used to follow him and provide for him when he was in Galilee were present at the crucifixion. The most prominent of the women followers of Jesus was Mary from the town of Magdala in Galilee. She may have interpreted Jesus' freeing her from some serious disorder (Luke 8:2) as the equivalent of a call to follow Jesus. Her name is common to all the lists of women followers of Jesus.

The gospels give no story where Jesus calls women to follow him, quite possibly because the evangelists had no such stories in the traditions from which they drew their material. Yet it would have

---

[34] Daniel J. Harrington, *The Gospel of Matthew*, ed. Daniel J. Harrington, Sacra Pagina (Collegeville, MN: Liturgical Press, 1991), 247–48n18.

been a cause of no small wonderment, if not a scandal, given the patriarchal orientation of ancient Israel, that women, some married, were among Jesus' followers who traveled with him and his male disciples. From this, one can reasonably assume that Jesus did in fact call women or at least gave positive acceptance to their following him and supporting him. Nor do the gospels call women "disciples" in any of the texts referring only to women followers. This may be explained by the lack of a feminine form of the word in either Hebrew or Aramaic and the unwillingness of the evangelists, writing in Greek, to use a feminine form of the Greek word where none existed in the other languages. Even granting this silence, women were among Jesus' disciples in fact if not in name.[35]

It is noteworthy that the memory of Jesus' extensive association with women was incorporated into gospels written at a time when such openness was beginning to be curtailed in the face of social pressure. While the actions of Jesus' women followers were startling by the standards of the day, recent scholarship cautions against seeing Jesus' positive attitude toward women as unique to him. Though notably difficult to date, some rabbinic sayings thought to come from the second century AD but possibly reflecting traditions of an earlier time give a more positive understanding of women than was generally the case. In the Diaspora, possibly as a result of influence by the Greco-Roman environment, Jewish women had some role in the life of the synagogue.

The disciples whom Jesus called to follow him, especially the Twelve with Peter as their spokesman, along with those who supported him, were the core of the Jesus movement. Jesus was not simply an itinerant preacher who attracted people to himself. He deliberately called others to associate with him and, in some way, have a share in his mission. Further, as we are seeing, the members of this movement had identifying characteristics that served to distinguish them within the Judaism of which they were still very much a part.

---

[35] John P. Meier, "Are There Historical Links between the Historical Jesus and the Christian Ministry?," *Theology Digest* 47 (Winter 2000): 312.

The Followers of Jesus and Their Contemporaries

We have further insight into the character of Jesus' followers by comparing them, even briefly, with three other groups, each a competitor in some way in the interpretation of first-century Judaism.[36]

There is no evidence that Jesus or his followers had contact with either the Essenes, gathered in sect-like communities in the towns of Palestine, or the community at Qumran, at the northwest corner of the Dead Sea.[37] The Essenes emerged in the second century BC as a separatist sect within Judaism, dissenting from the priestly and royal pretensions of the Hasmonean rulers. Both the Essenes and the more rigorous group at Qumran saw themselves as the true Israel, following the will of God as Israel approached its final days. The Qumranites saw themselves as already participating in the life and worship of the angels; Jesus celebrated the kingdom's presence in festive meals with sinners and social outcasts. The Qumranites rejected the Jerusalem temple; Jesus accepted the temple and its celebrations, though, we shall see, he looked to its replacement. Because of their great emphasis on proper legal and cultic observances and their rigorous study of the Law, the Essenes and, even more, the sectarians at Qumran had little interaction with ordinary Palestinian Jews. This was not the case with either Jesus or the Pharisees.

Jesus' major competitor in his attempt to guide Israel in its relationship to God and to interpret God's will for his people were the Pharisees.[38] While the precise origins of this group are not known, the Pharisees emerged around 150 BC as a devoutly religious group attempting to guide Israel in the aftermath of the attempt by the Seleucid king Antiochus IV (reigned 175–164 BC) to absorb Judaism into Hellenistic culture and by the Hellenistic leanings of some of the Hasmonean rulers. In the face of this challenge to Jewish religious identity, the Pharisees stressed the study and observance of Mosaic Law, developing an oral tradition to guide the Law's application to concrete circumstances. In the mind of the Pharisees, observance of

---

[36] Meier, *Marginal Jew*, 3: chap. 28 provides historical background.

[37] Ibid., 3:488–532, and Joseph A. Fitzmyer, "The Dead Sea Scrolls and Early Christianity," *Theology Digest* 42 (1995): 303–19.

[38] Meier, *Marginal Jew*, 3: chap. 28.

the Law marked Israel's identity as the chosen people of God. Those who observed the Law could look forward to God's raising them up on the last day. Some Pharisees related the Law's observance with the coming of the Messiah.

Jesus and the Pharisees shared some core issues of Jewish belief: the special place of Israel in God's design, the gift of the Law and the need to let it guide one's life, and the expectation that God would one day restore Israel, pronounce a final judgment, and raise the dead. Pharisees would have differed with Jesus' claims regarding his distinctive role in the unfolding of God's plan, his prohibition of divorce, his rejection of voluntary fasting, and his welcoming attitude toward sinners and those on the margins of society. The Pharisees zealously sought to inculcate their view of Judaism as widely as possible. In significant ways, Jesus and his disciples offered an alternate view.

Along with the Law, the temple in Jerusalem was a key symbol of Jewish religious identity. During his ministry, Jesus accepted it as such and participated in its worship, as did his followers after the resurrection. The temple was also a major factor in the economic and social life of the city and had political significance as well. The Jewish leadership of the temple served at the pleasure of the Roman overlords.

The temple leadership was in the hands of the priestly aristocracy and the party of the Sadducees (the name likely comes from Zadok, priest of Jerusalem at the time of David and Solomon).[39] Based on what we know of them, the Sadducees emerged as both a religious movement and a political party during the time of the Hasmoneans (134–63 BC). The Sadducees consisted of the old-time priestly families of Jerusalem and members of the lay aristocracy. They opposed the Hasmonean's usurpation of the office of the high priesthood. Under the authority of the Romans (after 63 AD), the Sadducees assisted the high priest in managing the ordinary affairs of Jews in Jerusalem and Judea. They had little interest in trying to influence the general populace. Jesus' interaction with the Sadducees during his public ministry was minimal, confined principally to the dispute over the resurrection of the dead mentioned in Mark 12:18-27 (par.).

---

[39] Ibid., 3: chap. 29.

Toward the end of his ministry, Jesus challenged the merchants in the outer court of the temple (Mark 11:15-17 par.; John 2:13-17 places the event at the beginning). The gesture confronted the unpopular and politically compromised religious authority associated with it, even if the scene may have been less dramatic than the gospels portray it. But, much more, the gesture was probably a symbolic, prophetic action to signal that with the dawn of the new age, the temple was about to be replaced.

In addition to this prophetic gesture, the Synoptics (Mark 13:1-2 par.) tell of Jesus' dire words about the fate of the temple sanctuary. A reference to that saying, implying that the sanctuary would be destroyed and replaced in the final age, appears in the scene where, after his arrest, Jesus is interrogated by the high priest and others of the Jerusalem leadership (Mark 14:58; Matt 26:61). As Jesus' saying appears in various versions (see also John 2:19 and Acts 6:14), it is difficult to determine its historical form. It is very likely that Jesus uttered a prophetic warning that the coming kingdom would dramatically change the status of the temple sanctuary. Diverse attitudes toward the temple would be a source of no little tension in the early Christian community.

Attitude toward the Gentiles

The disciples' attitude toward the Gentiles was a corollary of Jesus' mission to Israel. There is good reason to believe that Jesus' prohibitions of a Gentile mission in Matthew 10:5-6 and 15:24 have a firm historical basis, even if the gospel does not give us Jesus' actual words. When Matthew was written, the church was engaged in a universal mission (Matt 28:19). That very reason may well explain why the mission instructions in Mark 6:7-13 and Luke 9:1-6 omit any restriction concerning a Samaritan or Gentile mission. Matthew may refer to these prohibitions as a gesture of support to the Jewish Christians to whom he was writing and also because he felt obliged to respect the historical memory of Jesus' ministry.

The Synoptics tell of Jesus responding to the needs of Gentiles (the spirit-possessed Gerasene in Mark 5:1-20 par.; the Roman centurion appealing on behalf of his servant in Matt 8:5-13 par.; the Samaritan leper in Luke 17:11-19; and the Syrophoenician woman in Mark 7:24-30 par.), though the stories as we have them may be heavily influenced by the gospel editors. More important, perhaps, is Jesus' incorporation of the prophetic idea of reversal in his preaching: Gentiles would be included in the banquet, which symbolized God's final salvation, while those who did not accept his teaching would be excluded (Matt 8:11-12 par.). Jesus may also have thought of the salvation of the Gentiles in terms of the image from Isaiah of the great pilgrimage of all peoples coming to the mountain of the Lord in the final days (2:1-4; 49:12). Nowhere do we see that Jesus in his public ministry gave any specific instructions concerning the admission of Gentiles to be numbered among his followers.[40]

Jesus' Followers Called a Church?

Only twice in the gospels, in Matthew 16:18 and 18:17, does Jesus speak of *church*. In the first passage, the scene at Caesarea Philippi where Peter is called the rock on which Jesus will build his church, the term has a universal meaning. In the second, in the context of instructing the community on how to deal with an errant member, the term refers to the authority of the local community.[41] In both passages the Greek word for "church" is *ekklēsia* (based on the Greek "to call" or "to summon"). In ordinary usage, the term referred to a regularly assembled local body, such as a council called for a political meeting. In the Greek translation of the Scriptures, however, the term *ekklēsia* was used for the Hebrew word *qāhāl*, the assembly of Israel, chosen and gathered by the call of God. The use of the term in the two passages could mean that the gathering of Jesus' followers was the congregation of God, patterned after the Israelite congregation of former times.

Is it likely that Jesus himself used the term in its Aramaic equivalent? The fact that the term is not used in Mark or Luke gives pause. Many scholars (some would say a consensus) believe both passages in their entirety reflect post-Easter editing. Yet, that the Dead Sea

---

[40] On our understanding of Jesus and Jesus' knowledge, see appendix 2.
[41] Meier, *Marginal Jew*, 3:232, and Harrington, *Matthew*, 269n17.

community referred to itself as the "assembly of God" (*qĕhal 'el*) suggests that "there is no reason why Jesus could not have applied a similar term to his followers."[42]

The Last Supper

The disciples' final meal with the earthly Jesus holds a singular place in the story of Christian self-understanding. A look at that meal in the light of contemporary historical studies is an important part of our effort to summarize the historical roots of the church.[43] Later chapters will explore the theological relationship between Eucharist and the church.

Each of the Synoptics (Mark 14:22-25 par.) and the pre-Pauline tradition cited in 1 Corinthians 11:23-26 speak of this meal. The Fourth Gospel (John 13) refers to the meal without the specifics described in the other texts. The multiple references argue for the meal's historicity. Many scholars follow John rather than the Synoptics in thinking that the meal took place on the eve of Passover, so it would not have been the official Passover meal. Probably anticipating an imminent arrest and possibly sensing a betrayal by one of his inner group, Jesus sought to celebrate a final meal with his disciples even in such threatening circumstances. He did this by adding features of the Passover celebration to the meal he held on this earlier date. The meal quite probably took place in the home of an anonymous supporter living in Jerusalem.

Jesus used bread at the beginning of the meal and wine at its end to represent his anticipated death, seen as part of God's mysterious plan for the coming of the kingdom. The four versions of Jesus' words over the bread and wine (1 Cor 11:23-26; Mark 14:22-25; Matt 26:26-29; Luke 22:15-20) represent two traditions, one found in Mark and Matthew, the other in Paul and Luke, these latter containing the expression "new covenant." Scholars see liturgical influences in the texts as we have them, as well as editorial touches by the evangelists. The words in John 6:51—"The bread . . . is my flesh"—in the discourse on the bread of life may approximate more closely Jesus' actual

---

[42] Harrington, *Matthew*, 248n18.
[43] Meier, "The Eucharist at the Last Supper"; and Meier, "Jesus," NJBC 78:51.

words over the bread. Meier suggests that Jesus' actual words may have been something like the following: "This is my flesh [body]," and "This [cup?] is [= contains, mediates] the covenant [sealed] by my blood." The latter text calls to mind the text of Exodus 24:8 describing the ratification of the covenant. "Jesus therefore interpreted his death as the (sacrificial? atoning?) means by which God would restore the covenant with Israel at Sinai. Even to his death, Jesus saw his mission as the regathering and saving of all Israel in the final hour of its history."[44]

The Jewish prophetic tradition provides further insights into the significance of Jesus' actions at the Last Supper. The words and gestures of Israel's prophets were not simply signs but symbols containing the power of what they proclaimed. The words and symbolic actions of Jeremiah and Ezekiel, for example, initiated the events to which they pointed. Jesus' prophetic words and symbolic gestures "set in motion and revealed the deepest meaning of what was about to take place, while at the same time they already communicated something of the saving reality to those who shared the one bread and one cup of Jesus."[45] John Meier sums up the meaning of this last meal of the disciples with Jesus: "This last meal was a pledge that, despite the apparent failure of his mission, God would vindicate Jesus even beyond death and bring him and his followers to the eschatological banquet (see the eschatological note struck in Mark 14:25 and 1 Cor 11:26). Hence Jesus insists that the disciples all share his one cup rather than drink from their own cups. They are to hold fast to their fellowship with him as he dies, so that they may share this triumph in the kingdom."[46] This last note is based on Jesus' saying that he will not drink again of the fruit of the vine until he drinks it new (Matt adds "with you") in the kingdom of God (Mark 14:25 par.), a saying with a strong claim to historicity since it was very early on dropped from the church's liturgical tradition.

---

[44] Meier, "Jesus," NJBC 78:51.
[45] Meier, "The Eucharist at the Last Supper," 350.
[46] Meier, "Jesus," NJBC 78:51.

Jesus' Followers and the Death of Jesus

Assessing the effect on his disciples of Jesus' arrest and condemnation is complicated by varying traditions. Mark and Matthew tell us that after Jesus' arrest, all the disciples deserted him and fled (Mark 14:50; Matt 26:56); John 16:32 tells us something of the same. All four gospels tell us of Peter's subsequent denial (Mark 14:66-72 par.). The shamefulness of the stories of desertion and denial, written finally at a time when some of the same disciples were the church's most prominent leaders, is a strong argument for their historicity.[47] The Synoptics note the presence of women, "looking on from a distance" (Mark 15:40 par.), at the crucifixion scene; mention of "acquaintances" in Luke 23:49 presumably includes some of the disciples as well. As a historical account, the presence of the beloved disciple and the mother of Jesus at the foot of the cross in John 19:25-27 has many difficulties, one of which is its discrepancy with the Synoptic accounts. In any case, the "sophisticated and symbolic narrative" in John makes a very important point in Johannine theology that we will take up in chapter 4.[48] While the nature of our sources does not allow for a precise chronology of the appearances of the risen Jesus to his disciples, one could *hypothesize* that the Twelve, discouraged by the arrest and death of Jesus, returned to their homes and occupations in Galilee. How else account for what appears to be the first appearance of the risen Jesus to Peter on the shores of Lake Tiberias (John 21:1-14)?[49]

The Jesus Movement and the Beginnings of the Church

The story of the church has its beginnings in the self-giving love of God, first revealed in the mystery of creation and later in God's

---

[47] Dunn, *Jesus Remembered*, 774, and Raymond E. Brown, *Death of the Messiah: From Gethsemane to the Grave*, 2 vols. (New York: Doubleday, 1994), 1:614–21.

[48] Francis J. Moloney, *The Gospel of John*, ed. Daniel Harrington, Sacra Pagina (Collegeville, MN: Liturgical Press, 1989), 503–4; Raymond E. Brown and others, *Mary in the New Testament* (Philadelphia: Fortress Press, 1978), 208–10; and Brown, *Death of the Messiah*, 2:1028–29.

[49] Raymond E. Brown, *The Virginal Conception and Bodily Resurrection of Jesus* (New York: Paulist Press, 1973), 108–11. More on this in the following chapter.

choice of a specific people to be heralds and instruments in the unfolding of the divine plan inviting humankind to communion with and in the triune God. In that story, Jesus of Nazareth, his message and ministry, and the followers who were his companions and supporters have a unique place. Thanks to the refined methods of contemporary historical scholarship, what we know about Jesus and his ministry and how that relates to our understanding of the origins of the church has shifted dramatically in the past century. We cannot limit ourselves to a study of Jesus and his chosen companions prior to the time of his death. The foundation of the church also involves the mystery of Jesus' resurrection and the developments, guided by the Spirit of the risen Lord, that took place in the decades following that singular event.

At the time of his death, Jesus and his disciples constituted a *distinct* sociological and religious entity *within* Palestinian Judaism. The followers who responded to Jesus' call to leave home, family, and livelihood to accompany him on his itinerant ministry, and the special group of twelve among them were the core members. Others, notably the stay-at-home supporters of Jesus and his companions, were also important figures in what has come to be called the Jesus movement.

This movement could be identified by distinguishing characteristics: the practice of baptism, at least for a while, as a sign of one's joining Jesus and his followers; a distinct form of prayer, the Our Father or the Lord's Prayer; the prohibition of voluntary fasting and, its opposite, the festive meals at which those looked down upon morally or socially were welcomed (the lack of fasting and the festive meals understood as anticipations of the joyful banquet of the final days). Acceptance that the final days of God's saving plan were at hand and the rejection of divorce and possibly of oaths and vows further characterized the group gathered around Jesus. While the group had a distinct identity within Judaism, it did not adopt the stance of a separatist sect; in fact, it was through his disciples that Jesus sought to reach out to all of Israel and gather it into the community of the end time. It seems fair to assume, also, that the group gathered around Jesus shared his expectation, based on the vision articulated by the Jewish prophets, that at the consummation of God's plan for Israel the Gentiles would come to be included (Matt 8:11-12 par). The distinguishing factors listed in this summary may accurately be considered embryonic structures of the religious movement centered on Jesus. The group was not highly organized; neither was it an amorphous mass. That there were embryonic structures of this sort is not inconsistent with the belief that the end times were dawning, for they had not yet fully come.

That Jesus' followers saw themselves as a community so quickly after the resurrection tells us that they felt themselves bonded to Jesus and to one another before Jesus' death. If we cannot say that prior to his death Jesus founded the church as we see it at the end of the New Testament period, a distinct religious entity apart from Israel, neither can we deny continuity between Jesus and his companions during his ministry and that later church. It is not uncommon to speak of a "living, organic continuity" between the Jews who put their trust in Jesus during his ministry and those who, putting their faith in the crucified and risen Lord, formed the early church. Meier likens this continuity to an embryo that in due time becomes a twenty-, a fifty-, and later a seventy-year-old human in which there is "tremendous transformation and discontinuity within [an] organic continuity."[50] We shall review both the organic unity and transforming discontinuity in the following chapters.

---

[50] Meier, "Are There Historical Links?" 313.

CHAPTER TWO

The First Christian Churches

This chapter and the next two outline the story of how the first two generations of the risen Jesus' followers saw themselves, or were encouraged to see themselves. In essence, they were a community of faith, drawing life from the Risen One and, by the power of his Spirit, continuing the mission he entrusted to them. We look first at the apostolic period, from the earliest post-Easter communities to the deaths of James, Paul, and Peter in the early 60s, concluding with mention of the fall of Jerusalem and the destruction of the temple. Chapters 3 and 4 review the subapostolic period, roughly the final third of the first century, as the increasingly Gentile Christian communities charted their course following the end of Second Temple Judaism.

Our historical overview is limited by the number of our sources, principally the New Testament writings, less historical records than documents of faith meant to guide the early believing communities. As we read them now, hopefully they serve the same purpose, to guide the believing communities of our day.[1] This chapter draws on the Acts of the Apostles, the companion volume to the Gospel according to Luke, and the letters of St. Paul. Acts was written as an account of the growth of the Christian community, but with evangelical, theological, and even some apologetic concerns.[2] The insights in the letters

---

[1] See Sandra M. Schneiders, *The Revelatory Text: Interpreting the New Testament as Sacred Scripture* (New York: HarperSanFrancisco, 1991), 167–69.

[2] James D. G. Dunn, *Christianity in the Making*, vol. 2: *Beginning from Jerusalem* (Grand Rapids, MI: Eerdmans, 2009), 64–87; and Joseph A. Fitzmyer, *The Acts of the Apostles: A New Translation with Introduction and Commentary*, Anchor Bible (New York: Doubleday, 1998), 124–28. Both volumes are important studies of the

of Paul and Acts and what we can see of the way early believers saw themselves are ultimately more important for our study than the basic lines of historical development that might be reconstructed from a careful study of the texts.[3] We begin with an event that itself is *beyond* history yet pivotal to the way Jesus' disciples understood themselves throughout the New Testament period.[4]

Jesus' Resurrection and His Commission to His Disciples

The death of Jesus disillusioned many of his followers. Experiencing him as alive after his death or coming to believe that he was raised up transformed the disciples and decisively influenced their understanding of Jesus and of themselves. In the narratives of the appearance of the risen Jesus in 1 Corinthians and in the gospels, the frequent use of the Greek verb for "appear" implies some type of revelatory action on the part of God. These accounts insist on continuity between the crucified Jesus and the Jesus who had been raised up bodily by the power of God. They point as well to his unmistakable transformation: with his resurrection, Jesus entered a new manner of existence, unique to the experience of those to whom he appeared.

In the religious framework of his disciples, Jesus' resurrection was an event of God's final saving action, initiated in Jesus' proclamation of the dawning of the kingdom. Theologians today speak of Jesus'

---

book of Acts. See also Raymond E. Brown, *An Introduction to the New Testament*, Anchor Bible Reference Library (New York: Doubleday, 1997), 319–22.

[3] Frederick J. Cwiekowski, chaps. 4–8, "Early Church: Church in the New Testament," *The Beginnings of the Church* (New York: Paulist Press, 1988), gives a more extensive treatment of this material. See also Arthur G. Patzia, *The Emergence of the Church: Context, Growth, Leadership and Worship* (Downers Grove, IL: InterVarsity Press, 2001). A brief account is given by Raymond E. Brown, "Early Church," in *The New Jerome Biblical Commentary* [henceforth NJBC], ed. Raymond E. Brown, Joseph A. Fitzmyer, and Roland E. Murphy (Englewood Cliffs, NJ: Prentice Hall, 1990), art. 80, sec. 10–20. N. T. Wright, *Christian Origins and the Question of God*, vol. 1: *The New Testament and the People of God* (Minneapolis: Fortress Press, 1992), 341, makes the point: "We know far less about the history of the church from AD 30–135 than we do about second-temple Judaism."

[4] See Raymond E. Brown's treatment of the resurrection in "Aspects of New Testament Thought," in NJBC 81:118–34.

resurrection as an *eschatological* event, or as a *transhistorical* event, one standing outside of space and time as we know them yet impacting his disciples in their human and historical existence.⁵ Jesus' followers were convinced that, in raising Jesus, God had "clothed [him] with divine glory and given [him] a heavenly status as the plenipotentiary God"⁶ and, through him, had definitively inaugurated the restoration of Israel in the final time of salvation. The twin beliefs that Jesus was indeed the Anointed of God (Messiah) and that the end time had dawned in him became identifying characteristics of the earliest post-resurrection disciples.

Many of the appearance narratives tell of the risen Jesus commissioning the disciples to proclaim him to others (e.g., Luke 24:9-10; Matt 28:16-20; Mark 16:14-15; John 20:17, 21). The earliest exercise of this mission seems to have been directed to fellow disciples scattered after Jesus' death. Peter seems to have had an important role in bringing the Eleven to resurrection belief.⁷ When the gospels were written some decades later, specifics of the Christian mission that only gradually came to consciousness were added to the appearance narratives concluding each of the gospels (e.g., Matt 28:19; 16:19; Luke 24:47; John 20:22-23). The tradition that the risen Jesus appeared in the context of a meal may not only recall such appearances but express the conviction that the church in any age encounters the risen Christ at Eucharist (Luke 24:30, 41-43; John 21:9-13; Mark 16:14; cf. Acts 10:41). This is especially true of the Emmaus account in Luke 24:13-35. This tradition, the memory of the Last Supper, and Jesus' meals during his ministry would contribute to the development of the understanding of the Eucharist in Paul and in the early church.

---

⁵ Sandra M. Schneiders, "The Resurrection: Story, Reality, or the Real Story?," *Offerings: Journal of Oblate School of Theology* 10 (2017): 22–24.

⁶ Larry W. Hurtado, *How on Earth Did Jesus Become a God? Historical Questions about Earliest Devotion to Jesus* (Grand Rapids, MI: Eerdmans, 2005), 194.

⁷ This may stand behind the passage in Luke 22:31-32 where Jesus prays that after his failure Peter would again turn to the Lord and then strengthen his brothers.

Although Luke gives separate attention to Jesus' ascension (Luke 24:51 and Acts 1:1-9),[8] scholars reason that the resurrection and ascension of Jesus may originally have coincided.[9] John 20:17 supports such a view and Luke's gospel itself implies the ascension took place on Easter evening (Luke 24:51). Luke's more extended treatment of the ascension in Acts is probably inspired by theological reasons, to distinguish the time of Jesus from the time of the church and to account for both the absence of Jesus in his risen body and his continued presence in the church through his life-giving Spirit (Acts 2:4; cf. John 20:22).

Quite likely drawing on a pre-Lucan tradition, Acts tells us that between the ascension and Pentecost Matthias was chosen to replace Judas (Acts 1:15-26). Given the symbolic role of the Twelve in Jesus' ministry and the belief that the end time had dawned with Jesus' resurrection, it is understandable that the early community would want to restore the Twelve to its full number. Expectation that a further revelation of God's final saving events might come soon could have motivated the selection. The use of lots to discern the will of God is consistent with Jewish tradition (1 Chr 24:5; 26:13-14; cf. Luke 1:9). As the Twelve were to have a role in God's restoration of Israel in the last days, it was necessary to discern God's will in the choice of a replacement for the one no longer with them. The story of the election may also have served Luke's purpose in wanting to assure a largely Gentile readership that in Jesus and in the growth of the church God was fulfilling his promises to Israel.

The Gathering at Pentecost

As Jews who believed that at the feast of Passover that year God had initiated the final saving work, Jesus' followers may have expected that God might give some further revelation at the feast completing the Passover celebration. The nucleus of these believers seems to have been the Eleven or the reconstituted Twelve, along with members of Jesus' family, some of the women from Galilee

---

[8] Reflected also, it seems, in Mark 16:19 in an appendix to the original gospel.
[9] Dunn, *Beginning*, 138–49.

(Luke 23:49), and some others who came from Galilee to Jerusalem. Collectively they experienced at Pentecost some type of ecstatic spiritual presence and interpreted the experience as a further divine disclosure of God's saving plan.[10] As this second feast was a celebration of God's gift of the covenant at Sinai and the beginning of Israel as God's chosen people, Jesus' disciples quite likely experienced a new sense of themselves as the restored Israel. In the phenomenon of ecstatic speech, they felt a new missionary impulse to proclaim in a more public way Jesus' resurrection and God's saving plan unfolding in him. Though the Pentecost events and the positive response to the earliest preaching may have been less dramatic than Luke portrays them and may have taken place over a period of time, Pentecost remained an important moment in the early community's self-understanding (Acts 20:16 and 1 Cor 16:8). Acts refers to other experiences of the Spirit as well (4:8, 31; 8:14-17; 9:17; 10:44; 13:9; 19:6). The Pentecost experience inspired a missionary outreach to Jews who had not been followers of Jesus or who had heard him but had never committed themselves to him.

Peter's Pentecost sermon in Acts 2:14-36, ending with a call to be baptized, and other sermons attributed to him in the early chapters of Acts may reflect the substance of early apostolic preaching.[11] Three features of the Pentecost sermon are noteworthy. First, the sermon affirms the continuity between God's acts on behalf of Israel and what God has done in Jesus. Passages from the prophets and the psalms are cited to make the point. Second, the sermon insists that in Jesus' death and resurrection and the sending of the Spirit, as in the prophetic preaching of Jesus' followers, God's end-time saving events were being fulfilled. Third, it focuses on the risen Jesus himself as the anointed and promised of God (the Messiah or the Christ) and God's vice regent (the Lord) in the unfolding of God's final saving plan. This last feature signals an important shift between Jesus' preaching and that of his followers after the resurrection. It is as if the early preachers could not speak of the kingdom of God until they

---

[10] Dunn, *Beginning*, 156–71.

[11] On the historical character of many speeches in Acts, see Dunn, *Beginning*, 87–89.

had spoken of him through whom it was made present.[12] Even so, the kingdom of God remained a basic feature of post-Easter preaching and teaching, in continuity with Jesus' own ministry (e.g., Acts 14:22; 19:8; 20:25; 28:23, 31).[13]

Community Names / Baptism in the Name of Jesus

The early believers identified themselves and were known by several names, none of which, importantly, connote a break with Judaism.[14] Some terms clearly seem to have been self-designations. "Believers," the first collective term used (e.g., Acts 2:44; 4:32; 10:45; 1 Thess 1:7; 2:10), points to a distinguishing feature of the earliest group. After Easter, faith became distinctively focused on Jesus, especially in his death and resurrection, whereas in the gospels Jesus elicits or commends a faith that is more a trust in God's power to heal or to respond to prayer.[15] "Those who call upon the name of the Lord," presumably inspired by the Greek text of Joel 2:32 (Acts 2:21), "has the ring of a self-description in a number of passages"[16] (e.g., Acts 9:14, 21; 1 Cor 1:2). Significantly, while in Joel the term "Lord" refers to Yahweh, after the resurrection the early believers used the same term to refer to the risen Jesus. "Brothers" (often without gender-specific restriction, though some texts, e.g., Rom 16:1; 1 Cor 7:15, have the actual term "sister") was often used; its familial resonance gives an important indicator of the early group's self-perception of having a relationship based not on blood but on common adherence to Jesus. Beginning with Paul, "brother" became a common term for a fellow Christian.[17] Two other terms, "the saints" and "the elect," also used early on, lay claim to the group's being part of the heritage of Israel. Interestingly, the term "disciple" does not seem to have been much

---

[12] Brown, *Introduction*, 285.

[13] Note Luke's *inclusio* in Acts 1:3 and 28:31.

[14] Dunn, *Beginning*, 8–13.

[15] James D. G. Dunn, *Christianity in the Making*, vol. 1: *Jesus Remembered* (Grand Rapids, MI: Eerdmans, 2003), 501.

[16] Dunn, *Beginning*, 10.

[17] John P. Meier, *A Marginal Jew: Rethinking the Historical Jesus*, vol. 4: *Law and Love* (New Haven, CT: Yale University Press, 2009), 569.

used by the early believers, either in speaking to or about one another. Outside the gospel use of the term in the quite specific way described in the previous chapter, the term is not used in any New Testament writing other than the book of Acts, and here, in all cases but one (Acts 15:10), only in the narrative (e.g., Acts 6:1-2, 7; 9:10, 26). This may be Luke's conscious attempt to underscore continuity with the earlier teacher-disciple relationship with Jesus; later the term became a title of honor for the original disciples.

Other terms were used of the group by those outside the group, though in one important instance also by the group itself. This latter was the term "the Way" (Acts 9:2; 19:9, 23; 22:4; 24:14, 22). The term probably had its basis in the text of Isaiah 40:3, which looked to Israel's return from exile to the Promised Land on the way prepared by God. Its use could imply that the group saw itself continuing Jesus' mission to Israel, preparing the way for the coming reign of God. The sectaries at Qumran also referred to themselves as the Way, underscoring their own self-understanding as those who, by observance of the Law, prepared the way of the Lord. As the followers of Jesus grew in number, they were perceived by others as a sect or the sect of the Nazarenes (Acts 24:14; 28:22; 24:5); in the minds of their contemporaries, they would have been thought to be another group alongside the sect of the Pharisees (Acts 15:5) or the sect of the Sadducees (Acts 5:17) within Second Temple Judaism. At Antioch Jesus' followers were first called "Christians" (Acts 11:26), Christ-people. More on this last term presently, as well as on the term "church," widely used in the letters of Paul.

From the very beginning baptism marked the entrance into the new community.[18] Most probably given as a command received in a revelation experience of the risen Christ, baptism may have been seen as a reworking of John's baptism, with two new and very distinctive features. Baptism was performed "in the name of Jesus Christ" or "in the name of the Lord Jesus" (Acts 2:38; 8:16; 10:48; 19:5) and generally (see Acts 8:16) involved the gift of the promised Spirit.[19] As an initia-

---

[18] Dunn, *Beginning*, 185–89.

[19] The Matthean baptismal formula (Matt 28:19) in the names of Father, Son, and Holy Spirit reflects a later tradition, the liturgical practice known by the

tion rite, it signaled the transfer of the baptized into a new community committed to Jesus, acknowledging that he was indeed the one sent by God and submitting to his lordship. Ritual baptism was a tangible way of expressing adherence to him and to the community who lived in his memory. By its association with the forgiveness of sins (Acts 2:38), the nascent church was saying that what Jesus did during his ministry he now did through the actions of the church. That the Spirit was given to all who called on the Lord's name affirmed a fundamental equality of all believers prior to any differentiation. Seen at this early stage as the mark of a group within Judaism, baptism bore within it the seed that, joined with others, would contribute one day to the community's separate identity distinct from Judaism.

Community Life in Jerusalem

Acts 2:42 gives an idealized glimpse of the earliest Jerusalem community, though its elements are consistent with what is known of the community from other texts.[20] Luke's summary has four elements: "They [the newly baptized] devoted themselves to the apostles' teaching and fellowship, to the breaking of bread and the prayers." The apostles' teaching would have centered on the teaching of Jesus, especially what he expected of his followers, and the teaching about him as passed on by those who were his close companions during his ministry. These teachings were fundamental to the early community's identity and a basic means of instructing new converts. These early years and the next few decades saw the development of the oral tradition that would play so important a part in the formation of the gospels. The Jewish Scriptures, especially the Law and the Prophets, were no less important an element of the apostles' teaching. The bulk of ethical teaching came from the Jewish Scriptures. A preeminent authority would have been given to Jesus' teaching when it differed from the Law or the oral tradition of the Pharisees or when

---

evangelist when the gospel was written. Its basis, though, is probably a memory of the revelation experience mentioned above. Dunn, *Beginning*, 186.

[20] Brown, *Introduction*, 87–89; Dunn, *Beginning*, 189–202; and Fitzmyer, *Acts*, 268–71.

his teaching was applied to new circumstances. The Jewish Scriptures played a key role as a means of interpreting who Jesus was and the meaning of his suffering and death.

(Only in the second century did Christians speak of their own writings as a *New Testament* alongside the sacred writings of the Jews, now called the *Old Testament*. The term "testament" relates to the covenant relationship God made with Israel and, as Christians saw it, the renewed or "new" covenant God made through Jesus. Present-day Christian reference to the books of the Bible shared by Christians and Jews is not consistent. Because the terms "old" and "new" might suggest that the new replaces the old and deprives it of lasting value, some modern writers use the terms First Testament and Second Testament. This is not totally satisfactory, since the Second Testament might still seem to render the First Testament less valuable. Others choose to refer to the Old Testament as the Jewish Scriptures. Such a designation rightly respects the value of the Jewish tradition, but the Jewish Scriptures are also Christian Scriptures. Christians must respect and reverence the Jewish tradition in itself as well as the Jewish background of Jesus and of the church.[21] This present work uses the terms "Old Testament" and "New Testament." Jewish readers refer to their Scriptures as the Hebrew Bible or as TANAK, an acronym for its three parts: *Torah* [Law], *Nebi'im* [Prophets], and *Ketubim* [Writings].)

A second feature of the life of the early believers was the sense of fellowship or communion by which members felt bonded to one another. Luke's sole use of the word *koinōnia*, (related to *koinos*, "common") has the sense of "fellowship" or "community" (i.e., com-union, union with). Paul uses the term much more frequently, in key instances with the meaning of "participation in" (e.g., 1 Cor 10:16, participation in the body of Christ; 2 Cor 13:13 and Phil 2:1, participation in the Spirit). Luke's use of the term seems to be derivative, an outcome of the shared participation of which Paul speaks, though as a sequel to the Pentecost narrative Luke could be intending a

---

[21] See the 2001 statement of the Pontifical Biblical Commission, *The Jewish People and Their Scriptures in the Christian Bible* (Boston: Pauline Books and Media, 2002).

community brought into being by a sharing in the one Spirit. The basis for the community's fellowship was primarily theological, a common faith in the risen Lord and the conviction that all in the community shared in the gift of his Spirit. The sense of fellowship also involved a sharing of goods (Acts 2:44-45; 4:32-35). Though Luke's portrayal is no doubt idealized (see 4:36–5:11), a similar practice of such sharing took place in the community at Qumran. The followers of Jesus gathered at Jerusalem may well have expected the fullness of salvation to come soon and so regarded personal wealth of little consequence. The letters of Paul, written in the 50s, tell us about a collection he was gathering for the needs of the Jerusalem church, a gesture heightening a sense of interrelationship among the various communities (1 Cor 16:1-3; Gal 2:10; Rom 15:26). This common sharing reflects the thought that wealth was or could be an obstacle to the kingdom (see Mark 10:23; Luke 1:53; 6:24; 2 Cor 8:9; Jas 5:1) and may have been an impetus for the development of the Christian ethic of giving to the poor.[22] Administering the goods of the community would come to be one of the requirements of community leadership (1 Pet 5:2; 1 Tim 3:4-5).

The third item in Acts 2:42 is "the breaking of bread." While the same expression in Acts 2:46 seems to refer to common meals, verse 42 may refer to the Lord's Supper or to Eucharist, though neither of those terms appears in Acts. The fact that Jews who believed in Jesus continued to go to the temple at regular hours (Acts 2:46; 3:1; 5:12, 21, 42) implies that they saw no break with the worship of Israel but rather added to that their own worship gatherings.

Paul gives the earliest record of the Lord's Supper in 1 Corinthians 11:23-26, saying he received the tradition of the meal "from the Lord." Quite probably Paul received the tradition from the believing community, but in the conviction that the Lord acts in and through the community, Paul attributes the source of the tradition to Jesus. (This is a key principle in speaking of Christ's foundation of the church.) The Eucharist took place in the context of a meal, presumably at the home of one of the wealthier Christians in Corinth. Bread was broken and the cup shared in memory of the Lord. Paul's assertion that eating

---

[22] Raymond E. Brown, "Early Church," in NJBC 80:14.

the bread and drinking the cup "proclaim[s] the Lord's death until he comes" "*may* echo the Jewish pattern of Passover re-presentation . . . making present again the great salvific act, now shifted from the exodus to the crucifixion/resurrection."[23] That the cup was "the new covenant in my blood" quite likely alludes to the "new covenant" foretold by the prophet Jeremiah (Jer 31:31-33). In the prophet's text, "new" has the connotation of "renewed." The earliest believers in Jesus may have had that same understanding, though in time they would come to see the covenant God made through Jesus in a quite distinctive light. Paul's comment about needing to discern the body (v. 29) points to the presence of Christ in the Eucharist. There is good reason to think it also refers to the body of Christ, the church (more on this presently) brought about by participating in the "breaking of the bread" (see 1 Cor 10:16b). The "until he comes" may have its origin in the Jewish expectation of the Messiah's presence at the eschatological banquet, though it may also reflect the belief in the Lord's presence at "the breaking of the bread."[24] A religious meal proper to those who believed in Jesus was a major expression of community. In time it would contribute to giving Christians a distinct religious identity with regard to Judaism and came to be seen as constitutive of the being of the church.

Acts 2:46 mentions that the "breaking of bread" took place every day. While "fellowship meals" may have taken place daily in the early community, we do not know that that was also true of the Eucharist. The discovery of the empty tomb on early Sunday morning must have served to associate the Eucharist with Sunday. Since Sabbath travel restrictions ended at sundown, Jewish Christians would be free, after Sabbath observance, to gather in the home of one of the believers to break bread in the Lord's name. Later on, Christians had a celebration on the night between Saturday and Sunday. The most significant of such celebrations was and remains the Easter Vigil.

---

[23] Brown, *Introduction*, 288. Italics in the original.

[24] These details and the comment about proclaiming the Lord's death served as antecedents to the later theology concerning the real presence of Christ at Eucharist and Eucharist as sacrifice. Ibid., 289n24.

The final element in the Lucan summary is prayer. We have seen that the disciples participated in the prayer of the temple. Going to the temple at the ninth hour (Acts 3:1) is especially significant: at that hour, a male lamb was sacrificed for the continuing welfare of Israel. Two of the oldest prayer forms of Jesus' followers, one from Jesus himself (*abbā*) and another used by the earliest Jewish believers (*Marana tha*, "Come, Lord Jesus"; 1 Cor 16:22), were retained in their Aramaic forms even in Greek-speaking communities. The *abbā* prayer (Gal 4:6-7; Rom 8:15-17) was a distinctive feature of the earliest Christian worship; it attests to the conviction that the Christian pray-ers shared a sonship with Jesus (Gal 4:7), one derived from him.[25] *Marana tha* (1 Cor 16:22; Rev 22:20 in Greek) bears the eschatological outlook of the Lord's Prayer. The two forms of the Lord's Prayer (Matt 6:9-13; Luke 11:2-4) reflect the lived worship of different communities. Though the prayer is similar to synagogue prayers of the time, the familiarity of its address lacks the liturgical gravitas of typical Jewish worship.[26] The Lord's Prayer remains a staple, of course, of Christian worship. The canticles of Mary and of Zechariah (Luke 1:46-55, 68-79) show distinct Christian touches, though they are similar in structure and theme to Jewish hymns composed in the period between 200 BC and AD 100. These Lucan canticles may be examples of early Jewish Christian hymns or, if written later, hymns that preserve the piety of early Jewish Christians. (The centuries-old Christian use of these canticles in morning and evening prayer of the Liturgy of the Hours preserves the memory of the church's early Jewish Christian roots.) And, in a gospel written approximately forty years into the life of the community, Jesus utters the great Jewish prayer, the *Shema Israel*: "Hear, O Israel: the Lord our God, the Lord is one" (Mark 12:29; cf. Deut 6:4-5). Acts also suggests there were opportunities for spontaneous prayer as well as the use of fixed forms (Acts 4:24-30; 12:5; 13:3). Gradually, distinctly Christian hymns, centered on Jesus' saving work, were composed and incorporated into the prayer of the community.

---

[25] James D. G. Dunn, *Did the First Christians Worship Jesus? The New Testament Evidence* (Louisville, KY: Westminster John Knox, 2010), 98–99.

[26] Dunn, *Jesus Remembered*, 228.

The four elements in the Lucan summary show both continuity with Judaism and distinctively new elements. The continuity is consistent with our understanding of Jesus' own sense of mission and with the symbolism of the Twelve. Even after the resurrection, the earliest followers of Jesus saw themselves and were seen as Jews; they would not have thought to see themselves in any other way. Other Jews would have regarded as eccentric their twin beliefs—that Jesus was the awaited Messiah and that the promised last days had dawned—but tolerated them, especially if they continued to revere elements of Jewish belief and practice. Only when their preaching pressed the distinctiveness of Jesus and made heightened claims about him did they encounter opposition (Acts 3:1–5:42).

The Hellenists: Theological Diversity / New Structures

Notwithstanding Luke's focus on the single-mindedness of the earliest community (Acts 4:32-35), within what scholars think was its first year a dispute arose between the "Hellenists" and the "Hebrews," ostensibly over the distribution of the goods of the community (Acts 6:1-6).[27] The problem was apparently solved by appointing Hellenist leaders to attend to this special need. Scholars today are rather unanimous in thinking there was considerably more at issue.

Scholars hypothesize that the "Hellenists" refer to immigrant Jews from the Diaspora now living in Jerusalem, believers in Jesus, who spoke (only?) Greek and who were influenced by Hellenist culture. They interpreted Jesus' saving work in a way that led to a neglect or rejection of temple worship (Acts 7:48-50), thought by them to reflect a cultic nationalism they did not share. They may have welcomed converts who shared their views and who may have influenced them in the direction of their thinking. They may also have lived in a separate part of the city, somewhat isolated from the Aramaic-speaking believers. These factors put them at odds with the "Hebrews," the Hellenists' term for Jewish believers in Jesus who mainly spoke Ara-

---

[27] Dunn, *Beginning*, 242–57; Brown, *Introduction*, 293–95; Fitzmyer, *Acts*, 343–49.

maic and Hebrew (though possibly some Greek) and who continued to worship in the temple. Differences of language and culture and, probably more important, differences of theological outlook apparently led the Hebrews to slight the Hellenist widows in sharing the common funds. The Hellenists complained.

To remedy the situation, the Twelve called together the community as a whole (or perhaps those of the community who could vote) and proposed that seven men of good reputation, "full of the Spirit and of wisdom," be chosen to minister to the needs of the Hellenist community. Clearly, the seven did not confine themselves to administrative tasks alone. One of them, Stephen, emerged as a powerful preacher who articulated the Hellenists' theological outlook. Another, Philip, went to preach in Samaria and was later identified as "the evangelist, one of the seven" (Acts 21:8).

The story of the Hellenists and the Hebrews is important for several reasons. First, the outlook of the Hellenists, articulated in the lengthy sermon of Stephen (Acts 7:1-53), alerts us to the presence of diverse interpretations of the meaning of God's work in Jesus. Some believers, in the early years of the Jerusalem community, joined their belief in Jesus with a continuing insistence on the religious significance of Judaism. They would have felt that they were being faithful to Jesus by continuing his mission within the confines of Judaism. The Hellenists took a very different view of the place of the temple, yet both groups remained united by their shared fundamental faith in Jesus: "Better to tolerate certain differences of practice and thought rather than to destroy a *koinōnia* based on christology."[28]

Second, the Twelve, symbol of the renewed community, endorsed cultural and theological diversity within a common faith. The decision of the Twelve in this instance points to their unique role in preserving communion among the believers.

Third, new structures were developed to deal with a new situation. The Hellenists were accorded a ministerial leadership to meet their needs. (The Twelve do not attend to the distribution of the community's resources; that was not their role.) There is reason to think that the Hebrew Christians may have adopted new leaders for themselves

---

[28] Brown, *Introduction*, 294.

at the same time; from this point on, Acts makes references to the leadership of James and the elders (Greek, *presbyteroi*) in the Jerusalem community (Acts 11:30; 12:17; 15:2, 4, 22; 21:18). From a sociological viewpoint, one could say the development of new structures was necessarily caused by increasing numbers and differences of culture and theological outlook. In the faith perspective of the early community, however, the development of new leaders or elders in the church was guided by the Spirit of the risen Lord and reflected his will. The community held to the conviction that the will of Christ was discerned in and through the Spirit-guided community and its leaders.

(The James who is leader of the Jerusalem Christian community is described by Paul as "the Lord's brother" [Gal 1:19]. This is almost certainly the James whom Mark 6:1-6 and Matthew 13:54-58 speak of as "brother" [*adelphos*] of Jesus. The Greek term may mean "blood brother" [Mark 1:19-20] or "half-brother" [Mark 6:17], though the term can also be used in a figurative sense. Catholic teaching, developed from the assumption of Mary's perpetual virginity in Matthew [1:23-25] and Luke [1:34-35], sees James as a close relative but not a blood sibling of Jesus. While James seems not to have been a believer during Jesus' ministry [Mark 3:21-22, 31-35; John 7:5], he later came to believe [see 1 Cor 15:7] and emerged as leader of the Aramaic-speaking Jewish Christians in Jerusalem.)

There are resemblances between the emerging structures in the Christian community and those of other contemporary groups. The meeting that resolved the issue resembles meetings at Qumran, for example, which involved "the many" and a group of twelve. The number of Hellenist leaders may reflect that of the Jewish town council. Structures within the church would often be influenced by structures outside the church, as we shall see. (In the Spirit, the church needs to discern the appropriateness of structural adaptation.) While not called elders, the functions performed by at least some of the seven resemble more closely those of the elders (presbyters) and overseers (*episkopoi*) whose development we shall track as we proceed.[29] In sum, the story of the Hellenists tells us of diversity of out-

---

[29] It is probably inaccurate to speak of the seven in Acts 6 as the first deacons. John N. Collins, *Deacons and the Church: Making Connections between the Old and*

look within a shared belief in Jesus and of the development of new structures, guided by the Spirit, to meet new needs.

Missions to the Gentiles

The "radical" views of the Hellenists with regard to the temple provoked intense opposition from diaspora Jews who did not believe in Jesus but who strongly held to the temple and its significance for Jewish life. Stephen may have made some efforts to evangelize these Jews in their synagogues (Acts 6:9-10), emphasizing what was perhaps a neglected strand of the Jesus tradition that spoke of the destruction of the temple (Acts 6:14). The opposition led to his death (Acts 6:11-14; 7:54-60), probably not more than two or three years after Jesus' death and resurrection.[30] Other Hellenist leaders were driven from Jerusalem at the same time. Because of their continued allegiance to the temple, the Hebrew Christians and the Twelve were not driven away. The possibility that the Hebrew Christians did not come to the aid of the Hellenist Christians may have further complicated relations between the Hellenists and the Hebrews, but not enough to provoke a schism. The departure of the Hellenist Christians from Jerusalem may also have contributed to making the community at Jerusalem the center of more conservative attitudes regarding bringing the Gospel of Jesus to the Gentile world.

Hellenists expelled from Jerusalem (Acts 8:4-5) went to Samaria, where mixed-race people did not accept the Jerusalem temple as the only place of worship. They also went to Phoenicia (modern-day Lebanon), to the island of Cyprus, and, significantly, to Antioch in Syria (11:19), the third largest city in the Roman Empire and its major metropolis in the East. At Antioch, probably in the second half of the 30s, the Gospel was preached to Jews first and then to "the Greeks," either Greeks by birth or Greek-speaking Gentiles, but clearly

---

the New (Harrisburg, PA: Morehouse, 2002), 47–58; International Theological Commission, *From the Diakonia of Christ to the Diakonia of the Apostles* (Chicago: Liturgy Training Publications, 2004), 10–11, 93.

[30] Scholars offer competing chronologies of these early years: Brown, *Introduction*, 428–29; Fitzmyer, *Acts*, 138–41; Dunn, *Beginning*, 257n68, and 510–12. Here we follow the majority opinion, given in Brown.

non-Jews. The Hellenists generally adopted a more open policy both in the content of their preaching and with regard to those whom they addressed. The former proselytes (converts to Judaism) among them—Acts 6:5 tells us that Nicholas from Antioch was a convert to Judaism—might have been especially eager to preach the Gospel to other Gentiles. A special group among the latter might have been the "God-fearers," who, though not converts to Judaism, associated themselves to some degree to (some of) the synagogues in Antioch. Hellenist missionaries welcomed these Gentiles to their faith community and did so, momentously, without requiring circumcision as demanded by Jewish Law. In Antioch—Luke adds almost as a footnote—the disciples were first called "Christians" (11:26). These *Christianoi*, from the Latin *Christiani*, a neologism coined by Roman authorities "mildly contemptuous" of those who were perceived as members of the "Christ-party,"[31] were still regarded as within the orbit of Judaism.

Luke's use of a Hellenist tradition (Acts 6:1–8:40 and 11:19-26) into which he inserts other traditions concerning Paul's conversion and Peter's missionary work, helps us appreciate the key role of the Hellenists in the Gentile mission. In his concern to uphold the leadership of Peter and the Twelve, Luke would not likely attribute such a role to the Hellenists were that not part of the tradition. His account suggests that the missionary effort came less from a considered plan thought out by community leadership than from unanticipated circumstances. Jewish religious leadership welcomed God-fearers and proselytes and looked to the influx of the nations as part of the eschatological unfolding of God's plan, but they did not try to convince non-Jews to join them. The Hellenists' deliberate outreach to Gentiles without demanding circumcision gave a distinctive note to the early Christian movement and so initiated "one of the most crucial transitory phases in the emergence of Christianity."[32] But not without challenge, as we shall see.

---

[31] E. A. Judge, "Judaism and the Rise of Christianity: A Roman Perspective," *Tyndale Bulletin* 45 (1994): 363, cited by Dunn, *Beginning*, 304n266.
[32] Dunn, *Beginning*, 245.

Before completing his account of the Hellenist mission, Luke tells of Saul's conversion and preaching in Damascus (Acts 9:1-30) and Peter's ministry in Samaria (8:14-25), in the heavily Jewish cities of Joppa and Lydda on Judea's coastal plain, thence to the largely Gentile port of Caesarea (10:1–11:18). At Joppa, a vision calls Peter to a radical rethinking of the food laws, another sign of separatist Jewish identity in Second Temple Judaism.[33] At Caesarea, Peter responds to the call of a devout God-fearer, the Roman centurion Cornelius. When Peter and his companions recognize the Spirit's descent on Cornelius and his household (all Gentiles), Peter authorizes them to be baptized in the name of Jesus Christ. On returning to Jerusalem, however, Peter is called to justify his actions before the circumcised believers who confront him on his breach of Jewish Law. The vigorous outreach of the Hellenists and of the convert Paul, meanwhile, made of Antioch a second Christian center that openly welcomed Gentiles.

Increasing association with Gentile converts may have been a factor in a second Christian persecution in Jerusalem (Acts 12:1-19) in the late 30s and early 40s. To win support from the nationalist Jews of the kingdom of Judea, King Herod Agrippa I persecuted the Christian leadership and executed James, son of Zebedee, one of the inner circle of the Twelve. Peter was imprisoned and later forced to flee. James, the leader of the Jerusalem community, was allowed to stay, possibly because of his pronounced Jewish leanings. The James who was executed was not replaced as one of the Twelve, probably because the role of the Twelve diminished as the Christian mission expanded.

And expand it did, notably, as far as our records allow us to see, in a mission from Antioch led by Barnabas and Saul/Paul and their companions (in AD 46–49). The group went to Cyprus, then to what is now the southeastern part of Turkey. In his narrative of the mission (Acts 13–14), Luke begins consistently to use the name Paul rather than Saul and places Paul before Barnabas, indicating Paul's status

---

[33] One might think that Peter would have remembered the pronouncement of Jesus in Mark 7:15 concerning unclean foods. It seems most likely that the saying in Mark is a Christian formulation meant to support the practice of the church in ca. AD 70 by basing it in the teaching of Jesus. Meier, *Marginal Jew*, 4:398–99.

as the great proclaimer of the Gospel.[34] Even though Saul's encounter with the risen Jesus inextricably associated his conversion with a commission to take the Gospel to the Gentiles (Acts 9:15; 22:15, 21; 26:16-18), Paul and Barnabas went first to the synagogues, taking advantage of the presence of Gentile sympathizers and "God-fearers." In the face of hostility from some of the synagogues, they then took their appeal to the Gentiles and did so with marked success, as they reported upon their return to Antioch. The report was not welcomed by all among the Jerusalem believers. Accepting a few Gentiles into a predominantly Jewish Christian community was very different from seeing entire communities of Gentile Christians embrace the faith without following what was regarded as a God-given sign (circumcision) of the covenant people (Gen 17:9-14).

By the late 40s, the experience of the Christian mission and reflection on the relationship of salvation in Christ to the Law and Jewish cult led to discernibly different attitudes among Jewish Christians and their Gentile converts.[35] One view held that Gentile converts, in addition to belief in Jesus, must accept full adherence to the Law, including circumcision. This view was held by Christian Pharisees (Acts 15:5) or the circumcision party (Acts 11:2). A second view, associated with James, the leader of the Jerusalem community, and to some extent with Peter, did not require circumcision of Gentile converts but held that they were bound by certain regulations from the Pentateuch (Lev 17–18) concerning foreigners living with Jews (Acts 15:20, 29; Gal 2:12). A third viewpoint, represented by Paul, did not require Gentile converts to accept circumcision or observe Jewish laws regarding association with foreigners. Those who held this view continued to observe some cultic practices associated with the great Jewish feasts and made no request that Jews joining the community abandon the custom of circumcision. Luke writes that Paul himself observed some of these Jewish religious practices (Acts 20:16; 21:26; 24:11). If such details in Acts are historically accurate, such a stance would be consistent with what Paul would say about the abiding value of the Jewish cult in Romans 9–11.

---

[34] Brown, *Introduction*, 303.
[35] Raymond E. Brown, "Church in the New Testament," in NJBC 80:17.

A fourth point of view, maintained by the Hellenists, was openly critical of the Law and of the temple cult. Stephen's speech in Acts 7:1-53 articulates this theological outlook. Later expressions of this view would come in the Letter to the Hebrews and in the Fourth Gospel. Significantly, up to this point, those who held these various viewpoints did not break from communion with one another, even if at times relations between the various groups were strained. But the effectiveness of the Christian mission called for a common policy.

The Conference at Jerusalem

Acts 15 and Galatians 2 tell how the tensions produced by these viewpoints were resolved.[36] Scholars believe that Luke merged two events in his account. The first (Acts 15:1-12) refers to the Jerusalem assembly that decided against the necessity of full observance of the Law for Gentile converts. Participating in this meeting were the leaders of the Jerusalem community, James and Peter, and leaders of the Gentile mission, Paul, Barnabas, and other emissaries from the church at Antioch. A public discussion with representatives of those who demanded that Gentile converts accept circumcision and the Mosaic Law took place before the entire assembly. Scholars believe that this meeting, sometimes called the council of Jerusalem, occurred in AD 49. Paul's stance on Christian evangelization and observance of the Law was accepted as policy. The consequences of this decision were monumental. Freed from a narrow tie with Judaism, the early church became open to a universal mission and, ultimately, to becoming a distinct religious community. For this reason, this may well be "the most important meeting ever held in the history of Christianity."[37]

It is significant that none of the participants invoke the teaching of Jesus. Peter and Paul both cite their experiences of the Spirit's presence and activity among Gentiles: Peter in his dealings with Cornelius

---

[36] Fitzmyer, *Acts*, 538–69; Dunn, *Beginning*, 446–69, 1059–61; Brown, *Introduction*, 305–9. A "significant minority" (Dunn) holds that Gal 2:1-10 refers to the meeting mentioned in Acts 11:30/12:25. See Dunn, *Beginnings*, 446–50, and Ben Witherington III, *The Acts of the Apostles: A Socio-Rhetorical Commentary* (Grand Rapids, MI: Eerdmans, 1998), 439–45.

[37] Brown, *Introduction*, 306.

and his household (Acts 10:1–11:18), and Paul in his missionary work. If anything, those who demanded fidelity to the practice of circumcision might have insisted that Jesus did not authorize such a bold departure from the Law of Moses. The church was dealing with a question not faced by Jesus during his ministry. The assembly is confident, however, that the Holy Spirit guided them to know the mind of Christ in responding to a new question arising from a new situation. That the assembly made its decision without specific authorization from Jesus' words is an important lesson. "If Jesus did not solve the most fundamental question of the Christian mission, we may well doubt that his recorded words solve most subsequent debated problems in the church."[38]

Paul's account of the Jerusalem meeting cites an addendum to the basic agreement: "that we remember the poor" (Gal 2:10). Doing such was not only a distinctive feature of Jewish Law and tradition and a basic expression of covenant piety but also a feature of Isaiah's eschatological vision concerning Gentiles bearing gifts to Mount Zion (Isa 18:7; 45:14; 60:11).[39] Such a stipulation would satisfy traditionalist believers that, even without circumcision, Gentile believers would be binding themselves to the people of God and not be disqualified from membership into that holy body.

Sometime after the Jerusalem meeting, the issue of what to ask of Gentile converts was again the subject of discussion. Under James's leadership, another meeting took place with the apostles, the elders, and the entire assembly (Acts 15:13-29).[40] This second meeting determined that Gentile Christians should observe regulations of the Law concerning foreigners living among Israel. A letter concerning this decision was sent to the churches of Antioch, Syria, and Cilicia (southeast section of modern Turkey adjacent to Syria), all areas where James and the Jerusalem church had influence. It appears that Paul had already set out on another mission before the letter arrived and only later learned of its existence (Acts 21:25).

---

[38] Ibid., 331.
[39] Dunn, *Beginning*, 458–61.
[40] Ibid., 1080–83.

It was over the issue of Jewish and Gentile believers eating together—an issue not dealt with at the Jerusalem meeting—that led to Paul's confronting Peter at Antioch in the famous scene described by Paul in Galatians 2:11-14. It may be that Peter, mindful of his mission to fellow Jews, wished only to accommodate the scruples of Jewish believers and to avoid placing obstacles in the way of that mission. Paul would show a similar pragmatism, without denying principles, in his dealing with the Corinthians (1 Cor 8:4-13).

There is good reason to believe that, in spite of his confrontation with Paul, Peter maintained unity between the adherents of James, of Paul, and of the Hellenists. The special role accorded to Peter in Matthew's gospel, written some thirty years later, seems to reflect such a role.[41] That gospel was evidently written to guide the church, quite likely at Antioch, in integrating the various groups of Jewish Christians and Gentile converts.

The Letters of Paul: Theological Reflections on the Church

After the events of Acts 15, Luke focuses on the Pauline mission to the important cities on or near the Aegean Sea where Paul pursues an authorized circumcision-free Gentile mission. It was during these years of mission, the 50s and early 60s, that Paul wrote 1 Thessalonians, Galatians, Philippians, 1 and 2 Corinthians, Romans, and Philemon. In his pastoral concerns Paul inevitably had much to say, sometimes indirectly, about the nature of the church. In so doing, he leaves an invaluable legacy. That understanding and, implicitly, what the early Christian communities thought of themselves will be our focus for much of the remainder of this chapter.[42]

We begin with the very word "church," *ekklēsia*, the term Paul most regularly uses to speak of the corporate identity of those who came to have a personal relationship with Christ through faith and

---

[41] See Martin Hengel, *Saint Peter: The Underestimated Apostle*, trans. Thomas H. Trapp (Grand Rapids, MI: Eerdmans, 2010).
[42] See Dunn, *Beginning*, chaps. 30–33, and Wayne A. Meeks, *The First Urban Christians: The Social World of the Apostle Paul*, 2nd ed. (New Haven, CT: Yale University Press, 2003).

baptism.[43] While the term (literally "assembly" or "those who have been called out") was used in common parlance for an assembly of citizens entitled to vote, Paul almost certainly intended to use the term in the sense of the Septuagint (Greek translation of the OT, often indicated by LXX), which uses *ekklēsia* to translate the Hebrew *qahal Yahweh/Israel*, (assembly of God/Israel; e.g., Deut 23:1-3).[44] The Hebrew term was also used of the Israelites gathered in official prayer (1 Kgs 8:55; 1 Chr 29:10). Use of the term links the Christian community with the covenant people of old. We see this in Paul's oft-used expression "church (or churches) of God" (1 Thess 2:14; 1 Cor 1:2; 11:16; Gal 1:13). Paul was not the first to use the term, but the majority of its New Testament uses are in the Pauline corpus and in Acts, after Paul becomes its major focus, suggesting, perhaps, that it took some time before the community saw itself as *ekklēsia*.[45] Paul's writings show a development in the use of the term. Initially, the term is used of a local community (e.g., 1 Thess 1:1 or 1 Cor 1:2) or as a term of predilection for the community in Judea (1 Thess 2:14). In some instances in 1 Corinthians, Paul seems to be moving toward a more general sense of church (e.g., 12:28). Such a sense becomes more explicit in the deutero-Pauline Colossians and Ephesians.

The Greek term—though not its English translation—not only points to the continuity of the Christian church with the "People of God" of the Old Testament but also refers both to the gathered community and to the process by which it is summoned. It is God who calls and who continues to call the church into being, to receive the gift of God's life and to proclaim the offer of that gift to others. The church is a voluntary community only in the sense that faith is a gift to which one freely responds. We *are* church; we are always *becoming* church. The church is "a *convocation* before being a *congregation*."[46]

---

[43] James D. G. Dunn, *The Theology of Paul the Apostle* (Grand Rapids, MI: Eerdmans, 1998), 537–43.

[44] Dunn, *Beginning*, 600.

[45] Joseph A. Fitzmyer, "Pauline Theology," in NJBC 82:133. Only three times is the term used in the gospels: Matt 16:18 and twice in Matt 18:17.

[46] Henri de Lubac, *Catholicism: Christ and the Common Destiny of Man*, trans. Lancelot C. Sheppard and Elizabeth Englund (San Francisco: Ignatius Press, 1988), 64. De Lubac places the italicized words in Latin.

(The word *ekklēsia* is the root for the term "church" in the Romance languages: Latin *ecclesia*, Spanish *iglesia*, Italian *chiesa*, French *église*. Germanic languages draw on another Greek expression, *kyriakos*, "belonging to the Lord": German *kirche* and English "church.")

The term *ekklēsia* underscores corporate identity in continuity with historic Israel. Other expressions speak of incorporation into Christ, so emphasizing what is new and most distinctive.[47] Paul encourages his converts to see the church as a community of people incorporated—literally "embodied"—in Christ. Those who by faith or baptism enter "into Christ" are "symbolically plunged into Christ himself."[48] Paul's many uses of "in Christ" point to the union between Christ and the Christian, "an inclusion that connotes a symbiosis of the two."[49] Paul's references to life "in Christ" are at one with his speaking of the church as community, *koinōnia* or *koinōnia pneumatos*, often translated as "fellowship" or "communion" in the Spirit, though recent scholarship prefers "participation" or "participation in the Spirit."[50] The church is constituted by a shared experience of the Spirit, not simply by common membership in a congregation. Related to the notion of church as *koinōnia* is the image of the church as body of Christ. The latter is a "co-referent in corporate terms" to the phrase "in Christ" and the "dominant theological image" in Paul's theology of the church.[51]

Paul associates the baptized with "the body" of Christ in two ways. First Corinthians 12:12-27 suggests that the baptized, with their spiritual gifts, form a type of moral union with Christ. Such gifts of the Spirit are to be used for the good of all, just as the various parts of a body serve the good of the whole. Romans 12:4-8 carries a similar meaning. Of the undisputed letters, the Corinthians text comes closest to explicitly referring to the church as body of Christ, though it

---

[47] Fitzmyer, "Pauline Theology," in NJBC 82:116–21; see also Dunn, *Theology of Paul*, 396–412.
[48] Fitzmyer, "Pauline Theology," in NJBC 82:115.
[49] Ibid., 82:121.
[50] Thirteen of the nineteen occurrences in the New Testament appear in the undisputed Pauline letters. Dunn, *Theology of Paul*, 561 and note 152.
[51] Dunn, *Beginning*, 528–29. On body of Christ, see Fitzmyer, "Pauline Theology," in NJBC 82:122–27; Dunn, *Theology of Paul*, 548–52.

falls short of such a designation. Many scholars think Paul may be drawing on the Hellenistic notion of the state as the body politic where individual citizens agree to work together.

A second, more profound meaning seems to be implied in two other passages. First Corinthians 6:15 suggests that Christ and the Christian share in a union that is not only corporate (as the union in 1 Cor 12) but also corporal.[52] Believers are, in some way, members of Christ. A similar point seems to be made in 1 Corinthians 10:16-17 about sharing in the Eucharist: "Because there is one bread, we who are many are one body, for we all partake of the one bread" (v. 17). The point of these passages is to say that by the gift of the Spirit, we become one body with Christ (1 Cor 12:13). Only once, in 1 Corinthians 11:3-9, an obscure passage about head covering in the liturgical assembly, is there mention of Christ as head, with no reference to the metaphor of the body. Paul may be suggesting that Christ is the source of a believer's new being through her or his new life in Christ. The emphasis is less on unity with Christ than on subordination to Christ. The deutero-Pauline letters join the two metaphors, body and head, in speaking of the church.

Before looking at those letters, two further comments and a question. First, what Paul says about Eucharist in 1 Corinthians 11:23-29 serves as a compendium of teaching about the church: The church is a community that remembers the Lord, a community covenanted with God through the blood of Christ. It is called to fidelity to that covenant in all the aspects of its life, to recognize Christ giving himself in the Eucharist, and to see itself as the body of Christ. Romans 12:1–13:14 complements this text: The Christian's life in the world is worship in the Spirit offered to God. Romans 12 and 13 spell out this cult in concrete detail. Further, Paul sees his ministry as a "priestly service . . . so that the offering of the Gentiles may be acceptable, sanctified by the Holy Spirit" (Rom 15:16).

A second comment: Given Paul's key role in the Christian church's becoming predominantly Gentile, his thoughts concerning his former coreligionists, especially in Romans 9–11, are especially noteworthy. Chapter 9 begins with Paul's recognition of God's many gifts to his

---

[52] Fitzmyer, "Pauline Theology," in NJBC 82:123.

chosen people, the greatest of which is Christ himself. Paul laments that many Israelites have not accepted Christ and asks how God's saving work applies to them. God has most certainly not rejected his chosen people (11:1); in the mystery of God's ways, all Israel will be saved, "for the gifts and the calling of God are irrevocable" (11:29). Further, Gentile Christians should not boast; they are the wild olive shoot grafted onto the rich root of the olive tree and are supported by it (11:17-24).

One might ask: How realistic is Paul's vision of the church?[53] Paul was very aware of the tension between the present and a fulfillment yet to come. He articulated his vision, in part, to challenge those to whom he wrote. He was, after all, striving "to incorporate all-too-recently pagan Gentiles into [the] holy assembly of the last days."[54] Many times he speaks of the difficulties in overcoming the old self to put on the new. But guided by the Spirit, he boldly puts forth the principles, as he sees them, of communion in Christ and of being the body of Christ in the present.

The Church in the Letters to the Colossians and to the Ephesians

Pauline thought on the church is considerably developed in the deutero-Pauline texts of Colossians and Ephesians. (At present some 60 percent of biblical scholarship holds that Colossians was written by a Pauline disciple; 70 to 80 percent say the same of Ephesians.[55]) In many ways the two letters are similar, though the focus on the church is more pronounced in Ephesians. Because of its more extensive treatment and its lofty and inspiring vision of the universal church, Ephesians might almost be called "the church's first treatise on ecclesiology."[56] In the undisputed letters the church is always subordinate to salvation in Christ, Paul's central theological concern.

---

[53] Dunn, *Theology of Paul*, 562–64.

[54] Meier, *Marginal Jew*, 4:41.

[55] Brown, *Introduction*, 610, 629. Colossians: if by Paul or a disciple just after his death, in the mid-50s or early 60s; if not, in the 80s. Ephesians: if by Paul, in the early 60s; if not, in the 90s.

[56] Raymond F. Collins, *Preaching the Epistles* (New York/Mahwah, NJ: Paulist Press, 1996), 31.

Colossians and Ephesians place the church with Christ at the center of God's plan, according it a constitutive place in that plan. (In both letters, building on Pauline treatment in 1 Cor and Rom, God's plan is spoken of as *mystērion* [mystery], hidden in times past but now revealed in Christ: e.g., Col 1:26-27; Eph 1:9-10. The term, later translated into the Latin *sacramentum*, would have an important place in later liturgical and theological tradition.) In the Christ-hymn in the first chapter of Colossians (1:15-20), Christ is first spoken of as the image of God, the first-born of all creation, then further identified as head of the body, the church. As his body, the church is "the means by which Christ [the risen Lord] makes actual tangible encounter with wider society."[57] The same theme, the cosmic roles of Christ and church, appears in the magnificent hymn and prayer in the opening chapter of Ephesians (1:3-14, 15-23). In the final verse of the prayer, God is said to have made Christ "the head over all things for the church, which is his body, the fullness of him who fills all in all." With Christ and in him and his Spirit, the church has a central place in God's creative purpose for the world and all its peoples. As Christ's body, the church is a cosmic reality, encompassing all creation in a new unity where all the powers of evil will be overcome.

Akin to this emphasis on the role of the church is the virtual identification of the church with the kingdom of God's Son. In the two verses before the hymn in Colossians 1, the author affirms that God "has rescued us from the power of darkness and transferred us into the kingdom of his beloved Son, in whom we have redemption, the forgiveness of sins" (1:13-14). In the undisputed letters Paul describes himself as a minister of God (2 Cor 6:4), an apostle set apart for the Gospel of God (Rom 1:1-3); in Colossians, "Paul" is a minister of the church (1:24-25).

Developing Paul's figure of the church as a body, Colossians and Ephesians explicitly identify the church as the body of Christ and Christ as head of the body. Besides the references to these themes in the opening hymns in each letter (Col 1:18; Eph 1:23), Ephesians expands the use of the imagery. In chapter 4, for example, the author incorporates details from contemporary medical understanding: "We

---

[57] Dunn, *Theology of Paul*, 564.

must grow up in every way into him who is the head, into Christ, from whom the whole body, joined and knit together by every ligament with which it is equipped, as each part is working properly, promotes the body's growth in building itself up in love" (4:15-16). Christ is the source and goal of the church's growth, even as each member has a part in the growth of the whole. The longest sustained reflection on the church as the body of Christ occurs in Ephesians 5:23-33. Christ is head of the church, the church is his body, and the church is subordinate to him. Using baptismal and nuptial imagery, the author joins the images of church as body to church as bride.[58] As bride, the church is cleansed by Christ so that she may be presented to him "in splendor, without a spot or wrinkle or anything of the kind . . . holy and without blemish" (v. 27; cf. 2 Cor 11:2). In the "great mystery" of Christ and the church (v. 32), Christ loves the church because its members are members of his body.

The use of nuptial imagery to speak of the relationship between Christ and the church has antecedents in Israel's prophetic tradition: the eighth-century prophet Hosea (chap. 2); the exilic prophet Ezekiel (chap. 16); and a section of Isaiah that comes from the same period (Isa 54:6). The same image occurs in the bridegroom saying of Jesus (Mark 2:19-20) and in the parables of the marriage feast (Matt 22), of the places of honor (Luke 14), and of the wise and foolish virgins (Matt 25). In the Fourth Gospel, John the Baptist uses the bridegroom image in his final witness to Jesus (3:29); bridal imagery may also inform the symbolic narrative in the story of Jesus and the Samaritan woman in John 4.[59]

The juxtaposition of the two images, the church as body of Christ and the church as bride of Christ, are complementary. The first emphasizes the church's oneness with Christ; the second, the distinction between Christ and the church and the subordination of the

---

[58] Margaret Y. MacDonald, *Colossians and Ephesians*, ed. Daniel Harrington, Sacra Pagina (Collegeville, MN: Liturgical Press, 2000), 324–42.

[59] Sandra M. Schneiders, *The Revelatory Text: Interpreting the New Testament as Sacred Scripture*, 2nd ed. (Collegeville, MN: Liturgical Press, 1999), chap. 7, and *Written That You May Believe: Encountering Jesus in the Fourth Gospel* (New York: Crossroad, 1999), chap. 8.

church to him. Any image, of course, has limits: accepting that the church is subordinate to Christ does not entail acceptance of the subordinate status of women presupposed in the bride image adopted by the author of Ephesians.[60]

The image of the church in the deutero-Pauline letters is more stable and settled, concerned with describing its place in the cosmic plan of God (Eph 2:13-33). Expectation of the future completion of God's plan is retained (Eph 1:14, 21; 2:7; 4:30; 5:5-6), coupled with attention to the church's continued growth toward her final consummation (Eph 2:21-22; 4:13, 15-16). Ephesians 4:1-16 is a powerful plea for unity in the church: verses 4-6 list seven links that make the church one, while verses 7-16 speak of diverse gifts to serve the body's growth and its oneness in love. With Christian adaptations, household codes, so important in promoting social order in the Greco-Roman world, are included in Colossians 3:18-24 and Ephesians 5:21–6:9. These adapted codes probably served a double function. They would have served an apologetic purpose in a social world suspicious or even hostile to Christian emphasis on equality (Gal 3:28), on authority granted to apostles, prophets, and teachers (1 Cor 12:28), and on new and exclusive forms of worship. The codes may also have been meant to nurture cohesive community life, as loving service of others was promoted as an expression of love for Christ.[61]

The exalted and idealized view of church in Colossians and Ephesians has had a strong influence over the centuries, with both advantages and liabilities.[62] The personalized view of church as the beloved bride of Christ inspires devotion to the church. If "Christ loved the church and gave himself up for her" (Eph 5:25), if "Paul" rejoices in his sufferings for the sake of the church, "completing what is lacking in Christ's afflictions for the sake of his body"

---

[60] See MacDonald, *Colossians and Ephesians*, 341. Vatican II relates its treatment of the church as body of Christ to notions of diversity of members and functions, Christ as head, the Spirit who gives life to the body, and the church as bride of Christ. Dogmatic Constitution on the Church 7.

[61] Brown, *Introduction*, 608–10, 623–24.

[62] Raymond E. Brown, *The Churches the Apostles Left Behind* (New York/Ramsey, NJ: Paulist Press, 1984), chap. 3.

(Col 1:24), then others may be inspired to do likewise. Emphasis on the holiness of the church has also promoted a positive image. The author of Ephesians likely knew many of Paul's letters telling of failings and sin in the church; yet, he tells us, in Paul's name, that the church is "holy and without blemish" (5:27). Faith in the "holy catholic Church," as the Apostles' Creed expresses it, has helped people over the ages to maintain an association with the church even in the face of sinfulness, scandal, and administrative blunder and wrongdoing.

Nevertheless, those very advantages can also be liabilities. Emphasis on the holiness of the church can lead to hiding what is wrong, sinful, and misguided in the church or can blind one to areas calling for reform. At Vatican II and in the Jubilee of the Year 2000 church officials were more willing to admit errors and sinfulness in the church and to recognize that the holiness of which Ephesians speaks is yet to be realized. In its Decree on Ecumenism 6, Vatican II spoke of Christ's summoning the church to "continual reformation of which she always has need, insofar as she is a human institution here on earth." Colossians and Ephesians emphasize the universal church in such a masterful way that one could neglect to appreciate the theological significance of the local church. Both themes have an essential place in an integral ecclesiology. Finally, consideration of the church as the object and goal of God's saving plan can overlook the existence of other religions and of the millions of people who do not share Ephesians' belief in a cosmic salvation centered in Christ and the church. Contemporary reflection on the church is much involved with a consideration of other religious traditions.

Charisms and Ministry in the Pauline Communities

Paul's letters speak of both charisms (Greek for "gifts") and ministries in the church.[63] He describes the many types of charisms the Spirit distributed to the community at Corinth (1 Cor 12:8-10) and at

---

[63] Daniel J. Harrington, *The Church According to the New Testament: What the Wisdom and Witness of Early Christianity Teach Us Today* (Franklin, WI: Sheed & Ward, 2001), 148–62, and Patzia, *Emergence of the Church*, chap. 4.

Rome (Rom 12:6-8).[64] He also insists, in the face of rivalry and competition in the use of these gifts, that they are given for service to the community and its mission. The ministry of leadership is listed among the gifts of the Spirit.

Paul does not give a detailed picture of ministerial roles within the community; clear structures emerged some decades later. His letters do indicate the first steps toward the development of leadership positions in the church. First, there is the role of apostle as missionary leader who preaches about Christ and in so doing sometimes helps to found a local community. In this context Paul uses such expressions as "to lay foundations," "to build," or "to plant." These apostles are given principal positions in the lists in 1 Corinthians (12:28) and in the Letter to the Ephesians (4:11). A second role is that of "fellow worker" or "co-worker" (e.g., Phil 4:3; Rom 16:3, 6); a third, that of local leader. Paul calls for respect for "those who *labor* among you, and *have charge of* you in the Lord and *admonish* you" (1 Thess 5:12). The italicized verbs may refer to diverse functions of such leaders. That such ministry was done "in the Lord" points to the conviction that Jesus was the norm and guide for ministry in the church. Paul does not tell us who presided at Eucharist, though Acts 20:11 may indicate that he presided on the occasion of his stay at Troas.

Paul gives other insights into a theological understanding of ministry. In the opening lines of his letters, Paul often bases the credentials of his apostolate on a call from God (e.g., 1 Cor 1:1: "Paul, called to be an apostle of Christ Jesus by the will of God"; see also Gal 1:1). In addition to affirming a divine origin for his mission, he associates it with God's raising Jesus from the dead and suggests continuity between his call and the divine vocation given to figures in Israel's past. The heart of Paul's ministry consists in proclaiming Christ to others and encouraging their response in faith. Ministers act as "servants of Christ and stewards of God's mysteries" (1 Cor 4:1). The terms suggest both subordination to Christ and an official position in the community; the first term also implies responsibility for the

---

[64] Fitzmyer, "The Letter to the Romans," in NJBC 51:115; and Joseph A. Fitzmyer, *Romans: A New Translation with Introduction and Commentary*, Anchor Bible (New York: Doubleday, 1993), 647–49.

community's authentic belief. In 2 Corinthians 5:17-20 Paul sees himself being given an integral part of God's work in Christ: "in Christ God was reconciling the world to himself . . . and entrusting the message of reconciliation to us. So we are ambassadors for Christ, since God is making his appeal through us." The Father, ultimate author of salvation, accomplishes "a twofold effect in one action," reconciling us to himself through Christ and instituting the ministry of reconciliation.[65] A complement to this text is given in Ephesians 4:7-16.[66] Paul also recognizes the human dimension of ministry: "But we have this treasure [the knowledge of the glory of God in the face of Christ] in clay jars, so that it may be made clear that this extraordinary power belongs to God and does not come from us" (2 Cor 4:7). Paul's own example suggests how ministry was to be exercised: To those whom Paul calls "believers" and "brothers and sisters" he compares his ministry to "a nurse tenderly caring for her own children" and "a father [dealing] with his children" (1 Thess 2:7b-12; see also 1 Cor 4:15).

Paul clearly recognized the presence of women in various ministerial positions, most notably in Romans 16:1-16.[67] Among them, he mentions a Mary who "worked very hard" among the Christians in Rome, revealing "how highly he thought of the work of such Christian women on behalf of the gospel."[68] Other texts also cite the contribution of women (1 Cor 11:5; 16:19; Phil 4:2-3; see also Acts 18:26; 21:9). Counter indications might seem to appear in two texts in 1 Corinthians (11:2-16 and 14:33b-36), though in these texts Paul may have been seeking to protect Christian gatherings from being confused with the secret, orgiastic oriental cults, present in Corinth and elsewhere, that were regarded as undermining public order and decency. In this case, the texts should be seen as addressing a specific

---

[65] Gisbert Greshake, *The Meaning of Christian Priesthood* (Westminster, MD: Christian Classics, 1989), 33–35, at 34.

[66] The meaning of Eph 4:11-12 is not totally clear. Much depends on whether in translation a comma is placed after the word "saints." See John N. Collins, *Are All Christians Ministers?* (Collegeville, MN: Liturgical Press, 1992), chap. 2.

[67] Fitzmyer, *Romans*, 728–42.

[68] Ibid., 735. See also 1 Cor 15:10; Gal 4:11; Phil 2:16.

cultural situation rather than giving any theological directive.[69] Given the generally accepted later date assigned to them, the Letter to Titus and the two Letters to Timothy, completing the Pauline corpus, will be considered in the next chapter.

The End of a Generation / Time of Transition

The decade of the 60s and the year AD 70 mark important transitions, both for the Christian church and for Judaism, with consequences concerning the way each saw itself in the following decades. The early 60s saw the deaths of the three major Christian leaders; the later 60s, the Jewish revolt against Rome; and, in AD 70, the destruction of the temple. James, the leading figure in the Jerusalem church for some twenty years, was killed after the Sadducean high priest accused him, in AD 62, of breaking the Law, probably because of Jewish Christian claims about Jesus. The Letter of James, thought by most scholars to have been written pseudonymously in the 80s or 90s, consists largely of moral exhortation and the importance of prayer. It remains a valuable Christian witness to both the respect for and the use of the Jewish wisdom tradition of Second Temple Judaism in embryonic Christianity and to the community's continuity with the teaching of Jesus.[70]

Peter and Paul met their deaths in Rome within the next couple of years, possibly during the anti-Christian pogrom in 64 during the reign of the emperor Nero (AD 54–68). The death at Rome of these two great apostles was the major factor, more so than the city's political or economic prominence, that would lead Rome to become the major center of the church in the West in the following centuries. The deaths of Peter, Paul, and James and of other leaders of the first generation of the church posed new challenges in maintaining fidelity to the vision and teaching of Jesus. Each of the three major figures continued to influence the church and its self-understanding after their deaths, not least in the letters written by others in their name. "The three principal leaders of the first generation can properly be

---

[69] See Patzia, *Emergence of the Church*, 178–79.
[70] Dunn, *Beginning*, 1137–47.

said together to represent the enduring character and range of first-generation Christianity—a Christianity integrally Jewish/OTish in character, with a gospel of salvation for Gentile as well as Jew, embracing both Jew and Gentile on the common ground of faith in Messiah/Christ Jesus, inspired by the mission and teaching, the death and resurrection of Jesus, devoted to the one God through this Christ, and motivated by the same Spirit."[71]

The presumed year of Peter's death in Rome—and possibly Paul's—coincided with the beginning of a Jewish revolt against Rome's dominion in Judea.[72] The Roman field commander Vespasian, succeeded by his son Titus, led the imperial forces against the mutinous province. In the spring of 70 Titus entered the city of Jerusalem. Although he intended to spare the Jerusalem temple, in the melee it was destroyed and the city taken. (Commemorating the victory, the Arch of Titus, with its portrayal of the great temple candlestick, was erected in the Roman Forum where its ruins remain to this day.) With the temple's destruction, the symbolic center of Second Temple Judaism was no more. The event had momentous implications for Judaism; it was also a factor in the development of Christian self-understanding, as we shall see in the following chapter.

---

[71] Ibid., 1175. Dunn underscores a common finding of present scholarship, that we understand early Christianity only if we recognize its roots in Judaism and its appreciation of the writings of the Old Testament.

[72] Joseph A. Fitzmyer, "A History of Israel," in NJBC 75:181–88, and Martin Goodman, "Jewish History, 331 BCE–135 CE," in *The Jewish Annotated New Testament: New Revised Standard Version Bible Translation*, ed. Amy-Jill Levine and Marc Zvi Brettler (New York: Oxford University Press, 2011), 511–13.

CHAPTER THREE

The Church: AD 70 to the End of the First Century—Part 1

This chapter and the next focus principally on the church in the final three decades of the first century AD. This chapter will consider thinking about the church in the Synoptics and Acts, the Pastoral Letters, and the Letter of James. Chapter 4 looks at the Johannine writings, 1 Peter, the Letter to Hebrews, and the book of Revelation. We begin with a word on the situation of the church and of Judaism in the 70s. Chapter 4 concludes with a look at the relationship between Christianity and Judaism at the turn of the century and the early decades of the second century.

The destruction of the temple and the seizure of David's city by imperial Rome brought new challenges to the Jewish religious leadership.[1] The Pharisees who had not taken part in the revolt against Rome were free to establish a rabbinical school at the Judean city of Yavneh (Jamnia) on the Mediterranean coast, in present-day Gaza. The rabbis' principal concern was the Torah and its application in the new circumstances following the Roman takeover. Assuming the temple would be restored as it was after the Babylonian invasion, they also continued to be attentive to cultic issues. Under the rabbis, the Torah and the synagogue—with its partial adaptation of the temple liturgy—became focal points of Jewish religious identity. Though competing with a flourishing Jewish apocalyptic and a developing Jewish mysticism, and also with the claims of

---

[1] See James D. G. Dunn, *The Partings of the Ways between Christianity and Judaism and Their Significance for the Character of Christianity*, 2nd ed. (London: SCM Press, 2006), chap. 12.

Jewish Christianity, the rabbinate slowly extended its claim to be the authoritative interpreter of Jewish Law.

One feature of the rabbinical effort at Jewish reconstruction was an attempt to overcome the sectarian rivalry that, to some extent, was characteristic of Judaism prior to the revolt. Those who insisted on sectarian self-identification were gradually excluded. The Christian movement, with its growing Gentile membership, its increasingly exalted theology about Jesus, and its own claim to be the definitive interpreter of the Law, naturally became more and more suspect to rabbinic Judaism. In time, certain synagogues began excluding professed Jewish Christians.[2]

For their part, the Christians in the last decades of the first century were engaged in a period of transition and consolidation. A tradition preserved by the Christian historian Eusebius (ca. 260–ca. 340) has it that, either prior to the Jewish revolt or before the final Roman siege of the city, the Jerusalem Christians fled to the city of Pella in Transjordan. This dramatically lessened the influence of the conservative Jewish Christianity long associated with James, the leader of that community. The leadership provided by the Jerusalem community, with its strong sensitivity to its Jewish roots, would in time pass to the more dominantly Gentile church in Antioch and to other Christian centers in the Mediterranean. In addition, sub-apostolic Christian leadership came less from named individuals than from the apostolic tradition passed on in the gospels or from writings attributed to the apostles (e.g., 1 and 2 Timothy and Titus, quite probably the letters of James, Peter, and Jude). The period itself is marked less by missionary activity (images of fishing) than by pastoral concerns, seen in the shepherd imagery applied to both Peter and Paul (1 Pet 5:1-4; John 21:15-17; Acts 20:28-30).[3] To some of the principal theological insights of these New Testament writings we now turn.

---

[2] We see this reflected, for example, in John 9:22, 34; 12:42; 16:2.

[3] See Raymond E. Brown, "Early Church: Church in the New Testament," in *The New Jerome Biblical Commentary* (hereafter NJBC), ed. Raymond E. Brown, Joseph A. Fitzmyer, and Roland E. Murphy (Englewood Cliffs, NJ: Prentice Hall, 1990), 80:21–22.

The Gospel according to Mark

The death of those who provided a link with the ministry of Jesus and who were witnesses to his resurrection posed a new challenge: the need to preserve the memory of Jesus and to explore what he and his message meant in changing circumstances. A majority of scholarly opinion sees the Gospel according to Mark as the first text to bring together in a continuous narrative the story of Jesus, some of his teachings, and an account of his passion and death. Scholars believe Mark drew on oral and perhaps written traditions about Jesus to address the specific needs of the community, possibly at Rome, in the complex and turbulent situation of the late 60s or early 70s. In the turmoil of the times—earthquake and famine, bloody civil wars in which three emperors lost their lives, the Jewish revolt, and uprisings in Germany and Gaul—the author seems to be trying to bolster the faith of those who have suffered persecution and were saddened that some of their number abandoned the faith. In the face of this situation and the possibility of further persecution, the author tells the story of Jesus with special emphasis on his experience of opposition and on his passion and death. By adopting this strategy, which would be taken up in different ways by Matthew and Luke, Mark may be counted one of the most influential of the apostolic witnesses. His insights on the church come through his addressing the community for which the gospel was written.[4]

Discipleship: Community and Mission

Mark's gospel has two dominant themes: Jesus himself and the meaning of discipleship. Because the church is the community of disciples of Jesus, a correct understanding of Jesus is imperative. Mark articulates that understanding by the ways in which he speaks of Jesus and, even more, by the narrative of his ministry and of his

---

[4] See also Raymond F. Collins, *The Many Faces of the Church: A Study in New Testament Ecclesiology* (New York: Crossroad, 2003), chap. 7, and Kent E. Brower, "The Holy One and His Disciples: Holiness and Ecclesiology in Mark," in *Holiness and Ecclesiology in the New Testament*, ed. Kent E. Brower and Andy Johnson (Grand Rapids, MI: Eerdmans, 2007), 57–75.

passion and death. To follow Jesus as a disciple is to enter into community with him and to share in his ministry. The gospel gives three accounts of Jesus' call to others to follow him. The first call (1:16-20), to Galilean fishermen, follows Mark's summary of Jesus' proclamation concerning the coming of the end time and the dawning of God's reign (1:14-15). The call constitutes the inauguration of a new community that listens to Jesus' words and walks in his way. The subthemes of community and mission are continued in the second account, the call to the Twelve (3:13-19). Jesus calls those whom he has chosen; they come to him; they are "with him"—a basic characteristic of discipleship—and are to be "sent out to proclaim the message, and to have authority to cast out demons." The third account (6:7-13) with its injunction against taking food, belongings, or money on mission makes the point that the disciples are to rely not on their own means but on God's power. A further note on Mark's idea of community comes in Jesus' comment about who are his mother, his brothers, and his sisters (Mark 3:31-35). Jesus looks to an entire reordering of relationships among his disciples. The importance of Jesus' natural family is subordinate to those who become his "new family" by doing God's will: "Whoever does the will of God is my brother and sister and mother."

Parables about the Kingdom

One of the longest discourses of Jesus in Mark's gospel occurs in chapter 4. The bulk of the chapter consists of the three seed parables and the allegorical interpretation of the first of them. The chapter contains an important message to the church. The first parable, about the seed sown by the sower (vv. 3-9), tells of various failures but also of a wondrous yield. The second, about the seed growing quietly (vv. 26-29), reminds the hearer that the kingdom of God grows with a power that is beyond human understanding. The parable about the mustard seed (vv. 30-32) points to the difference between Jesus and his small group of disciples and the final community that will embrace a great multitude.

The allegorical interpretation (vv. 13-20) of the first parable reinforces the lesson that true discipleship comes only from hearing and accepting Jesus and his message. The difficult saying that some hear but do not understand (vv. 10-12) is best understood as Mark's recognition that many might not grasp Jesus' message and choose not to walk in his ways. As a whole, the chapter is a message of hope to the community, with a warning that not all who hear the proclamation of Jesus will bear good fruit. The kingdom of God depends on the power of God, but it also calls for our response. The concluding story of the calming of the sea (vv. 35-41) is the first of several accounts in the gospel of Jesus' mighty power. Rich in symbolism, the story recalls Old Testament images of God's power over the forces of chaos; it also tells us that Jesus, like God, rescues people when they are besieged with doubt or fear.

Lessons on Discipleship

Mark 8:22–10:52 stands at the center of the gospel. Repeated references to being "on the way" (Mark 8:27; 9:33, 34; 10:17, 32, 52) suggest that the evangelist used the term as a metaphor to emphasize that this segment of the gospel is an instruction on discipleship. The section is framed by two giving-of-sight stories. Within the section are three predictions of the passion, three misunderstandings on the part of Jesus' disciples, and three instructions by Jesus on the correct understanding of discipleship and leadership. The three instructions are our concern here.

The first instruction (8:34-38) follows Peter's rebuke to Jesus for speaking of his suffering and rejection. Jesus teaches that anyone (Mark's use of the singular emphasizes a personal challenge) who would be his disciple must "give up one's place at the center of things,"[5] be willing to make the gospel the center of their lives, evaluate their lives in terms of Jesus' life, and not be ashamed of him or his words. The second instruction (9:35-37) follows the second prediction of the passion and the disciples' discussion concerning which among them was the greatest. Jesus teaches that first among the disciples are those who serve others. Using the symbol of a child,

---

[5] John R. Donahue and Daniel Harrington, *The Gospel of Mark*, ed. Daniel J. Harrington, Sacra Pagina (Collegeville, MN: Liturgical Press, 2002), 263.

Jesus teaches that those who receive the powerless and the vulnerable in his name receive him and the God who sent him. Two further sayings follow: The first (9:38-41), following the disciples' concern about an unknown exorcist, challenges those disciples who would make exclusive claims to divine power and teaches that God's work can be done even by those who are not explicitly followers of Jesus. The second (9:42-50) warns about both the grave seriousness of giving scandal to others by inauthentic discipleship and the ineffectiveness of a leadership that is preoccupied with power rather than with self-sacrificing service.

The final instruction in this central section of Mark has two parts, Jesus' reply to two of the twelve (10:38-40) and his words to the other ten (10:42-45). After a third prediction of Jesus' passion, James and John, totally missing the point, ask for privileged places in the coming kingdom, perhaps at the final messianic banquet. Jesus' response: his disciples must identify with him in his passion and death, that is, be willing to accept suffering and possibly even death for God's kingdom. If Jesus' mention of baptism and the drinking of the cup (vv. 39-40) carry a sacramental allusion, the evangelist may be intending to remind the community that those who share in baptism and the Lord's Supper are accepting the way of the Lord, even if that way means the cross. Mark 10:42-45 continues Jesus' teaching on discipleship; he may also be speaking to community leaders. In responding to the indignant ten on hearing the request of James and John, Jesus contrasts the attitude of Gentile civic rulers who lord it over others with the attitude expected of his disciples and, according to some exegetes, their leaders. The domineering attitude attributed to political leaders of the day is the antithesis of the attitude of willing service expected of Jesus' disciples. Jesus himself, portrayed in the image of the servant figure of Isaiah 53:10-12, is the model and exemplar for the disciples.

A further word on discipleship appears in what is thought to be the original ending of the gospel (16:1-8).[6] The women's fear and

---

[6] Most scholars believe the original Mark, unlike the other gospels, did not end with an account of the resurrection. This lack so troubled the early Christian communities that various manuscripts came to append other endings, one

silence, even on hearing of the resurrection, may be the evangelist's way of saying that, even in the face of the resurrection message, one does not know Jesus apart from living in accord with Jesus' teaching and proclaiming the Gospel to others ("he is going ahead of you to Galilee; there you will see him"). Only thus do the church and its members find their identity.[7]

The Gospel according to Matthew

The last two decades of the first century were very significant ones in the church's development, both historically and theologically. Three themes were dominant: the life of the community, relations with Judaism, and efforts to find a place in the Roman Empire and in the Greco-Roman world. Aside from the letters of Paul and the Gospel of Mark, most of the New Testament writings come from this period.

Church communities in the 80s and 90s experienced a need for direction and consolidation. A major issue during this period concerned the relationship between growing numbers of Gentile converts and the Jewish background of the Christian church. Not only was there continuing tension between Jews and Christians; there were also tensions between Jewish and Gentile Christians of a more conservative stripe and those who were more independent in their attitude toward Jewish tradition. Matthew's gospel, probably written in the area around Antioch of Syria about AD 85, steers a careful path trying to relate Jewish Law and tradition to an increasingly Gentile Christian community. The gospel acknowledges Jesus' command to preach only to the house of Israel (Matt 10:5-6) and has Jesus say that he came not to destroy the law but to fulfill it (5:17-18), no doubt an effort to respect the sensitivities of those Jewish Christians who held

---

of which (Mark 16: 9-19), the so-called Longer Ending, came to be accepted as canonical Scripture.

[7] For the far greater part of the church's tradition, the Gospel according to Mark was largely ignored; that Matthew's gospel incorporates nearly 80 percent of Mark helps to account for this. Happily, the restoration of Mark into the readings of the liturgy provides redress. Mark's gospel is one of the charter documents of the church and a profound reflection on discipleship.

a deep respect for their Jewish heritage. But Matthew also recognizes that a new period of God's saving plan has been inaugurated with Jesus' resurrection and that the mission of the disciples is now directed to the people of all nations (28:16-20). Trying to promote the unity of all the members of the community for whom he is writing— Gentile Christians, Jewish believers who shared the outlook of Paul or the Hellenists, and Jewish Christians who shared the more conservative views of James—Matthew invokes the memory of Peter and makes him a symbolic center and norm of the church (16:16-19). There is no evidence that the Matthean community had any one individual who actually carried out such a role, but Matthew's portrayal of Peter would have an enormous influence on the development of a papal ministry in later centuries.[8]

Of the four gospels, the Gospel of Matthew has long been most closely associated with the church. It is the only gospel to give explicit attention to this theme. The structure of the gospel and its content make it a very apt guide for Christian life. Matthew has been as much a mainstay for Catholicism as Romans and Galatians have been guiding lights for Protestant Christianity. Until the liturgical changes after the Second Vatican Council, Matthew's gospel was used most frequently in the readings at Eucharist. With this historical background in mind, we look to see what Matthew might be saying about the church, inseparable always from what he says about Christ.[9]

Images of the Church

Like Mark, Matthew's gospel presents two key images of the church. The first is that of a community of disciples. The story of Jesus and the recounting of Jesus' discourses, formal and informal, are designed

---

[8] See Martin Hengel, *Saint Peter: The Underestimated Apostle*, trans. Thomas H. Trapp (Grand Rapids, MI: Eerdmans, 2010).

[9] See Raymond E. Brown, *The Churches the Apostles Left Behind* (New York: Paulist Press, 1984), chap. 8; Daniel J. Harrington, *The Church According to the New Testament: What the Wisdom and Witness of Early Christianity Teach Us Today* (Franklin, WI: Sheed & Ward, 2001), 104–8; Collins, *Many Faces*, chap. 8; Donald A. Hagner, "Holiness and Ecclesiology: The Church in Matthew," in *Holiness and Ecclesiology*, ed. Brower and Johnson, 40–56.

to guide the community in true discipleship. There is a fundamental equality among the disciples, even if there are also individuals with special roles. The gospel concludes with the commission, "Go . . . make disciples of all nations" (28:19). In this community of disciples, Jesus is the true interpreter of God's *Torah*, God's Law: there is one teacher, and everyone in the community is a learner (see 23:8). Several times in the gospel, Matthew also uses the image of a family, a second image, to describe the community of disciples. Matthew 12:46-50 describes the new family that Jesus' followers have become. The same theme appears elsewhere in Matthew (Matt 18:15, 21, 35; 23:8-9; 25:40; 28:10). Comparing the church to a family has been called a "hallmark" of Matthew's conception of church.[10]

Five Discourses: The Risen Lord's Instructions to His Church[11]

An outstanding feature of Matthew's gospel are the five discourses or sermons Jesus addresses to his disciples: the Sermon on the Mount (chaps. 5–7), the mission sermon (chap. 10), the sermon in parables (chap. 13), the sermon on the church (chap. 18), and the eschatological sermon (chaps. 24–25).[12] The editorial strategy underscores Matthew's intent to portray Jesus as the authoritative guide for the community. Jesus' teaching is in other sections as well.

The first of the five, the Sermon on the Mount, is the most famous. The sermon begins with the nine beatitudes (from Latin *beatus*, "blessed") that express both the actions and qualities to which Jesus gives priority in his vision of the kingdom of God. There is an activist cast to several of the beatitudes: blessed are those who show mercy to others, who commit themselves totally to the will of God, or who work for harmony within the community. The prohibition against anger in the next section, along with the beatitude on being a peacemaker, would have been especially applicable to the Matthean com-

---

[10] John P. Meier, *Matthew*, ed. Wilfrid Harrington and Donald Senior, New Testament Message (Wilmington, DE: Michael Glazier, 1980), 205.

[11] The phrase is from Frank J. Matera, "Theologies of the Church in the New Testament," in *The Gift of the Church: A Textbook on Ecclesiology in Honor of Patrick Granfield*, ed. Peter C. Phan (Collegeville, MN: Liturgical Press, 2000), 4.

[12] Titles from Brown, *Introduction*, 172.

munity in its need for reconciliation among its various groups. The climax to the first chapter of the sermon, and the motive underlying its demands, is the reminder of God's love for all (vv. 44-48). The community of disciples, children of the one heavenly Father, is to manifest God-like love in its inner relationships and, as well, in its dealings with those who do not offer love in return. The entire sermon is the Magna Carta of Christian discipleship. It describes a lofty ideal but also serves as a guide to all who strive to be disciples of Jesus in the church. A community living by Jesus' word is challenged to be a "contrast society" to those around it, acting as a light to the world and the salt of the earth (Matt 5:13-16).[13]

Some highlights from the other sermons: In the mission sermon, the assertion in 10:40, "Whoever welcomes you welcomes me, and whoever welcomes me welcomes the one who sent me," is fundamental to Matthew's Christology and to his ecclesiology. As the Father sends Jesus, so Jesus sends the disciples. The church cannot understand itself apart from its call to continue the mission of the Son. The command to proclaim the Gospel only to the house of Israel (Matt 10:6) is both delicate and complex. At the time of the gospel's writing, with the Gentile mission well under way, the disciples are specifically mandated to a universal mission (Matt 28:19). The directive to go only "to the lost sheep of the house of Israel" is surely a historical recollection of Jesus' own ministry and would have been a solace to the conservative Jewish Christians of Matthew's day. It might also have been the evangelist's plea for the increasingly Gentile community's continuing solicitude for Israel. In Matthew's mind the mission to Israel was not a question of calling Israel to convert from one religion to another; it was rather to suggest that, after the events of AD 70, "Christian Judaism was the best way to carry on the Jewish tradition."[14]

The pair of parables, in the third sermon, about the weeds among the wheat and about the dragnet (13:24-30, 36-43, 47-50) recalls Jesus'

---

[13] Reginald H. Fuller, "Matthew," in *Harper's Bible Commentary*, ed. James L. Mays (San Francisco: Harper & Row, 1988), 961.

[14] Daniel J. Harrington, *The Gospel of Matthew*, ed. Daniel J. Harrington, Sacra Pagina (Collegeville, MN: Liturgical Press, 1991), 143.

unwillingness to insist immediately on an unblemished community of followers. Including them serves the evangelist's desire to teach that the church is a community in which both the good and those who fall short are mixed together and will remain so until God's final judgment.

The fourth major discourse (18:1-35) focuses on the life of the church community.[15] Mindful of the tendency for human structures to absorb values from the world around it, Matthew intends to guard the increasingly structured community from attitudes at odds with the values of Jesus and the church's mission.[16] Much of the chapter may be directed to those who have pastoral responsibility within the church.[17] The symbol of the child in 18:1-5 is a call not to innocence but to complete dependence on God and openness to God's rule. Greatness in the kingdom is not measured by rank or power. The image of a child, a social "nobody" without status or social importance, challenges the community to avoid thinking in terms of social hierarchies.[18] The parable of the lost sheep, used in Luke to justify Jesus' eating with sinners, is here used to show that no effort should be spared in seeking out the person who has erred (vv. 12-14). The final injunction on dealing with the straying member of the community may refer to his being expelled (see 1 Cor 5:1-5); it may also mean that the sinner should be treated with special love in the manner of Jesus (Matt 11:19). Catholic Christians have devoted a great deal of attention to the power to bind or to loose given to Peter in Matthew 16. In chapter 18 the Matthean Jesus, using similar vocabulary, assigns to the entire community some role in so important a decision as isolating or excommunicating an unrepentant sinner.

The promise of Jesus to be present when two or three pray in his name (vv. 19-20) is a counterpart to the rabbinic tradition that when

---

[15] See Brown, *Churches the Apostles Left Behind*, 138–45.

[16] Raymond E. Brown, *An Introduction to the New Testament*, Anchor Bible Reference Library (New York: Doubleday, 1997), 192.

[17] Donald Senior, *Matthew*, ed. Victor Paul Furnish, Abingdon New Testament Commentaries (Nashville, KY: Abingdon Press, 1988), 204–6, titles the discourse "True Greatness within the Community" and reasons that Matthew is addressing "a core group within the community, if not its formal leaders."

[18] Harrington, *Gospel of Matthew*, 266.

two or three sat together to discuss the Torah, the *shekinah* (the divine presence) was with them. Jesus' answer to Peter's question about forgiveness and the final parable of the sermon make clear that "the Matthean Jesus has defined the unforgivable sin: it is to be unforgiving."[19] Peter's question at the end of the sermon and the disciples' question at the beginning show the evangelist's wish to make clear that all questions about the church must be addressed to Jesus.[20]

The fifth and final sermon functions as Jesus' farewell to his disciples (24:1–25:46). The sermon's teaching and moral exhortation mean to guide the community in the time between his resurrection and his return in glory. The three short parables in Matthew 24:37-44 make one basic point: Christian life must be lived in the perspective of the event that discloses its ultimate meaning, Christ's coming in glory to complete God's plan of salvation. Christ's disciples are to be vigilant, always ready for the Lord's coming. The three longer parables that follow reinforce this theme. The parable of the faithful and the unfaithful servants (24:45-51), presented as Jesus' warning to unfaithful religious leaders of his day, is directed now to the church, especially its leaders. The parable of the talents (25:14-30) calls Christian disciples, especially leaders, not only to preserve the gifts they have been given but to exercise them in faithful service.[21]

The discourse concludes with the great scene (25:31-46), found only in Matthew, of the final judgment likened to a shepherd separating sheep from goats. In one interpretation, Jesus, the "Son of Man" in the judgment scene, pronounces a verdict on the basis of one's treatment of the hungry and thirsty, the stranger and the naked, the sick and the imprisoned. The text, the Matthean Jesus' final word to the church, points to an essential element of Christian belief: that Christ is present in the needy and that care for them is a litmus test for Jesus'

---

[19] Brown, *Churches the Apostles Left Behind*, 145.

[20] This is not contradicted by what was said above about the decision taken in Acts 15. We learn of Jesus' will by discerning the gift of his Spirit guiding the church.

[21] On this last parable, see John P. Meier, *A Marginal Jew: Rethinking the Historical Jesus*, vol. 5: *Probing the Authenticity of the Parables* (New Haven, CT: Yale University Press, 2016), 306–10.

followers and for the church.²² The text, be it noted, does not support the claim that one's attitude toward the neighbor, *rather than* creed or worship or membership in the church, is all that matters. Another interpretation of the text sees it as referring to a judgment of the Gentiles, based on their treatment of Jesus' disciples and ultimately on Jesus himself who identifies with them. This interpretation draws on the Jewish tradition of separate judgments for Jews and Gentiles and Matthew's use of the terms "nation" and "the least of these" in the rest of the gospel. In this case, the text reinforces the notion of Jesus' identification with missionaries or ordinary Christians (Matt 10:40).²³

Petrine Ministry in the Church

Christ himself is the primary teacher and guide in the community of disciples or the new family in Christ that is the church. Matthew also recognizes a place for authoritative figures within the community, though he is equally concerned that their roles be rightly understood. Peter has the most prominent such role in the Matthean narrative. Matthew alone tells of Jesus giving Simon the name or nickname Cephas (Peter) after his profession of faith in Jesus as "the Son of the living God" (Matt 16:13-20). Simon Peter's faith becomes the human foundation stone of the new community. And Matthew alone tells of Jesus' commission to Peter concerning the "keys of the kingdom." Traditions of a change of name and of building on a rock are frequent in biblical literature (see Isa 51–52; Ps 118:22; Matt 21:42; Eph 2:20; Matt 7:24-25).²⁴ Jesus' bestowal on Peter of the keys of the kingdom, with the power to bind and loose on earth and in heaven, recalls the scene in Isaiah 22:15-25 where King Hezekiah makes Eliakim the vice regent, giving him the "the key of the house of David." Because Matthew's section on the keys follows a critique of the teaching of the Pharisees and Sadducees (Matt 16:5-12), it may

---

²² Meier, *Matthew*, 302–6.
²³ Harrington, *Gospel of Matthew*, 355–60.
²⁴ The desert community at Qumran also used the image of God's building on a rock foundation.

well be that the keys refer to Peter's positive teaching authority (the binding and loosing role of the local community in chap. 18 refers to *exclusion* from the community). Peter's role in the community is linked to his fidelity to the teaching about Christ, as the following verses (16:21-23) make clear. When Peter sets his mind on human things and not on the things of God he becomes a "stumbling-block." The scene in Matthew 14:28-31, where Peter is invited to walk on the water, reminds us that Peter shares in Jesus' power but only so long as he keeps his faith centered on Jesus.

In part because the saying about the keys of the kingdom is absent in Mark and Luke, many scholars suggest that it is based on an appearance of Jesus to Peter after the resurrection and in Peter's reaffirming the faith of the other disciples after the shattering experience of Jesus' death. Matthew uses his portrayal of Peter, quite probably based on the memory of Peter's role in the early decades of the church, as a *symbol of unity* meant to hold in communion the Jewish Christians and the Gentile converts of the 80s, a norm against any one-sided interpretations of the traditions associated with James or Paul or the Hellenists.

Authority in the Community

Two other passages deal with the issue of authority in the community. The first of these texts (20:20-28) is the Matthean parallel to Mark 10:35-45, about places of honor in the kingdom. Jesus clearly warns against adopting the style of Gentile rulers who lord it over others and who act like tyrants: "It will not be so among you" (Matt 20:25-26). The great are to be servants, just as Jesus came not to be served but to serve. The second text (23:1-36) is a lengthy denunciation of the scribes and Pharisees. The tension between Jesus and some of the Jewish religious leadership during his public ministry provides historical background. The gospel text recalls this memory and heightens it to serve Matthew's contemporary debate with the post-Jamnia Jewish leadership concerning claims to be the authentic and normative interpreter of the Law. The harsh language reflects the intensity of the debate between the Jewish leaders and the evangelist. Awareness of the historical situation in which the text was written and of the tradition of denunciations of Israel and its leaders by the prophets is necessary for a correct interpretation of the text with regard to Judaism. The text is no less a warning to the Christian community and its leaders in Matthew's day.[25] Matthew 23:1-12 addresses two distortions of true religion: saying one thing and doing another (v. 3) and doing things only for external show (vv. 5-7; see Matt 6:1-18). The Matthean Jesus mocks the concern for status symbols: special clothing, places of honor, obsequious greetings, and titles in public. Reminding the disciples that they are all equal in the new family of God (vv. 8-9), Jesus teaches that there is but one Father, God in heaven, of whom we are all children. There is but one teacher and one guide, Jesus the Messiah. Everyone in the community is to be a "servant" to one another. The prohibitions against calling disciples "father" or "rabbi" or "master" underscore both that all disciples are subordinate to God and to Jesus and that the community of disciples is not built on a patriarchal model. Catholic Christians who address their priests as "Father" draw from Paul's frequent use of parental imagery in describing his relation to those to whom he ministers (1 Thess 2:7, 11; also 1 Cor 4:15; Phil 2:22), even as he insists that there is only one God, the Father, and one Lord, Jesus Christ (1 Cor 8:6).

Sociological studies show that resistance to hierarchical structures is often a characteristic of new religious communities. Matthew's gospel uses chapter 23 to distance the Jewish-Christian community from Judaism and some of its traditional structures, though the same strategy weakens the case for leadership in the Christian community. What may serve well in a sect may be less suitable in a larger group needing inner cohesion and effective organization for its mission. Developed Christian churches will always need to respect both the basic common dignity that comes from baptism and institutional structures that serve ecclesial life and mission.[26]

The heart of the chapter in verses 13-36 consists of seven "woes" against hypocrisy and "lawlessness" (v. 28), the latter expressing underlying rebellion against God's will. The style of these woes is similar to prophetic denunciations against the powerful who abuse

---

[25] Senior, *Matthew*, 256–65, and Harrington, *Gospel of Matthew*, 319–30.
[26] Harrington, *Gospel of Matthew*, 323–24.

their positions (e.g., Isa 5:8-10, 11-14, 18-19; Jer 13:27; Ezek 16:23; Amos 5:18-20; Mic 2:1-4). Taken out of context, Matthew's text might seem to caricature Judaism itself as hypocritical and self-righteous; such an interpretation would be seriously misleading. The text also serves as a checklist for leaders in the Christian community. It warns against attitudes and practices such as undue emphasis on externals or casuistry that violates the spirit of the Law. Overall, Matthew's gospel shows a great respect for the Law and for authority in the church. Abuses that come from such an emphasis have an inbuilt corrective: Jesus is supreme interpreter of the Law, and all authority, relative always to him, must be exercised according to his standards.[27]

The Church and Judaism

Matthew 23, like other passages in the gospel, can be understood only in terms of the tension between the Christian church and the synagogue at the time of the gospel's composition. The evangelist writes for the Christian community, but he is also engaging in debate with "the synagogue down the street." Matthew often notes that events concerning Christ fulfill what was said in the Old Testament (Matt 1:22-23; 2:15, 17-18, 23; 4:14-16; 8:17; 12:17-21; 13:34-35; 21:4-5; 27:9-10). The use of these citations makes the claim that the Old Testament Scriptures point to Christ and find their fulfillment in him. The Matthean Jesus accepts much of the Mosaic Law, even if he himself, not the Law, is normative for the life of the community. Matthew has an abiding if qualified respect for the traditions of Judaism, for the Sabbath (24:20), for example, and for Jerusalem as a "holy city" (4:5; 27:53). At the same time, Matthew's attitude toward the synagogue and especially its leadership is often negative. Repeated references to "their [or your] synagogue[s]" (Matt 4:23; 9:35; 10:17; 12:9; 13:54; 23:34) heighten the sense of separation between church and synagogue. The parable of the tenants in Matthew 21:33-46, placed after the "cleansing of the temple," highlights the struggle with the synagogue, even if it also warns against Christian backsliding, and functions as an allegory of salvation history. Proper to Matthew is

---

[27] Brown, *Churches the Apostles Left Behind*, 135–38.

Jesus' comment at the end of the parable: "Therefore I tell you, the kingdom of God will be taken away from you and given to a people that produces the fruits of the kingdom" (v. 43). While the saying is sometimes taken to suggest that the Christian church replaces Judaism, the parable is really directed against the religious leaders who rejected Jesus and, in the period after the destruction of the temple, claimed to be the authentic interpreters of the Jewish faith. In Matthew's account, the vineyard is not destroyed, as it was in the poem in Isaiah 5:1-7, but the tenant farmers are replaced. Israel, Matthew contends, finds its truest guide in Jesus and in the leaders of the new community of his disciples.

The Great Commission

The final verses of Matthew's gospel (28:16-20), the commissioning of the disciples after the resurrection, have been called the key to understanding the whole of the work; they are also a fine summary of Matthew's idea of church. The eleven disciples (a sad allusion to the absent Judas) are a symbol of all disciples, but especially church leaders. The setting is in Galilee, the scene of Jesus' ministry and teaching. Seeing Jesus, the disciples give him homage, yet with hesitation, a pointer to enduring tension within their hearts (see Matt 14:31-33) and sometimes in ours. The mountain setting signals an imminent revelation. That all authority in heaven and earth has been given to Jesus tells of his exaltation over the entire universe and reminds the believer that he is the source and ground of all authority in the church. The restricted mission to the house of Israel (Matt 10:5-6) is now set aside: Jesus has been raised, the end time has dawned, and the Gospel is to be preached to "all nations," that is, all peoples, including Jews. The extent of the mission reflects Jesus' intent at the Last Supper, that the sacrifice of his life was "for many," a Semitism designating the collectivity, equivalent to "all." The disciples are to be initiated by baptism into relationship with Father, Son, and Spirit, the basis for the new community that is the church. The commission Jesus gives is an astonishing one, but Jesus, Emmanuel (Matt 1:23), pledges his abiding presence until "the end of the age." The Jesus who called disciples to be with him during his ministry and who promised to be with two or three disciples gathered in his name now promises to be with the church until his glorious return.

The Gospel according to Luke and the Acts of the Apostles

The Gospel according to Luke and the Acts of the Apostles are best read as two parts of a single work. Together they make the very important theological point that the story of Jesus continues in the church. This conviction is shared by all the evangelists, but none is as *explicit* about this as the author of the Third Gospel and the book of Acts. The latter work might well be called "a narrative ecclesiology."[28] Written about AD 85, perhaps a few years after Matthew's gospel, Luke and Acts may have been addressed to churches in Greece or Syria that were influenced by Paul or his coworkers. The author may have been a convert to Judaism before he became a Christian.[29] Our review of the theology of church in Luke–Acts will focus on several themes.[30] We have already seen a fair amount of Acts in the preceding chapter.

Jesus and the Church: Continuity in God's Plan

The author of Luke–Acts emphasizes continuity between God's work in Israel and his saving work in Jesus, and a continuity of mission between Jesus and the church. At the end of the gospel (24:44-49), Jesus grounds both his mission and that of the church in the will of God disclosed in the Law, the Prophets, and the Psalms, expressing the conviction that the divine plan disclosed in those writings is now being fulfilled. At the beginning of Acts, the risen Jesus tells the apostles: "You will receive power when the Holy Spirit has come upon you; and you will be my witnesses in Jerusalem, in all Judea

---

[28] Joseph Cardinal Ratzinger, *Called to Communion: Understanding the Church Today*, trans. Adrian Walker (San Francisco: Ignatius Press, 1996), 41.

[29] Brown, *Introduction*, 226.

[30] See Harrington, *Church*, 109–13; Brown, *Churches the Apostles Left Behind*, chap. 4; Collins, *Many Faces*, chap. 9; Matera, "Theologies of the Church," 6–7, 9–12; Richard P. Thompson, "Gathered at the Table: Holiness and Ecclesiology in the Gospel of Luke," in *Holiness and Ecclesiology*, ed., Brower and Johnson, 76–94.

and Samaria, and to the ends of the earth" (1:8). The book of Acts emphasizes the bridge role provided by persons in the gospel story (the Twelve, the mother of Jesus, and other family members) who also figure prominently in the story of the early church. The gospel describes Jesus' journey from Galilee to Jerusalem (9:51–19:27; note 13:22 and 17:11); Acts parallels that journey with the church's journey from Jerusalem (Acts 1:4, 12) to Rome (28:14), capital of the Empire, symbolically the ends of the earth (again, Acts 1:8).

We have already seen the emphasis on community in the early chapters of Acts. The statement in Acts 2:42-47, with its focus on the four features of church life (v. 42), is an idealized statement expressing Luke's deepest conviction about what is essential to church: "harmony, reverent care for one another, formal and informal prayer in common, and celebration of the Lord's Supper."[31] Yet this text and other summary statements in Acts (Acts 4:32-35; also 1:14; 6:7; 9:31; 12:24; 16:5; 19:20; 28:30-31), coupled with Luke's tendency to downplay elements of tension or struggle in the story of the church, may give the false impression that the community of the church was always at peace, experiencing constant growth and advancement. While expressing ever-valid ideals, Luke–Acts ill prepares one to deal with tensions as the community faces new questions; the author gives scant attention to setbacks or periods of decline in the church. The latter do not diminish the force of the former.

The entire book of Acts is testimony to the awareness of the sense of mission that guides the church. The sermons throughout Acts serve as paradigms of the central message of the church's evangelizing mission: God's saving word and action in Jesus Christ. Luke also reports that the church had to grow in understanding the nature of its mission (Acts 10, 11, and 15); Jesus' own example and the memory of his directives did not always provide a ready answer. The fateful decision of the Jerusalem assembly permitting the church to move from being a distinctive community within Judaism to being open

---

[31] Joseph A. Fitzmyer, *The Acts of the Apostles: A New Translation with Introduction and Commentary*, Anchor Bible (New York: Doubleday, 1998), 269, and *The Gospel According to Luke (I–IX): Introduction, Translation, and Notes*, Anchor Bible (Garden City, NY: Doubleday, 1981), 227.

to the Greco-Roman world may be a valuable paradigm for the present church's transition from being a predominantly Western European church to becoming a *world church*, embodied in diverse cultures.[32]

The Holy Spirit in the Church

Continuity, community, mission—all have their basis in "the distinguishing feature of Lucan ecclesiology . . . the overshadowing presence of *the Spirit*."[33] As in Spirit passages in the Old Testament, Luke represents the Spirit as a creative, prophetic, active force in Jesus and in the church. Luke's insistence that Jesus inaugurates a new age of salvation leads to his frequent mention of the Spirit in Jesus' conception, at his baptism, in his duel with the tempter, and in his inaugural sermon at the synagogue in Nazareth.[34] The Pentecost scene in Acts 2:1-41 parallels what the gospel says of Jesus himself: the church, too, is born of the Spirit. The Spirit's coming at the Jewish feast of Pentecost suggests a renewal of God's covenant with the disciples of Jesus. Filled with the Spirit, the disciples begin to preach. The Spirit moves a reluctant Peter to accept Gentile converts, who have already received the Spirit, to enter the community of the baptized. The same Spirit guides the assembly at Jerusalem to the momentous decision that has shaped Christianity ever since (Acts 15:8). The remainder of Acts shows the continuing place of the Spirit in the life of the church, sometimes directing its leaders in ways they did not expect (Acts 16:6, 7; 21:4). Generally, the Spirit is given in the presence of the Twelve or one of their number or a delegate. The one exception is Paul, probably because of Luke's wish to emphasize the extraordinary

---

[32] See Karl Rahner, "Basic Theological Interpretation of the Second Vatican Council," in *Concern for the Church*, trans. Edward Quinn, Theological Investigations 20 (New York: Crossroad, 1981), chap. 6.

[33] Brown, *Churches the Apostles Left Behind*, 65. Luke's gospel mentions the Spirit seventeen or eighteen times, compared to Matthew's twelve and John's fifteen; Acts mentions the Spirit fifty-seven times. Fitzmyer, *The Gospel According to Luke (I–IX)*, 227.

[34] Though not frequently so, there are reminders that Jesus' ministry is carried out in the Spirit: e.g., Luke 10:21-22; 11:13; 12:10-12.

grace given to him in light of his special role in God's plan. But in Acts the Spirit is given to the community as a whole, as well as to individuals in positions of leadership. Catholic tradition has long emphasized the link between the Spirit and the office of its pastors. The portrayal of the Spirit in Acts encourages a broadened understanding of the way the Spirit operates in the church.

Luke's emphasis on the Spirit in the church does not exclude interest in individual leaders or in developing church structures. The Twelve are prominent in the general oversight of the fledgling community, especially in the important decisions concerning the Hellenist leaders (Acts 6) and the Gentile mission (Acts 15). Paul and James are among the early church's principal leaders, though attention is also given to the Jerusalem elders, Barnabas (Acts 14 and 15), and Priscilla and Aquila (Acts 18). Emerging structures of office are also mentioned (e.g., Acts 6:1-7; 11:30; 20:17, 28). Paul and Barnabas are said to appoint presbyters to continue their work (Acts 14:23), though scholars question whether such formal appointments took place in Paul's day. Paul's sermon at Miletus (Acts 20:17-35) is especially important. Here, Luke outlines the role of Spirit-appointed leaders in the church. While Luke views the church as a Spirit-guided, organized community, he is more concerned with the growth of the church as a vehicle for proclaiming the Gospel than with ecclesial structures.

Far more than the other evangelists, Luke situates the story of Jesus and the church in the context of history. In the first three chapters of the gospel, the figures of Zechariah and Elizabeth, Simeon and Anna, and John the Baptist are bridge figures between Judaism and the fulfillment of God's promises in Jesus. The canticles of Zechariah, Mary, and Simeon in those chapters reflect the promise/fulfillment theme, as do Jesus' final words in the gospel and Peter's sermons in the first couple of chapters in Acts. Luke's concern to impart this theological pedigree to an increasingly Gentile community contrasts with Stephen's discourse in Acts 7. Luke also deliberately situates Jesus and the church in the Greco-Roman world of the day. Luke 2:1-2 relates Jesus' birth to the taking of the census; Luke 3:1-2 lists the political and religious leaders at the time of the Baptist's mission; and Paul tells King Agrippa (Acts 26:26) that Jesus' life and Paul's conversion did not take place "in a corner" (see also Acts 11:28; 18:12;

25:11; 27:1). How the church subsequently implemented that insight will be a major issue in its history. Another dimension of Luke's emphasis on the historical appears in his attitude toward the present. The evangelist maintains a lively awareness of Christ's second coming (e.g., Luke 10:9; 11; 22:32; Acts 3:19-21), but he is clearly more concerned to shift the emphasis to the "everyday" of Christian life. Only in Luke does Jesus tell his disciples to take up their cross *daily* (Luke 9:23; cf. Mark 8:34); Luke's version of the Lord's Prayer has the petition "Give us *each day* our *daily* bread" (Luke 11:3).

The Third Gospel and Acts also place a great emphasis on prayer. Besides the magnificent canticles of Mary and Zechariah in Luke 1, Luke frequently portrays Jesus at prayer.[35] The book of Acts does the same in describing the community: after the ascension and prior to the coming of the Spirit (Acts 1:14); in choosing a successor to Judas (1:24); in the several Lucan summaries of church life (Acts 2:42; see also Acts 3:1; 4:31; 12:12). The evangelist suggests that prayer is as important an apostolic service as ministry of the word (Acts 6:4).[36] Luke reinforces his emphasis on prayer by three parables, all proper to the Third Gospel (Luke 11:5-8; 18:1-8, 9-14). In the lesson on prayer in Luke 11:9-13, Jesus asks us to pray for the supreme gift we seek from God, the gift of the Spirit. Instructions on prayer come at the beginning and at the end of the "journey narrative" (9:51–19:27). Luke's focus on prayer functions as an instruction regarding a basic element of the Christian life of the community.

Concern for the poor and those on the margins as well as the disciples' need to use possessions wisely also enter into Luke's vision of discipleship in the church. In his inaugural sermon at Nazareth (Luke 4:16-21), Jesus draws on the prophet Isaiah (61:1-2; 58:6) in setting the agenda for his ministry in the context of a jubilee. Since the gospel does not further refer to the jubilee year (Lev 25:8-12)

---

[35] At his baptism (Luke 3:21); at reports of his healings (5:16); in choosing the Twelve (6:12); when asking his disciples what people thought of him (9:18); at the transfiguration (9:28-29); before teaching the disciples how to pray (11:1); at the beginning of the passion (22:41); and on the cross (23:46).

[36] Emphasis on prayer continues throughout the book of Acts: 9:11; 12:5; 13:3; 14:23; 20:36; 21:5; 22:17.

mentioned in Jesus' proclamation, the main point of the passage is not to suggest a program of economic or social reform but rather Jesus' special concern for the poor and the outcasts of society. Other texts express the same theme: Mary's canticle on the occasion of her visit to Elizabeth (Luke 1:46-55) and the first Lucan beatitude concerning the poor and the corresponding prophetic "woe" directed against the economically secure who see no need for God (Luke 6:20, 24). Almsgiving is stressed frequently in both the gospel and in Acts (Luke 12:33; 19:8; Acts 9:36; 10:2, 4, 31; 24:17). In Luke 14, Jesus speaks directly to issues of social status and the need to welcome the poor. His proposal for dinner guests, "the poor, the crippled, the lame, and the blind" (14:13), reflects the reversal of values that is a hallmark of God's coming kingdom.

Luke repeats warnings about the danger of wealth. Two parables proper to Luke take up these themes. The parable of the rich fool (Luke 12:16-21) follows a warning against greed and a saying that human life is not to be measured by the abundance of one's possessions (Luke 12:15). The rich man interacts with no one but himself, oblivious to the thought that the fruit of his harvest might be meant for anyone else. In the parable of the rich man and Lazarus (Luke 16:19-31), the rich man is judged not because he harmed Lazarus, the poor man at the gates of his house, but because, in his wealth, he never noticed him in his need. Indifference to the poor, the parable points out, can lead to separation from God. Luke's radical statements about wealth (Luke 6:35; 12:33; 14:33; 16:13) will inspire some in the church to an almost literal following. Passages that speak positively of those who help others with their means show that wealth as such is not evil, but its use must reflect the values of the kingdom and not blind us to others' needs (Luke 8:3; Acts 9:36; 10:2, 4, 31). Luke's gospel does not give ready answers to the many and complicated social and economic problems of our day when we are much more aware that systemic factors—economic, social, political, and even religious—cause poverty and in many instances contribute to injustice and marginalization. But Luke's writings, word of God to the community of disciples, remind us of the values and priorities of the kingdom. We who pray, at Jesus' command, for the coming of the kingdom, are called to keep those priorities and values before us as

The Church: AD 70 to the End of the First Century—Part 1   87

we see the Lazarus by our door and encounter the victims of robbers left naked, beaten, and half dead (Luke 10:29-37).

Last Supper Instructions

Our overview concludes with two other passages. The first (Luke 22:24-38), instructions at the Last Supper, constitutes a type of farewell discourse to Jesus' disciples on the eve of his passion. After the words over the cup and his word about the one who would betray him, Jesus responds to the squabble of the apostles over who should be the greatest (Luke's parallel to the disciples' misunderstanding in Mark 10:41-45 and Matt 20:25-28). Concern over prestigious places and rank in the kingdom is itself a form of betrayal.[37] The Christian community operates with other values: the most important among them—Luke presumes there is such a person—is to act like the least; leaders are to see themselves as servants. Expectations assumed in the political order are reversed in the community of believers: greatness is equated with the commitment to serve. Jesus' words to Peter (vv. 31-34), a prayer that when he turns back to Jesus after his betrayal he is to strengthen his brothers, may well refer to Peter's role in strengthening the resurrection faith of the Eleven after Jesus' death. In later church history, this text would be a key factor in the development of the Petrine ministry. The final three verses (35-38) of this Last Supper instruction actually alter earlier missionary directives (Luke 9:3; 10:4).[38] In view of the crisis confronting Jesus and anticipating the opposition the disciples will face in their ministry (in Acts and in the time after Acts), the disciples must be better prepared. Now they need purse, bag, and sword where before they did not. Jesus' statement is a metaphor that the disciples do not understand. They are too ready to depend literally on such means for their mission: they have two swords! In disheartened frustration at their lack of comprehension, Jesus says, "It is enough!" Centuries later the saying about the "two swords" and Jesus' response would take on a meaning far removed from the evangelist's

---

[37] See the related theme in Luke 9:46-48; 14:7-11; 20:45-46.
[38] Joseph A. Fitzmyer, *The Gospel According to Luke (X–XXIV): Introduction, Translation, and Notes*, Anchor Bible (Garden City, NY: Doubleday, 1985), 1428–31.

intent: the swords would become symbols of religious power and secular power, and canonists and theologians would debate the church's right to call on the secular sword.

On the Road to Emmaus

Our final passage is the famous Emmaus story, found only in Luke (24:13-35). The evangelist uses the story to strengthen communities unable to see the risen Jesus in the difficulties they experience as they walk in the way of the Lord (another reference to the journey theme). The story has a dialogue narrative with its reflection on the Scriptures and a meal narrative. Both point to constitutive elements of the church's worship and of the church itself. The Scriptures nourish us and are indispensable in our coming to know Jesus. But only when the disciples offer hospitality to the stranger, when they engage in the *blessing, breaking,* and *giving* that were at the heart of Jesus' ministry, do they see the presence of the risen Lord in their midst. The three terms recall Luke's story of the feeding of the five thousand (9:16) and his account of the Last Supper (22:19). When the disciples realize they have encountered the risen Jesus, they return to Jerusalem, announcing that they came to know him in "the breaking of the bread," the same term used in Acts 2:42. The tradition of the Emmaus supper and the other post-resurrection meals probably had a major influence in the development of the belief in the presence of the risen Lord in the Eucharist. The Emmaus story incorporates many of the themes of Luke–Acts and for good reason has long been seen as a guide to the church.[39]

The Pastoral Letters

Luke–Acts looks to missionary expansion; the Letter to Titus and 1 and 2 Timothy look to the care of established communities.[40] Except

---

[39] See Louis-Marie Chauvet, *Symbol and Sacrament: A Sacramental Reinterpretation of Christian Existence,* trans. Patrick Madigan and Madeline Beaumont (Collegeville, MN: Liturgical Press, 1995), 161–70, and *The Sacraments: The Word of God at the Mercy of the Body* (Collegeville, MN: Liturgical Press, 2001), 20–27.

[40] Brown, *Introduction,* chaps. 29–31; *Churches the Apostles Left Behind,* chap. 2; Harrington, *Church,* 93–98; and Collins, *Many Faces,* chap. 6.

for the possible fragments of genuine Pauline material in 2 Timothy, the letters appear to have been written by a disciple of Paul or someone (often called "the Pastor") who wished to invoke his authority. Most scholars hold that Titus and 1 Timothy were written between AD 80 and 100, probably intended for churches in Crete and Ephesus. The outlook of these letters is heavily influenced by the need to confront "false teachers" (1 Tim 4:1-2; 2 Tim 3:1-6; Titus 1:10-11) and the confusion they were bringing to the churches for which the letters were written. Three issues stand out: the image of church, the presence of the Spirit in the church, and the pastoral strategy adopted in these letters.

The basic image of church in the Pastoral Letters is given in 1 Timothy 3:15: "the household of God . . . the church of the living God, the pillar and bulwark of the truth."[41] The church is imaged as the household of God, where God's truth is upheld, proclaimed, and shared. The household image also reflects the familial character of the early Christian churches. The next verse identifies that truth, "the mystery of our religion": "He [Christ] was revealed in flesh, vindicated in spirit, seen by angels, proclaimed among Gentiles, believed in throughout the world, taken up in glory." The proclamation juxtaposes the realms of earth and of the divine: incarnation (earthly realm), resurrection and ascension (divine realm), preaching of the Gospel and its acceptance (earthly realm), glorification at the end (divine realm). The formula cited by the author shows the distinctiveness and interrelationship of each realm in Christ. The same juxtaposition of the earthly and the divine is also fundamental to an integral understanding of church. The place of Scripture is at the heart of the church's teaching and the formation of its members (2 Tim 3:14-17).

As Paul and Luke–Acts gave attention to the Holy Spirit and the Spirit's place in the church, the Pastor does the same, though in a quite different way. Paul emphasizes the Spirit dwelling in the hearts of believers as the source of various gifts and charisms in the church, with administrative and leadership roles counted

---

[41] Collins, *Many Faces*, 78: "one of the richest ecclesiological statements in the entire New Testament."

among them. Luke–Acts portrays the Spirit as God's power and presence in Jesus and in the church, guiding the latter in its mission, sometimes leading it in unanticipated ways. The Pastoral Letters closely link the Spirit with officeholders responsible for continuity and stability in the community. Social sciences speak of this as "a routinization of charism." The term supposes a distinction between the charismatic spirit of a religious founder and perhaps the earliest group of followers and the later and inevitable channeling of that spirit to the community's leadership responsible for its ongoing life. Of the few references to the Spirit in the Pastorals, two are, perhaps, the most significant: 2 Timothy 1:7 and 1:14. The first refers to the gift of God given to Timothy by the laying on of hands: "a spirit of power and of love and of self-discipline," dispositions suited to one in a leadership position. In the second text, the Spirit is seen in terms of empowering Paul and Timothy: "Guard the good treasure [the apostolic teaching] entrusted to you, with the help of the Holy Spirit living in us." In both cases, the Spirit is related to the officeholder's tasks of overseeing, preserving the faith, and teaching it to others.

The Pastorals address an urgent need in some of the local churches toward the end of the first century: how to deal with the corrupting presence of teachings at odds with the Gospel? Leaders with authority, empowered by the Spirit, directed to teach the truth and guide the community are portrayed as the response to the church's need. The leaders are variously described as "overseer" (*episkopos*, from which we get our term "bishop") or "elder" (*presbyteros*, presbyter, from which our English word "priest" is derived), without a clear distinction between the two, as well as "deacons" (*diakonoi*). In making their case, the Pastorals were justified in appealing to the authority of Paul: Paul himself sought to correct errors of understanding and of practice, most clearly, perhaps, in 1 Corinthians. Most of his letters gave continuing guidance to communities he helped to found. But there is a downside to the Pastorals' approach. There are times that call for an energetic affirmation of the truth by authoritative leaders, when errors need to be named and excluded. But such a strategy can also lead to excessive control that may hinder the search for truth. A rightful awareness of the Spirit in the church's leaders may sometimes lead to the neglect, if not practical denial, of the Spirit's presence among the entire body of the faithful.

Some of those who accepted and disseminated the errors that so exercised the author of the Pastorals were women, possibly wealthy women who had the leisure to do so (see 1 Tim 5:6, 13). No doubt this contributed to the negative portrayal of women in these letters (e.g., 1 Tim 2:11; 5:11-15; 2 Tim 3:6-7). In the urgency of his response, the author draws on cultural stereotypes concerning women, seeking to restrict them to a domestic role at home and silence in the church (1 Tim 2:11-15; though 1 Tim 3:11 seems to refer to women deacons). Some scholars reason that the criticisms may be directed only to a group of wealthy women within the community, not to all women. The author may also have had the apologetic concern to deflect from the Christian community potential criticism for violating what many would have regarded as the canons of social acceptability. Allowing that the Fourth Gospel was written in very different circumstances, we shall see below that it held quite a different attitude toward women in the church.

The Letter of James

The Letter of James, we have seen, was written by an unknown author in the name of the admired leader of the Jerusalem community.[42] Most likely written in the 80s or 90s, the letter addresses increasingly settled communities who treasure their Jewish Christian traditions but who fail to reflect the ways of the Lord in their practical lives. Several points stand out. First, the letter corrects what the author regards as a misunderstanding of Paul's emphasis on the necessity of faith for our justification (Gal 2:16 and Rom 3:28). James insists that the followers of Jesus must not only hear the word but put it into practice (Jas 1:22-25; 2:14-26), a reminder of Jesus' teaching that not everyone who utters "Lord, Lord" enters the kingdom of heaven (Matt 7:21). Second, in the face of the almost inevitable tendency to show partiality to the rich in a community, James speaks against such a practice (2:1-9) and argues against discrimination

---

[42] Brown, *Introduction*, chap. 34.

based on status or wealth. Oppression of the poor constitutes blasphemy against the name of Christ. Third, James is especially insistent on the need to care for the poor and lowly. "Religion that is pure and undefiled before God, the Father, is this: to care for orphans and widows [biblical symbols for the poor and the defenseless] in their distress, and to keep oneself unstained by the world" (1:27). James decries those who would wish well to the hungry and naked but not provide for their necessities (2:15-16). He warns against the corrosive character of wealth (1:9-11; 5:1-6) and the injustice to which it sometimes leads. Woe to the wealthy who withhold proper wages from those who work in their fields or harvest their crops (5:4). Fourth, James offers guidance to life in community (5:12-20): he echoes Jesus' prohibition of oaths, urges prayer, shows special concern for the sick and for those who have failed to live by the ideals of the community.

Because of its brevity and its paucity of christological references (only 1:1 and 2:1), James can easily be overlooked as a resource for ecclesial self-understanding. That would be a serious loss: the Epistle of James is "the most socially conscious writing" in the New Testament.[43] In contrast to James, the understanding of Christ is front and center in the Fourth Gospel, to which we turn in the next chapter.

---

[43] Ibid., 725.

CHAPTER FOUR

The Church: AD 70 to the End of the First Century—Part 2

We turn now to the vision of church in some of the later books of the New Testament. After looking at the Johannine writings, 1 Peter, Hebrews, and Revelation, the chapter concludes with remarks on the development of the church's self-understanding during this foundational period of its life.

The Gospel of John

At first glance the Fourth Gospel so emphasizes Jesus and the disciples' personal relationship to him that it seems to say little about church. The gospel says little explicitly about the sacraments and, though it mentions the Twelve, never mentions the term "apostle."[1] In the past, some scholars have suggested that this gospel was offering a critique, even an alternative, to a church becoming increasingly interested in internal organization and structure, as seen, for example, in the Pastorals. Contemporary scholarship offers a more nuanced view.[2] Scholars estimate that the body of the gospel (John 1–20) was

---

[1] The word is used in John 13:16, but not in the technical sense.
[2] Raymond E. Brown, *The Churches the Apostles Left Behind* (New York: Paulist Press, 1984), chap. 6, and *An Introduction to the New Testament*, Anchor Bible Reference Library (New York: Doubleday, 1997), chap. 11; Daniel J. Harrington, *The Church According to the New Testament: What the Wisdom and Witness of Early Christianity Teach Us Today* (Franklin, WI: Sheed and Ward, 2001), 115–22; John P. Meier, "The Absence and Presence of the Church in John's Gospel," *Mid-Stream* 41, no. 4 (2002): 27–34; Raymond E. Brown, *An Introduction to the Gospel of John*, ed. Francis J. Moloney (New York: Doubleday, 2003), 221–34.

probably completed in the 90s by someone other than one of the Twelve. Its principal authority, though not necessarily its author, is "the disciple whom Jesus loved" (John 13:23; 19:26; 20:2; 21:7, 24). The three Letters of John are generally presumed to have been written by another author around the turn of the century, before chapter 21 and possibly the prologue were added to the gospel by a final editor (redactor) perhaps just after AD 100. The evangelist (conventionally called John), the presbyter-author who wrote the Letters of John, the final redactor, and the Beloved Disciple, the source of the tradition, are sometimes referred to as the Johannine School.[3] The gospel and the letters are addressed to a specific group, the Johannine community, shaped by the distinctive christological insights given in the gospel. Many scholars think the community was located in the area of Ephesus, in Asia Minor, though some suggest Syria.

The gospel brings three basic insights to our understanding of church: the church as a community adhering to Jesus; discipleship as the fundamental category in speaking of persons in the church; and the risen Christ's presence in all the members of the community through the Paraclete-Spirit. Each insight reflects the fundamental theme that the person of Jesus is central to ecclesial life and self-understanding.

In John's gospel Jesus is God's preexistent Son, the incarnate Word, through whom the world was made and in whom God offers divine life to those who believe in him. In the Synoptics, Jesus gives insights concerning the reign of God in parables that liken the kingdom to a shepherd who cares for his sheep, to yeast a woman puts in a mass of dough, or to the owner of a vineyard who hires people at different times of the day and then pays them all the same wage. In the Fourth Gospel Jesus tell us that *he* is the living bread who nourishes all who believe in him (6:51-58; a reference to the Eucharist), that *he* is the good shepherd who knows and cares for his sheep (10:11-18), and that *he* is the vine who gives life to the branches who remain in him (15:1-10). All three images are symbolic of a community adhering to Jesus, even though, unlike Paul's image of the body (1 Cor 12), they say nothing about members having different roles. Members relate

---

[3] Brown, *Introduction to the Gospel of John*, 189–99.

to one another only through their adherence to Jesus. In several instances—the dialogue with Nicodemus (John 3), the second part of the bread of life discourse (6:51b-58), and in the story of the man born blind (chap. 9)—the evangelist implies that one encounters Jesus now in the sacraments as others once encountered him in the flesh.

In John's understanding of church, primacy is given to the category of disciple with no evident interest in the category of apostle or in specific charisms. In the first twenty chapters of the gospel, if there is a special place assigned to one figure, it is to the "Beloved Disciple." Relationship to Jesus is more significant than any role or charism in the church. Two texts especially point to the theme of discipleship, the footwashing scene in John 13:1-20 and the scene at the foot of the cross in John 19:25-27. In the first text, Jesus' washing the feet of his disciples is a symbol of his giving of himself to God and to his followers in his approaching death. It is also a call to his disciples to a loving friendship that expresses itself in mutual service. As the gospel reading for Holy Thursday, the text calls disciples to pledge themselves to imitate the action of our "Teacher and Lord" (John 13:13). The second text is richly symbolic: the crucified Jesus brings his mother and the disciple whom he loved into a mother-son relationship. The Beloved Disciple is a figure of the Christian believer. The mother of Jesus, possibly evoking the image of Lady Zion giving birth to God's messianic people, suggests the church, giving birth to new disciples of Jesus, and the love that is to bind them to their mother. Jesus' work is completed in the church's giving birth to disciples of Jesus. With this, Jesus utters his final word from the cross, "It is finished," and hands over his Spirit to the community he leaves behind (John 19:30); water (signifying baptism) and blood (signifying Eucharist) flow from his pierced side. The community then becomes the "place of encounter between Jesus and his disciples," and it is the task of the community "to *be*, through love, Jesus' bodily presence, and thus the giver of his Spirit, to all who will come to believe down through the ages."[4]

---

[4] Sandra M. Schneiders, *Written That You May Believe: Encountering Jesus in the Fourth Gospel* (New York: Crossroad, 1999), 62.

96   *The Church*

Emphasis on discipleship may well have influenced the fourth evangelist's positive attitude toward women.[5] The Samaritan woman in chapter 4 leads her townspeople to belief in Jesus (4:39). The same chapter includes the intriguing note (4:27) about the disciples being "astonished" or "shocked," in one translation, at seeing Jesus speaking with a *woman* but not daring to ask about it. It may be that this detail in the written gospel was being directed to community members unsettled by the roles of Christian women in the church in their day, with the implicit suggestion that they let themselves be guided by the will of the Lord rather than by their own expectations.[6] In the Lazarus story Martha gives a profession of faith in Jesus (11:27), a parallel to the profession of faith by Peter in the much more quoted text from Matthew 16. In the Fourth Gospel Mary Magdalene is the first to see the risen Jesus and is sent by Jesus to proclaim him to the apostles (20:17-18), earning her for many centuries the title *apostola apostolorum*, "the apostle of the apostles." If the Fourth Gospel is roughly contemporary with the Pastorals, we see a dramatic difference of outlook on the role of women in the two writings.

A third major element of John's theology of the church is its teaching on the role of the Paraclete-Spirit in chapters 14–16. This theme relates to the gospel's emphasis on adherence to Jesus as the basis of community and the primacy of discipleship. Through the Paraclete the risen Jesus remains with the disciples, "preserving what he taught but interpreting it anew in each generation . . . surely one of the greatest contributions made to Christianity by the Fourth Gospel."[7] We have noted the attention given to the Spirit in Paul, in Luke–Acts, and in the Pastorals.[8] In the Fourth Gospel, the Spirit is distinctively portrayed in personal terms and is the gift of the risen Lord to *every*

---

[5] Raymond E. Brown, "Roles of Women in the Fourth Gospel," in *The Community of the Beloved Disciple: The Life, Loves, and Hates of an Individual Church in New Testament Times* (New York: Paulist Press, 1979), 183–98; Schneiders, *Written That You May Believe*, chaps. 6 and 8.

[6] Schneiders, *Written That You May Believe*, 103–4, 141–42.

[7] Brown, *Churches the Apostles Left Behind*, 121.

[8] Raymond E. Brown, *Biblical Exegesis and Church Doctrine* (New York: Paulist Press, 1985), 106–10, and *The Gospel According to John (XIII–XXI)*, Anchor Bible 29A (Garden City, NY: Doubleday, 1970), 1135–44.

believer. In John the Spirit is called *paraklētos*, Paraclete, from the Greek roots *klētos*, "called," and *para*, "alongside," literally, "one called alongside to help"; it is a personal term and calls for the use of personal pronouns. The word, found only in John in the New Testament writings, has been variously translated: Advocate, Intercessor, or Consoler. One could make a case for each translation based on the use of the word in the gospel, though it seems preferable to retain the word Paraclete, keeping in mind its different meanings but recognizing the forensic or legal sense in which it is often used. In part, the Johannine teaching about the Paraclete responds to the question: How are the disciples who no longer see (or who have never seen) Jesus to have contact with him?

The Paraclete texts are few but they say a great deal (John 14:16, 26; 15: 26; 16:7-14). Two points are essential. First, almost everything said about the Paraclete parallels what is said about Jesus in other parts of the gospel. In effect, the Paraclete, identified with the Spirit in John 14:26, is the post-resurrection presence of Jesus in his disciples, continuing the work he did when he was in the flesh. Second, two special functions are attributed to the Paraclete present in believers individually and in community. The first function is to enable believers to do the works that Jesus did and even greater works (14:12) because through the Spirit "Jesus will be *present in his absence.*"[9] Acting *in believers*, the Paraclete convicts the world of sin in its refusal to believe in Jesus; of righteousness that comes about not through Jesus' being sent to a disgraceful death but in his return to the Father; and of condemnation, not of Jesus, but of Satan, the ruler of the world's evil (16:8-11).[10] The second function enables the community of disciples, along with disciples individually, to become "the real symbolic presence of the glorified Jesus in the world."[11] The church does not simply point to an absent reality, the risen Jesus; the church makes the glorified Jesus *present* because and to the extent that it participates in the life he offers. Yet the church is limited in this

---

[9] Francis J. Moloney, *The Gospel of John*, ed. Daniel J. Harrington, Sacra Pagina (Collegeville, MN: Liturgical Press, 393–400, at 396 (italics in original).

[10] Brown, *Gospel According to John (XIII–XXI)*, 711–14.

[11] Schneiders, *Written That You May Believe*, 69.

re-presentation; it does so in a sensible mode as a *symbol* that both reveals and conceals a transcendent reality. In the Spirit and always dependent on and subordinate to the Spirit, the church and the individual disciple share in the sacramental or symbolic economy inaugurated by the incarnation, the Word of God become flesh (John 1:14). This line of thinking, along with the Pauline theme of the church as the body of Christ, will lead to an understanding of the church itself as a sacrament and not simply as an agent of sacramental actions.

The three themes just mentioned are the glories of the Johannine vision of church. One might also reflect on Jesus' long farewell discourse in John 13:31–16:33 followed by his final prayer in chapter 17, where the same themes are present, at least implicitly.[12] Most notable in the latter, perhaps, is Jesus' prayer that those who come to believe in Jesus through the word of his disciples may be one as he and the Father are one (17:20-21). Both the farewell discourse and the prayer follow the footwashing scene in John 13:1-17: "a symbolic action that reveals Jesus' limitless love for his own" and that, at Jesus' direction, is to be imitated by the disciples in their own self-giving service to others.[13]

The Letters of John and John 21

The lofty insights of the Fourth Gospel concerning both Christ and the church were developed in tension and, indeed, polemic both with other Christians who did not affirm its lofty Christology and with post-Jamnia Judaism, which saw in that Christology an abandonment of Israel's belief in one God. This led to a heightened attention to some insights but attenuated others and opened the gospel to one-sided interpretations and misunderstandings. The Letters of John reflect these difficulties.[14] It appears that some members of the Johannine community espoused a particular interpretation of certain teach-

---

[12] Johan Ferreira, "Johannine Ecclesiology," *Journal for the Study of the New Testament, Supplement Series* 160 (1998): 14, sees John 17 as "the Gospel's most significant statement on ecclesiology."

[13] Moloney, *Gospel of John*, 372–79, at 375.

[14] Brown, *Community of the Beloved Disciple*, 93–144, and *Introduction to the New Testament*, 373–76 and chaps. 12–14.

ings of the gospel, forming a splinter group and urging others to join them. The author of the First Letter of John believes that the teaching of the secessionists erred on two major points. First, in so insisting on the preexistent Word in their understanding of Jesus (John 1:1, 14), the splinter group gave little room to the humanity of Jesus or to the importance of his ministry. Second, consistent with this neglect, members of the group became indifferent to the moral significance of their own activity and had little regard for the commandments. In their view, the only sin was the failure to believe. The First and Second Letters of John—the first is actually a treatise—address the communities experiencing the schism. The letters oppose the splinter group's interpretation of the gospel and insist that the letters are the sure guide to the message of the gospel (1 John 1:5; 3:11).

Several practical lessons can be learned from the experience of the Johannine community.[15] First, insights, however valid, of a theology shaped in the heat of polemic can lead to one-sidedness and division. Second, polemics with the synagogue with gospel references to "the Jews" and "their law" (John 15:25) could lead to an unwarranted Christian neglect of Jewish traditions that are rightfully and necessarily theirs as well. Third, polemics in theology or ecclesiology can encourage hostility toward those with whom one does not agree. The gospel's hostile comments about "the Jews" (John 8:43-47, 55; 12:37-40) have been misunderstood and used to justify all sorts of evil. The Johannine Letters also show that hostility between differing viewpoints can be present within the Christian community itself. The fourth lesson may be the most unsettling: the conviction that the Paraclete dwelt in the heart of every believer could also lead to divisions within the community. But the Jesus of the gospel never tells us what to do when believers, gifted with the Paraclete, disagree among themselves. The Letters of John indicate the sorry possibility that sometimes the very communion so strongly urged by Jesus (John 13:34-35; 15:9, 12-13) can be broken. Unlike the author of Titus (Titus 1:11; 2:1), the author of 1 John can only remind his readers that "the anointing that you received from him [the Holy Spirit] abides in you, and so you do not need anyone to teach you" (1 John 2:27) and that

---

[15] Brown, *Churches the Apostles Left Behind*, 110–23.

one must test the spirits to discern whether they are of God (1 John 4:1). Ultimately that was not enough: both the author of the Letters and the secessionists could make the same claim, on the basis of the gospel. The Third Letter of John tells us that in one of the Johannine communities Diotrephes sought to solve such an impasse by guiding the community in the interpretation of the tradition. Like the author of the Pastorals, he saw the need for authoritative leader-teachers in the community. That stance would be reinforced by the appendix to the Fourth Gospel.

There is good reason to believe that what is now the final chapter of the Fourth Gospel, chapter 21, was written shortly after the Third Letter of John, probably by an editor other than either the evangelist or the author of the Letters. This epilogue to the gospel gives a final word about the Johannine community and, indirectly, a further word about the problems that led to the composition of the Letters. Chapter 21 is important for both historical and theological reasons. The chapter also provides one of the major New Testament texts concerning Peter.

A good number of the Johannine community, it appears, followed the secessionists (1 John 4:5). It seems likely that, faithful still to the Fourth Gospel as they interpreted it, the secessionists evolved into a form of Gnosticism, of which there were several groups in the second century. Christian Gnostics were generally dualistic in outlook, denied the humanity of Jesus, emphasized access to secret apostolic revelations, and equated salvation with privileged knowledge about God and human destiny. Those of the Johannine community whose views were represented by the author of the Letters consolidated with what came to be called the *church catholic* (from *katholikos*, "universal"), associated with Peter and Paul.[16] The author of John 21 encourages this consolidation by means of two stories. The first, in verses 1-14, tells of a miraculous catch of fish in which Peter plays a prominent role; it points to the missionary success of bringing many peoples to one community. The second story, in verses 15-19, tells of Jesus' three questions to Peter and of his appointing Peter to be shepherd in the community. The dignity and the memory of "the disciple whom Jesus loved" is preserved (21:7), but it is to Peter that the risen

---

[16] The term comes from Ignatius of Antioch, *Letter to the Smyrneans* 8:2.

Jesus gives the commission of pastoral authority. The story seems to represent a Johannine acceptance of church structure, influenced perhaps by the impasse described in the Letters of John. The final editor knows this goes against the grain of the Johannine tradition, so the proposed change is put in the form of a story in which Jesus authorizes Peter's role, but only after Peter meets the criterion of discipleship, love of the Lord Jesus, even after Peter's threefold denial (18:17-27). Acceptance of human pastors in the church does not erase the clear affirmation that Jesus is and remains *the* shepherd of the church and the only door to the sheepfold (John 10). The flock continues to belong to Jesus: they are his lambs, his sheep.

The Johannine writings have an important place in the canon of our Scriptures and in the New Testament vision of church. That vision has grandeur but also limitations. Chapter 21 of the gospel offers a partial correction to the Johannine tradition. What John 21 does for the Johannine tradition, the Johannine writings do for the New Testament as a whole. By the late fourth century, the church in the Greek East and Latin West had come to widespread agreement as to which of its writings constituted the list of holy books, the canon of Scripture. The decision to include the Johannine writings had monumental consequences. There are insights in John that are not found at all or are not found with the same emphasis in the other New Testament books. It is true that Johannine insights stand in tension with some of the teachings and emphases in other New Testament writings. Significantly, our forebears in the faith did not eliminate those tensions but chose to keep them for the benefit of us all. The Catholic Church has, for understandable reasons, often emphasized the place of structures and authoritative leaders in the church. Often that emphasis has served the church well as it navigated its way through history. But these emphases, valuable as they are, must be complemented by other insights from the New Testament writings. The Fourth Gospel gives three perspectives on church that are foundational: the centrality of Jesus and the importance of a personal relationship, in community, to him; the primacy of discipleship in the church; and the indwelling of the Paraclete-Spirit in each disciple—gifts by which the church must be ever challenged and for which she must be ever grateful.

The First Letter of Peter

In its reflection on living a Christian life, the First Letter of Peter has been called "one of the most attractive and pastorally rich writings in the [New Testament]."[17] Probably written in Rome between AD 70 and 90 by a disciple of Peter, the letter means to encourage Christians in northern Asia Minor (modern Turkey). Believers there were experiencing a sense of isolation, seeing themselves as "aliens and exiles" (1 Pet 1:1; 2:11) because of their minority religion and possibly also from their status as foreigners or immigrant workers. The use of baptismal imagery leads some to ask if the letter originated as a baptismal homily or in association with a baptismal liturgy.[18] The letter may seek to encourage Christian immigrants but also to challenge Christians who have become so socially and culturally acclimated that their religious distinctiveness is scarcely noticed by themselves or by others. Two issues stand out: the letter's designation for the church and its comments on authority in the church and in civil society.

The author of First Peter draws on Old Testament imagery in an attempt both to encourage a sense of dignity in his hearers and to guide their ecclesial self-understanding. Themes of Jewish Passover, the exodus, and the desert wandering are applied to baptized Gentiles. In that context, the author encourages them: "Let yourselves be built into a spiritual house, to be a holy priesthood, to offer spiritual sacrifices acceptable to God through Jesus Christ" (2:5). This is followed by one of the key passages in the letter: "You are a chosen race, a royal priesthood, a holy nation, God's own people, in order that you may proclaim the mighty acts of him who called you out of darkness into his marvelous light" (2:9). The four titles in the second citation are taken from Exodus 19:6 (Greek translation) and Isaiah 43:20-21. The author then applies to the Christian community (1 Pet 2:10) what Hosea (2:23) once said of Israel: "Once you were not a people, but now you are God's people." Canadian Dominican J.-M.-R. Tillard's translation (vv. 9 and 10) helps us appreciate the text: "But

---

[17] Brown, *Introduction to the New Testament*, 706.

[18] Brown, *Churches the Apostles Left Behind*, chap. 5, and *Introduction to the New Testament*, 705-24.

you, you are the chosen race, the priestly community of the king, the holy nation, the people won by God so that you may proclaim the mighty acts of the one who called you out of darkness into God's marvelous light, you who once were not God's people but now are God's people." That passage, he says, "is without doubt one of the most important of the New Testament,"[19] certainly in what it says about the church.

It is important to recognize that the text speaks of the people as a whole or as a unity. One is baptized into a community. As in Exodus so in 1 Peter, the people exercise their priestly character by the way they live. By the "spiritual sacrifices" of their lives, the baptized manifest themselves as a holy people and move others to praise God. By its use of this central theme of the exodus tradition, 1 Peter also points to the continuing influence of Jewish Christianity in the Roman capital. The special status accorded to the "aliens and exiles" by the lofty designation does not imply a special worthiness, even if it does point to God's choice of them for a specific role in his saving plan. The exclusiveness inherent in the notion of the "people of God" does have some "troublesome corollaries."[20] The text in 1 Peter says nothing about the term's prior application to the Jewish people and could lead, as it did for some in the next century, to the erroneous conclusion that the Jews were no longer the people of God, replaced, as they were, by Christians. Also, the notion that holiness comes with belonging to the church says nothing about the holiness of those outside the church apart from the assertion that Gentiles who have not been converted will glorify God at the judgment (2:12). Both issues are important concerns in contemporary reflection on the church.

First Peter also speaks to the issue of authority. As in Exodus so in 1 Peter, that the entire people are a priestly people does not exclude the presence of those who have specific priestly roles within the community. In the Levites, Judaism had a cultic priesthood; the Christian community had its own shepherding roles, as 1 Peter itself indicates. The exhortation to pastoral leaders, elders, in 1 Peter 5:1-4 is

---

[19] J.-M.-R. Tillard, *Flesh of the Church, Flesh of Christ: At the Source of the Ecclesiology of Communion* (Collegeville, MN: Liturgical Press, 2001), 22.

[20] Brown, *Churches the Apostles Left Behind*, 82–83.

yet another expression of concern for a proper understanding of leadership roles in the church. Two items suggest a degree of development in the office by the time the letter was written. The phrase about exercising the office "not under compulsion but willingly" implies that some type of designation or election was in place. The prohibition against "sordid gain" implies that a salary was being paid (see 1 Tim 5:17). The injunction that elders not "lord it over" those in their charge shows affinities with the passages in Mark 10, Matthew 20, and Luke 22 where Jesus contrasts the behavior of Gentile rulers and what he expects of his disciples. This repeated attention to leadership roles in the church shows the high degree of concern that these roles not be contaminated by elements foreign to the nature of service in the church.

The First Letter of Peter also includes a word about civil authority (2:13-17). Reminiscent of Paul's words in Romans 13:1-7, the author of 1 Peter encourages obedience to civic officials. Both texts may be inspired by the concern to silence critics who saw Christians as inimical to the good order of the state. The book of Revelation takes a very different stance on this issue, as we see presently. The church's relation to the state will be another important issue to be dealt with.

The Letter to the Hebrews

The Letter to the Hebrews is a masterful reflection on Christ's death and resurrection, expressed in terms of priesthood and sacrifice. It also gives insights on the church. The text of Hebrews contains few clues regarding authorship, addressees, or place of origin. By analyzing the text itself, scholars reason that the work, really a written sermon, was composed by a second-generation Christian in the 80s, possibly to Christians at Rome. One *hypothesis* suggests that the sermon may have been addressed as a corrective to conservative Jewish and Gentile Christians who, attracted by idealized values of Jewish worship, were perhaps wavering in their faith in Christ.[21] In this view,

---

[21] Raymond E. Brown and John P. Meier, *Antioch and Rome: New Testament Cradles of Catholic Christianity* (New York: Paulist Press, 1983), 139–42, 213; Brown, *Introduction to the New Testament*, 693.

the author of Hebrews shares the theological outlook of the Hellenists described in Acts 6–7, emphasizing the superiority of Christ and his replacement of the Jewish temple and its cult. Three themes in the letter are of interest to our study

The first section of Hebrews (1:1–4:13) reflects on Jesus and his place in God's saving plan. Jesus is God's Son. Through him God has spoken in a way that gives Jesus priority over the angels (called "sons of God" in Jewish tradition) and over Moses as well. Inaugurating the last days, Jesus surpasses all God's previous communications (1:2). Hebrews reaffirms the central place of Jesus in our ecclesial identity and our need to trust in him. At one with the portrayal of Jesus as God's exalted Son is the affirmation that by his incarnation Jesus is "not ashamed" to call us his brothers and sisters (2:11-13). And Jesus, "tested" (tempted) in his own life and again before his suffering and death, is able to help us who are tempted in our lives (2:18; 4:15). The church is a community of Jesus' brothers and sisters who can expect of him compassion and understanding.

Second, the principal christological reflection of Hebrews centers on Christ as high priest of a new covenant. Hebrews is unique in the New Testament in its explicit treatment of Jesus as priest. By his one sacrifice, begun on the cross and completed in heaven, Jesus atones for sin once and for all (9:12). In doing so, Jesus established a new covenant (8:7-13, citing Jer 31:31-34) that renders the former covenant "obsolete" (8:13). He is "mediator of a new covenant" (9:15); he has taken away the first covenant to establish the second (10:9). It is a mark of later New Testament writings to think more in terms of *replacement* of the covenant with Israel, rather than of its renewal, though the attitude of Hebrews has also been understood more as the author's desire to help Christians appreciate the value of Christ's priesthood and sacrifice in the aftermath of the temple's destruction than by any intent to speak specifically to the status of Judaism.[22] The

---

[22] Alan C. Mitchell, *Hebrews*, ed. Daniel J. Harrington, Sacra Pagina (Collegeville, MN: Liturgical Press, 2009), 25–28. See also Vatican Commission for Religious Relations with the Jews, " 'The Gifts and the Calling of God Are Irrevocable': A Reflection on Catholic-Jewish Relations," *Origins* 45, no. 30 (December 24, 2015): 18.

letter clearly differs from Romans 11:29, which affirms that the gifts and call of God to Israel are irrevocable. The presentation in Hebrews also differs from what scholars believe was Jesus' *renewal* of the covenant at the Last Supper.

In Hebrews, we have the second explicit Christian use of "priest" in the New Testament: here the term is used for Christ; in 1 Peter, the term "priesthood" is applied to the entire people of God. The theme of the priesthood of all the baptized may predate the treatment of Christ's priesthood, though the former has come to be understood in relation to the latter. How these two priesthoods are related to each other and to an ordained priesthood will be an important issue in an understanding of church.[23] Hebrews also makes extensive use of the category of sacrifice, the most developed in the New Testament. Hebrews is not alone in speaking of Christ's redemptive work as a sacrifice. The Last Supper accounts relate Jesus' final meal and the renewal of the covenant with his death on the cross. Romans 3:25 speaks of the "sacrifice of atonement by [Jesus'] blood" and 1 John twice speaks of the "atoning sacrifice" of Jesus (2:2 and 4:10). Catholic theology gives an important place to the sacrifice of the Mass and to the ordained priesthood. Any reflection on these themes must keep in mind the teaching of Hebrews on the once-and-for-all character of Christ's sacrifice and the uniqueness of Christ's priesthood.

Third, Hebrews 3:7–4:13 uses Psalm 95:7-11 to invoke the image of ancient Israel's forty years of wandering in the desert as a type of the Christian community. Israel of old sought rest in the land of Canaan, though some did not reach that goal because of disobedience and unbelief. The Christian community is portrayed as God's people in Christ on a journey or pilgrimage looking to a heavenly rest, life with God. This follows only through fidelity to the word of God "living and active, sharper than any two-edged sword . . . able to judge the thoughts and intentions of the heart" (4:12). The same theme continues in the final chapters of the letter. Chapter 11 remembers "so great

---

[23] See Ronald D. Witherup, "The Biblical Foundations of the Priesthood: The Contribution of Hebrews," in *Ministerial Priesthood in the Third Millennium: Faithfulness of Christ, Faithfulness of Priests* (Collegeville, MN: Liturgical Press, 2009), chap. 1.

a cloud of witnesses" (12:1) who, even if they would not receive what was promised until the coming of Christ, are examples of faith for us. The supreme example of faith is Jesus himself (12:2). The exhortation of the final chapter looks to the life of the community, remembering leaders of the past, "those who spoke the word of God to you" (13:7), and those of the present (13:17). Through Christ, believers are to offer to God their own "sacrifice of praise," confessing his name, doing good for others, and sharing what they have.

The Book of Revelation

The final book of the New Testament, though not the last written, is the book of Revelation. Much of the book is written in the apocalyptic genre with heavy use of visions and symbols, purporting to interpret present times and events and intending to give a message of hope. Passages in this same genre appear in several Old Testament books: Ezekiel, Joel, Zechariah, Isaiah, and, most especially, Daniel.

The author of Revelation was an otherwise unknown Jewish Christian prophet named John (1:1, 4, 9; 22:8), who writes in exile on the island of Patmos (1:9), off the coast of Asia Minor. While there are some affinities between Revelation and the Johannine literature, scholars do not believe the author is the same as that of the Fourth Gospel or of the Letters of John. Revelation was probably written between AD 92 and 96, at the end of the reign of the Roman emperor Domitian (AD 81–96). The book is divided unevenly into two parts. The letters in the first part (chaps. 1–3) are addressed to particular churches in seven well-known cities in Asia Minor, though they seem to have been meant for all the churches of the region. The visions and the revelatory experiences in the remainder of the book (chaps. 4–22) are also addressed to the Christians of the seven cities. The churches to which Revelation is addressed faced a twofold set of problems. Internally, they suffered from a loss of enthusiasm, complacency, or divisive teachings. Externally, they had to deal with their relationship to the state and to the surrounding culture. Called to participate in the imperial cult to demonstrate their political loyalty, some Christians were tempted to accede to this request, reasoning that the cult was but a political convention. Recalling the earlier and much more extensive persecutions under Nero and thinking they might well be repeated, the author of Revelation dramatically rejects any compromise. He casts his response in terms of a clash between the rival claims of Christ and of the empire, a struggle on earth reflecting a cosmic drama taking place in the heavens. Revelation calls the churches to an uncompromising acceptance of Jesus who alone is "King of kings and Lord of lords" (Rev 19:16).

The seven letters in chapters 2 and 3 describe the strengths and weaknesses of the churches to which they are written and give encouragement or calls to reform. While many of the observations on the individual churches are time-conditioned, the strategy used by the author has enduring value. In its own local situation, every church needs to look at how it responds to the call and grace of God and how it might address those areas where it may be falling short. In that sense, the seven letters contain an abiding lesson for the church.

Much like 1 Peter, Revelation applies images from the Jewish tradition to the church with the assumption that only in Christ do they find their full meaning. Several images are pressed into service, especially in the penultimate chapter: "I saw the holy city, the new Jerusalem, coming down out of heaven from God, prepared as a bride adorned for her husband" (Rev 21:2). This is followed by a voice from the throne of God proclaiming the covenant formula: "See, the home of God is among mortals. He will dwell with them as their God; they will be his peoples [some manuscripts read the singular: people], and God himself will be with them" (21:3; see also Lev 26:11-12; Ezek 27:27; 2 Cor 6:16). The holy city is portrayed as engaged in warfare with evil Babylon (Rome), a warfare that is played out in the churches of Asia Minor and in the hearts of every Christian. Revelation 21:10-14 says the heavenly city has twelve gates, inscribed with the names of the twelve tribes of Israel, and twelve foundation stones, inscribed with the names of twelve apostles of the Lamb. (Jesus, the Paschal lamb without blemish, is the principal christological title in Revelation.) The symbolic role assigned to the Twelve in Revelation is congruent with the purpose of the Twelve in the saying attributed to Jesus in Matthew 19:28 and Luke 22:28-30.

The symbol of the church as the bride of the Messiah, synonymous with the holy city, the New Jerusalem, is also prominent in the closing chapters of Revelation.[24] Besides the identification mentioned in Revelation 21:2, the image recurs in 21:9, where the angel says to the seer, "Come, I will show you the bride, the wife of the Lamb." Earlier, in Revelation 19:6-8, the bridal image was also used to stand in sharp contrast to the harlot, the city of Babylon, portrayed in chapters 17 and 18. The image of church as bride represents the eschatological union of Christ with the faithful who have persevered in their fidelity to him. As in other biblical references to this theme, the image of church as bride is combined with other images (body, temple, city, or nation). Because of this, the bridal image is considered an ancillary biblical image of the church.[25] Such a view is corroborated by the logical tension between the bridal image and the image of the wedding feast where the disciples are described as guests of the bridegroom (Mark 2:19) or attendant maidens (Matt 25:1-13). The variety of images, sometimes in tension with one another, reminds us that the reality of the church far exceeds images used to describe it. Each image offers its own contribution and has its own limitation.

Revelation associates the notions of kingdom and priesthood in an opening doxology (1:6) and in the account of the visions following the letters to the churches (Rev 5:9-10). In a third passage (20:4-6), the priestly people is associated with two other ideas, Christ's second coming and mention of a thousand-year reign, the "millennial kingdom," before the final consummation of God's plan. The notion of a temporary earthly messianic reign comes from the author's attempt to reconcile two traditions: the prophetic tradition, developed during the Babylonian exile, that there would be a restoration of the house of David in an earthly, historical kingdom; and the apocalyptic expectation that the final stage of God's plan would be a restoration, by God's power alone and without any mention of the Davidic kingdom, of the divine primordial authority over all.[26] The author of Revelation tries to preserve both traditions, relating them to belief in Christ's definitive victory over the powers of evil. The author's resolution of

---

[24] The same depiction is also found in 2 Cor 11:2 and Eph 5:21-31.
[25] Paul S. Minear, *Images of the Church in the New Testament* (Philadelphia: Westminster Press, 1960), 54–56.
[26] Brown, *Introduction to the New Testament*, 800–802.

these traditions awkwardly doubles some events, a twofold struggle with and victory over Satan, for example, and a first and second resurrection, with the millennial kingdom in between. (A similar concern to relate Jewish tradition to belief in Christ is reflected in 1 Cor 15:22-28.) While we do not hold to a literal understanding of a thousand-year reign, Revelation is a forceful reminder of belief in the ultimate victory of Christ over all the forces of evil and of the finality of history in Christ and in God. The royal priestly people will share in that victory.

Revelation's vision of the final times includes the expectation of "a new heaven and a new earth" (21:1). The author associates this image with those of the holy city, the bride adorned for her husband, and the people with whom God dwells. The image of the new heaven and new earth comes from Isaiah 65:17 and 66:22, where it refers to the transformed cosmos of God's final salvation. In its closing chapters, Revelation 21–22 makes this image one of many in the poetic description of God's ultimate victory over evil and chaos. Again, those who are faithful to God will participate in that victory. Recent Catholic social teaching on the mission of the church uses the image of a new earth in speaking of Christian responsibility and earthly progress in the world of our time.[27] Continuity exists between the present world and the world to come, though the new world is qualitatively different because of the nearness of God's presence (21:6-7) and the absence of evil.[28]

A final consideration from Revelation: How do the followers of Christ relate to the political and cultural milieu to which they belong? Two of the major challenges of the early church concerned its relationship to Judaism and its desire to preach Christ to the Greco-Roman world. Luke–Acts clearly situates the Christ-event in the political and social world of the empire. The letters to the Colossians and the Ephesians proclaim the cosmic significance of Christ and of the

---

[27] See, for example, Vatican II's Pastoral Constitution on the Church in the Modern World 39.

[28] Second Peter 3:10-13 also speaks of new heavens and a new earth to come with God's final judgment, though it seems to suggest a fiery destruction of the present heavens and earth rather than their transformation.

church. The author of Revelation looks to the church as the heavenly Jerusalem but is very clear that the church stands in fierce opposition to the earthly Babylon (Rome). For Revelation, Christians are a group apart. Facing the danger of compromise with the culture and cult of the empire, the seer insists that Christians avoid any contact that would threaten their purity. The 144,000 who alone can learn the hymn to be sung before the throne of the lamb are *virgins* who have preserved themselves from idolatry (Rev 14:4-5). They would have to form their own social relationships, their own trade associations, their own burial societies. Christianity would represent a sectarian withdrawal from association with non-Christians. There could no middle ground.[29] The stance taken by Revelation differs from that of 1 Peter and Romans. The earlier writings call on believers to honor civil rulers and to respect their authority (1 Pet 2:13-17; Rom 13:1-7). It also differs from Jesus' saying in the Synoptics (Mark 12:17 and parallels) that we give to the emperor what belongs to the emperor but to God what belongs to God. The varied contexts in which these texts were written helps explain such differences. That the church did not embrace a sectarian stance does not lessen the contribution Revelation makes in its warning against compromising fidelity to Christ in its social and political interactions. Doing that, of course, calls for no little discernment.

Summary and Retrospect

Chapters 3 and 4 have reviewed some of the principal New Testament insights into the nature and mission of the church. Themes discussed in one text appear in another, at times with marked differences. The preceding paragraph noted one instance of such. There are other examples. As the church grew in number and saw that it faced an indeterminate future, increasing attention was given to officeholders, though this development coincided with the Fourth Gospel's heightened emphasis on personal adherence to Jesus and the primacy of discipleship. The Acts of the Apostles tells of growth

---

[29] Pheme Perkins, *Reading the New Testament: An Introduction*, 2nd ed. (New York: Paulist Press, 1988), 326.

and development in the church; the Letters of John (and the Letter of Jude) show intense tensions, even unto schism. John's emphasis on our loving others in the community must be seen with the call in Luke–Acts and James to care for the poor and the lowly who are not always part of the community. The prominence of the Spirit in Luke–Acts and John's teaching about the Paraclete are important reminders of the experience of the Spirit in the life of the community, its worship, and its missionary activity.

Not surprisingly, the relation between the Christian community and Judaism continued to receive attention. Matthew and Luke–Acts see Christianity as a fulfillment of Judaism; the Fourth Gospel and Hebrews tend to see the relationship in terms of replacement. Yet the Letter of James (and the Letter of Jude) and 1 Peter remind us of the continued veneration of Judaism among certain Christian communities and the readiness to apply to the church important Jewish symbols. Probably the most pronounced contrast in the writings we have been looking at concerns the attitude toward the empire in Luke–Acts and in the book of Revelation. We saw other differences as well. The Pastorals' perspective on the role of the Spirit in the church is quite different from that in Luke–Acts or John. The Pastorals' outlook on the role of women is very different from that of the Fourth Gospel.

A few general observations may help draw all of this together. First, the risen Jesus, one, of course, with the Jesus of the ministry and the passion and death, was regarded as the center and the foundation for the church. The Holy Spirit initially received less attention, in part because of the early church's preoccupation with Christ who once walked in their midst and who alone was the Word of God in the flesh. The early church shared with Judaism belief in the Spirit, though the understanding of the Spirit and the Spirit's role in the church became more refined through the post-Easter experience of prayer and community and through reflection on the totality of the Christ-event.

Second, in and with Christ and the Spirit, the church saw itself as a community called to continue the mission of Christ. The notions of community and mission were inseparable, even if they received different emphases in different writings. Third, while preserving the basics of faith, the early church witnessed great diversity of outlook on the several matters mentioned above. Some of this theological diversity may be explained in part by the local character of the churches, along with the history of their foundation and the background of those who comprised them. Being a local church did not take away from belonging to the *great church*, signified especially by sharing common faith and Eucharist. Unity also came in the acceptance of the authority of Peter and Paul and in seeing the church's beginnings in the apostolate of the Twelve and those associated with them. Later theology of the church will speak of the great church or the church universal as being a communion of local churches. The New Testament writings stand at the beginning of that development.

The Christian Church at the End of the Century

Four considerations describe the Christian church at the end of the first century: its development as a structured community; its relation to Judaism; its emerging identity as a new religion; and its relation to the Roman Empire. We see the first in the many writings in the 80s and 90s and in the development of ministerial structures. Both were meant to guide the church in preserving its roots in the teaching and ministry of Jesus and guiding it as it faced new challenges coming from its growth, misunderstanding of its teaching,[30] its changing demographics, and the local situations in which it found itself. As regards the church's changing relation to Judaism, we recognize that the Christian break with Judaism did not take place *tout court* with the destruction of the temple and the fall of Jerusalem; nor was there a single parting of the ways.[31] In its attitude toward the temple, we saw a first fissure in the Stephen episode and its aftermath. An "irreparable breach"[32] came with Paul and the Gentile mission, though Paul himself held to belief in Israel's election. The Johannine teaching in

---

[30] Besides 1 and 2 John and James, see also 2 Peter 3:15-16.
[31] James D. G. Dunn, *The Partings of the Ways between Christianity and Judaism and Their Significance for the Character of Christianity*, 2nd ed. (London: SCM Press, 2006), chap. 12.
[32] Ibid., 302.

the 90s that Jesus was the divine Word incarnate had to be intolerable for Jewish monotheism, especially when interfaced with the distinctive interpretation of Scripture being developed by post-Jamnia rabbinic Judaism. By the time of the second Jewish revolt in AD 132–34, with its claim that the leader bar Kokhba (from Num 24:17, "son of the star") was the true Messiah, the break between Christianity and Judaism became "clear-cut and final,"[33] though in different areas contacts between adherents of the two traditions continued into the next few centuries.

A third point: We have already seen that early Christians made ample use of the Jewish Scriptures to unpack the meaning of Christ and his work and to see in them the fulfillment of the words of the prophets. They did the same in speaking of the church, most notably in 1 Peter but in many other places as well. Gradually Christians came to see the Eucharist as the unbloody sacrifice replacing the sacrifices once offered in the temple. The Eucharist came to be regarded as the fulfillment of the words of the prophet Malachi, that a perfect offering would be made from the rising of the sun to its setting (Mal 1:11).[34] It would be one step further—though it was not a step made in the New Testament writings—when those who presided were called "priests." This was but another indication that by the turn of the century, the Christian church was well on the way to becoming a religious entity distinct from both Judaism and the religions of the Greco-Roman world.

A final point: Early Christians probably benefited from being regarded as a sect within Judaism (Acts 24:5, 14). Since Jews were exempt from the Roman call to worship civic deities, Christians shared the same exemption so long as they were seen as a group within Judaism. But as Christians became increasingly distinct from Judaism and were excluded from the synagogue, they lost this official protection and had to stand on their own. Refusing to engage in the civic worship of pagan gods or of a deified emperor, Christians could expect the possibility of persecution and, at times, death. The book of Revelation speaks to Christians in such a situation. In contrast to

---

[33] Ibid., 312.
[34] First found in the *Didache*, written toward the end of the first century.

that book's attitude toward Rome, a desire to promote good relations with official Rome may have been a factor in Luke's editing of the passion narrative. Even though Pilate ultimately sends Jesus to the cross, three times the prefect affirms that he finds Jesus not guilty of the various charges brought against him (Luke 23:4, 14, 22). A similar motive may be present in Luke's citing official Roman declarations of Paul's innocence (Acts 23:29; 25:25; 26:30-32). Neither Jesus nor Paul, nor the Christian community at the end of the century, the evangelist implies, seeks to overthrow Roman secular power. In the patristic period, discussed in the following chapters, relations between Christianity and Rome will become a major issue.

This ends our story of how the church saw itself or was seen by others in the New Testament period. The length of this treatment was guided by the long-held belief that "the study of the sacred page should be the very soul of sacred theology" and that "all the preaching of the church, as indeed the entire christian religion, should be nourished and ruled by sacred scripture."[35]

---

[35] Vatican Council II, Dogmatic Constitution on Divine Revelation 24 and 21.

CHAPTER FIVE

Christian Antiquity—Part 1: The Second and Third Centuries

This chapter and the next look at the theological understandings of the church in the period extending from the early second century to the early seventh century in the West and the mid-eighth century in the East. The period, often called the patristic period or the age of the fathers, is marked by those leaders and teachers of the early church who had a major role in preserving the unity and integrity of the church.[1] Some of them made monumental contributions in exploring and developing the insights of Paul and the author of the Fourth Gospel as they sought to communicate the Christian message to the Greco-Roman cultural world. Within this period, the second and third centuries form a first part; the reign of Emperor Constantine in the early fourth century introduces the second part, the remainder of the period.

Extended reflection on the church was very rare in the East during the patristic period and, outside of Cyprian and Augustine, only minimally the topic of extensive reflection in the West. The church was a part of believers' daily lives, a lived reality at one with their efforts, in the Spirit, in trying to be followers of the risen Lord in the community of faith. Historical studies have often so

---

[1] Many of the fathers were bishops, but not all. Justin Martyr (d. ca. 165) and Prosper of Aquitaine (d. ca. 463) were laymen; Jerome (d. 420) and Origen (d. 253) were priests; Ephrem (d. 373), a deacon. From the end of the fourth century, the term was used of those whose doctrinal teaching was seen as especially important. On mothers of the church, see Mike Aquilina, *The Fathers of the Church: An Introduction to the First Christian Teachers*, exp. ed. (Huntington, IN: Our Sunday Visitor, 2006), 251–59.

focused on institutional aspects of the church and its struggles with secular powers that the heart of the church's self-understanding has sometimes been given less attention than it deserves.[2] That understanding was expressed most clearly when Christians gathered at worship, to hear the word of God and to celebrate the saving covenant that gave meaning and order to their lives. The age of the fathers has deservedly been spoken of as a time when the Christian tradition and the church was lived with particular intensity; as such, it remains a key resource in the never-ending task of ecclesial renewal. Our treatment begins by looking at the understanding of the Christian life entered through baptism and nourished at Eucharist.

Baptism and Eucharist: New Life in Christ and the Church

The church's baptismal theology was its earliest theology of the church.[3] In the spirit of 1 Peter, baptism was said to give one a new identity as a member of the body of Christ and the people of God. The church was viewed as mother, whose baptismal waters, impregnated by Christ (recall the symbolic ritual of the paschal candle at the Easter Vigil), gave birth to new Christians. A fifth-century poem inscribed on the walls of the baptistery of St. John Lateran, the cathedral church of the city of Rome, beautifully expresses this church-mother imagery:

> Here a people of godly race are born for heaven;
> the Spirit gives them life in the fertile waters.
> The Church-mother, in these waters, bears her children
> like virginal fruit she has conceived by the Holy Spirit.[4]

---

[2] Henry Chadwick, *The Church in Ancient Society: From Galilee to Gregory the Great* (Oxford and New York: Oxford University Press, 2001), 212.

[3] Gerard Austin, "Restoring Equilibrium after the Struggle with Atheism," in *Source and Summit: Commemorating Josef A. Jungmann, S.J.*, ed. Joanne M. Pierce and Michael Downey (Collegeville, MN: Liturgical Press, 1999), 37.

[4] Cited by ibid., 38. Translation taken from the Cathedral baptistery, Brisbane, Australia.

Up to the third century, baptism was said to incorporate one into the Christian "brotherhood."[5] The same idea appears in the oldest description of the eucharistic celebration, in Justin Martyr, written in the mid-second century.[6] Such a manner of referring to one another expressed the inner cohesion of the community, even as believers were urged to have a brotherly attitude to their persecutors.[7] The new identity in baptism would be described very boldly by St. Augustine: "Let us rejoice and give thanks: We have not only become Christians, but Christ himself. . . . Stand in awe and rejoice: We have become Christ."[8] St. Cyril of Jerusalem would say much the same: "Having been baptized into Christ, and put on Christ, you have been made conformable to the Son of God . . . [and] are properly called Christs."[9]

Through oneness with Christ and membership in a new community, the baptized entered into a new way of life. We see three fine examples describing that life in the *Didache*, the *Letter to Diognetus*, and *The Shepherd*. The first, the "Teaching [or Training] of the Twelve Apostles," whose second title reads: "Teaching [Training] of [the] Lord through the Twelve Apostles for the Gentiles," comes from late first- or early second-century Syria.[10] A short work, the *Didache* describes the program by which a Gentile convert was prepared for and introduced into the life of the church. The first chapters call for a decisive change in the "habits of perception and standards of judg-

---

[5] So Tertullian in his *Baptism*, written between the years 200 and 206. Cited in Joseph Cardinal Ratzinger, *The Meaning of Christian Brotherhood*, 2nd Eng. ed. (San Francisco: Ignatius Press, 1993), 37.

[6] St. Justin Martyr, *The First and Second Apologies*, 65, trans., intro., and notes by Leslie William Barnard, Ancient Christian Writers 56 (New York: Paulist Press, 1997), 70.

[7] Ephesians 10.3 in *The Epistles of St. Clement of Rome and St. Ignatius of Antioch*, trans. James A. Kleist, Ancient Christian Writers 1 (Westminster, MD: Newman Press, 1961), 64.

[8] Austin, "Restoring Equilibrium," 38.

[9] Cited by Perry Cahall, "*Lectio Divina*: The Fathers of the Church and Theological Pedagogy," in *Seminary Theology: Teaching in a Contemplative Way*, ed. James Keating (Omaha, NE: IPF Publications, 2010), 78.

[10] Some scholars put the date of composition in the 50s or 60s of the first century. See Aaron Milavec, *The Didache: Text, Translation, Analysis, and Commentary* (Collegeville, MN: Liturgical Press, 2003), 110–14.

ment of novices coming out of a pagan lifestyle."[11] The section begins with the familiar Jewish theme of "two ways": one of life and one of death. The former is described in terms of one's relationship to God and to neighbor; the latter includes not showing mercy to the poor, being murderers of children, turning away the needy, being advocates of the rich and lawless judges of the poor.[12] Preparation for baptism included a lengthy instruction in the way of life by a spiritual mentor. Baptism, in flowing water, if possible, was given in the name of the Father and the Son and the Holy Spirit. The candidate, stripped at the moment of baptism, received a white tunic upon emerging, was embraced by his or her new ecclesial family, and then, with them and arms raised and facing East (facing the rising sun, a symbol of Christ), prayed the Our Father for the first time. The initiation was completed with a celebration of thanksgiving.

A second early catechetical work is given to us in *The Shepherd*, written during the first half of the second century in Rome and by far the longest of the writings from this early period. The work was widely used in the second and third centuries. The author, Hermas, was at one time a Christian slave, later a penitent. *The Shepherd* stresses the necessity of penance and the possibility of forgiveness of sins after baptism. Throughout, the work emphasizes the need for holiness in the church. It also describes the church as the first of God's creations, an idea that may have been inspired by the New Testament passage that God chose us in Christ before the foundation of the world (Eph 1:4).

The *Letter to Diognetus*, an apology directed to a pagan of high social or political standing, is generally thought to have been composed mid- or late second century. Analogous to the Platonic view of the soul in an alien body, *Diognetus* speaks of the church as a foreign group living in the cities of the empire: "What the soul is in the body, that the Christians are in the world."[13] "They reside in their respective

---

[11] Ibid., 39.
[12] *Didache* 5.2, in Milavec, *The Didache*, 17.
[13] *Epistle to Diognetus* 6, in *The Didache, The Epistle of Barnabas, The Epistles and the Martyrdom of St. Polycarp, The Fragments of Papias, The Epistle to Diognetus*, trans. James A. Kleist, Ancient Christian Writers 6 (Westminster, MD: Newman Press, 1961), 139.

countries, but only as aliens. They take part in everything as citizens and put up with everything as foreigners. Every foreign land is their home, and every home a foreign land. . . . They spend their days on earth, but hold their citizenship in heaven."[14] At the same time, by God's design, the church, like the soul, holds the world together. By the witness of their lives, a witness to the divine power in them, believers increase their numbers. "Such is the important post to which God has assigned them, and they are not at liberty to desert it."[15] The *Letter* seeks to explain the church's identity and its concern for its own discipline and purity. It explains as well why Christians referred to themselves as *hagioi*, a people who were holy or sacred, and *paroikoi* or *paroikountes*, "resident aliens" or "settled migrants."[16]

Baptismal initiation was completed in the celebration of the Eucharist. Here especially is Christian evidence from the second and third centuries limited, in part to avoid incriminating evidence in the intermittent persecutions to which Christians were subject.[17] Passages in the *Didache* (chaps. 9–10 and 14) may refer to the Eucharist or to the celebratory meal following baptism, though themes present in them appear in later reflections on the Eucharist and contain important implications for an understanding of the ecclesial community.[18] The Greek word *eucharistia* ("thanksgiving") could mean an ordinary meal of the community, celebrated in thanksgiving, or the Eucharist itself, or a combination of both: an *agapē*-Eucharist.[19] Several elements are noteworthy. First, the prayers in the *Didache* are closer to Jewish prayers and to forms of later Jewish liturgy than other early Christian

---

[14] *Epistle to Diognetus* 5.

[15] *Epistle to Diognetus* 6.

[16] Rowan Williams, *Why Study the Past? The Quest for the Historical Church* (Grand Rapids, MI: Eerdmans, 2005), 37 and 33.

[17] Norman Tanner, *New Short History of the Catholic Church* (London: Burns & Oates, 2011), 13.

[18] See the treatment of the *Didache* in Dennis Billy, *The Beauty of the Eucharist: Voices from the Church Fathers* (Hyde Park, NY: New City Press, 2010), 47–56.

[19] The word *agapē* (Greek for "love") used in John and Paul for God's or Christ's love for us and, derivatively, our love for God and for one another. By the end of the second century the *agapē* meals, to benefit the poor and foster Christian concord, were completely separate from the Eucharist.

liturgies.[20] Second, the meal or the Eucharist promotes unity in the local church with a mindfulness as well of the extended church: "As this piece [of bread] was scattered over the hills and then brought together and made one, so let your Church be brought together from the ends of the earth into your Kingdom."[21] This last image is often repeated in the later sermons of the Eucharist. Third, the two references to *sacrifice* on the Lord's Day, followed by a reference to the text of Malachi about the offering of a pure sacrifice, could refer either to the community's sacrifice or to Christ's sacrifice on the cross, or to both. The juxtaposition of the two uses may "convey a deeper sense of the mystery that takes place in the worship of the Christian community" in that the "Eucharist (or 'Thanksgiving') of the believing community is deeply rooted in Christ's total offering of self."[22]

The church's relation to the Eucharist is very prominent in the letters (ca. AD 115–17) of Ignatius, bishop of Antioch. The letters were written to different churches in Asia Minor as the bishop was being taken to Rome for execution during the persecutions under Emperor Trajan (emperor 98–117). In Ignatius's view, the Eucharist is a *synaxis* (a "gathering together," a term used to distinguish Christian worship from that of the synagogue), understood in light of the New Testament expectation of the eschatological gathering of the dispersed people of God. Salvation and eternal life come only by participating in this end-time community, manifested in the eucharistic assembly under the leadership of the bishop, presiding in the place of Christ or of God.[23] In the *Letter to the Philadelphians*, thought to contain "the fullest résumé"[24] of Ignatius's belief, we read: "Take care, therefore, to participate in one Eucharist (for there is one flesh of our Lord Jesus

---

[20] Diarmaid MacCulloch, *Christianity: The First Three Thousand Years* (New York: Viking, 2009), 120.

[21] *Didache* 9.4, trans. in Billy, *Beauty of the Eucharist*, 49.

[22] Billy, *Beauty of the Eucharist*, 54.

[23] John D. Zizioulas, "The Early Christian Community," in *Christian Spirituality: Origins to the Twelfth Century*, ed. Bernard McGinn, John Meyendorff, in collaboration with Jean Leclercq, World Spirituality: An Encyclopedic History of the Religious Quest, vol. 16 (New York: Crossroad, 1985), 32.

[24] James A. Kleist, notes in *The Epistles of St. Clement of Rome and St. Ignatius of Antioch*, 137.

Christ, and one cup which leads to unity through his blood; there is one altar, just as there is one bishop, together with the presbytery and the deacons, my fellow servants), in order that whatever you do, you do in accordance with God."[25] Francis A. Sullivan notes, "The sequence 'one Eucharist, one altar, one bishop' shows that for Ignatius the unity of the church is profoundly rooted in the 'one flesh and one cup' of the Eucharist and in the person of the bishop who presided at it."[26]

Other writings give further indications of the Eucharist-church relationship. The earliest extant description of a eucharistic service in Rome, and, given the author's travels, surely true of other places as well, is found in the *First Apology* (ca. 152–155) of Justin Martyr (d. ca. 165). Reflecting a time when the Eucharist was becoming separate from community meals, Justin, a layman, twice emphasizes the importance of the congregation's *Amen* to the prayer of the presider, carrying over the community spirit and sense of oneness previously expressed when the celebration of the two were joined.[27]

Considered the founder of Christian theology, Bishop Irenaeus of Lyons (130–ca. 200) incorporates reflection on the Eucharist in his most famous work, *Against Heresies*, written between 180 and 190. The treatise was written to counter Gnostics in the area of Lyons whose strongly dualistic outlook opposed an evil material world, created by the God of the Old Testament, against a spiritual world, into which Jesus was said to introduce believers by imparting to them a secret knowledge. Drawing on Paul, the deutero-Pauline letters, and the Fourth Gospel, Irenaeus articulates a theory of recapitulation by which Christ, after the fall of Adam and Eve spoiled God's plan, inaugurated a new creation in a single divine plan encompassing creation, redemption, and sanctification. The saving unity of flesh

---

[25] Ignatius, *Letter to the Philadelphians* 4. Translation in Francis A. Sullivan, *From Apostles to Bishops: The Development of the Episcopacy in the Early Church* (New York: Newman Press, 2001), 116.

[26] Sullivan, *From Apostles to Bishops*, 116.

[27] Joseph A. Jungmann, *The Mass of the Roman Rite: Its Origins and Development (Missarum Sollemnia)*, trans. Francis A. Brunner, 2 vols. (New York: Benziger Brothers, 1951), 1:23.

and spirit brought about by Christ is embodied in the church's Eucharist. Formed from the dust of the earth, our bodies, sharing even now in the power and glory of God through the Eucharist, witness to the new creation. In Irenaeus's mind, the Eucharist is so closely tied to the apostolic tradition that it becomes "a universal symbol of the Church's unity of belief and practice" and "a concrete sign of God's redemptive grace at work in our hearts and in the world."[28]

A similar vision is supposed in the segment on Eucharist in the *Apostolic Tradition*, attributed, probably incorrectly, to Hippolytus (ca. 170–ca. 235), presbyter of Rome.[29] Much of the present Eucharistic Prayer II of the current Roman Missal is closely drawn from a prayer in the *Apostolic Tradition*. As the oldest extant eucharistic prayer available, it was probably intended as a guideline for a more developed prayer by the presider. The first paragraph of the prayer embraces themes of creation, redemption, and incarnation and thanks God for the Son's obtaining "a holy people" for himself. It concludes by asking God to send the Holy Spirit upon those gathered so that they might be "incorporated in Jesus' sacrificial offering and become a living oblation, a 'holy church.' "[30] Coming toward the end of the prayer, the church's holiness is seen as coming from its participation in the paschal mystery of Christ. The church is holy as it dies to sin and lives by the Spirit and because, united to Jesus, it continues to do the will of the Father.

Our final word on the Eucharist-church relation in this early period comes from Cyprian, the bishop (ca. 248–258) of Carthage in North Africa.[31] His teaching on this matter comes in what seems to be an encyclical letter to other bishops of the area. The letter, the first extant extended reflection on the Eucharist, seeks to correct the custom in some areas of offering only water in the eucharistic cup. In the mingling of water (representing "God's people") and wine ("the blood of Christ"), Cyprian insists, "the union between Christ and the

---

[28] Billy, *Beauty of the Eucharist*, 67–75, quotations at 72 and 74.
[29] John F. Baldovin, "Hippolytus and the Apostolic Tradition: Recent Research and Commentary," *Theological Studies* 64 (2003): 520–42.
[30] Billy, *Beauty of the Eucharist*, 98–108, at 102.
[31] Ibid., 119–28.

Church" is brought about. In this commingling, "the people are made one with Christ and the multitude of believers are bonded and united with Him in whom they have come to believe."[32] While seeking to clarify what he sees as an erroneous practice, Cyprian helps lay the groundwork for a eucharistic ecclesiology that later would be summed up in the phrase "the Eucharist makes the Church."[33] The belief of the fathers and so much of what they wrote was "anchored in regular, indeed habitual, participation in the church's worship" and what they taught was confirmed by how they prayed.[34]

The Church's Scriptures and Rule of Faith

If members of the church were introduced into a new way of life received in baptism and nourished by the Eucharist, no less important was the place of the Scriptures in the life of the church. The church saw in the Scriptures its link to Jesus and his teaching and a guide for its own life. So Irenaeus: "It behooves us . . . to flee to the Church, and be brought up in her bosom, and be nourished with the Lord's Scriptures." The church, he says, has been planted as a garden (*paradisus*) in the world, and the Spirit says it may eat from every tree of the garden (Gen 2:16), from "every Scripture of the Lord."[35] The great biblical exegete and theologian, Origen (ca. 184–ca. 254), is equally clear: "We are said to drink the blood of Christ not only when we received it according to the rite of the mysteries, but also when we receive his words, in which life dwells."[36] But which Scriptures were

---

[32] *Letter* 63, 13.1, in *The Letters of Cyprian of Carthage*, vol. 3: *Letters 55–66*, trans. G. W. Clarke, Ancient Christian Writers 46 (New York: Newman Press, 1986), 105.

[33] The phrase was coined by Henri de Lubac in his work *Corpus Mysticum* (1949).

[34] Robert Wilken, *The Spirit of Early Christian Thought: Seeking the Face of God* (New Haven, CT: Yale University Press, 2003), 26–27.

[35] Irenaeus, *Against Heresies* 5.20.2, in *Saint Irenaeus of Lyons, Against Heresies*, ed. Alexander Roberts and James Donaldson, new ed. (Ex Fontibus Co., 2010), 607.

[36] Origen, *Homilies on Numbers* 16, 9, cited in Olivier Clément, *The Roots of Christian Mysticism: Texts from the Patristic Era with Commentary* (Hyde Park, NY: New City Press, 1993), 97.

to guide the church? In the mid-second century, Marcion (d. ca. 160) adopted the Gnostic belief in an opposition between the God of Law in the Old Testament and the God of love in the preaching of Jesus. Accordingly, he eliminated from the Scriptures all of the Old Testament and all but the letters of Paul (excluding the Pastoral Letters) and a revised text of Luke's gospel and adopted the exegetical principle of absolute contrast between Law and Gospel.[37] On the other side of the spectrum, a Jewish Christian sect, the Ebionites (from *Ebionim*, "the Poor," a self-designation), so emphasized the binding character of the Mosaic Law that they rejected the letters of Paul. The claims to secret traditions and revelations by the Gnostics and assertions by the Montanists—a movement of ecstatic prophesy making claims to special revelation uttered by Montanus and two women associates—were further catalysts in determining which documents were to be regarded as foundational for the church.

The process by which the canon of the New Testament was determined was complicated.[38] A text's apostolic origin, real or putative, was very important, as was the community to which the writing was addressed. The community at Antioch, for example, very probably contributed to Matthew's prominence, as Ephesus and Greece likely promoted the writings of Paul and John. Conformity with what was emerging as the basics of the faith, a rule of faith, was also a factor leading to a work's acceptance or rejection: the Gospel of Peter, used to support a docetic understanding of Christ, was rejected, as were writings that denied that Jesus truly died on the cross. Eminent figures associated with one church sought to be guided by what was being used in the liturgy of other churches. The very process of determining which of the early Christian writings were to be received as the word of God contributed to the growing sense of what Ignatius of Antioch referred to as the *church catholic* (universal). Ultimately it was probably the sense of the church (the *sensus ecclesiae*), an intuition

---

[37] Chadwick, *Church in Ancient Society*, 89–92.
[38] Luke Timothy Johnson, with the assistance of Todd C. Penner, *The Writings of the New Testament: An Interpretation*, rev. ed. (Minneapolis: Fortress Press, 1999), 595–619, and Raymond E. Brown, *An Introduction to the New Testament* (New York: Doubleday, 1997), 10–15.

as to which writings were the word of God, that was the major factor in determining the question of canonicity. "We shall never know all the details of how the twenty-seven books were written, preserved, selected, and collected; but one fact is indisputable. Joined as the [New Testament], they have been the single most important instrument in bringing untold millions of people from different times and places into contact with Jesus of Nazareth and the first believers who proclaimed him."[39]

In the course of the second century, the Christian books regarded as normative came to be called the *New Testament*, from the Greek word *diathēkē*, which means both "covenant" and "testament." The idea of a first and second covenant was already mentioned in the Letter to the Hebrews (8:7). The Hebrew Scriptures then came to be called the *Old Testament*, though no less the Word of God. By the end of the fourth century, the twenty-seven books in what has become the New Testament had become widely accepted, though universal agreement came only in the seventh century. The church saw itself, we have seen, as the new covenant people of God

Two other interrelated questions faced the church: How interpret the Old Testament in its relationship to the New, and how interpret the Scriptures whose anthropomorphic texts were so problematic to those learned in Greek philosophical thought?[40] The first was answered in large part by the use of a "typological" reading of the Old Testament: events, persons, and things in the Old Testament were seen as "types" foreshadowing the realities, the "antitypes," of the New. Paul, for example, sees Adam as a type of Christ; the passing through the Red Sea was seen to prefigure baptism.[41] Insisting that both Old and New Testaments were a seamless whole, Irenaeus used such a method, as did the catechetical school at Alexandria. This method helped Christian believers embrace the Old Testament even as they proclaimed its fulfillment in the actions described in the New.

---

[39] Brown, *Introduction to the New Testament*, 15.
[40] See Wilken, *Spirit of Early Christian Thought*, chap. 3.
[41] See a fine example of typology in the adapted translation of a passage from *Peri Pascha* ("On Passover" or "On Easter") by Melito (d. ca. 190), bishop of Sardis, Asia Minor, in Aquilina, *Fathers of the Church*, 77–79.

Sharing in the concern to help Christians own the Old Testament as well as in an effort to speak of the Scriptures with those trained in Greek culture, Clement of Alexandria (d. ca. 215) and even more so Origen, successive leaders of the catechetical school at Alexandria, developed typology into an allegorical method of interpretation. Allegorical exegesis (from the Greek *allos*, "other," and *agoreuein*, "to speak publicly") looks beyond the literal sense of the text to its "spiritual" meaning.[42] This method of exegesis had antecedents in Greek reflection on the writings of Homer and in the efforts of the observant Jewish exegete Philo (d. ca. 50) who sought "to demonstrate the compatibility between the spiritual meaning of the Hebrew Scriptures and the loftiest insights of Platonic philosophy."[43] In Origen's words: "All the things in the visible category can be related to the invisible, the corporeal to the incorporeal, and the manifest to those that are hidden. . . . This relationship does not obtain only with creatures; the Divine Scripture itself is written with wisdom of a rather similar sort."[44]

Among his extant works, the best example of Origen's use of the allegorical method is his commentary and two homilies on the Song of Songs, or the Canticle of Canticles. Though not the first to compose a commentary on the Song of Songs nor the last—several others in the next few centuries did the same—his was by far the most profound. The Song may be read, Origen says, in three senses, corresponding to the three levels of human existence mentioned in 1 Thessalonians 5:23, "spirit and soul and body": a "bodily" or literal sense, in which the Song is seen as lofty love poetry; corresponding to the soul, a sense that looks to the bridal union of the *Logos*, Christ, and the

---

[42] Gerald O'Collins and Edward G. Farrugia (*A Concise Dictionary of Theology* [New York: Paulist Press, 2000], 5), see the Greek root as "speaking under the guise of something else."

[43] Sandra M. Schneiders, "Scripture and Spirituality," in *Christian Spirituality: Origins to the Twelfth Century*, ed. Bernard McGinn and John Meyendorff, in collaboration with Jean Leclerq, World Spirituality: An Encyclopedic History of the Religious Quest, vol. 16 (New York: Crossroad, 1985), 10.

[44] Origen, *The Song of Songs: Commentary and Homilies*, trans. and annotated by R. P. Lawson, Ancient Christian Writers 26 (Westminster, MD: Newman Press, 1957), 223.

human soul; and a spiritual sense that sees in the Canticle the mystical nuptials of Christ and the church. Readings in the latter two senses, always conjoined, are based on "the compenetration of the life of the Church and the life of the soul, of the mystery of the Church and our life under grace."[45] Origen sees the kiss mentioned in the first verse of the Canticle and the kiss at the Eucharist as figures of Christ's kiss (love) of the church.[46] For Origen, and later for Denys the Areopagite and, even more so, for Gregory of Nyssa, there is a "mutual co-inherence of the mystical and the ecclesiological . . . though it is a pervasive colouring rather than a specific theme."[47]

The school at Antioch preferred a more literal reading of the biblical text, but allegorical exegesis became widely adopted in the church in the East and, through Ambrose and Augustine, had a strong influence in the church of the West, well into the Middle Ages. Our own day sees a renewed appreciation of some of the insights of an allegorical approach to the Scriptures, especially in the liturgy.[48]

The early church's efforts to maintain the integrity of its apostolic heritage was three-pronged. In addition to settling which Scriptures the church considered its own, professions of faith were also designed to ensure fidelity to its apostolic tradition.[49] Baptismal professions of faith that led to the early creeds were based on the threefold baptismal command at the end of Matthew's gospel. The earliest extant form of such, used most likely in Rome, is preserved in the *Apostolic*

---

[45] See the introduction in ibid., 15.

[46] Paul J. Griffiths, *Song of Songs*, Brazos Theological Commentary on the Bible, ed. R. R. Reno (Grand Rapids, MI: Brazos Press, 2011), 9–10.

[47] Andrew Louth, *The Origins of the Christian Mystical Tradition: From Plato to Denys*, 2nd ed. (Oxford: Oxford University Press, 2009), 196.

[48] Jason Byassee, *Praise Seeking Understanding: Reading the Psalms with Augustine*, Radical Traditions: Theology in a Postcritical Key, ed. Stanley M. Hauerwas and Peter Ochs (Grand Rapids, MI: Eerdmans, 2007), chap. 1, and Andrew Louth, *Discerning the Mystery: An Essay on the Nature of Theology* (New York: Oxford University Press, 1983), chap. 5.

[49] Luke Timothy Johnson, *The Creed: What Christians Believe and Why It Matters* (New York: Doubleday, 2003), 21–32. See also Berard Marthaler, *The Creed: The Apostolic Faith in Contemporary Theology*, rev. ed. (Mystic, CT: Twenty-Third Publications, 1993), 1–36.

Tradition of the early third century. It seems quite certain that the earliest form of the third question was simply: "Do you believe in the Holy Spirit?" By the end of the second century, the third question was changed to "Do you believe in [*eis*] the Holy Spirit in [*en*] the holy Church?" which became the most common form of the third element in the baptismal creed. Other forms omitted the second "in" and simply listed the church as the first of the works of the Spirit: "Do you believe in the Holy Spirit, the holy catholic church . . . ?" It is worth noting that in the second form cited above, a distinction is made between belief in Father, Son, and Holy Spirit and belief in the church. The point of the distinction was to emphasize that baptismal faith centers on the triune God, a faith expressed in the context of the church community. The church is not the object of belief the same way in which God is the object of faith. Belief in the Holy Spirit, however, involves "believing in" the church community that is the work of the Spirit and in which one encounters the triune God. Also, once mention of the church was included in these early baptismal creeds, it was always after the profession of faith in the Holy Spirit and never without the adjective "holy." Scholars suggest the most likely reason for mention of the church in the creed was to counter the Gnostic scorn for the churches over which the bishops presided. Irenaeus insisted, for example, that only in the holy church was the Holy Spirit to be found. Local variations in the profession of faith are found over the next few centuries. In the seventh century, Rome accepted as its own the Apostles' Creed, recommended now for Masses on the Sundays of Lent and Easter and used in the rosary.

A third means of safeguarding the apostolic heritage of the church in these early centuries came in the recognition of a need for authoritative teachers, given that both biblical texts and, later, doctrinal statements were susceptible to very divergent interpretations. We shall look at this matter after the following section.

Early Christian Views of the Church

We have already encountered several ways of understanding the church in the writings that have been mentioned: church as mother, for example, or as bride, as body of Christ (more on this in the following chapter) and people of God, as soul of the world, and as having, in Christ, a central place in God's plan of recapitulation and bringing about a new creation. These next paragraphs focus on some of the principal theological understandings of church in the second and third centuries with some overlap to the later period.

The fathers of the church gave major attention to seeing the church as "spouse" or "virginal bride," as "mother" or "virginal mother." The church as spouse or virginal bride were foundational: the church is first of all related to Christ, expressed in the nuptial imagery that has its roots in the Old Testament and in the New, most especially in Ephesians 5:32. Origen's commentary and homilies on the Song of Songs, mentioned above, are the most outstanding examples of patristic reflection on Christ as the bridegroom and the church as virgin bride, expressions of the mutual love between Christ and the church. In that love, the church is seen as mother. She is *virginal* mother "because she bears us, not by a human father but by the Spirit," says Bishop Ambrose of Milan (d. 397).[50] She is virginal *mother* because of her fecundity in giving life to those reborn in baptism. Early authors saw the church's motherhood with different, though not exclusive, emphases: Hippolytus saw the church as mother through baptism, looking to the new life brought by the sacrament; Clement of Alexandria saw the church as a virgin mother who nurses her children with holy milk, the *Logos*. The Latin North African apologist Tertullian (d. ca. 222) gave attention to the church's introducing the baptized into a new pattern of life, including worship and sacraments, but put greater stress on the ethical and canonical aspects of the church's order or "discipline." Those who separate themselves from the church, Tertullian noted, are "without mother."[51] Origen is credited with developing most profoundly the image of church as mother "who is ceaselessly giving birth. The preaching of the Word, the administra-

---

[50] Ambrose, *De virginibus* 1.6.31, in Boniface Ramsey, *Beginning to Read the Fathers*, rev. ed. (New York: Paulist Press, 2012), 112.

[51] Karl Delahaye, *Ecclesia Mater chez les Pères des trois premiers siècles*, trans. P. Vergriete and E. Bouis (Paris: Editions du Cerf, 1964), 99. See also Henri de Lubac, *The Motherhood of the Church: Followed by Particular Churches in the Universal Church*, trans. Sergia Englund (San Francisco: Ignatius Press, 1982), 62–65.

tion of baptism, prayers, and various works: everything is the activity of the Church giving birth to, developing and carrying to completion in the heart of believers this gift from God which is eternal life."[52]

Many patristic writings—the so-called Second Letter of Clement (the earliest extant homily, written about AD 150 by someone other than the author of 1 Clement); *The Shepherd* of Hermas; texts of Origen, of Bishop Methodius of Olympus (martyred ca. 311), and, later, of Augustine—speak of an original "spiritual church" founded "before the moon and the sun" (Second Letter of Clement). The basic insight of these writings, suggests Swiss theologian Hans Urs von Balthasar, is the conviction that "the deepest origins of the Church are to be traced right back through the broad sweep of creation and salvation history into the very source of love: God."[53] The church is also compared to the moon because of the latter's association with woman (fecundity) and because its light is borrowed from the sun, symbol of Christ the true light (think paschal candle). "It is darkness and light both at once. In itself it is darkness, but it sends out light from another whose light is transmitted through it."[54] In the moon's periodic changes the fathers saw a symbol of the historical condition of the church, showing weakness but also renewal. As the sun/moon imagery was also given a nuptial interpretation, it relates to yet another image, that of the harlot chosen and purified after being called. The harlot Rahab (Josh 2), for example, was seen as a figure of the church.[55] The church was imaged also as ark (Gen 6–9) with

---

[52] Delahaye, *Ecclesia Mater*, 120, trans. in de Lubac, *The Motherhood of the Church*, 65.

[53] Brendan Leahy, *The Marian Profile in the Ecclesiology of Hans Urs von Balthasar* (New York: New City Press, 2000), 106–7.

[54] Joseph Ratzinger, "Why I Am Still in the Church," in Hans Urs von Balthasar and Joseph Ratzinger, *Two Say Why*, trans. John Griffiths (Chicago: Franciscan Herald Press, 1971), 77.

[55] Yves Congar, *True and False Reform in the Church*, trans. with intro. Paul Philibert (Collegeville, MN: Liturgical Press, 2011), 70–71 (the volume translates Congar's revised edition of 1968), and Ramsey, *Beginning to Read the Fathers*, 109. See also the lengthy essay by Hans Urs von Balthasar, "Casta Meretrix," trans. John Saward, in *Explorations in Theology*, vol. 2: *Spouse of the Word* (San Francisco: Ignatius Press, 1991), 193–288.

varying takes on its symbolism: it is the ark that guarantees salvation (Maximus of Turin, d. 408/23); as ark, it carries within it both clean and unclean animals, signifying the good and those not so good; or, in carrying all kinds of animals, it indicates the church's embrace of all nations (Augustine).[56]

Aware of the limitations and imperfections in their concrete experience of church, the fathers tried to take them into account even as they maintained the ideals of their ecclesial understanding. Clement of Alexandria and Origen, for example, were both very likely influenced by the Platonic doctrine of forms, that "each empirical thing has its perfect pattern and its true reality in the eternal world."[57] Clement distinguished between the church on earth, with its preaching and sacraments guiding its members on the road to holiness, and the spiritual church, whose members are the true Gnostics (those who have authentic knowledge) given over to contemplation of God. In Clement's words, "The earthly Church is the image of the heavenly."[58] Origen makes a similar distinction, in his case, between "the true church" and the church as a historical institution. The latter involves the church whose members share a priestly baptismal anointing and a call to offer God sacrifices of praise. Origen applies to the church the Matthean parable of the weeds among the wheat (Matt 13:36-43). Drawing on the image of the church "without a spot or wrinkle" (Eph 5:27), Origen also speaks of the spiritual church or "the true church" or "the heavenly church" that existed before the creation of the world. The church on earth prepares the baptized for a place in the heavenly church.[59]

Related to these distinctions was the question concerning the place in the church for those who had sinned. In the face of laxity in the church or compromise in times of persecution, one approach so stressed the need for purity and holiness that the church was understood in perfectionist terms, as a community of saints that must

---

[56] Ramsey, *Beginning to Read the Fathers*, 111.
[57] Eric G. Jay, *The First Seventeen Centuries*, vol. 1 of *The Church: Its Changing Image Through Twenty Centuries* (London: SPCK, 1977), 59.
[58] Ibid., 59–60.
[59] Ibid., 60–64.

exclude sinners. Tertullian, in his later Montanist years, adopted a stance of distinguishing between the church joined to the Spirit and the "Church which consists of a number of bishops."[60] A rigorist stance was also taken by Hippolytus, who opposed what he thought was the Bishop of Rome's unacceptable readmittance, after doing penance, of one who had committed adultery. The bishops of Rome had adopted a more flexible approach regarding repentant sinners. As did Origen, they saw themselves guided by the biblical parable of the weeds in the field of wheat. This second stance became normative in the church, though not without opposition from those who insisted on a more rigorous stance.

The letters of Ignatius of Antioch provide us with "some of the richest resources for the understanding of Christianity [read: church] in the immediate 'postapostolic' period."[61] Ignatius refers to his own devotion to the unity of the church (Philad. 8.1; Magn. 1).[62] The ultimate foundation of this unity is "a union based on the flesh and spirit of Jesus Christ, our enduring life, a union based on faith and love—the greatest blessing; and most especially, a union with Jesus and the Father" (Magn. 1). On the practical level of the local church, union is to be centered on the bishop, assisted by presbyters and deacons. The letters of Ignatius show "a sort of constant and fruitful dialectic between two characteristics of Christian life": on the one hand, the fundamental unity of all the faithful in Christ; on the other, the structure of the ecclesial community.[63] All members of the community, including its leaders, are to conform themselves to God's ways, to respect one another, to regard no one by outward appearances only,

---

[60] Tertullian, "On Modesty," in *The Ante-Nicene Fathers: Translations of Writings of the Fathers down to A.D. 325*, ed. Alexander Roberts and James Donaldson, American reprint of the Edinburgh edition, vol. 4 (Grand Rapids, MI: Eerdmans, 1982), 100.

[61] Rowan Williams, *The Wound of Knowledge: Christian Spirituality from the New Testament to Saint John of the Cross* (Cambridge, MA: Cowley Publications, 1990), 24–32, at 24.

[62] Citations taken from *The Epistles of St. Clement of Rome and St. Ignatius of Antioch*.

[63] Pope Benedict XVI, *The Fathers* (Huntington, IN: Our Sunday Visitor, 2008), 16.

134 *The Church*

but to love one another at all times in Jesus Christ (Magn. 6). The eucharistic self-giving of God is to be reflected in an ordinary life of selfless service of others. Given the time in which he lived, Ignatius saw the supreme example of that self-giving in martyrdom. The stories of the martyrs up to the mid-third century were "an essential part of the Church's self-identification" as a community of aliens whose ultimate loyalty lay outside the social and political system in which they lived (recall the *Letter to Diognetus*).[64] The witness of the martyrs, combined with the commonly recognized call given to all Christians to evangelize, contributed greatly to the rapid growth of the church across the Mediterranean world in these early centuries.

We also have indications of the church's attitude toward Judaism in this early period. New Testament writings that emphasized lines of continuity between Judaism and Christianity were preserved in the second and third centuries, true, but the church was clearly coming to see itself as constituting a new religion. Jews and Christians continued their debates, often using the Greco-Roman polemical style of defaming one's opponent. Even though their numbers were increasing, Christians often wrote with the defensiveness of a minority religion facing what seemed a still powerful rival.

Apparently, to counter the idea that Christians and Jews shared a common covenant and to discourage any sympathy toward the practices of Judaism, a letter written in the name of Barnabas, the missionary colleague of Paul, delivered a strong attack on Judaism. Using an allegorical interpretation of the Scriptures strongly critical of Jewish literalism, the letter argued that Christianity was the perfect fulfillment of the Jewish tradition. The work, the first explicitly to speak of Christians as "the new people" (no longer a renewed Israel), is thought to have been written in the early second century, possibly at Alexandria.[65]

A more positive assessment of Judaism appears in the *Dialogue with Trypho* by Justin Martyr.[66] Cast in the form of a conversation with a learned Jewish scholar, the work accepts that Jewish Scriptures are

---

[64] Williams, *Why Study the Past?*, 36–37, at 36.
[65] Chadwick, *Church in Ancient Society*, 56–57.
[66] Ibid., 93–99.

an inspired authority but argues that Judaism was a temporary dispensation until the coming of the true people of God. Justin sees fulfilled in the Eucharist the prophecy of Malachi 1:11 about a true sacrifice being offered to God from all peoples. The *Dialogue* seems to have been directed to Jewish readers, though it may also have been meant to help Gentile pagans see the difference between Judaism and Christianity.

The homily *Peri Pascha* ("On Passover" or "On Easter), composed around 165 by Melito, Jewish-born bishop of Sardis in Asia Minor (modern Turkey), is yet another type of writing.[67] The city of Sardis had a well-established Jewish community with a magnificent synagogue that held some fifteen hundred persons. In its shadow, the fledgling Christian congregation may well have felt unsure of itself and insecure in accepting the Christian claims. During the community's celebration of Easter, held on the same day as the Jewish Passover following the custom of the churches of Asia Minor, Melito delivered a skillfully crafted homily in which he portrayed the exodus and the Jewish Passover as types of the true saving Passover, which took place in Jesus. In the rhetorical climax of the homily, Melito asks who it was who murdered the God sent to save us. His answer: "The King of Israel is destroyed by an Israelite hand." The homily was meant to differentiate Christianity from Judaism and bolster the Christian identity of the local congregation, but its dramatic conclusion, taken up by others centuries later, would have tragic consequences.

Ministry in the Church / Apostolic Succession

We have seen two of the three means developed to safeguard the apostolic heritage of the church; the third concerned authoritative teachers and leaders.[68] At the end of the first century and the beginning

---

[67] Aquilina, *Fathers of the Church*, 74–79, and Mary C. Boys, *Has God Only One Blessing? Judaism as a Source of Christian Self-Understanding*, Studies in Judaism and Christianity: Exploration of Issues in the Contemporary Dialogue between Christians and Jews, ed. Helga Croner (New York: Paulist Press, 2000), 50–53.

[68] See Daniel J. Harrington, *The Church According to the New Testament: What the Wisdom and Witness of Early Christianity Teach Us Today* (Franklin, WI: Sheed and Ward, 2001), chaps. 11 and 12, and Sullivan, *From Apostles to Bishops*.

of the second, both the forms of ministerial leadership and their designations were fluid. Besides mentioning both bishops and deacons, but not presbyters, the *Didache*, for example, lists "apostles" (itinerant missionaries), "prophets" (who spoke in ecstasy), and "teachers" (catechists).[69] Chapter 15 of the *Didache* seems to reflect a process of transition from itinerant ministers to a stable ministry of bishops and deacons, both to be elected by the people, a custom continuing well into the Middle Ages.[70] The *Didache* is clearer than the New Testament in saying that the appointed leaders also presided at the community's Eucharist.

Roughly contemporary with the *Didache*, the First Letter of Clement (written ca. 96) uses the terms *episkopoi* and *diakonoi* (the same terms used in Phil 1:1) when it speaks of appointments made by the apostles, though the letter ordinarily refers to church leaders as *presbyteroi*.[71] The letter was written by Clement on behalf of the Church of Rome to the community at Corinth to settle a conflict that arose when a group in the community opposed some of the local presbyters. The letter appeals to an orderly succession of community leaders, a group of elders (presbyters) rather than a single individual. The apostles, the letter says, appointed their first converts as bishops and deacons in the community and instructed them to appoint others who, in turn, would succeed them. The New Testament evidence suggests the process of selection and designation of ministers was much more complex, though rough antecedents exist in the letters of Paul and in the Pastorals.[72] First Clement witnesses to the conviction that ministry in the postapostolic community has its foundation in and continues the ministry of Jesus and of the early church. To bolster his argument, Clement appeals to order in the created universe and the ordered structures of imperial Rome, finding in the

---

[69] Sullivan, *From Apostles to Bishops*, 81–90.

[70] James A. Kleist, in *The Didache, the Epistle of Barnabas, the Epistles and the Martyrdom of St. Polycarp, the Fragment of Papias, the Epistle of Diognetus*, 164n91.

[71] Sullivan, *From Apostles to Bishops*, 91–102.

[72] Raymond E. Brown concludes that Clement "has generalized an apostolic practice that was occasional but not consistent or universal" (Raymond E. Brown and John P. Meier, *Antioch and Rome: New Testament Cradles of Catholic Christianity* [New York: Paulist Press, 1983], 175).

latter an exemplar for organizational elements in the Christian community. The letter also appeals to the order in the Jewish priesthood and appropriates to Christian leaders the terms "high priests," "priests," and "Levites." This the New Testament did not do. Clement recognizes the role of the whole community in the appointment of its leaders as well as the community's role in judging the performance of its officials.[73]

Some twenty years after Clement's letter, the letters of Ignatius of Antioch indicate further developments in ecclesial structures.[74] To meet the challenges to the faith coming from the Docetists (from *dokeo*, "appear"), who denied the full humanity of Christ and the reality of Christ in the Eucharist, and possibly to guide the church in face of persecution, Ignatius promotes the value of a threefold ministry consisting of a single bishop, a council of presbyters, and a "council" of deacons who assist the bishop and the presbyters, all ordered to service of the community as a whole. The New Testament, we saw, does not so clearly differentiate the first two offices. Ignatius's emphasis on the importance of this threefold pattern, especially on the role of the bishop, suggests he was promoting a structure that had not yet taken firm hold, even in the churches of Asia Minor. The churches in Alexandria, Philippi, Corinth, and Rome are thought to have been led by a college of presbyters well into the second century. A threefold ministry gradually became the norm for the church, though probably universally so only around AD 175. The "strong collegial element in Ignatius's view of ministry"[75] seen in his associating the council of elders with the single bishop in the leadership of the community suggests a need to qualify what has sometimes been spoken of as Ignatius's "monarchical" episcopacy. Better to speak of his promoting a "mono-episcopal" structure. Ignatius speaks of the bishop imaging Christ or presiding "in the place of God" but somewhat awkwardly sees the presbyters functioning "as the council of the Apostles" (so

---

[73] Sullivan, *From Apostles to Bishops*, 97.
[74] Ibid., 104–25.
[75] William R. Schoedel, *Ignatius of Antioch: A Commentary on the Letters of Ignatius of Antioch*, ed. Helmut Koster (Philadelphia: Fortress Press, 1985), 46, cited by Sullivan, *From Apostles to Bishops*, 107.

linking them rather than the bishops with apostolic imagery) and deacons "entrusted with the ministry of Jesus Christ" (Smyr. 8; Magn. 6; see Trall. 3.1). Roughly a century later, the ordination rite of the *Apostolic Tradition* clearly unites both christological and apostolic imagery with the person of the bishop.[76] Where Clement of Rome stresses the historical continuity between the sending of Christ, the sending of the apostles, and the subsequent episcopate, Ignatius makes no such argument but sees Christ and the Twelve permanently present in the person of the bishop with his presbyters. "Ignatius regards the Christian community assembled around the bishop in the midst of presbyters and deacons as the *actual* manifestation in the Spirit of the apostolic community."[77] The views of Clement and Ignatius are complementary; they call for seeing apostolic succession both in terms of historical continuity and as an actual spiritual reality. Consistent with what he asks of all the baptized, Ignatius calls the bishop to pattern his authority on the pattern set by God: "Bear all men as the Lord bears you. Endure everyone in love. . . . Speak to each one in the particular manner appropriate to him, as is God's way with us."[78] The importance of the bishop comes from his being head of the eucharistic community rather than from his simply having an office.

Bishop Irenaeus of Lyons adds distinctive touches in his concern to preserve the integrity of the apostolic tradition, not only in the role of bishops but in the faith and apostolicity of the entire community as well.[79] Bishops linked to the apostles in historical succession serve as guarantors of the authentic faith and teaching of the church. At the same time, "succession of episcopal office served as the visible corollary or sign of the community's faith and continuity with the

---

[76] Paul G. McPartlan, "Priesthood, Priestliness, and Priests," in Ronald D. Witherup and others, *Ministerial Priesthood in the Third Millennium: Faithfulness of Christ, Faithfulness of Priests* (Collegeville, MN: Liturgical Press, 2009), 72.

[77] *Baptism, Eucharist and Ministry*, Faith and Order Paper No. 111 (Geneva: World Council of Churches, 1982), 29, from segment on ministry, Commentary (36). Italics in original.

[78] Ignatius to Polycarp 1, in Williams, *The Wound of Knowledge*, 26.

[79] Sullivan, *From Apostles to Bishops*, 144–53.

apostles."[80] These two elements—episcopal succession and the faith of the community—are conjoined in the famous text in which Irenaeus speaks of the church at Rome: To avoid the cumbersomeness of checking the list of bishops of every church, it would suffice to show harmony between a given church and the tradition of "that very great, oldest, and well-known church, founded and established at Rome by those two most glorious apostles Peter and Paul," a tradition received from the apostles and passed on through its succession of bishops. The teaching of the Roman Church is normative not only because of its "outstanding pre-eminence" but because "the apostolic tradition is preserved in it by those from everywhere,"[81] that is, the presence in Rome of faithful from all the provinces of the empire. Irenaeus's emphasis on the teaching role of the bishop was a further step in recognizing a teaching office in the church, a development that has a basis in the New Testament texts themselves. The earliest insignia of the bishop was the *kathedra*, the seat or throne from which he taught (so the term *cathedral*, the church of the bishop).[82] (In Latin the official seat of the bishop was the *sedes*, from which comes the word "see," the place where the seat was located. The "Holy See" is now used exclusively of the Church of Rome.) Irenaeus was the first to elaborate a theory linking authenticity of teaching, authoritative teachers, and apostolic succession. As much as Irenaeus stresses the need for a clear canon of truth in the church and the means to ensure it, he gives pride of place to the love we encounter in Christ and learn from him. Truth without love, Irenaeus insists, is sterile.[83]

---

[80] Francine Cardman, "Myth, History, and the Beginnings of the Church," in *Governance, Accountability, and the Future of the Catholic Church*, ed. Francis Oakley and Bruce Russett (New York: Continuum, 2004), 39.

[81] Translation from Cyril Richardson, *Early Christian Fathers* (New York: Macmillan, 1970) in Cardman, "Myth, History, and the Beginnings of the Church," 40.

[82] The synagogue had a similar "seat of Moses," a symbol of the authority of teachers whose interpretation of the tradition ensured a link with Moses, the supreme lawgiver and teacher.

[83] Several similarities exist between the teaching of Irenaeus and that of Tertullian, though the latter emphasized the role of apostolic churches or those in communion with them rather than the role of the bishops in witnessing to the apostolic tradition; Sullivan, *From Apostles to Bishops*, 169–70.

The most important voice in articulating an understanding of episcopal office in the church, but also of the role of the laity, was that of Cyprian (ca. 200–258), bishop of Carthage, North Africa, at the time the second most important see in the West.[84] Only a few years after he became a Christian, he was appointed a bishop in 248 at the insistence of the people. His understanding of church, focused on the local church and addressing very practical issues, is expressed in a collection of eighty-two letters, of which sixty were written by himself; six conciliar letters; and several treatises, among them *On the Unity of the Catholic Church* and *The Lord's Prayer*. In what was a rarity for Latin authors, his writings were translated into Greek. Many of his views, as those of Augustine, influenced the understanding of the church in the West for centuries.

Within months of Cyprian's election as bishop, Emperor Decius (249–251), after decades of relative peace, mandated under threat of persecution that all persons must sacrifice to idols or a statue of the emperor. In this first major persecution of the entire church, not a few Christians bribed officials to obtain a certificate of compliance (*libellus*) even though they did not offer the sacrifice. Some of those who suffered for their faith equated this ploy with apostasy, long considered an unforgivable sin. What to do when those who capitulated, the *lapsi* (the "fallen"), sought forgiveness? Largely against this backdrop, and schisms arising therefrom, Cyprian developed many of his ideas about the church. Four points deserve notice.

First, against rigorists insisting on a church of the holy and awaiting a decision of the African bishops gathered in synod, Cyprian argued for forgiveness, but only through the authority of a bishop in lawful succession in an established local church. To support his position that the bishop is the visible symbol of unity within the church, Cyprian cited the Petrine text of Matthew 16:18-19 and the text of John 20:20-23, where the risen Jesus imparts the Spirit for the forgiveness of sins. In Cyprian's view, all bishops were successors of Peter, signs of unity in their own dioceses, hence his adage, "No bishop, no church." Only an authorized bishop could ordain or authorize baptism, forgiveness, or Eucharist. While the idea was not original to

---

[84] Ibid., chap. 10, and Chadwick, *Church in Ancient Society*, 145–60.

him, Cyprian especially became associated with another adage, "Outside the church [with the established bishop], no salvation." (The warning was directed to Christians who persisted in separating themselves from the lawful bishop; it was not addressing the issue of non-Christians, still the vast majority in the Roman Empire.)

Second, Cyprian promoted a collegial view of episcopal ministry. One of his principal writings, the relatively short work *On the Unity of the Catholic Church*, was occasioned by threats of schism, in Carthage and in Rome, when bishops broke ranks with each other. In his response, Cyprian attached singular importance to the unity among the bishops. As the apostles formed a college or corporate body, each sharing in the responsibility of the group, bishops did the same. From his legal background, Cyprian coined what became a classic formula: "The episcopate is one, of which a part is held by each [bishop] in solidarity [with all other bishops]." The expression "in solidarity" (*in solidum*) was a legal phrase used for joint ownership in which each party possesses rights concerning the whole and is responsible for the whole. The original text of *On the Unity of the Catholic Church* referred to the "primacy given to Peter" to show that there is but one church and one chair. If one were to desert the chair of Peter, Cyprian asks, could one be confident that one was in the church? Cyprian uses the term "primacy" in its original sense of *priority*: the power was first given to Peter but later given to all the Twelve and thence to the bishops. "In Cyprian's mind, the legitimate bishop of *every* see occupied a place in the 'one chair' which Christ inaugurated with Peter."[85]

Third, though not the first to do so, Cyprian frequently used the term *sacerdos* ("priest") in referring to bishops, though he clearly associates presbyters with such priestly functions as Eucharist and reconciling penitent sinners. He drew a parallel between Christian bishops and the Old Testament cultic priesthood: as Jewish high priests and priests were sanctioned by divine authority, so too were ministers of the new covenant. The Old Testament in this instance was no longer seen as foreshadowing a fulfillment in Christ's

---

[85] Maurice Bévenot, cited by Sullivan, *From Apostles to Bishops*, 196. Italics in original.

priesthood but as a divine prescription for the present.[86] Cyprian no longer employed the word "brother" for all Christians but restricted its use to address bishops, clerics, and confessors. Coming from the upper class himself, he also adapted the conventional aristocratic manner in addressing bishops as "your holiness," though preachers in Christian antiquity commonly used the same address referring to their listeners.[87] Cyprian's letters describe a pastoral ministry in which liturgical and spiritual ministry had a very important part.[88] Third-century bishops were also expected to perform certain social roles, settling tax disputes, for example, or difficulties with the law. Adopting Paul's injunction against Christians suing one another in the courts (1 Cor 6:1-8), bishops were expected to provide arbitration in such cases.[89]

Fourth, Cyprian's understanding of the role of the bishop is always a part of his view of church unity and the place of the church in the plan of God. In his *Treatise on the Lord's Prayer* he relates unity in the church to its ultimate source: "The greatest offering we can make to God is our peace, harmony among fellow Christians, a people united with the unity of the Father, the Son and the Holy Spirit."[90] In what became a slogan in the early church, Cyprian also insisted: "You cannot have God for your Father, if you have not the Church for your mother."[91] His favorite image of the church was that of a mother who joins all her children in one family.

---

[86] Thomas F. O'Meara, *Theology of Ministry*, rev. ed. (New York/Mahwah, NJ: Paulist Press, 1999), 95.

[87] Chadwick, *Church in Ancient Society*, 146; see also Boniface Ramsey's introduction in Augustine, *Homilies on the First Epistle of John*, trans. Boniface Ramsey, The Works of Saint Augustine: A Translation for the 21st Century (Hyde Park, NY: New City Press, 1990), 19n1.

[88] Sullivan, *From Apostles to Bishops*, 203–5.

[89] Chadwick, *Church in Ancient Society*, 147.

[90] *Treatise on the Lord's Prayer*, 23. Translation in *The Liturgy of the Hours According to the Roman Rite*, vol. 3: *Ordinary Time: Weeks 1–17* (New York: Catholic Book Publishing, 1975–1976), 377.

[91] "The Unity of the Catholic Church," chap. 6, in St. Cyprian, *The Lapsed and the Unity of the Catholic Church*, trans. Maurice Bévenot, Ancient Christian Writers 25 (Westminster, MD: Newman Press, 1957), 48–49.

Cyprian is also important for what he says about the role of laity in decision making in the church.[92] He spoke of the laity's role in the selection of bishops as a practice "based on divine teaching and apostolic observance."[93] He also recognized the laity's role in the appointment of clergy, in conciliar decisions, and in the reconciliation of the lapsed.

Considering Origen and Cyprian as representative figures, one can see the difference between the Greek approach to the church through its reflection on the Song of Songs, linking the church to Christ in the image of bride and groom, and the many practical Latin concerns about the life of the community or, drawing on the pattern of the Roman family, seeing the bishop as the head of the Christian family, guiding it and protecting it.[94]

The Church at Rome

Already at the dawn of the second century, the church at Rome had a distinct spiritual prominence in the wider Christian community. Ignatius's letter to the church at Rome testifies to the esteem with which that church was held. The basis for this respect was the unchallenged tradition that both Peter and Paul died for their faith in the Roman capital. The witness unto death of the "Apostle to the Jews" and the "Apostle to the Gentiles" was thought to have endowed the church at Rome with a distinct spiritual importance: Peter was revered because he had received from Christ the commission to bind and to feed; Paul's authority was rooted in the Gospel he received from God.[95] The community at Rome, for its part, showed a sense of pastoral solicitude for the other churches.

---

[92] Francis A. Sullivan, "St. Cyprian on the Role of the Laity in Decision Making in the Early Church," in *Common Calling: The Laity and Governance of the Catholic Church*, ed. Stephen J. Pope (Washington, DC: Georgetown University Press, 2004), 39–49.

[93] Letter 67, 4.1–5.2, cited in ibid., 40–41.

[94] Vittorino Grossi, "*Episcopus in Ecclesia*: The Importance of an Ecclesiological Principle in Cyprian of Carthage," *The Jurist* 66 (2006): 11.

[95] Eamon Duffy, *Saints and Sinners: A History of the Popes* (New Haven, CT: Yale University Press in association with S4C, 1997), 13.

The Church at Rome seems to have been governed by a group of presbyters well into the second century. Only with Anicetus (ca. 155–ca. 166) do we see a single ruling bishop clearly in place. The author of 1 Clement seems to have been one of a group of presbyters governing the church at Rome, a "first among equals" who, after the mid-second century, came to be called bishop and third successor to Peter. (The title *pope*, "father," was used by many bishops in the early church; only in the sixth century was its Latin use restricted to the bishop of Rome.[96])

The importance of the link between the church of Rome and the two great apostles became heightened as a result of the debates with the Gnostics. In the face of Gnostic claims to special apostolic revelations given only to the elite, pressure built to identify the list of the authentic Scriptures and the pedigree of episcopal leadership. Sees associated with apostolic founders were accorded special importance: Antioch, Thessalonica, Corinth, Philippi, Ephesus, and Rome were all regarded as "apostolic sees." By its association with the two great apostles, Rome had a special place among the apostolic sees, though before the mid-third century its status differed in degree rather than in kind. As it was the only see with such a pedigree in the West, Rome became the apostolic see for all of Italy and for the Latin territories in North Africa and Gaul. That Rome was the capital of the empire added to the prestige of the church in that city, but that was not the principal reason for its ecclesial importance. From the mid-third century, a joint feast of Peter and Paul was celebrated in Rome on June 29.

In the course of the second and third centuries, the standing of the Roman Church among the various churches was also enhanced by its part in several decisions that affected the entire church. One decision regarded the date of the celebration of Easter. Following the Jewish calendar, some churches in Asia Minor and Christians from those churches residing in Rome celebrated Easter, the Christian Passover, on the fourteenth day of Nisan, on whatever day of the week it occurred, hence the term *Quartodeciman*, from the Latin word for "fourteenth." Originally the church in Rome had no separate ob-

---

[96] Ibid., 15.

servance of Easter since it regarded every Sunday as a celebration of the resurrection;[97] in time, it came to celebrate Easter on the Sunday following the Passover in the Jewish calendar. Consulting synods in various Christian centers and seeing that the majority sided with the general Roman practice, Victor I (pope 189–198) sought to make that practice universal and threatened to break communion with congregations who maintained the Quartodeciman tradition. Irenaeus insisted that all churches must agree with the Church of Peter and Paul on doctrinal matters but not on liturgical practice. It appears that Victor withdrew his threat, but the incident shows the emerging belief that the Roman See enjoyed a special authority in the church.

A second debate involving the authority of Rome concerned the recognition of baptism administered in churches in schism. Cyprian, three synods of African bishops, and some bishops in the east refused to recognize baptisms celebrated outside the visible communion of the church. Pope Stephen (254–257) and the church at Rome held that any baptism performed in the name of the Trinity was valid, even if the presiding minister was in schism or heresy. One so baptized could be restored to communion by the penitential laying on of hands. Stephen sought to impose this Roman understanding on the churches of Africa and Asia Minor who thought otherwise and did so under the threat of excommunication, though he died before carrying out his threat. The pope appealed to the text of Matthew 16:18, apparently the first to do so to support the bishop of Rome's authority over other churches. The debate was the first instance in which the bishop of Rome sought to exercise an authority qualitatively different from and superior to the authority of other bishops. Cyprian, in turn, issued a second edition of his *On the Unity of the Catholic Church* in which he excised the passages referring to the primacy given to Peter, though he never denied Rome's position as the symbol of unity of the episcopate. The standoff was resolved when, shortly after Stephen's death, Cyprian was executed in the persecution under the emperor Valerian. The subsequent development of church authority often involved the interplay between claims of the bishops of Rome and

---

[97] Richard P. McBrien, *Lives of the Popes: The Pontiffs from St. Peter to John Paul II* (New York: HarperSanFrancisco, 1997), 40.

the varying reception given them by other bishops.[98] The debate over baptism is also significant for the weight it gave to the view that the efficacy of a sacrament depends on the action of Christ and not on the personal holiness of the minister.

Rome did not alone decide the matters just mentioned, but its part in working toward a solution increased its prominence among the churches. Rome also played a notable part in establishing the canon of the New Testament and in providing an opportunity for penance and forgiveness of even very serious sins. It opposed a rigorist view of church and insisted that the church must be ready to receive sinners and those who are weak.

By the end of the third century, the church saw itself as a communion of churches sharing the same faith in the crucified and risen Christ, sharing a common baptism and Eucharist, and united by a college of bishops in communion with each other. When the number of bishops became too numerous to permit individual contact, major sees would gradually emerge as centers of communication, and so of communion: the bishop of Alexandria, for example, for the bishops of Egypt, and the bishop of Antioch for the bishops of Syria. Provinces coinciding with the administrative provinces of the empire formed around these and other major sees. Provincial synods enabled the bishops of a given region to ensure their fidelity to the apostolic tradition and resolve common pastoral questions. In the third century, the three most important sees were the churches of Rome, Alexandria, and Antioch. The Roman Church's prominence and its special responsibility among the churches always presupposed solidarity with the entire church. In the course of the century, the church at Rome grew as a Christian community and its influence as an apostolic see extended to Spain as well as to North Africa and Gaul.

At the end of the third and the beginning of the fourth centuries, the church experienced a watershed moment to which we turn in the next chapter.

---

[98] Sullivan, *From Apostles to Bishops*, 216.

CHAPTER SIX

Christian Antiquity—Part 2: Constantine to Gregory I and John Damascene

This second chapter on the patristic period, from the early fourth century to the period's end, will be organized broadly around two basic considerations: first, the impact of the church's becoming the official religion of the empire and, second, the various reflections on the theology of the church during the period. Some overlap is inevitable in the two considerations.

The fourth century opened with major events that would have a profound impact on the church's self-understanding. In 286, Emperor Diocletian reorganized the vast Roman Empire into a Greek-speaking East and a Latin-speaking West, each with its own imperial leadership. Constantine became emperor of the West after the defeat of his Western rival in 312.[1] Attributing his victory to the power of Christ and adopting in some way the faith of his Christian mother, Constantine and the Eastern emperor in 313 declared freedom of worship and a restoration of Christian properties confiscated during Diocletian's "Great Persecution" in 303.[2] While religious toleration (the so-called Edict of Milan) extended to all, Constantine clearly favored Christianity and granted it special privileges. "Few events," writes Jesuit historian John O'Malley, "more radically changed the Christian church than Constantine's recognition of it and his granting it a privileged status

---

[1] Henry Chadwick, *The Church in Ancient Society: From Galilee to Gregory the Great* (Oxford: Oxford University Press, 2001), chap. 27.
[2] An edict of toleration concerning Christians had been issued in 311 by the dying emperor Galerius, Diocletian's successor in the East, though persecutions still continued on a smaller scale after his death.

in his empire."³ Constantine became sole emperor in 324 and held that position until his death in 337. In 380 Emperor Theodosius declared Christianity the official and only lawful religion of the empire.

The Church in the Empire

An immediate sign of Christianity's new prominence in the empire was the construction with imperial funds of basilicas for Christian worship.⁴ The basilica ("hall of the king," from Greek *basileus*, "king") was a rectangular structure, sometimes flanked by columns, often with a rounded apse at one or both ends. Romans used the basilica structure for audience halls, business offices, and other civic purposes. Christians built simple basilicas before the fourth century, but with Constantine's accession to power, magnificent basilica structures were erected, powerful and lasting symbols of the new alliance between church and empire.⁵ Replacing the emperor's throne, the bishop's throne was often placed in the center of the apse with benches on either side for the college of presbyters. A freestanding altar around which the faithful could gather was placed in front of the apse. Often decorated with mosaics or frescoes, the apse frequently portrayed an image of the glorious Christ, seated on a throne, surrounded by the apostles, saints, and angels of the heavenly court. The scene provided a visual ecclesiology and supported the idea, popular in the West but especially so in the East, that through the Eucharist the assembly entered into the heavenly sanctuary and participated in its liturgy.

The structure of the basilica lent itself to a more imperial style of worship. Signs and gestures used to show respect to the emperor were incorporated into the liturgical rites: the use of incense; proces-

---

³ John W. O'Malley, "'The Hermeneutic of Reform': A Historical Analysis," *Theological Studies* 73 (2012): 517.

⁴ Allan Doig, *Liturgy and Architecture: From the Early Church to the Middle Ages* (Hampshire, England: Ashgate, 2008), chap. 2; and Edward Foley, *From Age to Age: How Christians Have Celebrated the Eucharist*, rev. ed. (Collegeville, MN: Liturgical Press, 2008), 79–93.

⁵ Peter Brown, *The Rise of Western Christendom: Triumph and Diversity, A.D. 200–1000*, 2nd ed. (Malden, MA: Blackwell Publishing, 2003), 77.

sions; choirs used, in part, to add solemnity to the processions; the introduction of luxurious vestments. As liturgical rites became more solemn and less personal and familial and the ranks of the clergy more institutionalized, references to "holy mother church" contributed to a process of personifying the church so that it would come to be seen as "an entity apart from and beyond the people who make it up," which would in turn lead to identifying the church with its clerical ministers.[6]

In addition to the basilica, baptisteries and buildings called *martyria*, over the tombs of the martyrs, were also built. These buildings often took the form of round structures modeled after the burial mausoleums in the pagan tradition. Christian belief in baptism as a participation in the death of Christ served to link the architectural similarity between baptisteries and the *martyria*. Christians in the East came to favor these central-plan domed church buildings. Under Constantine's direction, churches of this second type were built in Byzantium, the new capital of the empire rebuilt and inaugurated as Constantinople in 330, and in Jerusalem. The style was most developed during the sixth-century reign of the emperor Justinian and became the pattern for churches in the Eastern Empire.

Other developments also influenced the church's self-understanding. The marked increase in Christian numbers that came with religious toleration led to many more local congregations of various types, many of them called parishes. Used as early as the second century, the Greek term *paroikia* (Latin *paroecia*) was used of local congregations of believers. The term meant "those living near" or "beside" or "in the same neighborhood," though its secondary meaning, "resident aliens, foreigners, nonnative sojourners," was also operative when the term was first put to Christian use.[7] Assigned by the bishop, presbyters who ministered in local congregations in villages and market towns along the trade routes or in rural areas began to

---

[6] David Bohr, *The Diocesan Priest: Consecrated and Sent* (Collegeville, MN: Liturgical Press, 2009), 39; and Bernard Cooke, *Ministry to Word and Sacraments: History and Theology* (Philadelphia: Fortress Press, 1976), 66–67.

[7] James A. Coriden, *The Parish in Catholic Tradition: History, Theology, and Canon Law* (New York: Paulist Press 1997), 19.

be called priests (*hiereus* or *sacerdos*). In this development, the sense of a corporate presbyterate with collegial responsibility with the bishop gradually diminished. Mindful of the lack of clear distinction between *episkopos* and presbyter in the New Testament, the biblical scholar Jerome (d. 420) held that priest and bishop were equal in their power to consecrate the Body and Blood of Christ; differences centered on the bishops being seen as successors of the apostles, their power to ordain, and in the authority that came to them through church custom.[8] Again the apostolic and christological imagery diverged (recall Ignatius of Antioch): the bishop was regarded as apostolic in his authority; the presbyters, christological in their priesthood. In later centuries, the bishop came to be seen less as eucharistic presider and, in fact, more a manager of eucharistic communities. Orthodox theologian Alexander Schmemann wrote that this change "represents one of the most radical changes that ever took place in the Church."[9]

In the early centuries, the church used the term *ordo* (order) in the general sense in which it was used in Roman society, to designate specific groups within a larger society. Christians belonged to different orders in the church: porters charged with maintenance and security; lectors who read at worship; exorcists who assisted at rites of initiation and repentance; acolytes who initially were secretaries and messengers for the bishop. There were orders of catechumens, of teachers, of widows or virgins, as well as the orders of deacons, presbyters, and bishops. In the fourth century that began to change. As Constantine and his successors granted special privileges to the bishops and as they were expected to take on the responsibilities of governors, judges, and servants of the state, the notion of *ordo* in a more restricted sense began to be used either of the entire body of the clergy or of particular grades within the clergy, with heightened emphasis

---

[8] Cooke, *Ministry*, 80, and Bohr, *Diocesan Priest*, 45.

[9] Alexander Schmemann, "Towards a Theology of Councils," *St. Vladimir's Quarterly* 6 (1962): 177, cited in Paul G. McPartlan, "Priesthood, Priestliness, and Priests," in Ronald D. Witherup and others, *Ministerial Priesthood in the Third Millennium: Faithfulness of Christ, Faithfulness of Priests* (Collegeville, MN: Liturgical Press, 2009), 74–75, at 74.

given to rank or dignity. This contributed to an increasingly pronounced distinction within the church between those in ecclesiastical orders and those who lacked them, roughly parallel to the more restricted use of *ordo* for Roman senators, distinguishing them from the mass of the people (*plebs*). Even as the fourth century began, some bishops were already adopting a manner of exercising authority that resembled that of Roman governors.

The church's changed status also affected its relations with Judaism. As the church gained public support and then official status in the empire, Jewish critiques of Christianity ceased, although during the short reign of the emperor Julian (361–63) there were sharp tensions between church and synagogue. Julian's efforts to rebuild the temple in Jerusalem and the discovery that many Christians in Antioch were attending Jewish Sabbath services and observing Jewish festivals led John Chrysostom (d. 407) to deliver a series of anti-Judaic homilies—a lamentable element of his otherwise notable legacy. Yet both he and Bishop Ambrose of Milan encouraged their congregations to emulate Jews in their prayer and their study of the Scriptures.[10] Gradually Roman laws from earlier periods protecting Jews were undermined, and political authority tolerated sporadic Christian persecution of the Jews. The goal of church and civil legislation seems to have been directed at isolating Jews and preventing their influence over Christians. Prior to the seventh century, the concept of a "Jewish witness" first proposed by Augustine (d. 430) seems to have generally guided policy toward the Jews: with restrictions, Jews were to be tolerated and not harmed, witnesses, it was thought, to their own wickedness and to the Christian truth, until they came to accept Christ at his second coming.[11]

The Church of the Empire

Constantine decided to make Byzantium, now Constantinople, both the Eastern imperial capital and a "new Rome," a Christian city unlike old Rome with its pagan monuments and culture. Even so, he

---

[10] Chadwick, *Church in Ancient Society*, 362 and 480.
[11] Kevin Madigan, *Medieval Christianity: A New History* (New Haven, CT: Yale University Press, 2015), 27–28.

accepted many elements of the pagan system, giving him a sovereign position in both religious and civil affairs. In effect, he nurtured, especially in the East, "a concept of a Church within the framework of the Empire,"[12] relating the whole life of the church to him and to his authority.

Constantine regarded church unity as a valuable means of maintaining political unity in the empire. Almost immediately at the outset of his rule as emperor of the West, church unity was fractured by schism in Roman North Africa, a result of continuing disagreement concerning the return of those who capitulated during the Diocletian persecution. Efforts to resolve the schism through countils of bishops were unsuccessful. Some years later, in the very year Constantine became sole emperor and was about to move the imperial capital to Byzantium, a major theological dispute erupted concerning the status of the *Logos*, the Word of God incarnate in Jesus. A priest and popular preacher in the city of Alexandria, Arius (ca. 250–ca. 336), attracted a large following by preaching that the *Logos* was a divine intermediary created by the Father and subordinate to him, but not fully divine. His bishop, along with others, argued that Arius's teaching was not faithful to the Scriptures: only if the Word were divine could humankind be saved. Eager to see the debate brought to an end lest it endanger civic unity so close to the capital city, Constantine summoned the bishops to Nicaea (modern Iznik, across the Bosporus, in the Asian part of Turkey). The gathering at Nicaea brought together an estimated 250 to 300 bishops, mostly from the Greek-speaking Eastern Church, but some from both Greek and Latin North Africa, a few bishops from the West, and two priest delegates representing the bishop of Rome. The council produced a creedal statement and a rejection of any who held the Arian teaching. It also promulgated twenty canons, short prescriptive ordinances, sometimes including punishment for failure to comply. The use of this genre, at Nicaea and in many subsequent councils, as in regional councils before it, reflects the communicating style of the Roman

---

[12] Yves Congar, *After Nine Hundred Years: The Background of the Schism between the Eastern and Western Churches* (New York: Fordham University Press, 1959), 7–8, at 7.

Senate, a legislative-judicial body.[13] While the decisions of the council were made by the bishops, Constantine, not yet baptized, involved himself in the working of the council. (He insisted, for example, that the compromise term *homoousios*, "of the same substance" or "consubstantial," be included in the creed.) He confirmed the council's work and sought to enforce it, in part by banishing bishops refusing to accept its decrees. In this the emperor set a precedent for civil intervention even in matters of church teaching.

Though local councils continued to be held, some convoked by imperial order, the gathering at Nicaea introduced a new structure, a universal council, representing the church in its entirety. The Council at Chalcedon (also on the Asian side of the Bosporus, presently a district of Istanbul), again convoked by the emperor, established a list of what came to be regarded as the first four general councils: that at Nicaea in 325; a local council of Constantinople in 381, given status as a general council because of its creed; a council in Ephesus in 431; and the Council at Chalcedon in 451. The teachings of these councils came to be accepted as having binding authority in matters of faith. The four councils were designated ecumenical councils, distinguishing them from local councils of lesser authority. The word "ecumenical" ("inhabited world" from *oikein*, "to inhabit," and *oikos*, "house") refers to the whole "inhabited" Christian world. In these councils, and in the three that followed, imperial authority had an important role, both in their convocation and in the promulgation of their decrees. The councils were largely composed of bishops, though some who were not ordained also participated. A belief that the Spirit was guiding them and the desire for unanimity, or quasi-unanimity, were important features of the conciliar decision-making process, principles held to the present day.

These major councils raised a crucial question: Who holds ultimate decision-making authority in the church?[14] Pope Leo I (440–461) held

---

[13] John W. O'Malley, *What Happened at Vatican II* (Cambridge, MA: Belknap Press of Harvard University Press, 2008), 44–45.

[14] Robert B. Eno, *The Rise of the Papacy*, Theology and Life Series, vol. 32 (Wilmington, DE: Michael Glazer, 1990), 115–17.

that the decision of the bishop of Rome was definitive at the Council at Chalcedon: the council was not to debate his decision but to ratify it. In the Eastern view, a general council should take such a decision into account but come to a judgment after its own deliberations. Gradually, the East came to accept that Rome's approval of a council was necessary, but only in the context of unanimity with the other major sees. The bishop of Rome and the more collegial-minded bishops of the East participated in subsequent councils, each with quite different views on this matter.

The many benefits that Constantine brought to the church led many to speak of him in almost biblical terms. In the popular mind, many thought the messianic age foretold by the prophets appeared on the verge of being fulfilled. Constantine was regarded as God's anointed, the new head of the Christian people. The most prominent, if uncritical, appreciation of the emperor came from his friend and biographer, the learned historian Eusebius, bishop of Caesarea in Palestine (ca. 260–ca. 340).[15] Though initially sharing in this assessment, Augustine's enthusiasm cooled over time and he ultimately reversed himself on this question.[16]

The Church in the East and in the West

Growth of the church led to greater sophistication in its structural organization, often adapted to the jurisdictional divisions of the empire: in the West, divisions were according to *diocese* (from the Greek for "administrative division"); in the East, *eparchy* (from the Greek for "province"). Metropolitan sees (Greek *meter*, "mother," and *polis*, "city") exercised certain provincial responsibilities. Already in the third century the sees of Rome, Alexandria, and Antioch had acquired major prominence and were recognized as such at the Council of Nicaea. The Council of Constantinople in 381 placed the see of

---

[15] Diarmaid MacCulloch, *Christianity: The First Three Thousand Years* (New York: Viking, 2009), 196.

[16] Robert Markus, *Christianity and the Secular*, Blessed Pope John XXIII Lecture Series in Theology and Culture (Notre Dame, IN: University of Notre Dame Press, 2006), 34–38.

Constantinople as second after Rome. Jerusalem, for historical importance, was added to the others. In the fifth century, the terms "patriarchate" and "patriarch" (from Greek for "father" and "ruler") began to be used with reference to these five sees. While Rome never accepted all of Constantinople's prerogatives affirmed at Chalcedon, an idealized view of a single and undivided church governed by the five patriarchates, the Pentarchy, persisted through much of the first millennium, especially in the East. Besides exercising a supervisory function over the dioceses or eparchies of the region, these sees became centers of development in liturgy, theology, and church discipline, contributing to the rich diversity characteristic of the church during these early centuries. Regional diversity, at times, led to tensions, especially between Rome and Constantinople.

The bishops at Constantinople decreed that the See of Constantinople was to have preeminence in honor after the Church of Rome since Constantinople was the "new Rome." Pope Damasus (366–84) and his successors resisted the implication that Rome's importance came from its being the former capital of the empire rather than from its association with the apostles Peter and Paul. They insisted that Rome had a primacy over all the churches because of Christ's promise to Peter (Matt 16). As Constantinople became a major Christian center, it also became a political and an ecclesiastical rival to Rome, seriously curtailing Rome's influence on the church of the East but leaving the bishop of Rome to increase his authority not only in Italy but in the entire church of the West. These developments contributed to significant differences in ecclesial understanding.[17] The basic convictions about the church—the basic role of faith, baptism, Eucharist, the sacramental and hierarchical structure—were fundamentally the same throughout. But the Latin West saw the church as a whole with Rome as its center; the Greek East understood the church of the empire as an ellipse with two foci, Rome and Constantinople, virtually equal in jurisdictional authority in their respective domains but with a primacy of honor to be granted to the bishop of Old Rome as

---

[17] Congar, *After Nine Hundred Years*, 57–73.

representative of the Latin West.[18] Further, Rome based its conception of church on apostolic principle, while the ecclesiastical domain of the church at Constantinople coincided with the political and cultural domain of the empire.[19]

After Constantine's death, the bishops of Rome sought to recast the former imperial capital, still the center of the Mediterranean world, in a Christian light and to further the integration of Christianity with the empire and its culture. Since the late third century Latin had replaced Greek as the language of the Western Church. New Christian churches, observance of Sunday as a public holiday, and Christian festivals gave the city a more distinctively Christian character and led the Christian populace to see themselves as Roman.[20] With what were probably mixed motives—an element of worldliness along with genuine Christian convictions—Pope Damasus was particularly forceful in trying to "Latinise the church, and Christianise Latin."[21] Under his direction, the learned biblical scholar Jerome made a new Latin translation of most of the Bible. The translation, known as the *Vulgate* (Latin *vulgata editio*, "popular edition"), used the language of Roman law courts to translate the covenant legislation of the Old Testament. Roman legal terms "binding" and "loosing" were used in translating Jesus' promise to Peter in Matthew 16:19.[22]

At times, bishops of Rome consciously adopted the style and procedures of the Roman state, most significantly in their manner of

---

[18] Chadwick, *Church in Ancient Society*, 189. See Brian E. Daley, "Position and Patronage in the Early Church: The Original Meaning of 'Primacy of Honour,'" *The Journal of Theological Studies*, new series, 44 (1993): 529–53.

[19] Congar, *After Nine Hundred Years*, 57.

[20] Basil Studer, "The Situation of the Church," in *The Patristic Period*, ed. Angelo de Berardino and Basil Studer (Collegeville, MN: Liturgical Press, 1996), 255.

[21] Eamon Duffy, *Saints and Sinners: A History of the Papacy* (New Haven, CT: Yale University Press in association with S4C, 1997), 29.

[22] Ibid., 30. See also Jaroslav Pelikan, *Whose Bible Is It? A History of the Scriptures Through the Ages* (New York: Viking, 2005), 124–25, and MacCulloch, *Christianity*, 294–96.

Christian Antiquity—Part 2: Constantine to Gregory I and John Damascene 157

responding to queries sent to them from other churches.[23] The form was that of a decretal, modeled on imperial rescripts and providing authoritative rulings that were meant to establish legal precedents. This specific form of reply encouraged a legal mind-set that would strongly influence segments of Western thought about the church. Assuming a role as the church's supreme lawgiver, rescripts of Rome's bishops were placed on the same level as synodal decrees that until this time were the chief means of creating church law. These rescripts from Rome, especially to other churches in the West, would become the substance of papal canon law. Though originally claiming preeminence from its bonds with both Peter and Paul, fourth-century Roman bishops increasingly emphasized the Petrine foundation of the Roman See, insisting on Rome's headship over other churches and its primacy among the bishops. Damasus customarily referred to Rome as the "apostolic see"; Pope Siricius (384–399) claimed that in official statements Peter was speaking through him.[24] As emperors in Constantinople gave more of their attention to the Eastern part of the empire, bishops of Rome often filled the power vacuum created by their neglect or by weak Western emperors. Later papal claims to civil authority invoked the exercise of such authority during this period as a basis for those claims.

The Church and the Bishop of Rome

A focus on the church of Rome and its bishop and their place in the universal church was much the concern of three Roman bishops in the latter part of the patristic period. The first of these, the very gifted Leo I, provided the formula of faith adopted at the Council of Chalcedon. He also continued the process begun by Popes Damasus and Siricius in the latter half of the fourth century in developing the doctrine of Roman primacy.[25] Leo drew on both the three classic

---

[23] Duffy, *Saints and Sinners*, 31.
[24] Richard P. McBrien, *Lives of the Popes: The Pontiffs from St. Peter to John Paul II* (New York: HarperSanFrancisco, 1997), 62–68.
[25] Klaus Schatz, *Papal Primacy: From Its Origins to the Present*, trans. John A. Otto and Linda M. Maloney (Collegeville, MN: Liturgical Press, 1996), 28–38. See also John Meyendorff, *Imperial Unity and Christian Divisions: The Church 450–680*

Petrine texts in the New Testament mentioned earlier (Matt 16:18-19; Luke 22:32; John 21:15-17) and Roman law to make his case for the bishop of Rome's authoritative role. From Roman law he invoked the provision concerning legal inheritance: the rights and duties of the deceased passed undiminished to the heir. Leo did not claim to be an equal of Peter and spoke of himself as his "unworthy heir" or Peter's "vicar" or "representative," as Peter was the vicar of Christ. He is seen to mark the final stage of "the translation in *juridical terms* of the apostolic *parádosis* ['tradition'] as ultimate reference for the *communio* of the Church."[26] On the fifth anniversary of his ordination, Leo spoke of his sharing with his brother bishops a care "for all the churches" (2 Cor 11:28). At other times, he spoke of his having the "fullness of power" and responsibility in the church, though he only intervened to safeguard the truth or to uphold respect for local church law. He also affirmed a Petrine "succession" in the episcopate in each province of the church and by the faithful of the entire church.[27] Leo varied the exercise of his primacy in different regions of the West; his claims regarding primacy were only partially accepted in the East.

Later in the century, Pope Gelasius (492–496) sought to distinguish ecclesial authority from imperial authority, especially in the areas of dogma but also in the areas of church law and discipline. In his famous letter to Emperor Anastasios in 494, the pope spoke of "two powers," both divinely established: the sacred authority of the bishops and the royal power of temporal affairs, the former being pre-eminent. Gelasius saw a hint of these two powers in Luke 22:38, the passage about the two swords in Jesus' instruction before his arrest. In theory, the two powers were to cooperate for the welfare of all; in practice that was often not the case.

A.D. (Crestwood, NY: St Vladimir's Seminary Press, 1989), 148–58, and John Jay Hughes, *Pontiffs: Popes Who Shaped History* (Huntington, IN: Our Sunday Visitor, 1994), chap. 2.

[26] Klaus Schatz, "Historical Considerations Concerning the Problem of the Primacy," in *Petrine Ministry and the Unity of the Church: "Toward a Patient and Fraternal Dialogue,"* ed. James F. Puglisi (Collegeville, MN: Liturgical Press, 1999), 5 (italics in original).

[27] Olivier Clément, *You Are Peter: An Orthodox Theologian's Reflection on the Exercise of Papal Primacy*, trans. M. S. Laird (New York: New City Press, 2003), 30.

Pope Leo's theory about the primacy was implemented practically during the pontificate of Pope Gregory I (590–604).[28] He also sought, by the exercise of his administrative decisions, to give a greater theological grounding to the Petrine primacy. Gregory was given the epithet "the Great" because of his noble character, his selfless ministry, and the impact of his writings. He fully accepted the notion that the bishop of Rome's primacy over the universal church was inherited from the apostle Peter and saw that primacy as one of solicitude and responsibility. He saw a clear difference between his authority regarding the bishops of his province and his authority regarding the church at large.[29] To the patriarch of Alexandria who, in the exaggerated Eastern use of titles, addressed him as "universal pope," he wrote, reprovingly: "My honour is the honour of the universal Church. My honour is the solid strength of my brothers. Then I am truly honoured, when honour is not denied to each one [of the bishops] to whom it is due."[30] In a title taken from Augustine, he referred to himself as the *servus servorum Dei*, "servant of the servants of God." A monk himself before being called to official service in the church, Gregory saw in the monastic life the embodiment of the gospel ideal of discipleship and the paradigm of the Christian life. He spoke of a tripartite ordering within the church: the ordained cleric, the monk, and the layperson. His best-known work, *Regula pastoralis* (*Pastoral Rule*), emphasized the role of preaching and sought to give priests and bishops a counterpart to the monastic Rule of St. Benedict, encouraging thereby a separation of the clergy from the laity. In giving advice to questions from mission areas, Gregory urged flexibility, the Christianization of pagan shrines, not their destruction. The pope's many efforts to serve the people of Rome and Italy led to his de facto temporal authority, so

---

[28] Jaroslav Pelikan, *The Emergence of the Catholic Tradition (100–600)*, vol. 1 of *The Christian Tradition: A History of the Development of Doctrine* (Chicago: University of Chicago Press, 1971), 352–55; Chadwick, *Church in Ancient Society*, 658–74.

[29] Clément, *You Are Peter*, 30–31.

[30] J. M. R. Tillard, *The Bishop of Rome*, trans. John de Satgé (Wilmington, DE: Michael Glazier, 1983), 52–53, at 53. See the discussion in Meyendorff, *Imperial Unity*, 304–7.

contributing to the foundation of what would become the temporal power of the papacy.

The Monastic Vision of Church

Mention of Gregory I's upholding the ideal of monastic life as a paradigm for the church may introduce the second principal consideration of this chapter, the varied theological understandings of church in the patristic period under discussion. Monasticism (from Greek *monachos*, "solitary") antedates Gregory by some centuries: it had its origins in the second-century ascetics, living in the towns and villages of Egypt.[31] The appeal of some type of monastic life greatly increased in the fourth century, influenced by the renown of the hermit Antony of Egypt (d. 356) and the widely read *Life of Antony* of Bishop Athanasius of Alexandria (d. 373). While many monks withdrew from society, others combined ascetical renunciation and contemplative prayer with active ministry to the urban poor and sick. (Along the Nile the desert may be only a few hundred feet away from villages alongside the river.) The *Life of Antony* sought to promote integration between the urban churches and those practicing the ascetic life. In the face of a rapidly growing church with a lessened observance of earlier ideals, monastics sought a distinctive life, meant to imitate the spirit of the primitive church in the early chapters of Acts. Basically a lay movement, early monasticism in the fourth, fifth, and sixth centuries "must be reckoned as a distinctive mark of classical Christianity along with the Eucharist and baptism, bishops, creeds, and the canon of Scripture."[32] The movement influenced the church's self-understanding by upholding gospel ideals and at times promoting reform.

The desire to return to a simpler life and more familial relationships, lost in the shift from house churches to the great basilicas, influenced the growth of monasticism in the West as well. Monasticism

---

[31] Robert Louis Wilken, *The First Thousand Years: A Global History of Christianity* (New Haven, CT: Yale University Press, 2012), 260–63 and chap. 10, and Chadwick, *The Church in Ancient Society*, chap. 42.

[32] Wilken, *The First Thousand Years*, 108.

was well established before Benedict (ca. 480–ca. 550), but in time the extraordinary influence of Benedictine monasticism is attributable to the moderation of Benedict's Rule (ca. 540), especially in the eighth and ninth centuries when it received royal support. Drawn from earlier rules and written in vernacular Latin, the Rule sought to guide the life of the community in a way of life more closely resembling the gospels. Another, less positive, influence came when clerics and monks, both men and women, came to be seen as the more committed members of the Christian community. In addition, besides the restricted use of "brother" to clerical groups, mentioned above, only in the monastic communities did the terms "brother" and "sister" live on. The familial terms lost meaning as the church became swollen with great new numbers, introducing, so Joseph Ratzinger noted on the eve of the Second Vatican Council, a state of affairs lasting for centuries "with all its inevitably damaging effects."[33] This, of course, does not take away from the contribution of monasticism over the centuries to the church of which it is so integrally a part, both in the East and in the West.

Theological Reflection on the Church

Increased numbers joining the church in the fourth and fifth centuries also led to the golden age of the catechumenate in which the entire community assumed responsibility for those preparing for their full incorporation into the body of Christ. The homilies of the great bishop-preachers given during the period of initiation before and after baptism at the Easter Vigil are among the most important expressions of the theology of the church during this period. Theirs was a theology of the church understood very much in terms of the sacraments of baptism and Eucharist and the new community life in Christ. (Only in the West about this same time did the chrismation associated with baptism become a separate sacrament of confirmation reserved to the bishop.) Insights into a theological understanding of church are also present in the homilies and commentaries on the

---

[33] Joseph Cardinal Ratzinger, *The Meaning of Christian Brotherhood* (San Francisco: Ignatius Press, 1993), 39–40. Original German edition published in 1960.

Scriptures given by the great bishop-theologians and exegetes of the time. If the canons of the councils and rescripts from the bishops of Rome reflected the Roman juridical tradition, the rhetoric of the fathers was cast in the classical rhetorical genre of panegyric, "the painting of an idealized portrait in order to excite admiration and appropriation."[34] That genre must be kept in mind in reading their texts. Examples of such reflections appear in the twenty-four catechetical lectures, considered "one of the most precious treasures of Christian antiquity,"[35] of Cyril of Jerusalem (d. 386); the fifteen homilies on the Song of Songs of Gregory of Nyssa (ca. 330–ca. 395); the homilies on the Letters of Paul and the Gospels according to Matthew and John by the brilliant orator and bishop of Constantinople, John Chrysostom (Greek for "golden-mouthed"); the *Commentary on St. John's Gospel* by Cyril, the patriarch of Alexandria (ca. 375–444). To these must be added the many sermons and treatises of Augustine of Hippo, the letters and sermons of Pope Leo I, and the poems on Israel the betrothed and the church as bride, expressed in paradox and symbolism, of Ephrem the Syrian (d. 373).[36]

Several themes emerge in these writings. A major theme in both Eastern and Western reflection was the church as the body of Christ, a conscious development of the Pauline teaching on baptism and the church as body. This theme appeared in earlier patristic writings but came to full flower in the fourth and fifth centuries. Development of the theme took place in a threefold direction.[37] First, using the Pauline theme of Christ as the Second Adam, the fathers saw in the incarna-

---

[34] John W. O'Malley, "Vatican II: Did Anything Happen?," in *Vatican II: Did Anything Happen?*, ed. David G. Schultenover (New York: Continuum, 2007), 74. See also John W. O'Malley, *Four Cultures of the West* (Cambridge, MA: Belknap Press of Harvard University Press, 2004), chap. 3.

[35] Johannes Quasten, *Patrology*, vol. 3: *The Golden Age of Greek Patristic Literature, from the Council of Nicaea to the Council of Chalcedon* (Westminster, MD: Newman Press, 1960), 363.

[36] Sebastian Brock, *The Luminous Eye: The Spiritual World Vision of Saint Ephrem*, Cistercian Studies 124 (Kalamazoo, MI: Cistercian Publications, 1992), chap. 7.

[37] The next few paragraphs draw on the essay of Walter Burghardt, "The Body of Christ: Patristic Insights," in K. E. Skydsgaard and others, *The Church as the Body of Christ* (Notre Dame, IN: University of Notre Dame Press, 1964), 69–101.

tion Christ's becoming one with all of humanity. That initial oneness was completed on the cross, when the church, a new Eve, was born from Christ's pierced side; as Eve was taken from the side of Adam to become his wife, two in one flesh, so on the cross, Augustine says, the church was wed to Christ and the two became one, receiving life by the gift of the Spirit. From a sermon of Augustine: "What the soul is to the body of a man, this the Holy Spirit is to the Body of Christ, which is the Church: what the soul does in all the members of one body, this the Holy Spirit does in the whole Church."[38] The church's identity in Christ reaches its final stage in the resurrection and ascension: in Christ, the church is raised to the Father so that "we too might be called sons through Him and children of God."[39] Second, the church lives the life of the body through baptism and the Eucharist: by baptism the Spirit incorporates us into Christ; through the Eucharist the church lives as the body of Christ. Third, the fathers see the body of Christ expressed in a life lived in love of others.

A commentary on the Gospel of John by Cyril of Alexandria illustrates patristic thought on the church as the body of Christ:

> The Only-begotten, through the wisdom which is his and through the counsel of the Father, found and wrought a means by which we might come into unity with God and with one another. . . . For by one body, and that his own he blesses those who believe in him by a mystical communion and makes them of one body with himself and one another. . . . For if we all partake of the one loaf, we are all made one body; for it is not possible that Christ be divided. Therefore the Church is called "Body of Christ" of which we are individually members, according to Paul's understanding. For we are all united to the one Christ through his holy body, inasmuch as we receive him who is one and undivided in our own bodies.[40]

---

[38] Augustine, *Sermon* 267, 4. Trans. in Burghardt, "Body of Christ," 78.

[39] Cyril of Alexandria (d. 444), *Commentary on John*, cited in Burghardt, "Body of Christ," 81.

[40] Cyril of Alexandria, *Commentary on the Gospel of John* 11:10, in Eric G. Jay, *The Church: Its Changing Image Through Twenty Centuries*, vol. 1: *The First Seventeen Centuries* (London: SPCK, 1977), 79.

From the same commentary, Cyril speaks about our unity in the Spirit:

> With regard to our unity in the Spirit, we may say . . . that all of us who have received one and same Spirit, the Holy Spirit, are united intimately, both with one another and with God. Taken separately, we are many, and Christ sends the Spirit, who is both the Father's Spirit and his own, to dwell in each of us. Yet that Spirit, being one and indivisible, gathers together those who are distinct from each other as individuals, and causes them all to be seen as a unity in himself. Just as Christ's sacred flesh has power to make those in whom it is present into one body, so the one, indivisible Spirit of God, dwelling in all, causes all to become one in spirit.[41]

The understanding of church was closely related to the concern for holiness and, especially in the East, to the notion of "deification" that comes through participation in Christ through the liturgy and ministry of the church. Much was made of the text in 2 Peter 1:4, which speaks of our becoming "participants of the divine nature." Gregory of Nyssa, for example, speaks of our human nature becoming divine by the "conjoining" of the divine and human in Christ. In a short exposition on 1 Corinthians 15:28, he extends that to the church: by "being conjoined to the one body of Christ by participation, we become his one body." At the consummation (1 Cor 15:28), Christ will be subjected to the Father "mingled with his own body which is the Church."[42]

Added to the ideas about the holiness of the church and its unity and apostolicity was an affirmation of its catholicity. The four terms, later known as the notes of the church, were specifically mentioned in the addition to the creed at the Council of Constantinople in 381. An example of the breadth of the church's catholicity is seen in one of the twenty-three *Catechetical Lectures* of Cyril, bishop of Jerusalem.

---

[41] Cyril of Alexandria, *Commentary on the Gospel of John* 11:11, in *The Liturgy of the Hours According to the Roman Rite*, 4 vols. (New York: Catholic Book Publishing Co., 1975–1976), 2:890.

[42] Jay, *The Church: Its Changing Image*, 1:78.

> The Church is called Catholic or universal because it has spread throughout the entire world, from one end of the earth to the other. Again, it is called Catholic because it teaches fully and unfailingly all the doctrines which ought to be brought to men's [sic] knowledge, whether concerned with visible or invisible things, with the realities of heaven or the things of earth. Another reason for the name Catholic is that the Church brings under religious obedience all classes of men, rulers and subjects, learned and unlettered. Finally, it deserves the title Catholic because it heals and cures unrestrictedly every type of sin that can be committed in soul or in body, and because it possesses within itself every kind of virtue that can be named, whether exercised in actions or in words or in some kind of spiritual charism.[43]

Patristic writings about the church included very practical demands regarding the love of others, very especially in the many sermons on the topics of poverty and wealth, quite probably the most pressing social issue facing the church.[44] These were addressed, in part, to wealthy Christians aware of New Testament sayings about wealth as a potential impediment to salvation or to those who thought wealth was in itself evil, as well as to the wealthy who did not share with the poor or were blind to the temptation of avarice. In a powerful passage from a homily on Matthew's gospel, John Chrysostom challenges the congregation to see the uselessness of weighing down Christ's table in church with golden cups when neglecting Christ in the poor who were dying outside. The altar table may be adorned with cloths woven of gold thread, yes, but only after one has provided Christ in the poor with the clothing he needs.[45] Chrysostom's argument for almsgiving is based on his conviction of "the mystical identity of the poor with Jesus."[46]

---

[43] Trans. in *Liturgy of the Hours*, 3:555–56.
[44] See Boniface Ramsey, *Beginning to Read the Fathers*, rev. ed. (New York: Paulist Press, 2012), chap. 10.
[45] John Chrysostom, Homily on Matthew 50.3-4 in *Liturgy of the Hours*, 4:182–83, and *A Select Library of Nicene and Post-Nicene Fathers of the Christian Church*, vol. 10 (Grand Rapids, MI: Eerdmans, 1978), 313.
[46] Burghardt, "Body of Christ," 96.

The Eastern understanding of church had other elements. While mindful of the universal church, a strongly eucharistic ecclesiology emphasized the local church, though sometimes this led to bitter rivalry between local churches or, in later centuries, to an unhealthy nationalism. A strong synodal tradition—a canon of Nicaea called for twice-yearly synods in each province—helps explain Eastern resistance to placing decrees of the bishop of Rome on a par with decrees of local synods. Both the Eastern emperor and the Christian populace generally accepted the Roman tradition of the emperor's responsibility for both temporal and spiritual welfare. In the East, this continued in one way or another for a thousand years, until the fall of Constantinople to the Turks in 1453.

Western Approaches to the Church

As in the East, perhaps even more so in the West, the church as the body of Christ—manifested, sustained, and made more itself by the Eucharist—was basic to patristic preaching and teaching. There were other insights as well. We see some of these in Ambrose of Milan (ca. 339–397), bishop of the administrative capital of the Western empire for twenty-four years and the most important figure in the church in the West in the final quarter of the fourth century.[47] Ambrose placed a fundamental importance on the study of the Scriptures and was instrumental in introducing the allegorical method of interpretation to the West. As a means of addressing the laxity of some of the lay faithful, he emphasized the entire body of believers as a priestly people. To promote the unity of the congregation, he composed Latin hymns meant to be sung by all, women and men, ordinary folk and the rich and powerful. Ambrose promoted the authority of the church in Milan, but he insisted that he was acting on behalf of the Church of Rome and promoted the cult of Peter and Paul as a way of emphasizing the place of the Diocese of Rome. "The primacy," he said, "is one of confession, not of honor; of faith, not jurisdiction."[48] He main-

---

[47] Wilken, *The First Thousand Years*, chap. 13, and Chadwick, *Church in Ancient Society*, chap. 39.

[48] Ambrose, *De Spiritu Sancto*, cited by Clément, *You Are Peter*, 29.

tained the local customs of the church at Milan regarding fasting and the veneration of martyrs and expected that visitors would not try to supplant them with Roman practices. Though probably predating Ambrose's episcopacy, the Ambrosian Rite of the Milanese diocese continues to be used to this day.

In contrast to the Eastern manner of relating to the emperor, Ambrose exemplifies what became a more typically Western approach, even if not always successful: he sought to ensure the autonomy of the church from imperial interference, anticipating Gelasius by a hundred years. In clashes with Theodosius, Ambrose forced the emperor to yield. Ambrose is the first church father to explicitly assert Mary as *type* and personification of the church.[49]

By far the major figure in the West, both in theology in general and in theological reflection on the church, was Augustine, the bishop of Hippo (modern Annaba, northeast coast of Algeria) from 395 to his death in 430.[50] He wrote no special work on the church, but the topic appears frequently in his major works and in his treatises, sermons, and letters, most especially in his writings on John's gospel and in his sermons on the Psalms.[51] Augustine's conception of the church is marked by paradoxes and tensions. By way of introduction to his understanding of church, it is helpful to keep in mind Augustine's distinction, on the one hand, between the church on earth as a community "gathered under the word of God and born of the sacraments," a "mixed" body whose members are compared to wheat and weeds, good fish and bad (Matt 13:24-31, 47-48), and, on the other, the church as a "fellowship of the holy," those living truly Christian lives, the "Body of Christ, alive by his Spirit, united under genuine love."[52]

---

[49] Hilda Graef, *Mary: A History of Doctrine and Devotion*, 2 vols. (Westminster, MD: Christian Classics; London: Sheed & Ward, 1963, 1965), 1:77–89.

[50] MacCulloch, *Christianity*, 301–12; Wilken, *The First Thousand Years*, chap. 19; Desmond O'Grady, *Beyond the Empire: Rome and the Church from Constantine to Charlemagne* (New York: Crossroad, 2001), chap. 8.

[51] See an analysis of Joseph Ratzinger's study of Augustine in Aidan Nichols, *The Thought of Pope Benedict XVI: An Introduction to the Theology of Joseph Ratzinger*, new ed. (London: Burns & Oates, 2007), chap. 2.

[52] Joseph A. Komonchak, *Who Are the Church?* (Milwaukee, WI: Marquette University Press, 2008), 53–54.

Augustine understands the church in relationship to both Christ and the Spirit. Christ is the Word of God, equal to the Father; he is the God-man, mediator and head of the church; and, with those united to him, he is the *totus Christus*, the "whole Christ," the fullness of the church, head and body, in a particular place and throughout the world (Sermon 341).[53] Even though Christ is whole and entire without us, Christ has chosen to be whole with us. As body of Christ, the church embodies Christ on earth after his death and resurrection. An exposition of Psalm 34 relates the image of body to that of bridegroom: "We hear Christ's voice in it [the psalm]: the voice, that is, of Christ's Head and body. When you hear Christ mentioned, never divorce Bridegroom from bride, but recognize that great sacrament, *they will be two in one flesh*" (with references to Eph 5:31 and Gen 2:24).[54] Unlike Ambrose, who applied the image of bride and bridegroom to the individual soul and Christ, Augustine more generally uses the spousal image to describe the relationship between the church and Christ.[55] A sermon instructs the neophytes regarding the communion rite at Eucharist: "You hear the words 'body of Christ,' and you answer 'Amen.' Then *be* a member of the body of Christ, that your 'Amen' may be true" (Sermon 272).[56] As bishop, Augustine directed his preaching to help his hearers be more like the Christ whose body they were.[57]

---

[53] Augustine, *Sermons (341–400) on Various Subjects*, The Works of Saint Augustine: A Translation for the 21st Century, III/10, ed. John E. Rotelle, trans. and notes by Edmund Hill (Hyde Park, NY: New City Press, 1995), 19–29. Unless otherwise noted, translations of Augustine will be taken from this series.

[54] Augustine, *Expositions of the Psalms 33–50*, vol. III/16, trans. Maria Boulding, 59. Italics in original.

[55] John C. Cavadini, "Feeling Right: Augustine on the Passions and Sexual Desire," *Augustinian Studies* 36 (2005): 215n53.

[56] Translation from Jay, *The Church: Its Changing Image*, 1:85. Complete sermon in Augustine, *Sermons (230–272B) on the Liturgical Seasons*, III/7, 300–301. The liturgical prayer after communion on the memorial of St. Augustine (August 28) incorporates this idea.

[57] See Michael C. McCarthy, "An Ecclesiology of Groaning: Augustine, the Psalms, and the Making of Church," *Theological Studies* 66 (2005): 23–48.

The church as body and the church as the fellowship of the Holy Spirit, a fellowship of love, are one. Drawing on the notion that the human body is enlivened by the soul, Augustine saw the body of the church receiving life from the gift of the Spirit. As the Spirit is the bond of love within the community of the divine persons (an element of Augustine's trinitarian theology), so the Spirit is the bond of love in the church. In sum, the church is a fellowship of love created by the Spirit, a fellowship of those who love God and one another in Christ.

As Tertullian and Cyprian before him, Augustine also describes the church as a mother, one who gives birth to her children, who nurses and cares for them, and who is pained when they stray. When by baptism we are born as members of Christ in "Mother Church," we become sisters and brothers of Christ; when we draw others to the font of baptism and life in Christ, we have it in our power to become ourselves "mothers of Christ" (Sermon 72A.8).[58] As did other patristic writers, Augustine variously speaks of the church's beginning at Pentecost, at the cross, or at the incarnation. The ultimate foundation of the church lies in the triune God. Inasmuch as the Word of God and activity of the Spirit precede the historical beginnings of Christianity, the church existed from the time of Abraham, justified by his faith, or even from the time of Abel, the just one (Gen 4:1-11). Continuity exists between the church from the time of Abel and the church at Pentecost, but there is also a difference. With Pentecost, the Spirit is more abundantly given, and the church becomes both a particular and universal community, an instrument of God bringing the life of the Spirit to others by proclaiming what God has done in Christ and the Spirit.

Augustine dealt with very practical issues and developed his thinking on the church in his debates with the Donatists and with the teachings of Pelagius. The Donatists, so named from Donatus, the second of their leaders in the early fourth century, were a rigorist group who separated themselves from bishops or priests who gave in to imperial demands at the time of the Diocletian persecution.[59]

---

[58] Augustine, *Sermons (51–94) on the New Testament*, III/3, 281–90. See translation in *The Liturgy of the Hours*, 4:1572–74.

[59] Robert F. Evans, *One and Holy: The Church in Latin Patristic Thought* (London: SPCK, 1972), chap. 3, and Chadwick, *Church in Ancient Society*, 382–93.

Claiming Cyprian as their authority, Donatists judged that sacraments celebrated by a defiled bishop or priest must be invalid since their effectiveness depended on the holiness of the minister. Donatists saw themselves as the church of the righteous, inspired both by Christian martyrs and by the attitudes of orthodox Jews toward the Torah. The Donatists alone were the "True Israel," uniquely *catholic* in that they preserved the totality of the Christian law.[60] Over time, the group grew to become a rival schismatic church.

Almost immediately upon becoming bishop, Augustine was forced to deal with the century-old issues raised now by the Donatists. For Augustine, rival claims to be church were intolerable. Drawing on ideas initially advanced by Optatus (fl. 370), bishop of the nearby Diocese of Milevis, Augustine argued that Donatists of North Africa broke catholic unity by rejecting communion with the universal church throughout the world, especially with the Church at Rome, the premier apostolic see. In so doing, Donatists forfeited their right to call themselves church. Augustine reasoned that the church's catholicity was not only temporal, from Abel to the last justified person, but geographic as well. Further, unlike Donatists, who envisioned themselves as an alternative to the society around them, Augustine viewed the church as empowered by God to live in the world without losing itself. That the church could do so depended on the promises of God and the efficacy of the sacraments.[61] Augustine also rejected the notion that a sacrament's validity depended on the personal holiness of the minister. Sacraments are first of all acts of Christ. Augustine recognized the validity of episcopal ordinations by Donatist bishops, even if they were not in full communion with the universal church. This teaching, taken up by Thomas Aquinas in the thirteenth century and the Council of Trent three centuries later, is fundamental to the Catholic understanding of sacraments.

In seeing the church as a "mixed" body including both saints and sinners, Augustine saw the biblical description of the church as being without spot or wrinkle (Eph 5:27), fulfilled only at the end of time.

---

[60] Peter Brown, *Augustine of Hippo: A Biography*, new ed. (Berkeley: University of California Press, 2000), 213.

[61] Ibid., 209.

As mentioned earlier, he distinguished the celestial church, the community of those united to Christ, and the terrestrial church, whose members may or may not be living in relationship to Christ and the Holy Spirit. This thought was likely influenced by the Platonist distinction between eternal and unchanging essences and their imperfect earthly embodiments. The celestial church and the church on earth are interconnected, though they do not coincide; the church on earth is a work in process, attaining its goal only when Christ fulfills God's saving plan. Reacting to Donatist persecution of Catholics and drawing on the Lucan parable of the great feast, "Go out into the roads and lanes, and compel people to come in, so that my house may be filled" (Luke 14:23), Augustine justified state persecution of the Donatists on behalf of the church.[62] In his view, the state had a responsibility to guarantee the freedom of the church to pursue its mission and to protect it from its enemies.

Augustine's teaching on the church continued in his reaction to Pelagius, a British monk and a leader of another effort in the expanding ascetic movement of the fourth century.[63] In late fourth- and early fifth-century Rome, Pelagius sought to challenge what he perceived as Christian laxity in the practice of the faith. He and his followers insisted that perfection attainable through self-discipline and asceticism was both possible and demanded by God. His followers in both the West and the East received a sympathetic hearing by insisting that exemplary lives in a church of the holy would inspire a positive regard in pagan public opinion. Augustine and the bishops in Latin North Africa learned of these ideas when a disciple of Pelagius, the outspoken Caelestius, began to preach in Carthage. Six propositions of his radical preaching were condemned by the African bishops. In the propositions and their supporting arguments, Augustine saw and opposed what he thought, perhaps without sufficient nuance, was a very defective understanding not only of people's need for God's

---

[62] Defending the truth with the use of methods not in keeping with the Gospel was one of the items that figured in the Service Requesting Pardon conducted by Pope John Paul II on the First Sunday of Lent in the Jubilee Year 2000. *Origins* 29, no. 40 (March 23, 2000).

[63] Brown, *Augustine of Hippo*, chaps. 29–31.

grace but also of the nature of the church. He opposed the implicit claim of the reformers that by virtue of self-discipline and the exercise of unimpeded human freedom, the church could be "holy and without blemish," a church of elite Christians. Instead, Augustine viewed the church as existing to redeem a humanity burdened by sin and the effects of sin, a church open to all in their common need for God's grace as they engaged in the slow and not always steady process of healing. By God's grace, some were heroes in the church, but, as with all the faithful, they too were like the wounded man in the parable of the good Samaritan, saved by baptism but needing a long convalescence in the "inn" that is the church.[64]

In his anti-Pelagian writings, Augustine developed his theory of predestination, that the number of those saved by means of the church and its sacraments would replace the fallen angels who once populated the primordial heavenly church and that their number was predetermined by God. Later church councils and papal teaching modified Augustine's teaching on grace and subordinated it to Augustine's anti-Donatist teaching on the church. Humankind needed grace but possessed the power and the responsibility to cooperate with grace, aided too by the grace of the sacraments.[65]

The Church in History: Augustine's *City of God*

As he was dealing with the Pelagian controversy, Augustine also began his monumental work, *On the City of God*.[66] The work was written at intervals between 413 and 427, after the sack of Rome in 410 at the hands of the Visigoth chief Alaric, a former general under Emperor Theodosius. In writing the book, Augustine sought, in part, to refute the populist charge that Rome's official abandonment of its traditional deities lay behind the recent calamity. More important,

---

[64] Sermon 131.6, in Augustine, *Sermons III/4 (94A–147A) on the New Testament*, 320.

[65] Francis Oakley, *The Western Church in the Later Middle Ages* (Ithaca, NY: Cornell University Press, 1979), 134–36, 159–61, and 206–8.

[66] Brown, *Augustine of Hippo*, chaps. 26–27; Evans, *One and Holy*, 108–28; Benedict J. Groeschel, *Augustine: Major Writings* (New York: Crossroad, 1995), chap. 6.

he found in the event an occasion to reflect at length on the origin, progress, and destinies of the "earthly city" and the "heavenly city" and his vision of the church of Christ as the entry point to the "city of God" (Ps 46:4; 48:1), to which all peoples were called and in which alone one ultimately finds one's true homeland. In effect, he looked at the church within the context of a theological understanding of history.[67]

While Augustine affirmed the legitimacy of Christian responsibilities in the Roman state and the state's claims on Christian loyalty, true justice can ultimately be found only in the City of God, where the love of God reigns supreme. Though that city will be achieved only in the afterlife, by the power of Christ it also exists on earth. The City of God exists in tension with the earthly city, marked often enough by self-love and not ordered to God as its ultimate end. God wishes us to live with this tension, Augustine reasons, rather than allowing us to be totally assimilated to the present culture or to think that we can be a community of saints living apart from a world touched by sin. Augustine sometimes identifies the city of God with the church, though here especially the tensions in his use of the word come into play. As a mixed society, the church includes members marked both by love of God and by love of self. Not everyone who is publicly a member of the church belongs to the City of God, and many who do not profess the Christian faith belong to it unawares. Like the wheat and the weeds of the parable, the two cities are inextricably mixed, to be separated only at the end. The church on earth, through Christ, is the pilgrim part of the heavenly City of God and of the glorious church that will be manifest at the end of time. That end, he describes in the book's final passage, will be "the Lord's day . . . an eighth and eternal day, consecrated by the resurrection of Christ, and prefiguring the eternal repose not only of the spirit, but also of the body. There we shall rest and see, see and love, love and praise."[68]

Augustine's *City of God* challenged the views of other Christian writers, most notably Bishop Eusebius of Caesarea, who promoted

---

[67] Mary T. Clark, *Augustine of Hippo* (London: Continuum, 1994), chap. 9.
[68] Saint Augustine, *The City of God*, trans. Marcus Dods, intro. Thomas Merton (New York: Random House Modern Library, 1950), 867.

the thesis that with the accession of Christian emperors, Old Testament prophecies about the messianic age were on the verge of being fulfilled. Ambrose of Milan held something of this idea, as did Augustine in an earlier period. In his later years, Augustine thought this view too simplistic. In his mind, the two cities, each guided by its distinctive love, would perdure until the final judgment. Augustine cited biblical texts calling for obedience to civil authority and saw the virtue of patriotism as a religious obligation. With other early writers, he cited Romans 13:1-7 as an inspiration for his thinking.

Building on the thinking of Tertullian, Cyprian, and Optatus, Augustine's teachings on the church had a dominant influence on Western Catholic theology. In his study of Augustine, Joseph Ratzinger pointed out—so observes Aidan Nichols—that "whereas in the Greek East theology was centered on the concepts of God, his *Logos* and his Spirit, with the Church tacitly omitted from an account of the inner reality of salvation, Augustine makes the Church 'an inner-dogmatic affair.'"[69] This is not, of course, to deny the lived eucharistic theology of the church in Eastern thought or its oft-expressed link between Christ and the church in the image of the groom and the bride.

Three Fathers of the East

The patristic period in the West is generally thought to have come to a close with the deaths of Gregory I and two prominent bishops of Seville in Visigothic Spain, Leander (d. ca. 600) and Isidore (d. 636). Westerners see the period extending in the East for another century and a half, though Eastern Orthodoxy sees itself continuing the traditions of the fathers even to the present day.[70] Three major figures warrant a place in our study.

Our first is an unknown author, very probably a Syrian monk, known to us as Denys (Dionysius) the Areopagite. For a long while the author was thought to be one of the few converts from Paul's

---

[69] Nichols, *Thought of Pope Benedict*, 29.
[70] Andrew Louth, "Postpatristic Byzantine Theologians," in *The Medieval Theologians*, ed. G. R. Evans (Malden, MA: Blackwell, 2001), 37.

mission to Athens (Acts 17:34), though present scholarship places him at the end of the fifth and the beginning of the sixth centuries.[71] Our interest centers on two of his works, the *Celestial Hierarchy* and the *Ecclesiastical Hierarchy*. The first gives the meaning of hierarchy (from Greek *hier*, "sacred," and *archē*, "source or principle"), a term coined by the author himself. Hierarchy is a God-given ordering, involving either angelic choirs (celestial hierarchy) or human beings or the sacraments (ecclesiastical hierarchy), meant to bring about assimilation to God and union with him. Originating in God's self-giving love, the hierarchies mediate the "descent" of divine illumination and human "ascent" leading to divinization or deification. The ecclesiastical hierarchy consists in the triad of sacraments, ministers, and those to whom they minister, each triad again forming a triad. The first and most important triad of "mysteries" or sacraments speaks of baptism, Eucharist, and the consecration of chrism and all the sacraments incorporating an anointing with oil. The second triad comprises three orders of clergy: bishops, priests, and deacons, having, respectively, a triple, double, or single power to purify, to illuminate, and to unify. The third triad consists of monks, laity, and catechumens or public penitents. God's love extends to us through these holy orderings and "to depend on God and his love means to depend on other people."[72] Those who mediate purification, illumination, and perfection themselves stand in need of those same gifts. The hierarchy is both a community that is being saved and one that mediates salvation. The church with its sacraments and rituals are vehicles of God's revelation; the liturgy is very much the context for Denys's theology. He draws language and categories from Neoplatonic thought, but his thinking is distinctively Christian.[73]

Denys's teaching that the church's worship is a response to the beauty of God's manifestation in the cosmos was given architectural expression not long after in the magnificent church of Hagia Sophia

---

[71] See the introduction to the author and his intellectual world in Andrew Louth, *Denys the Areopagite*, Outstanding Christian Thinkers, ed. Brian Davies (London: Continuum, 1989), chap. 1.
[72] Ibid., 41.
[73] Ibid., 10–14.

(Divine Wisdom) in Constantinople.[74] Dedicated by Emperor Justinian (emperor 527–565) in 537, the church became the model for Eastern church architecture (and, later, for Islamic mosques). Built in the domed style of the fourth-century Church of the Holy Sepulcher in Jerusalem, the central dome was built above a gallery of windows, permitting sunlight to come down from the heights. The light and multicolored marbles were meant to suggest that heaven had come down to earth. Its liturgy, suggesting that in Christ we are given a share in the heavenly liturgy, let itself be influenced by the architecture.[75] (In Justinian's church of San Vitale in Ravenna, the principal center of his rule in Italy, the lush fern-like green surrounding the many holy figures portrayed along the walls was meant to remind the worshipers that in church they had entered a Garden of Paradise where holy souls would find their rest. The liturgy's generous use of incense, lights, and chanting were meant to suggest the smells, the sights, and the sounds of Paradise.[76])

The church's liturgy, along with ascetic, cosmological, and anthropological concerns, is central to the thought on the church of Maximus the Confessor (ca. 580–662), called "the real father of Byzantine theology."[77] Through his writings many of the principal traditions of previous Eastern thought, including those of Origen and Denys the Areopagite, were preserved within Eastern Christianity. Maximus's *Mystagogy* is an important example of the mystical interpretations of the church and its liturgy produced by many Eastern theological writers.[78] Understood as the new creation in Christ, the church is a

---

[74] Andrew Louth, "'Beauty Will Save the World': The Formation of Byzantine Spirituality," *Theology Today* 61, no. 1 (2004): 69.

[75] Marcel Metzger, *History of the Liturgy: The Major Stages*, trans. Madeleine Beaumont (Collegeville, MN: Liturgical Press, 1997), 75.

[76] Brown, *Rise of Western Christendom*, 401.

[77] John Meyendorff, *Christ in Eastern Christian Thought*, 2nd ed. (Crestwood, NY: St Vladimir's Seminary Press, 1975), 131–32; see St. Maximus the Confessor, *The Church, the Liturgy and the Soul of Man*, trans. Julian Stead (Still River, MA: St. Bede's Publications, 1982).

[78] Jay, *The Church: Its Changing Image*, 1:148–49, and Yves Congar, *L'ecclésiologie du haut Moyen-Age: De Saint Grégoire le Grand à la désunion entry Byzance et Rome* (Paris: Editions du Cerf, 1968), 324–28.

"mystery of unity," an image (icon) of God and of the cosmos, and of humankind as God intends us to be. By its uniting people of every age, condition, and race, the church images God who is all in all and preserves all things in unity. In its union of visible things (hierarchy and sacraments) as symbols of invisible realities, the church is also an image of the cosmos. As Maximus sees it, the very church building and its liturgy unite the earthly (the nave) and the heavenly (the sanctuary). The nave, the sanctuary, and the altar of the church, representing, respectively, the body, the soul, and the mind, image humanity as it is called to approach God. Denys and Maximus, along with Origen and Gregory of Nyssa, share an important feature of many of the fathers, "the mutual co-inherence of the mystical and the ecclesiological."[79] Their primary interest may be our union with God, but it is a union achieved in and through the church.

A third major figure is the last of the Eastern fathers, John Damascene (d. ca. 750), an Arab Christian, at one time a court official for the caliph of Damascus (following the Arab conquest in 635), later a learned monk in a monastery near Jerusalem and a prolific writer. Given our interests, two items stand out. His most important work, *The Orthodox Faith*, itself part of a larger work, *Fount of Wisdom*, is a comprehensive treatment of the teaching of the Greek fathers on the Trinity, creation, the incarnation, the sacraments, Mary, and the use of images. (In the patristic period, the term "orthodox" was used to designate the christological and trinitarian faith of the early councils. After the schism between Eastern and Western churches in the fifteenth century, "Orthodox" came to refer to the churches united to Constantinople.) Reflecting the writings of which *Orthodox Faith* is a summary, there is no separate section on the church. His work is another reminder that patristic thought on the church, especially in the East, is really one with the whole of the Christian life.

John also wrote three treatises in defense of images (Greek *eikon*, "icon"), opposing the attack on the devotional use of such images and their destruction (iconoclasm) ordered by Emperor Leo III

---

[79] Andrew Louth, *The Origins of the Christian Mystical Tradition: From Plato to Denys* 2nd ed. (Oxford: Oxford University Press, 2007), 196.

in 726.[80] The veneration of icons had been part of public worship and private devotion since the fifth century, though in some instances devotion fell into outright superstition. The emperor's reasons for his opposition are not clear: he may have been influenced in part by a desire to follow the prohibition of images in Exodus 20:4-5 and by strains of thought that minimized the humanity of Christ; he may also have wished to counter Islamic claims to be the true and incorrupt religion in their opposition to images. In response, John claimed for images "the same unambiguous ability to represent the unseen that earlier authors had claimed only for the liturgy and for the sacraments of the Church."[81] Drawing in part on the teaching of Denys the Areopagite, that God created the material world as an icon, a symbol of God, John centered his argument by pointing to the incarnate Christ as the image of the Father, to human beings made in the image of God, and to visible elements in Christian worship used to draw humankind to God. Since the iconoclasts argued that the use of icons was a later and unauthorized development, John and his successors insisted that images venerated in their time had been venerated in the same form since the days of Christ and the apostles. The anachronistic argument seriously weakened a sense of history and recognition of development in the life of the church.[82] Though more appreciated after his death, John's powerful defense of icons was implicitly a strong endorsement of the principle of sacramentality in the church. The basics of John's teaching were accepted at the Second Council of Nicaea in 787, the last council accepted by both the church of the East and that of the West. The council ended the first phase of the iconoclast controversy. (A second phase of the controversy, begun in 815, ended with a ceremony, the "Triumph of Orthodoxy," in 843, annually celebrated to this day by the Orthodox Church on the First Sunday of Lent.)

---

[80] Andrew Louth, *Greek East and Latin West: The Church AD 681–1071* (Crestwood, NY: St Vladimir's Seminary Press, 2007), chaps. 2 and 6, and Brown, *Western Christendom*, chap. 17.

[81] Brown, *Western Christendom*, 398.

[82] Ibid., 399.

Christian Antiquity—Part 2: Constantine to Gregory I and John Damascene 179

Yves Congar summarizes the fathers' vision of church in three notes: "The Church is contemplated as a Spirit-moved, Spirit-known and Spirit-defined reality, as the Body whose living Soul is the Spirit of Life. The Church is contemplated in Christ, as Christ is contemplated in the Church. And the inward Church is not separated from the outward Church, which is its sacramental veil and vehicle."[83] The basic lines of the Eastern theological understanding of the church were fairly set at the end of the patristic period; such shifts that did occur we shall note as we proceed. The theology of the church in the West was considerably more volatile; to that we turn in the next chapter.

---

[83] Yves Congar, *The Mystery of the Church*, trans. A. V. Littledale (Baltimore: Helicon Press, 1960), 117.

CHAPTER SEVEN

Medieval Understandings of Church

This present chapter covers developments in the long period from the early seventh century to the late fifteenth century. For that reason, it is somewhat longer than the other chapters. Recognizing the limits of so doing, it may help to think of this period in the West in three segments, without the first having a clean break from the ancient world.[1] A first section (ca. 600–1050) focuses on the theology of church in the Carolingian period and in feudalism, along with a debate that emerged concerning church authority. The second major segment (ca. 1050–1300) looks at the understanding of church in the period beginning with the mid-eleventh-century reform efforts and extending through developments in the twelfth and thirteenth centuries. The final portion (ca. 1300–1500) reviews the church as seen in the struggles between the papacy and the emerging monarchs and then in the efforts to deal with the Great Western Schism. The chapter concludes with a word on developments in the East.

Historical Setting of the Transition to the Medieval Period

By the end of the fifth century, much of what had been the Western Roman Empire was taken over by waves of northern peoples—many of them farmers fleeing the nomadic Huns—who moved south and set up their own local kingdoms. Bergundians and Franks settled in Gaul, Ostrogoths in Italy, Visigoths in Spain, and Vandals in North Africa. Rome was sacked in 410 by frustrated immigrant Visigoths and again in 455 by the Vandals. In 476, the last emperor of the West,

---

[1] See Kevin Madigan, *Medieval Christianity: A New History* (New Haven, CT: Yale University Press, 2015).

by then a minor figure, was deposed by a Germanic warlord. The Eastern empire continued to exist and, in the sixth century and early seventh century, saw its fortunes rise under the emperors Justinian (emperor 527–565) and Heraclius (emperor 610–641), only to change dramatically with the astonishing spread of Islam beginning in the mid-seventh century. Within a hundred years of Muhammad's death (632), his followers took over Syria, Palestine, all of North Africa, and much of Spain and parts of France before being stopped in 732 near Tours by Charles Martel, the Frankish Mayor of the Palace (the de facto prime minister) of the Merovingian kingdom. The Eastern empire maintained its claim to be the Roman Empire but in effect was "an island surrounded by enemies on all sides,"[2] though it lasted for another eight hundred years. The centers of Christianity at Antioch, Jerusalem, and Alexandria fell under Muslim rule. The patriarch of Constantinople emerged as leader of Eastern Christianity.

Threats against Italy in the late 730s by yet another group, the Lombards, led the popes, no longer able to rely on help from the emperor in Constantinople, to look to the north, to the Franks, Nicene Christians since the conversion of Clovis in 496. Frankish help would come after Pippin III (Pippin the Short), son and successor of Charles Martel in what had become the ineffectual reign of the Merovingians, appealed to the pope in 750 to recognize his having the royal title. The pope consented, and Pippin was anointed the following year. When the Lombards captured Ravenna, ending exarchate rule in northern Italy, and were making their way toward Rome, Pope Stephen II successfully appealed to Pippin for military assistance. In 756, after taking Ravenna and freeing Rome from Lombard control, Pippin donated the territories he conquered in Italy, including the exarchate of Ravenna, to the pope. In doing so, he created what came to be known as the "patrimony of Peter," making the bishop of Rome a temporal ruler. To counter protests from the East at these several changes, a forged document known as the *Donation of Constantine* was produced, according to which Constantine granted to the pope "all the provinces, districts and cities of Italy

---

[2] Alexander Schmemann, *The Historical Road of Eastern Orthodoxy*, trans. Lydia W. Kesich (London: Harvill Press, 1963), 169.

and the Western regions" and, momentously, over all other churches, including the four other patriarchal sees.[3] The bond between the Western church and the Frankish kings became even closer during the long reign (768–814) of Pippin's son, Charles or, after his death, Charlemagne.[4] In return for confirming and extending the papal territory, Charles looked to ecclesiastical collaboration for the good of the realm, extending, after 785, over much of what was the Western Roman Empire.

In December 800, Charles presided at an assembly in Rome that enunciated the principle—invoked in later centuries to support papal claims—that no one could sit in judgment on the successor of Peter.[5] On Christmas Day of that year, Pope Leo III (795–816) anointed Charles "Emperor of the Romans," seeing him as a new Constantine, protector of the faith under papal guidance in a theocratic state. Charles claimed to be emperor by divine right and to have a divinely given role in holding the church accountable to its mission. Easterners regarded the Christmas coronation as sacrilegious arrogance, a denial of the Eastern emperor's claims over Western territory and his historical role in the church, and a hostile challenge to Eastern ecclesial and political self-understanding.

Understanding of Church in the Carolingian Period

Desiring to promote the well-being of the church, but also with an eye to a renewed and unified church as a way to political unity, Charles, even before that eventful Christmas, had undertaken a program of *correctio* (the term used) for the church, a "correcting, shaping

---

[3] Colman J. Barry, ed., *Readings in Church History*, vol. 1: *From Pentecost to the Protestant Revolt* (Westminster, MD: Newman Press, 1960), 239.

[4] See Diarmaid MacCulloch, *Christianity: The First Three Thousand Years* (New York: Viking, 2009), 346–62, and Robert Louis Wilken, *The First Thousand Years: A Global History of Christianity* (New Haven, CT: Yale University Press, 2012), chap. 35.

[5] Accepting that principle, papal historian Walter Ullmann suggests, was "far more important" than the events that followed. Walter Ullman, *A Short History of the Papacy in the Middle Ages* (London: Methuen, 1972), 82.

up, getting things in order again."⁶ This was continued by his son and successor, Louis the Pious (814–840), and by others after him. The application of the *correctio* varied widely in what was beginning to be spoken of as "Europe," but it did have a broad influence. An important indication of the understanding of church in this development is seen in Charles's *Admonitio Generalis*, the "General Warning," promulgated in 789. While respecting the local laws of each region, Charles saw "Christian Law" as the universal law of his realm. That law comprised a written law, the texts of the Bible, liturgical texts, the canons of church councils, and the works of the Latin fathers of the church. Liturgical texts had a singular importance inasmuch as ecclesial life at this time was at the center of what has been called a "liturgical civilization."⁷ The church, through her ministers, was to provide a properly executed ritual pleasing to God, to the benefit of the individuals morally and legally obliged to attend and to the community as a whole. The work of priests was largely seen in terms of bringing God to his people, in the sacraments and in the many forms of blessings and prayers related to many aspects of daily life.

Other factors also entered into the church's self-understanding. Germanic fascination with the image of Peter as the heavenly gatekeeper and the belief that the traditions of the Roman Church best guaranteed a proper cult for putting believers in contact with God strengthened the tendency to look to Rome for guidance and to see the Frankish church as one with the universal church.⁸ Attitude toward Eastern Christians is shown in the court reaction to a faulty translation of the Second Council of Nicaea's affirmation of the value of icons. A memorandum, known in modern times as the *Libri Carolini* ("Books for Charles"), was prepared by Theodulph, a Visigothic refugee from the Islamic invasion of Spain, and was intended as a

---

⁶ Peter Brown, *The Rise of Western Christendom: Triumph and Diversity, A.D. 200–1000*, 2nd ed. (Malden, MA: Blackwell, 2002), 438–46.

⁷ André Vauchez, *The Spirituality of the Medieval West: From the Eighth to the Twelfth Century*, trans. Colette Friedlander (Kalamazoo, MI: Cistercian Publications, 1993), 15–19.

⁸ Klaus Schatz, *Papal Primacy: From Its Origins to the Present*, trans. John A. Otto and Linda M. Maloney (Collegeville, MN: Liturgical Press, 1996), 63–68.

rebuttal to the teaching of the council. The text was at pains to contrast the worldview of the Latins from that of "the Greeks."[9] The Christian people needed the "commands of the Lord" in "God's own Law," far more than the "little pictures" of the Greeks. Theodulph, later made the bishop of Orléans (798–818), and his colleagues saw God as a distant ruler, distant from creatures, relating to them by means of the gift of law. Emphasis was given to keeping apart the sacred and the profane, unlike Greek thinkers (e.g., Dionysius and John Damascene) who readily linked the invisible to the visible world. Charles's court also promoted the addition of the term *filioque* ("and [from] the Son") to the creed of 381 in an effort to emphasize the Son's equality with the Father and the full divinity of the Spirit. Eastern Christians regarded the addition as tampering with the established creed and, at the end of the ninth century, constituting a major theological difference as well.[10] The Frankish vision of church was also affected by anti-Arian concerns brought to Carolingian circles through the influence of Spanish teachers and their two-century opposition to residues of Arian thought among the Visigoths in the Iberian Peninsula. Anti-Arian stress on the divinity of Christ, for example, made it more difficult to see the baptized as *alter Christus*, "another Christ," and may be one factor in a diminishing appreciation of the church as body of Christ.[11] Earlier baptismal theology had viewed the church as a mother giving birth to new Christians and saw the newly baptized as other Christs in the church, the body of Christ.

Church buildings and liturgical practice in this Romanesque period also reflected an understanding of church.[12] During the eighth century,

---

[9] Brown, *Rise of Western Christendom*, 457–61.

[10] Edward Siecienski, *The Filioque: History of a Doctrinal Controversy* (New York: Oxford University Press, 2010), 91–93, 100–104.

[11] J. A. Jungmann, "The Defeat of Teutonic Arianism and the Revolution in Religious Culture in the Early Middle Ages," in *Pastoral Liturgy*, trans. Challoner Publications (New York: Herder and Herder, 1962), 58. See Gerard Austin, "Restoring Equilibrium after the Struggle with Heresy," in *Source and Summit: Commemorating Josef A. Jungmann, SJ*, ed. Joanne M. Pierce and Michael Downey (Collegeville, MN: Liturgical Press, 1999), 35–47.

[12] Robert Cabié, *History of the Mass*, trans. Lawrence J. Johnson (Washington, DC: Pastoral Press, 1992), 64–67, and R. Kevin Seasoltz, *A Sense of the Sacred:*

in the Frankish realm as elsewhere, it became common to have the apse and the altar at the eastern end of the church building, the entrance facing the west. Both the presider and the congregation faced the altar in the east, with the presider's back toward the people. The eastward stance reminded the community to look to Christ, the "light of the world" who would return one day as the risen Lord, though it reinforced a sense of separation of the congregation from the presiding priest. Some late Romanesque cathedrals and monastic churches had rood screens separating the chancel and the nave. ("Rood," from the Old English word for "cross," was often a prominent feature in the decoration of the screen.) Even modest church structures in rural areas, the church buildings used by most people, had a division between the sanctuary and the main body of the church. In practice, the church had two rooms, the sanctuary reserved for the clergy, perhaps also for the choir, and the nave, set aside for the laity now distanced from the sacred action, more spectators than participants. The use of Latin in the liturgy instead of the commonly used vernacular; increasing emphasis on the role of the priest, especially as mediator before Christ whose divinity was emphasized at the expense of his humanity; and his praying the eucharistic prayer of the Mass in a low voice all contributed to a distancing of the priest and the people. How the lay faithful experienced themselves in prayer affected how they saw themselves as church. Starting with this period one begins to see the word "church" increasingly identified principally with the clergy.[13]

Even as Latin was maintained as the liturgical language in the West and the translation of the Vulgate into the Romanic or Germanic tongue regarded as sacrilegious and useless for a mostly illiterate population, an opposite stance would be taken on behalf of the Indo-European Slavs who had moved into what is now Eastern Europe, southern Russia, and the Balkans. In 862 the king of one of the Slavic nations petitioned the Byzantine emperor Michael III to

---

Theological Foundations of Christian Architecture and Art (New York: Continuum, 2005), 119–24.

[13] Yves Congar, *L'ecclésiologie du haut Moyen-Age: de Saint Grégoire le Grand à la désunion entre Byzance et Rome* (Paris: Editions du Cerf, 1968), 98.

send missionaries who knew the Slavic language. The petition led to the groundbreaking mission of the Thessalonian brothers Cyril (d. 869) and Methodius (d. 885). The two not only initiated a way of writing, a simplified version of which later came to be known as the Cyrillic script still used among many Slavic peoples, but also laid the foundations for a Slavic-speaking church.[14] (In his encyclical letter *Apostles of the Slavs* (1985), Pope John Paul II referred to the work of Cyril and Methodius as "both a model of what today is called *inculturation*—the incarnation of the Gospel in native cultures—and also the introduction of these cultures into the life of the church.") It is noteworthy that approximately one hundred years later, under Prince Vladimir, who became their ruler in 980, the Kievan Rus accepted Byzantine Christianity, the beginning of both the Ukrainian and the Russian church. The conversion of the Slavs in the Balkans and among the Rus would have momentous consequences in the centuries to come.

Feudalism: The Proprietary Church

The Carolingian period and its reform efforts came to a practical end with the death of Charlemagne's grandson in 887 and a new round of invasions by Vikings in the north and by nomadic Saracens in Sicily and southern Italy. Facing threats from foreign invaders and a weakened central authority to protect them, many people looked to local lords for protection. In the ninth and tenth centuries, drawing on both Roman and Germanic influences, the feudal system (Latin *feudum*, "land") developed in many of the lands settled by the Germanic peoples. The church became part of this system. With exceptions, the most common type of church at the turn of the millennium were proprietary churches, numbering most likely in the tens of thousands, founded and governed by the local lay lord.[15] In the feudal system, the king or the landlord insisted on his right to choose the bishop, abbot, or pastor. As a sign of their feudal rights regarding bishops, the king or lord received the homage of the cleric at the time

---

[14] Wilken, *The First Thousand Years*, chap. 36.
[15] Madigan, *Medieval Christianity*, chap. 5.

of his appointment and, at the time of a bishop's ordination, invested him with the ring and the pastoral staff, symbols of his office.[16] In practice, the priest became "a cult-minister in the retinue of a feudal lord" and the bishop a "functionary of the Empire . . . concerned only secondarily with the ecclesial assembly."[17] This issue, and others, would fuel several reform movements that involved distinct understandings of the church. We look, first, at two other approaches to seeing the church, both related to the exercise of authority.

The Church: Collegial Authority or Papal Monarchy

As a means to control the entire episcopate, the Carolingian reform emphasized the role of archbishops or metropolitans. In this context, there arose two contrasting positions regarding authority structures in the life of the church. One position was notably represented by Hincmar, archbishop of Rheims from 845 to 882, the metropolitan of France, and the best canonist of his time.[18] In the face of political divisions following the death of Louis the Pious, Hincmar looked to the unity of the church. Following Augustine and reflecting the common understanding, he saw the church as a seamless robe, a people united under Christ the priest and king, in one faith, one baptism, and one Eucharist, constituting the body of Christ in a visibly ordered communion. Drawing on earlier church law, Hincmar saw this order centered on the pope and the bishops, each with proper responsibility but carefully avoiding anything that hinted of a papal monarchy. Reasoning that Christ chose twelve and gave them and their successors a role in church order, Hincmar sought to balance the papal use of Matthew 16 by applying Matthew 18 to a local body of bishops with their metropolitan, responsible as a group for church order and unity in a particular church. He valued the notion of "reception,"

---

[16] Ian McNeill, "Attitudes to Authority in the Medieval Centuries," in *Problems of Authority: An Anglo-French Symposium*, ed. John M. Todd (Baltimore, MD: Helicon Press, 1962), 160–61.

[17] Joseph Ratzinger, *Principles of Catholic Theology: Building Stones for a Fundamental Theology*, trans. Mary Frances McCarthy (San Francisco: Ignatius Press, 1987), 255.

[18] Congar, *L'ecclésiologie du haut Moyen-Age*, 166–77.

whereby a decision taken in one place is accepted in another, so becoming part of a common tradition. Only decisions receiving approbation by the pope and by all the bishops were to be regarded as the canons or laws of the church. By this same reason, he did not accept the decisions of the Second Council of Nicaea on the use of icons since the council's decisions were not received by all the churches. Both Hincmar and the second group to which we now turn were eager to place canonical structures within a doctrinal understanding of the church.

Other Frankish bishops sought to limit the power of the metropolitans as well as that of the king and of lay lords in the appointment of clerics in the proprietary church system and in the general affairs of the church. Looking to precedents in patristic literature and earlier ecclesiastical law, they argued for a strong papal authority as the source of jurisdiction in the church. From the circles of these bishops and perhaps other sympathetic clerics there appeared in the mid-ninth century a forgery now known as the *False Decretals*, purporting to be associated with the learned Spanish bishop Isidore of Seville. Many of the citations were fabrications, and interpolations were inserted into authentic texts. The entire collection gave legal underpinnings to a vision of church centered on the authority of the pope, limiting the power of the metropolitans and freeing the church from imperial control.[19]

The *Decretals* gave the bishop of Rome metropolitan authority over all the bishops of the church, even those of the East. What Pope Leo I said of his vicar in Thessalonica—that his vicar had a "share" of the pope's "fullness of power" over all the churches—was now said of all bishops, suggesting that they were the equivalent of papal representatives. Papal authority in teaching and in discipline was autonomous, not bound by the norms of tradition. In contrast to the commonly held position of the Eastern Church, the power of the keys was said to be given solely to Peter and his successors, with the "binding and loosing" of Matthew 16 applicable to any papal decision.[20] The *False Decretals* so emphasized the papacy in

---

[19] Schatz, *Papal Primacy*, 70–73.
[20] Congar, *L'ecclésiologie du haut Moyen-Age*, 228–30.

juridical categories that it lessened an appreciation of the papal office in charismatic or spiritual terms. By fabricating what were presented as ancient texts, the *Decretals* also obstructed an historical awareness of the development of the institutional structures of the church. The outlook of the *Decretals* was exemplified in the pontificate of Pope Nicholas I (858–67), probably the most forceful papal leader between Gregory I and Gregory VII in the eleventh century.[21] Relying on previous papal writings and, most probably, on the *False Decretals*, Nicholas saw the church as the one spouse of Christ whose care was entrusted to Peter and, following him, to the pope. In his view, the apostolic see had the right to regulate everything in the life of the church; its judgments suffered no appeal; it was the source of legitimacy for every law in the church. Nicholas held that this authority came to the Roman church, not through any council, but from Peter and ultimately from Christ himself. Claims for papal authority were expressed in a markedly juridical manner. Nicholas defended papal prerogatives in his dealings with emperors, archbishops, and regional councils. For Nicholas, the papacy was a pastoral monarchy; bishops had an especially important part, but only if they were strictly subordinate to the pope from whom they drew their power. In what was a complicated situation, Nicholas excommunicated the patriarch of Constantinople in 863 and the patriarch did the same to him in the year of Nicholas's death. Relations between Rome and Constantinople were restored after Nicholas's death, though the mistrust and suspicion between Rome and Constantinople only increased. Nicholas supported missionary efforts, notably those of Ansgar in Scandinavia and Cyril and Methodius in Moravia.

With exceptions, the papacy for roughly the hundred years after Nicholas's death entered a period of decline, many of the popes controlled by powerful Roman families.

---

[21] Ibid., 206–16, and Henry Chadwick, *East and West: The Making of a Rift in the Church: From Apostolic Times until the Council of Florence* (New York: Oxford University Press, 2003), chap. 16.

Eleventh-Century Reform and the Understanding of Church

The disorder following the collapse of the Carolingian empire, a period of general decline of the papacy, and three issues—the buying and selling of church offices (simony), the lay control of clergy appointments (investiture), and clerical marriage or concubinage—led to calls for a new order, a reform of the church.[22] Even as lay lords and kings were assuming increasing control of church affairs, movements of monastic reform were developing in France, Germany, and Anglo-Saxon England. Most prominent among these was the monastic foundation at Cluny, founded in 910 in Burgundy. Two important features in its charter had implications for thought about the church: the monastery's dedication to Saints Peter and Paul (so under papal control) and the stipulation that after the death of the first abbot, his successor should be elected solely by the community, not by any secular power. Monks in the many Cluniac monasteries in France, Germany, Italy, and Spain became strong opponents of simony and clerical marriage. Reform-minded clerics would see in Cluny's exemption from lay control a model of *libertas*, freedom from the control that, in their view, was so hindering church renewal.

Reform efforts in the mid-eleventh century began with a series of German popes, imposed or nominated by the German king, Henry III (d. 1056). The decision of three of them to use the names of popes of the early church (Clement, Damasus, Leo) signaled their desire to return to the ideals of early Christianity. Their doing so was part of an emerging vision of the church, centered on the image of Christ and the apostles in certain key texts of the gospels and the Acts of the Apostles.[23] Embracing the *vita apostolica* ("apostolic life") was proposed as the way to restore what was perceived to be the discipline and order of the primitive church. Relying on such texts as Mark 6:6-13 and Acts 4:32-35—the first speaking of wandering moneyless preachers, the second, the renunciation of property and sharing things in common—and drawing on ancient laws, the reformers sought to abolish simony and clerical concubinage. These widespread practices,

---

[22] Madigan, *Medieval Christianity*, chap. 8.
[23] Ibid., 124–26.

seen as contaminating the rituals that were at the core of the life of the church, were anathema to the reformers.

The most important of these German popes, Leo IX (1049–1054), called to Rome a group of reformers sharing his own concerns: Humbert, a monk from northeastern France, later a cardinal; the hermit Peter Damian who, once called on, eagerly promoted monastic reform and the apostolic life and poverty of the clergy; and another monk, Hildebrand. The group, all non-Romans, envisioned a strong papacy as a principal means of restoring the church to a more primitive purity. Almost simultaneously with the pontificate of Leo IX, the pope's responsibility was signified in the Latin neologism, *papatus*, "papacy," meant to indicate that his was an authority of a higher order than that of the episcopate (*episcopatus*). Leo exercised that authority not only in Roman synods but in councils held in cities north of the Alps, a novelty that reinforced the notion of extended papal authority. In his opposition to simony Leo insisted on the election of church officers by the clergy and laity. Regarding the church in the East, efforts failed to settle a dispute with the patriarch of Constantinople and to secure Eastern acceptance of Roman claims. Leo's delegate, the inflexible papalist Cardinal Humbert laid a bull of excommunication against the patriarch and his adherents on the altar of Hagia Sophia in July 1054 and was himself anathematized by the patriarch a couple of weeks later.[24] As Leo's death the preceding April made void Humbert's action and relations continued, if hesitantly, the events of 1054 were not a formal schism but rather symbolic of the deteriorating relations between East and West.

The most intense phase of the reform came when the monk Hildebrand, already working for reform for some twenty years, was elected Pope Gregory VII (1073–1085); from him the reform gets its name, though it began some years earlier and continued after his death.[25] Gregory developed an almost mystical vision of the papal

---

[24] Chadwick, *East and West: The Making of a Rift in the Church*, chap. 33.

[25] Eamon Duffy, *Saints and Sinners: A History of the Papacy* (New Haven, CT: Yale University Press in association with S4C, 1997), 94–98; John W. O'Malley, *Tradition and Transition: Historical Perspectives on Vatican II*, Theology and Life Series (Wilmington, DE: Michael Glazier, 1989), 82–106, and *Four Cultures of the*

office and saw it in the context of his understanding of the church as a corporate and public body of all the baptized, lay and cleric, transcending all boundaries of kingdom or feudal territory. Church leaders were to be freely chosen according to canonical norms, that is, elected by their clergy; they were to be chosen from those qualified for the office and free to exercise their office without interference from king or lay lord. Lay investiture was perceived as the antithesis of the church's freedom.

To achieve reform, Gregory sought a clearly articulated and effectively enforced legal system. He drew on a codification of law put together some years earlier by Humbert as well as other collections of law, all of them emphasizing the papacy's authority in the church. An indication of what apparently was to be yet another collection of legal texts, the *Dictatus Papae* ("Pronouncements of the Pope"), appears in the papal register for the year 1075.[26] The *Dictatus* lists twenty-seven propositions thought to be chapter headings for a collection of legal texts that was never completed. One proposition refers to papal rights over bishops and councils and to the rights of papal legates (often deacons) over bishops, so giving priority to the legal over the sacramental.[27] Another asserts that the pope alone is a universal bishop whose authority is not restricted to a single diocese or territory (contrast Gregory I). A third affirms that the Roman See has never erred nor shall ever err. For the most part, there is nothing historically new in the *Dictatus*, though it expresses papal rights in the boldest language yet. Gregory's concern, he wrote in his final missive, was "that holy church, our lady and mother, should return to her true glory and stand free, chaste, and catholic."[28]

West (Cambridge, MA: Belknap Press of Harvard University Press, 2004), 50–56; Yves Congar, *L'Eglise: De saint Augustin à l'époque moderne* (Paris: Editions du Cerf, 1970), 102–12; John Jay Hughes, *Pontiffs: Popes Who Shaped History* (Huntington, IN: Our Sunday Visitor, 1994), chap. 4.

[26] The propositions are cited in Patrick Granfield, *The Limits of the Papacy: Authority and Autonomy in the Church* (New York: Crossroad, 1987), 34–35.

[27] Bernard Lauret, ed., *Fifty Years of Catholic Theology: Conversations with Yves Congar* (Philadelphia: Fortress Press, 1988), 42.

[28] Cited in H. E. Cowdrey, "Pope Gregory VII (1073–85) and the Liturgy," *The Journal of Theological Studies* 55 (2004): 83.

The impact of the Gregorian Reform on the theology of the church was enormous. First, the reformers promoted a very papal-centered church as the most effective means to achieve the church's freedom. "Obedience to Peter [with whom the pope was seen to stand in mystical union] now becomes the epitome of ecclesiality."[29] Second, the arguments for reform cast the church in predominantly legal and juridical categories. Papal pronouncements came to adopt much the same outlook as the temporal power itself, that is, to see the church as a society, a legal institution. Combined with the shift in theological method in the next century, this juridical emphasis impoverished later lines of reflection on the church. Yves Congar sees in the reform begun by Leo IX and continued by Gregory VII a major turning point in the history of ecclesiology.[30] Here, the term "ecclesiology" is appropriate in that many voices in the reform focused immediately on the church itself. The enduring significance of the reform lay in its coming to see the church primarily in juridical terms rather than in the predominantly spiritual and anthropological terms characteristic of the first Christian millennium.[31]

Third, while the reforms meant to return to what was inexactly considered a primitive golden age, the use of counterfeit canons purporting to come from that period dulled appreciation of historical development in ecclesial structures. Finally, Gregory VII overturned the affirmation by Pope Gelasius, six hundred years earlier, that there were two divinely established authorities in the world, sacred authority and royal authority, the former having preeminence. By denying that the king or emperor was an anointed of God with responsibility regarding the church, Gregory desacralized their roles. In his view, there was one society with a single spiritual authority over everyone, even over the emperor or the king, an authority that belonged to the vicar of Peter. This dramatic

---

[29] Schatz, *Papal Primacy*, 89.

[30] Yves Congar, "The Historical Development of Authority in the Church: Points for Christian Reflection," in *Problems of Authority*, 136.

[31] Joseph A. Komonchak, *Who Are the Church?*, The Père Marquette Lecture in Theology 2008 (Milwaukee, WI: Marquette University Press, 2008), 46.

change leads some scholars to speak of the "Gregorian Revolution" rather than the "Gregorian Reform."[32]

Canon Law and the Understanding of Church

The heightened attention to legal texts—and the inconsistencies and even contradictions in the church's legal tradition, along with tensions between church law and imperial law—encouraged the systematic study of law as a distinct academic discipline, most especially at one of the earliest European universities, that at Bologna in the late eleventh century. The Italian jurist John Gratian (d. ca. 1160) made a major contribution by collecting and giving some order to existing church law. His *Concordia Discordantium Canonum* ("The Concordance of Discordant Canons"), later known as *Decretum Gratiani*, collected the legal tradition on both sides of a question and then offered a resolution on the issue. The common use of Gratian's text was a major factor in the development of administrative unity in the Western Church. Because it emphasized the role of the pope as the church's supreme legislator and judge, the text went a long way toward implementing Gregory VII's vision of papal authority, with the Roman curia as its administrative arm. Gratian cites the legal maxim, "The pope can be judged by no one," though he also includes the eleventh-century qualification, "unless he [the pope] is caught deviating from the faith."[33] In their commentaries on this last point, the Decretists (commentators on the *Decretum*) laid the foundations for fourteenth-century conciliarist thought on the corporate association of members of the church and their authority in the absence of an effective head.[34]

Two other features in Gratian's collection had a long-standing influence: the emphasis on two types of Christians in the church, clergy and laity, leading to an understanding of church "composed

---

[32] Christopher M. Bellitto, *Renewing Christianity: A History of Church Reform from Day One to Vatican II* (New York: Paulist Press, 2001), 48.

[33] Francis Oakley, *The Conciliarist Tradition: Constitutionalism in the Catholic Church 1300–1870* (Oxford: Oxford University Press, 2003), 108.

[34] Francis Oakley, *The Western Church in the Later Middle Ages* (Ithaca, NY: Cornell University Press, 1979), 164.

essentially of unequals"[35] and the development of a sacramental jurisprudence in which baptism, for example, was seen less as a sacramental act uniting one to Christ and more as a juridical act giving one rights and responsibilities in the church.[36] Canon law also played a major role in the conversion of proprietary churches into the beginnings of what would be territorial parishes as the fundamental unit of pastoral care, one of the medieval church's greatest achievements. Gratian's collection, and others like it, also performed the invaluable service of preserving in the church's corporate memory diverse traditions on a given topic, which might suggest alternatives to what became the accepted practice regarding the selection of bishops, for example, or the place of synods in the church. This service was partially offset by a neglect of the historical context from which the texts came. Less than a hundred years later, Bernard of Clairvaux (d. 1153), the saintly and very respected Cistercian abbot, was very critical of the developing imperial ways of the papacy, noting that the pope seemed more a successor of Constantine than a successor of Peter, and the Roman curia more concerned with the laws of Justinian than with those of the Lord.[37] The hierarchical structure of the church seemed to be engaged in an "intentional mimicry" of the secular system, the Petrine-hierarchical element reflecting the Constantinian-Carolingian hierarchy.[38]

Yet there were counterpoints. A letter from Peter Damian explained why a hermit, praying the monastic office alone, should not omit the greeting, "The Lord be with you [plural]" and the response, "And with your spirit." The words should be used, Peter wrote, because "the Church of Christ is so joined together by the bond of love that in many it is one, and in each it is mystically complete. Thus we at once observe that the whole Church is rightly called the one and only

---

[35] James H. Provost and others, *The Code of Canon Law: A Text and Commentary* (New York: Paulist Press, 1985), 140.

[36] Richard P. McBrien, *Catholicism*, rev. ed. (New York: HarperSanFrancisco, 1994), 622.

[37] Congar, *L'Eglise*, 127.

[38] Hans Urs von Balthasar, *Razing the Bastions: On the Church in This Age*, trans. Brian McNeil (San Francisco: Ignatius Press, 1993), 38. German original published in 1952.

bride of Christ, and we believe each individual soul, by the mystery of baptism, to be the Whole Church."[39] The letter—really a treatise— has been called "one of the most important ecclesiological works among all the theological literature of the middle ages."[40]

The Eucharist and the Church

The medieval understanding of church was also affected by debates concerning Christ's presence in the Eucharist.[41] Prior to the eleventh century, the church was referred to as the "true body of Christ" (*corpus Christi verum*), based on the teaching of St. Paul, while the consecrated body of the Lord in the Eucharist was called the "mystical body of Christ" (*corpus Christi mysticum*), *mysticum* understood more as the divine action bringing this about than the consecrated host itself. In the early centuries, those (especially bishops) who presided over the church, the (true) body of Christ, presided also at the celebration of the Eucharist by which the church expressed itself and was nourished. When medieval authors in the ninth and in the eleventh centuries so emphasized the sign aspect of the consecrated elements that they appeared to minimize or deny the actual presence of Christ, others countered by stressing Christ's *real* presence in the sacrament. The consecrated elements of the Eucharist came then to be called the "true" body of Christ, while the church was called the "mystical" body of Christ, in the sense that the identity of the elect, those who will ultimately be saved, is known only to God.[42] By the thirteenth

---

[39] Letter 28.11 in *Peter Damian: Letters 1–30*, trans. Owen J. Blum, The Fathers of the Church: Medieval Continuation, ed. Thomas P. Halton (Washington, DC: The Catholic University of America Press, 1989), 262.

[40] G. Miccoli, cited in *Peter Damian: Letters 1–30*, 255n1. See Henri de Lubac, *Catholicism: Christ and the Common Destiny of Man*, trans. Lancelot C. Sheppard and Elizabeth Englund (San Francisco: Ignatius Press, 1988), 315.

[41] The basic work on this topic is that of Henri de Lubac, *Corpus Mysticum: The Eucharist and the Church in the Middle Ages; Historical Survey*, trans. Gemma Simmonds, ed. Laurence Paul Hemming and Susan Frank Parsons (Notre Dame, IN: University of Notre Dame Press, 2006). The translation is that of the 2nd ed., 1949.

[42] Andrew Louth, *Greek East and Latin West: The Church AD 681–1071* (Crestwood, NY: St Vladimir's Seminary Press, 2007), 147.

century, "the mystical body" was used as a proper term, analogous to "holy church," *without* implicit reference to the Eucharist.[43] Gradually the presence of Christ was not so much seen in the ecclesial body of Christ, especially at worship, but in the consecrated elements in the Eucharist. Joseph Ratzinger noted that the gradual "separation of the doctrine of the eucharist and ecclesiology . . . from the 11th and 12th centuries onward, represents one of the most unfortunate pages of medieval theology (meritorious in so many other questions) because both thereby lost their center. A doctrine of the eucharist that is not related to the community of the Church misses its essence as does an ecclesiology that is not conceived with the eucharist as its center."[44] In the aftermath of these debates, the "eucharistic ecclesiology" so characteristic of the patristic period gradually fell "into general oblivion" in the West; the term "mystical body" would continue to be used, though in terms of analogy with a human body or a human society rather than with reference to the Eucharist.[45]

Correlative to this development, as priestly ordination was seen as receiving "power" to consecrate the Eucharist, episcopal consecration was regarded as not pertaining to the sacrament of orders but rather conferring juridical power to govern the mystical body of Christ, the church.[46] (When presiding at Eucharist, the bishop was regarded as functioning by virtue of his priestly ordination.) These distinctions between sacrament and jurisdiction and between liturgy and administration are further indications of the increasing impact of juridical thinking regarding the church. In the process, the church was increasingly understood as "a juridical instrument, a complex of laws, ordinances, [and] claims" to the detriment of "the essential identity of Church and liturgical assembly, of Church and *communio*."[47]

---

[43] Congar, *L'Eglise*, 168–69.
[44] Joseph Ratzinger., "The Pastoral Implications of Episcopal Collegiality," in *Concilium*, Dogma vol. 1: *The Church and Mankind* (Glen Rock, NJ: Paulist Press, 1965), 59.
[45] Walter Kasper, "Church as *Communio*," *Communio* 13 (1986): 107, and de Lubac, *Corpus Mysticum*, 114–17.
[46] Ratzinger, "Pastoral Implications," 58.
[47] Ratzinger, *Principles of Catholic Theology*, 255.

198   *The Church*

Twelfth-Century Reflections on the Church

Alongside the juridical considerations regarding the church, the twelfth and thirteenth centuries reveal a richness of theological reflection that is also an important part of our story. In glosses (marginal notes) and commentaries (heavy with patristic citations), medieval writers gave a special place to the Psalter, Job, and the Song of Songs in their considerations on the church.[48] The Psalms had a privileged role in that they were the only part of Scripture spoken or chanted by the entire community or by a choir representing the community. The Song of Songs also had an honored place in medieval reflection.[49] Following Augustine's emphasis on the basic role of *caritas*, love, in the life of the church, medieval theologians saw the bride in the Song as an especially apt image of the church, more suitable than others to convey the idea of the mutual love uniting Christ and his church. Medieval exegesis followed Origen in his allegorical interpretation of the work. The high point of medieval examples of this tradition is found in the eighty-six sermons on the Song of Songs by Bernard of Clairvaux.[50] The sermons are really a series of treatises on various issues facing the twelfth-century church. When Bernard reflected on the Song, he saw in the figure of the bride an allegory of both the individual soul and the church. The two are interrelated; both receive the love of Christ the bridegroom. The church is a community of believers united in that love and with that love reaching out to the needs of others as it makes its way to union with God. Bernard and many fellow Cistercians promoted this mystical understanding as a way of renewing the church. Two centuries later Dante's *Paradiso*, cantos 10–14, would use bridal images to describe the Church Militant and the Church Triumphant.[51]

---

[48] James R. Ginther, "The Church in Medieval Theology," in *The Routledge Companion to the Christian Church*, ed. Gerard Mannion and Lewis S. Mudge (New York: Routledge, 2008), 54–56.

[49] Paola Nasti, "*Caritas* and Ecclesiology in Dante's Heaven of the Sun," in *Dante's* Commedia: *Theology as Poetry*, ed. Vittorio Montemaggi and Matthew Treherne (Notre Dame, IN: University of Notre Dame Press, 2010), 216–17.

[50] Jean Leclercq's introduction in *Bernard of Clairvaux: Selected Works*, trans. G. R. Evans, Classics of Western Spirituality (New York: Paulist Press, 1987), 9–10, 21–22, and 45–54.

[51] Paola Nasti, "*Caritas* and Ecclesiology," 210–44.

Medieval Understandings of Church 199

The visions of the Rhineland mystic Hildegard of Bingen (d. 1179) portray the heart of the divine plan from creation to the end of time in the mysterious marriage of God and humankind. The incarnation and the cross are central to this view. Pope Benedict summarizes her vision on the church as bride of Christ and mother of the faithful: "On the tree of the Cross take place the nuptials of the Son of God with the Church, his bride filled with grace and ability to give new children to God, in the love of the Holy Spirit."[52] Through this union of Christ and the church, the baptized become "co-creators" with the incarnate Son in bringing about the unity of all reality in Christ and its participation in the trinitarian life of love.[53]

Alongside the patristic-monastic theology of Bernard and the symbolic theology of Hildegard, a new mode of theological reflection was developing in the cathedral schools and later in the universities: scholasticism, or the method of the schools.[54] With variations, its basic pattern consisted of stating a thesis (*quaestio*), followed by arguments for or against (*disputatio*), leading to a conclusion (*sententia*). Dialecticians who engaged in this approach aimed to see theology as a "science" alongside other disciplines, with its own method and structures. While early practitioners of the new method did not intend to separate theology from its spiritual goals, the use of the new method contributed to such a separation as its use became more widespread.

---

[52] Pope Benedict XVI, *Great Christian Thinkers: From the Early Church through the Middle Ages* (Minneapolis: Fortress Press, 2011), 229. See Hildegard of Bingen, *Scivias*, trans. Columba Hart and Jane Bishop, Classics of Western Spirituality, ed. Bernard McGinn (New York: Paulist Press, 1990), 169–74.

[53] Renate Craine, *Hildegard of Bingen: Prophet of the Cosmic Christ*, Crossroad Spiritual Legacy Series (New York: Crossroad Publishing Co., 1997), chaps. 7 and 8.

[54] I am indebted to Frederick Parrella of Santa Clara University for alerting me to the significance of this shift in methodology and its effects on the theology of the church: *Catholic Ecclesiology: An Historical Sketch* (class notes, December 1999), 63–67. See John W. O'Malley, *Four Cultures of the West* (Cambridge, MA: Belknap Press of Harvard University Press, 2004), chap. 2; Yves M.-J. Congar, *A History of Theology*, trans. and ed. Hunter Guthrie (Garden City, NY: Doubleday, 1968), 85–122; and Pope Benedict XVI, *Church Fathers and Teachers: From Saint Leo the Great to Peter Lombard* (San Francisco: Ignatius Press, 2010), chaps. 27 and 28.

Hugh of St. Victor (d. 1142) of the abbey school of St. Victor in Paris anticipates to some extent early scholastic reflection on the church, though both Hugh and the abbey school had strong reservations about the use of the dialectical method.[55] Hugh continued the monastic tradition in considering the church through typological reflection on biblical images, underscoring their implications for the Christian life. The church is a sacramental mystery, "a means of relating to and of manifesting the fullness of Christ."[56] Hugh respected the social, historical reality of the church and spoke of the church as the body of Christ in both its invisible and visible aspects, an integrated approach not always followed by theologians after him.

Peter Lombard (d. 1160), teacher at the cathedral school in Paris for nearly twenty years, popularized the scholastic method and influenced thirteenth-century theology of the church. His four *Books of the Sentences* gave no formal treatment of the church, nor do the hundreds of commentaries on his work.[57] Considerations on the church are interspersed in Lombard's reflection on grace and the sacraments. Christ is head of the church; possessing the fullness of grace, he is the source of grace for everyone in the church, seen as his body. This emphasis underlined the role of Christ in the church, though it sidelined the dynamic role of the Spirit. The church also figured in his contribution to scholastic reflection on the twofold reality of the Eucharist: one reality, the body of Christ born of Mary and the blood of Christ shed for us, is both signified and contained in the sacrament; the other reality, the unity of the church, is signified but not contained. So we see the link between the body of Christ in the Eucharist and the ecclesial body of Christ was not entirely lost from view. Benedictine theologian William of St. Thiery (d. 1148), abbot of the monastery in the Diocese of Rheims, continued the Augustinian tradition:

---

[55] Congar, *L'Eglise*, 159–61; Eric G. Jay, *The Church: Its Changing Image through Twenty Centuries*, vol. 1: *The First Seventeen Centuries* (London: SPCK, 1977), 115; Philip Timko, "Medieval Ecclesiology: From Body of Christ to Hierarchical Institution," *Chicago Studies* 49, no. 2 (Summer 2010): 204–6.

[56] Timko, "Medieval Ecclesiology," 205.

[57] Jaroslav Pelikan, *Reformation of Church and Dogma (1300–1700)*, vol. 4 of *The Christian Tradition: A History of the Development of Doctrine* (Chicago: University of Chicago Press, 1984), 71.

"Eating the Body of Christ is nothing else but becoming the Body of Christ."[58]

Scholastic reflection on the sacraments also influenced the understanding of church.[59] Twelfth-century scholastics viewed orders largely in terms of personally possessed sacramental power to consecrate the Eucharist rather than service in and for the community as the body of Christ, though this was offset in practice by confession, preaching, and the beginnings of catechetical instruction. As attention focused on the sacramental power conferred at ordination, the earlier notion that one was ordained to an order of priests or bishops was lost from view. Each of these emphases constituted a shift from the patristic and Augustinian view of the church. The church was increasingly seen as "a hierarchical and sacramental structure of mediation for the [lay] faithful."[60] Yves Congar represents this as a shift from a focus on two terms, (1) God/Christ and (2) the church (understood as the body of the faithful in which church ministers are organically a part, serving the faithful in their communion with God), to three terms, (1) God, (2) the church, seen as a structure of mediation, and (3) the people.[61] Gradually, the theme of church would become a separate treatise standing on its own, apart from treatises on Christ, grace, or sacraments.

Theology of the Church in Stone and Glass: Gothic Cathedrals

Another expression of church is also seen in the stone and glass of the Gothic cathedrals built in France and Germany, in England, in Scandinavia, in parts of Christian Spain, and, in the late medieval period, in areas of northern Italy.[62] In twelfth- and thirteenth-century France, some eighty cathedrals, five hundred larger churches, and

---

[58] Cited in Ratzinger, "Pastoral Implications," 59.
[59] Congar, *L'Eglise*, 169–74.
[60] Timko, "Medieval Ecclesiology," 209.
[61] Yves Congar, "L'ecclésiologie de S. Bernard," in *Saint Bernard théologien*, Analecta Sacri Ordinis Cisterciensis 9 (1953): 179.
[62] Seasoltz, *A Sense of the Sacred*, 136–42. See also Robert Barron, *Heaven in Stone and Glass: Experiencing the Spirituality of the Great Cathedrals* (New York: Crossroad, 2000), and Benedict XVI, *Church Fathers and Teachers*, chap. 30.

thousands of smaller churches were built in the Gothic style.[63] Entering a Gothic cathedral reminded people that, in the midst of their ordinary daily lives, they had access to the realm of the divine. The light from the windows and the awesome height of the walls and the ceiling above, all made possible by the new techniques of Gothic architecture, spoke of the transcendent world to which the church and the cathedral building gave access. If, as seems possible, the word "nave," for the body of the building, comes from the Latin *navis*, ship or boat, believers could see the church as the ship in which Christ carried them to safe shores. The many cathedrals named after Our Lady, symbol and mother of the church, may have suggested that, as Mary's womb gave birth to Christ, the church is the womb that gives the life of Christ to believers. The cruciform shape of the cathedral proclaimed that Christ and the cross are at the center of everything in the church. The figures on the stained glass and the sculptures along the walls recalled the holy men and women of the Old Testament and the place they have in the "church from the time of Abel." At the same time, figures chiseled in the walls of not a few cathedrals also mockingly portray Israel as a blindfolded woman, the synagogue, unable to see the light of Christ or accept his coming, an unfortunate aspect of the ecclesial self-image of the medieval period. Representations of the saints of the New Testament celebrated the union between them and the believers in the cathedral and reminded believers of their roots in the apostolic period. Within the church, the placing of altar, choir, and nave expressed a view of the church in which each person had a precise place in the ordered whole and through which a person related to God, creator, judge, and savior. Places of worship and instruction, these churches were also very much a part of the lives of those who lived near them and were treated with an easy familiarity. During times of unrest, they provided shelter, a refuge where one might bring one's livestock and household belongings. For the masses of the people there was no separation

---

[63] Roland H. Bainton, *Christendom: A Short History of Christianity and Its Impact on Western Civilization*, vol. 1: *From the Birth of Christ to the Reformation* (New York: Harper and Row, 1964), 195.

between the sacred and the profane, between the understanding of church and ordinary life.

Thirteenth-Century Theologies of the Church

Commentaries on the liturgy, a genre born in the Carolingian period, are another indication of thinking about the church. The genre reached a high point in the *Explanation of the Divine Liturgy* of William Durandus (c. 1230–1296), the bishop of Mende in southern France.[64] The first chapter of the book, published in final form between 1294 and 1296 and destined to become one of the most widely read works of the late Middle Ages, was really a treatise on the church. The work as a whole argues that "the Church is most truly itself in worship."[65] Durandus's exposition, using the type of spiritual exegesis often applied to the Scriptures, "moves without seam from the material building to the moral meaning of the church for the human person, to the allegorical meaning of the church as Christ, and to eschatological meaning of the church as the elect in heaven."[66] The analysis reflects the thinking of the first millennium. The four walls of the church building and the lime in the cement holding the walls together are a symbol of the church's unity; the altar and sanctuary, identified with the holy of holies of the Old Testament, the church's holiness; a church's roundness and its dome, any removal from which endangers the whole, suggests the church's catholicity, its presence throughout the world; the church's apostolicity is symbolized by the steps to the altar, symbol of Christ.[67] The importance of the work is twofold: it provided a means of passing on some of the patristic understandings of church and it shows the need to nuance the view that only in the early fourteenth century did there appear the first treatises on the church. Often these later treatises are more accurately seen as political tracts dealing with papal claims. The bishop of Mende also wrote

---

[64] Stephen Mark Holmes, "Reading the Church: William Durandus and a New Approach to the History of Ecclesiology," *Ecclesiology* 7, no. 1 (2011): 29–49.
[65] Ibid., 37.
[66] Ibid., 41.
[67] Ibid., 43–44.

juridical works in which he upholds a strong papal authority. The *Explanation* makes no mention of the papacy, reflecting as it does the earlier tradition.

Interest in returning to the ideals of the early church that inspired eleventh-century reform efforts continued to appeal to others in the twelfth and thirteenth centuries, among them the "Poor Men of Lyons," followers of Peter Waldo (later: Waldensians) and the Cathari (from the Greek for "pure") or the Albigenses, so called because of their strong presence near Albi and Toulouse in southern France.[68] The Cathari were dualists who sought to restore what they understood to be the purity of the early church. Because they rejected the Old Testament teaching on the goodness of creation, they rejected marriage and the use of anything material in church worship, including the Mass and the sacraments, and any temporal possessions belonging to the church. They vigorously opposed the notion of canon law, the authority of an ordained priesthood, and even special buildings for worship. Through their affinity with other evangelical renewal movements of the period, the appeal of their austere lives, and their opposition to wealth and laxity in the church, the Cathari attracted a wide following. By the end of the twelfth century, their views on the gospel life and the church posed a serious challenge.

Only slowly did church officials respond to Cathrai views, largely through conciliar condemnations and professions of faith. Three elements of the theological response are of interest.[69] First, the Cathari claim to be the true church and to embody the apostolic life occasioned reflection on what constituted the church and the meaning of its apostolicity. In the face of variant views on this matter, the apostolic life and the teaching of the church became closely linked to the apostolicity of its ministers. Second, the desire to preach, especially on the part of the "Poor Men of Lyons," led to an emphasis on the link between preaching and canonical mission and the need for a teaching authority in the church, even if an understanding of the latter was not fully elaborated. Third, responses to these reform

---

[68] Jean Comby, *How to Read Church History*, vol. 1: *From the Beginnings to the Fifteenth Century* (New York: Crossroad, 1985), 161–64, and Jay, *Church*, 1:123–25.

[69] Congar, *L'Eglise*, 205–9.

Medieval Understandings of Church   205

groups led to greater theological attention to the visible elements and the place of the sacraments in the life of the church. Regrettably, critical responses to these itinerant preachers did not make more of their genuinely religious concerns.

Francis of Assisi (1181/82–1226) and his earliest followers were the most prominent among the twelfth- and thirteenth-century reform movements among the poor, though Francis remained devoted to the church and had a deep respect for its judicial and sacramental life.[70] Francis and his companions were laymen who called themselves friars (from Latin *fratres*, "brothers"). They took their inspiration from the itinerant Jesus, who depended on the support of others in his ministry. Francis sought to minister to the poor of the new towns and cities. In 1210 Francis sought and received approval for himself and his followers from Pope Innocent III, who, by having them tonsured, made them clerics in the church, thus authorized to preach. The poor friar and the most powerful pope in history are portrayed in the famous thirteenth-century fresco attributed to Giotto (d. 1337), *The Vision of Innocent III*, in the Basilica of Saint Francis in Assisi.[71] The painting expresses an important truth about the church. Innocent III represents the continuity of the church without which there would be no Gospel and no Francis of Assisi; but the church needs always to be upheld and renewed by Christ, represented in the friar later known as "the second Christ."

Spanish-born Dominic de Guzman (c. 1172–1221) also sought to combine a simple, ascetic life with an apostolic ministry to others. In 1214 or 1215, with the blessing of the bishop of Toulouse, Dominic and his companions established a community of itinerant preachers in the manner of the apostles to work among the Cathari. He adopted a mendicant life less as a spiritual value in itself than as a means of getting a hearing among the Cathari and giving witness to an austere life within the church, so an alternative to condemnations and

---

[70] Lawrence S. Cunningham, *Francis of Assisi: Performing the Gospel Life* (Grand Rapids, MI: Eerdmans, 2004), 48–63.

[71] Jaroslav Pelikan, *The Illustrated Jesus through the Centuries* (New Haven, CT: Yale University Press, 1997), 153–55, and Benedict XVI, *Great Christian Thinkers*, 240–41.

persecutions in dealing with the errant sect. Because of their preaching mission, Dominic urged his followers, the Order of Preachers, to study theology and to become experts in church doctrine. A hundred years later, Dante saw the hand of Providence in sending mendicants Francis and Dominic to renew the church's love for her divine spouse.[72]

A valuable summary of practical ecclesiology in the West in the early years of the thirteenth century comes to us in the Fourth Lateran Council of 1215, the principal event of the pontificate of Innocent III (1198–1216) and the most important of the medieval councils.[73] Innocent called the council to foster church reform, to combat heresies, and to promote a crusade to the Holy Land. The first decree's stress on the visibility of the church was meant to combat the Cathars; another decree (the twenty-first) mandating annual confession of sins and communicating at Easter "probably did more to strengthen the adherence of Church members in the regular practice of their faith than any other canonical regulation of the Middle Ages."[74] This latter decree is also credited with being one element among others (e.g., the preaching of the mendicant friars) in promoting the idea that Christian perfection is not limited to spiritual elites.[75] The council also indicates the ways in which church leadership regarded Eastern Christians and Jews. Two statements concern Greek Christians. "On the Pride of the Greeks towards Latins" expresses the Latin church's desire to cherish the Greeks who return to the obedience of the "Apostolic See" and promises to respect Greek customs and rites, though it faults the Greeks for the antagonism between the two churches and makes no allusion to the sack of Constantinople only eleven years earlier. A statement on the dignity of the patriarchs

---

[72] *Paradiso*, Canto 11.28–36.

[73] Norman P. Tanner, *The Councils of the Church: A Short History* (New York: Crossroad, 2001), 52–64, and Norman P. Tanner, ed., *Decrees of the Ecumenical Councils*, vol. 1: *Nicaea I to Lateran V* (Washington, DC: Georgetown University Press, 1990), 230–71.

[74] William J. La Due, *The Chair of Saint Peter: A History of the Papacy* (Maryknoll, NY: Orbis Books, 1999), 123.

[75] Charles Taylor, *Dilemmas and Connections: Selected Essays* (Cambridge, MA: Belknap Press of Harvard University Press, 2011), 215.

asserts the ordinary power of the Church of Rome, the "mother and mistress of all Christ's faithful" over all other churches; it recognizes the ranking of the traditional Pentarchy, though the patriarchs are to take an oath of fidelity and obedience to the pope. Eastern Christians would have positively regarded the call for annual councils and synods. Four of the last five decrees of Lateran IV focus on the Jews and do so in a hostile tone. For almost a hundred years, papal policy was basically "a call to protect Jews even while disparaging Judaism."[76] That this policy was repeated sixteen times in the twelfth and thirteenth centuries suggests that the call to protect Jews was far from being observed.

The two most prominent theologians of the thirteenth century were Bonaventure (ca. 1217–1274), a Franciscan, and the Dominican Thomas Aquinas (ca. 1224–1274). Bonaventure[77] stands in the Augustinian tradition in his approach to theology: the goal of theology is to bring us to a loving union with God. We see this in his *The Journey of the Mind into God*, written after weeks of solitude on Mount Alverna where, having become minister general of the Franciscans, Bonaventure sought to enter more deeply into the spiritual world of the order's founder. (It was at Alverna that Francis had the vision of the six-winged Seraph in the form of the crucified Lord.) Written some years later, Bonaventure's *Lectures on the Hexaëmeron* (an allegorical interpretation of the six days of creation) outlined his theology of history and the place of the church in that history, the most significant attempt at such in the scholastic period.[78] The lectures sought to respond to the writings of the biblical exegete and mystic, Joachim of Fiore (ca. 1135–1202). The embrace of the latter's teachings by certain Franciscans was threatening to split the Order. Joachim proposed a trinitarian conception of history: the age of the Father was the age of the Law and of the married state; the age of the Son, the

---

[76] Mary C. Boys, *Has God Only One Blessing? Judaism as a Source of Christian Self-Understanding* (New York: Paulist Press, 2000), 59.

[77] Benedict XVI, *Great Christian Thinkers*, 257–68.

[78] Bernard McGinn, "The Significance of Bonaventure's Theology of History," *Journal of Religion* 58 (1978) Supplement: *Celebrating the Medieval Heritage: A Colloquy on the Thought of Aquinas and Bonaventure*, ed. David Tracy, S78.

age of the church and of the clerics; and the age of the Spirit, the age of the monks or contemplatives. Joachim stopped short of assigning a date for the third period, but some of his prophesies spoke of the dissolution of the sacraments and of the institutional aspects of the church in the final period. Some Franciscans, insisting that the final age had dawned with Francis of Assisi, would have the gospels and the institutions of the church abolished in this Joachimite age of the Spirit.

Bonaventure's response, drawing on Augustine, ideas from Joachim, and elements of medieval apocalyptic, took up the traditional idea, rooted in Augustine, that the mystical body of Christ had a life extending over six ages from Adam to the end of time.[79] The Franciscan general was convinced that the times in which he lived belonged to the end of the sixth age of the church and the dawning of the seventh age, marked by a period of crisis, then of Sabbath peace. This would be followed by the eighth age, that of eternity. He rejected both Joachim's schema regarding the three phases of history and the idea of the Spiritual Franciscans (those who opposed any modification of the Franciscan rule) who saw in Francis the beginning of a new church of the Spirit replacing the Gospel and the existing sacraments. Yet Bonaventure did see in Francis the figure of the apocalyptic angel (Rev 7:2-8) whose seal would mark the 144,000 from every tribe of Israel, symbol of the final people of God.[80] In a contemplative form of life realized earlier in Francis, this community would enjoy already in this world the peace of the seventh age, which would precede the Parousia of the Lord and the dawn of eternity. Bonaventure did not identify this people with the Order of Franciscans of his day but saw the Franciscan and Dominican Orders at the inauguration of a new period that would come one day by the power of God. When the final time came, it would be a time of contemplation, marked by the full understanding of Scripture, a time of the Holy Spirit leading to the fullness of truth in Christ. Against Joachim, Bonaventure saw Jesus as God's final word,

---

[79] See Joseph Ratzinger, *The Theology of History in St. Bonaventure*, trans. Zachary Hayes (Chicago: Franciscan Herald Press, 1971 and 1979), chap. 1.
[80] Ibid., 54–55.

though he recognized progress in understanding that word. The example of Christ's life in Francis relates to his seeing Christ as the *center* of all history, an innovation since the fathers of the church and most of his contemporaries saw Christ as the *end* of history. This allows Bonaventure to teach "the need for overall, even strict discernment, sober realism, and openness to the newness that Christ gives his Church through the Holy Spirit."[81] In the Franciscan general's view, Christian wisdom is "unthinkable and unintelligible without reference to the historical situation in which it has its place."[82] The apocalyptic and the generally optimistic elements in his theology of history are lacking in Augustine's *City of God*, though both theologians are one in their conviction "that the Church which hopes for peace in the future is, nonetheless, obliged to love in the present; and . . . that the kingdom of eternal peace is growing in the hearts of those who fulfill Christ's law of love in their own age."[83]

Not only did he reject the anti-institutional aspects of the Joachimite vision, Bonaventure was the thirteenth century's principal theorist of a papal monarchy.[84] He drew on Bernard of Clairvaux and the legal pronouncements of Gregory VII, giving the latter a metaphysical aura by reading them in light of Denys the Areopagite. Bonaventure describes the three dimensions of the power the See of Rome received from Christ: it alone has the plenitude of authority; its authority extends to all the churches; and it is the source of all authority held by others in the church, much as the glory of all the saints has its one source in Christ. Bonaventure uses the notion of participation to reason that as only through Christ does the church exist in its life of grace, so only through the vicar of Christ does the church exist in its canonical and social life.

Like Bonaventure, Thomas Aquinas saw theology's final purpose in promoting our union with God. Unlike Bonaventure, Thomas boldly drew on the pre-Christian philosophy of Aristotle and in his expository writings used the scholastic method mentioned above.

---

[81] Pope Benedict XVI, *Great Christian Thinkers*, 263.
[82] Ratzinger, *The Theology of History in St. Bonaventure*, 6.
[83] Ibid., 163.
[84] Congar, *L'Eglise*, 222.

Thomas has no specific treatise on the church; his thought on the topic appears in his masterworks, the apologetic *Summa contra Gentiles* (E.T.: *On the Truth of the Catholic Faith*) and the *Summa Theologiae* (*Summary or Compendium of Theology*), as well as in his commentaries on the *Sentences* of Peter Lombard and on the Scriptures. Dominican scholar Marie-Dominique Chenu summarizes Thomas's study of the church: "As with Bonaventure, Thomas's reflection on the Church both as institution and sacrament is developed within his theology of Christ and of the incarnation. The Church is the body of Christ, animated (given life) by the Spirit. Its organs are the apostolic institutions of various members under the leadership of the sovereign pontiff. At one and the same time, the Church is a body, a corporation in the sociological sense of the word, and the very mystery of Christ mystically and sacramentally extended in time and place."[85] Thomas also reflects the gradual distancing of church and Eucharist mentioned above; his analogy of the church as a mystical body is drawn from natural bodies rather than from the sacramental Body of Christ.[86] His emphasis on Christ as Head of the church and the grace of Christ as "grace of the Head" signals a change from earlier eucharistic views of the church, though he also sees the Eucharist as making us one in Christ.[87] The church is set within the schema of humanity's return to God (*Summa Theologiae*, part 2) in which the Spirit is the principal agent.[88]

In a short work, *Exposition on the [Apostles'] Creed*, Thomas comments on the four notes or properties of the church. The church is one because she is grounded in a single faith, hope, and love. She is holy because she is washed in the blood of Christ, anointed by the

---

[85] Marie-Dominique Chenu, *Aquinas and His Role in Theology*, trans. Paul Philibert, (Collegeville, MN: Liturgical Press, 2002), 71.

[86] De Lubac, *Corpus Mysticum*, 112–13.

[87] Michael Schmaus, *Dogma 4: The Church; Its Origin and Structure*, trans. Mary Lederer (New York: Sheed and Ward, 1972), 72–73.

[88] Yves Congar, "The Idea of the Church in St. Thomas Aquinas," in *The Mystery of the Church*, trans. A. V. Littledale (Baltimore: Helicon Press, 1960), 97–117, at 103. See also Avery Dulles, "The Church According to Thomas Aquinas," in *A Church to Believe In: Discipleships and the Dynamics of Freedom* (New York: Crossroad, 1982), chap. 10.

grace of the Holy Spirit, and because the Trinity dwells in her. She is catholic in her geographical diffusion, in her embrace of all peoples, and because she is universal in time, from Abel to the end of the world, after which she will endure in heaven. And she is indestructibly firm or, in the term used in the creed, apostolic because Christ is her principal foundation, the apostles and their doctrine a second foundation.[89] With Bonaventure, Aquinas was also an "architect" of the "new papalist ecclesiology" of the period, though Thomas took a more moderate line than did the Franciscan.[90] It may be that both were influenced by mendicant dependency on papal authority in university disputes with the secular clergy. Thomas defends the value of a single authority for both diocese and universal church, a reflection of the medieval idea that monarchy best imitates God's rule over the universe. But citing Aristotle's suggestion that a monarchy combined with elements of aristocracy and democracy would be a still better form of government and drawing on texts from Exodus and Deuteronomy, Thomas argues that God actually provided a mixed form of government for Israel by giving Moses a type of regal authority, making of the seventy-two elders an aristocracy, and providing a democratic element in elders selected from the people by the people.[91] Thomas never directly applied this latter line of thinking to the church, though the appropriateness of such a form of government would be advocated in the fourteenth and fifteenth centuries.

Twelfth- and thirteenth-century reflection and practice reveal an interesting note concerning the church's teaching authority or magisterium (from Latin *magister*, "master" or "teacher").[92] Thomas distinguished between the "magisterium of the pastors" or prelates based on a canonical mission, and the "magisterium of the teachers" based on recognized academic competency. In the latter part of the thirteenth century, the *studium* (the schools) had a recognized place

---

[89] Congar, "Idea of the Church in St. Thomas Aquinas," 99–100.
[90] Dulles, "The Church According to Thomas Aquinas," 161–63.
[91] Brian Tierney, "Church Law and Alternative Structures: A Medieval Perspective," in *Governance, Accountability, and the Future of the Catholic Church*, ed. Francis Oakley and Bruce Russett (New York: Continuum, 2004), 57–59.
[92] Dulles, *Church to Believe In*, 109–11 and chap. 11.

alongside the *sacerdotium* (the priests) and the *imperium* (civil leadership). The doctrinal decrees of the First and Second Council of Lyons (1245 and 1274, respectively) and the Council of Vienne (1311–1312) were submitted to the universities for vetting before official publication.

Fourteenth- and Fifteenth-Century Treatises on the Church

Friction between a papacy intent on preserving the prestige and authority it had under Innocent III and the ambitions of the rulers of the emerging nation-states of England, France, and Germany occasioned, in the early fourteenth century, new rounds of writings on the church and authority in the church. A first clash came when the kings of France and England attempted to tax their clergy without prior papal permission. In 1296, Boniface VIII (1294–1303) issued the papal bull *Clericis laicos* (from Latin *bulla*, the "lead seal" stamping the document) denying national sovereignty over church personnel or church goods. The bull opens with the famous introduction: "Antiquity shows us that the laity has always been exceeding [*sic*] hostile to the clergy; and this the experience of the present time clearly demonstrates, since, not content with their limitations, the laity . . . do not prudently observe that all control over the clergy, as well as over all ecclesiastical persons and their possessions is denied them."[93] When Philip IV (Philip the Fair), king of France (r. 1285–1314), expelled foreign clergy from France and cut off papal income, the pope capitulated. A second flare-up came when the same king accused a bishop of treason, so challenging both papal authority and the medieval alliance between throne and altar operative since the time of Charlemagne. After a war of words, Boniface issued another bull, *Unam Sanctam* (the first words of the bull), asserting that a lack of commitment to Peter and his successors is tantamount to admitting that one is not of Christ's flock and that earthly power is to be judged by spiritual power and spiritual power judged by God.[94] The bull

---

[93] Barry, *Readings in Church History*, 464.
[94] Ibid., 465–67.

contains nothing new in its claim for papal sovereignty, though its bold style is remarkable.

The conflict between the king and the pope occasioned what are often called the "first treatises" on the church, largely canonical tracts on the rights and privileges of the pope rather than comprehensive studies on the church's nature and mission.[95] They were written at a time when the speculative-spiritual synthesis characteristic of theological writing in the patristic period and in the writings of Bonaventure and Thomas was being divided into separate treatments on either the doctrines of the faith or spiritual theology. Three examples illustrate the types of issues being discussed. In 1301 or 1302, before the publication of *Unam Sanctam*, James of Viterbo, an Augustinian friar and archbishop of Naples (d. 1307/8), wrote what is often regarded as the first of these treatises: *De regimine christiano* (On Christian Government).[96] The work explains that "in our own time, and not without a reasonable cause, it is appropriate for the teachers of sacred doctrine to speak especially about" the doctrine concerning the Church.[97] Much of the work centers on the role of the pope in the church and in secular society, though it is the first to give extensive treatment of the four notes of the church: one, holy, catholic, and apostolic.

About the same time as James of Viterbo's work, another Augustinian monk, Giles of Rome (d. 1316), issued *De ecclesiastica potestate* (*On Ecclesiastical Power*), sometimes referred to as *De Summi Pontificis potestate* (*On the Power of the Supreme Pontiff*). The work, possibly used by Boniface VIII in his *Unam Sanctam*, gives a dominantly christological and hierarchical view of the church.[98] Giles stoutly defended the thesis of a papal theocracy and saw in it the fulfillment of the Augustinian city of God. The pope so represented the church that the word "church" could simply refer to him. One is not under Christ's rule if one does not submit to the pope, the universal vicar of Christ. Giles

---

[95] Congar lists thirty-two such treatises; see *L'Eglise*, 270–71.
[96] Congar, *L'Eglise*, 273–75.
[97] Cited by Pelikan, *Reformation and Church Dogma*, 71.
[98] Congar, *L'Eglise*, 272–73; Brian Tierney, *The Crisis of Church and State* (Englewood Cliffs, NJ: Prentice-Hall, Inc., 1964), 193–95.

allows for the existence of natural rights and lay power, though these are brought to perfection by the church, its sacraments, and its priesthood. The church is catholic in its universal dominion over all.

Dominican friar John of Paris or Jean Quidort (d. 1306) took an opposite tack: he focused on the entire body of the faithful in his reflections and supported the autonomy of the temporal order.[99] His *On Royal and Papal Power*, written about a year after the two works just mentioned, is moderate in tone.[100] The work is considered the ablest of those who opposed the thesis of a papal theocracy; it argued for constitutional restraints for both the royal and papal power.[101] John challenged the theory that all authority was entrusted to the church, which then granted temporal authority to the state, though he recognized the primacy of spiritual power when conflict arose between the two. John of Paris contributed to settling, at the end of the Middle Ages, the three abiding principles regarding church and state: the recognition of two authorities (Gelasius), the freedom of the church (Gregory VII), and the primacy of the spiritual.[102]

John's communitarian understanding of the church drew on Aristotelian thought on the social character of human existence. Ecclesial authority came from God, as did all legitimate authority, but God placed the selection of those who were to bear authority in the body of the faithful, to whom the leadership was responsible. The authority of a bishop or a pope is mediated through the church's election and consecration. John also taught that the faith of the church cannot be defined without a general council and hinted at the superior authority of a council over that of the pope. Rather than being above the church, the pope is its most important (*supremum*) member; his power

---

[99] Congar, *L'Eglise*, 283–85; Paul Avis, *Beyond the Reformation? Authority, Primacy and Unity in the Conciliar Tradition* (New York: T&T Clark, 2006), 43–47; Brian Tierney, *Foundations of the Conciliar Theory: The Contribution of the Medieval Canonists from Gratian to the Great Schism* (Cambridge: Cambridge University Press, 1955; reprinted, 1968), 157–78; Tierney, *Crisis*, 196–200.

[100] John of Paris, *On Royal and Papal Power*, trans. J. A. Watt (Toronto: Pontifical Institute of Medieval Studies, 1971).

[101] Tierney, *Crisis*, 197–98.

[102] J. Bryan Hehir, "Church and State," in *The HarperCollins Encyclopedia of Catholicism*, ed. Richard P. McBrien (New York: Harper Collins, 1995), 315.

is that of a bishop, given to him to serve the unity of the universal church. John opposed the idea of a papal monarchy and used the example of Moses and the elders to support the idea of a mixed government in the church. His work marks a turning point: until the end of the thirteenth century, attention was often focused on relations between spiritual and temporal authority; henceforth, increasing attention would be given to authority within the church.[103]

Another round of writings was occasioned by continuing tensions between the papacy and increasingly independent secular powers and by the papal residence in Avignon (1309–1377), both set in the tumultuous fourteenth century.[104] An important feature of these writings was the increasing use of the apostolic ideal of the primitive church as a criterion for viewing the church and looking for its reform. Appeals were made to the simplicity of life shared by Christ and the apostles, their lack of possessions and temporal authority and what was perceived as the absence of hierarchical ordering.[105] This was exemplified in the work of Marsilius of Padua (d. 1342), one-time rector of the University of Paris.[106] The second part of his *Defensor Pacis* (*The Defender of the Peace*, 1324) held that the church is the totality of the faithful who believe and invoke the name of Christ. Priest and bishop are basically equal; each ministers without any jurisdiction or power to coerce. The supreme authority in the church is a council called by the emperor and composed of bishops, priests, and lay faithful, so representing the entire body of believers. Its chief function is to clarify ambiguous passages of the Scriptures that alone are normative. Councils were to be responsible also for setting up dioceses, canonizing saints, or establishing and dispensing from church discipline, all matters heretofore reserved to papal authority. Papal primacy, in his view, was a purely human invention, without biblical support, and the biggest impediment to peace and unity in

---

[103] Tierney, *Foundations*, 178.

[104] Justo L. González, *The Story of Christianity*, vol. 1: *The Early Church to the Dawn of the Reformation*, rev. ed. (New York: HarperOne, 2010), chap. 33.

[105] Gordon Leff, "The Apostolic Ideal in Later Medieval Ecclesiology," *Journal of Theological Studies* 18 (1967): 58–82.

[106] Congar, *L'Eglise*, 287–90; Avis, *Beyond the Reformation?*, 50–54.

Christian society. The "defender of the peace" is the emperor; he alone has jurisdiction; the church and the pope are subordinate to him. Condemned three years after its publication, *Defensor Pacis* was one of the most famous writings of the fourteenth century; its ideas would surface in fifteenth-century debates, in the thought of some of the reformers, and in later writers who would make the church totally subordinate to the state.

The understanding of church in the work of English Franciscan philosopher, theologian, and polemicist William of Ockham (d. 1347) was guided in large part by his opposition to the Avignonese pope John XXII (pope 1316–1334), who condemned as heretical the idea of the Spiritual Franciscans that Christ and the apostles owned no property.[107] In so doing, Ockham thought the pope himself became a heretic, so bringing to the fore a case previously considered only hypothetically by medieval canonists. Ockham's *On the Authority of Emperors and Popes* accepts the divine origin of the papal monarchy, but only as a constitutional power, a ministry to serve the common good. The church itself is the congregation of all the faithful, faith being the constitutive note of the church, a faith held without error, so contrasted to the pope who did err. The Franciscan's writings show little interest in the relation between the community of believers and Christ or the Spirit; the church is more a social reality, the multitude of individual believers. Ockham's philosophical stress on the distinctiveness of each individual subject and his Franciscan evangelism led him to accord a central place to the freedom given by the Gospel, the first time a theological writer of note applied such a theme to the church.[108] Where the medieval world stressed natures, institutions, and laws, Ockham introduced an emphasis on persons and on freedom in the faith. The ultimate authority for the believer is the Word of God present in the Scriptures. Ockham's views on the institutional aspects of the church would influence many of the anti-papal writings of the fourteenth and fifteenth centuries and some of the reformers of the sixteenth century.

John Wyclif (ca. 1330–1384), Oxford priest, philosopher, and theologian, also challenged accepted thinking on the church. His writings,

---

[107] Congar, *L'Eglise*, 291–95; Avis, *Beyond the Reformation?*, 54–58.
[108] Congar, *L'Eglise*, 294.

though not always consistent, are set in the context of his view that the church of his day had undergone a serious decline from the practice of apostolic poverty and simplicity.[109] Wyclif's *De Ecclesia* (*On the Church*, 1378) uses the medieval language of "holy mother church" as the body and spouse of Christ and speaks of the three parts of the church: triumphant (in heaven), dormant (purgatory), and militant (on earth). His central idea, though, is shaped by his adopting in extreme form Augustinian ideas of predestination and the irresistibility of grace so that the church is the invisible body of the elect. Where the church in the fifth and sixth centuries subordinated Augustine's anti-Pelagian teaching on grace to his anti-Donatist teaching on the church, so allowing for the presence of sinners in the church on earth, Wyclif "went a long way toward subordinating his doctrine of the church to his doctrine of grace."[110] In this schema, there is little import attached to the visible, institutional church or to its sacramental ministries, in effect minimizing the mediatory role of the visible church in the unfolding of God's saving plan. Wyclif sees little theological connection between the mystical church known only to God and the visible church involving pope, bishops, and priests. The church might well have a papal leader—a human convention, in his view—but one whose authority depended solely on his embrace of apostolic simplicity. Clerical jurisdiction was contingent on virtuous living, hinting at and possibly being recognized at the time as a form of neo-Donatism. Wyclif accepted the idea that the visible church of a given territory would be supported and regulated by local lords or princes. In his work *On the Truth of Sacred Scripture*, he argued for the Bible's role as sole source of Christian teaching and practice, though he allowed that the meaning of the text may at times require a study of the church fathers. Wyclif's ideas influenced others in England, notably the so-called Lollards—a derogatory term—who produced the first entirely vernacular translation of the Bible. As we shall see below, Wyclif's ideas had an even greater influence in Bohemia.

---

[109] Congar, *L'Eglise*, 299–302; Avis, *Beyond the Reformation?*, 59–67; Madigan, *Medieval Christianity*, 387–95.
[110] Oakley, *The Western Church in the Later Middle Ages*, 206–8, at 208.

A contemporary of Wyclif, Dominican tertiary Catherine of Siena (1347–1380) expressed her thoughts about church in her many letters and in her *Dialogue*, written in the final years of her life. Drawing on her mystical experiences and influenced by her image of Christ as the bridge to God, she saw the church in the light of this basic image, as the bridge, identified with Christ, offered to humankind after Christ's ascension. While recognizing the important roles given to church ministers—though faulting bishops who ordained incompetent clergy and clerics who lived in luxury or engaged in ambitious career seeking—she recognized the light given by all the baptized to others also making their way on the same church bridge. Catherine distinguished three groups within the church: the clergy, in a restricted sense the "mystical body" because of their ministry of the sacraments; the "universal body" of all the baptized faithful and virtually all of humankind; and, between them, members of the religious orders, belonging to the charismatic character of the church, and "servants of God," those from any state of life tasked with praying and working for the salvation of the world and the renewal of the church.[111]

Conciliar Thought and the Understanding of the Church

Though Pope Gregory XI returned from Avignon to Rome in 1377, opposition to his successor led the cardinals to elect a second pope who returned to the papal fief in southern France. So began the Great Western Schism (1378–1417), a pope with his cardinals and curia in Rome and another with the same in Avignon.[112] Nations took sides in their allegiance, as did religious orders and universities. Attempts to settle the matter by force or by securing mutual resignations came to nothing. Early on, theologians at the University of Paris, mindful of earlier medieval councils and invoking both the principle that "what affects all should be approved by all" and Aristotle's principle

---

[111] Giuliana Cavallini, *Catherine of Siena* (London: Geoffrey Chapman, 1998), 89–107, and Giacinto D'Urso, *Catherine of Siena: Doctor of the Church*, trans. with intro. Thomas McDermott (Chicago: New Priory Press, 2013), 39–42.

[112] For historical background, see Norman Tanner, *The Church in the Later Middle Ages* (London: I. B. Tauris, 2008), chap. 1. See also Oakley, *Conciliarist Tradition*, chaps. 1 and 2; Avis, *Beyond the Reformation?*, chap. 6.

of *epieikeia* (equity) in the application of law in unforeseen circumstances, proposed that only a council could end the schism. Henry of Langenstein, theologian at the University of Paris, articulated the basic tenet of what became known as the conciliar theory: "The universal Church, of which a General Council is representative, is superior to the college of cardinals and to every other particular grouping [*congregatio*] of the faithful and to every single person of whatever dignity, even to the holder of the highest dignity or precedence, the lord pope."[113] In 1409, a council met in Pisa in northern Italy; it deposed the two existing claimants and elected a new pope, Alexander V. As the other two claimants refused to secede, there were now three popes. Pressure continued for another council to end the schism and promote reform in the church. Behind calls for a council lay thinking that had been developing since the late fourteenth century, with roots going back at least a century before that.

In the background of this development was the question of how to understand the unity of the church.[114] On the one hand there was the dominant high-papalist position, which saw the key to unity in the subordination of all the members of the church to a single papal head with universal jurisdiction. This position had been supported by mendicant theologians in their debates with the secular masters at the University of Paris in the mid-thirteenth century. Another theory, applied at first to an individual church, then at the beginning of the fourteenth century to the Roman Church and the church as a whole, saw the basis of unity in the corporate association of the church's members. This second theory figured in earlier canonical speculation regarding the possibility of a heretical pope but came to be seen as having a direct bearing on the situation of the schism and so became an element in conciliar thinking in the late fourteenth century. With variations that shifted with changing circumstances, mainline conciliar thought sought to uphold belief in a divinely instituted papal headship of the church while affirming the biblical and

---

[113] Henry of Langenstein, "A Letter on Behalf of a Council of Peace" (1381), in *Advocates of Reform: From Wyclif to Erasmus*, ed. Matthew Spinka (Philadelphia: Westminster Press, 1953), 118.

[114] Oakley, *The Conciliarist Tradition*, 65–81.

patristic understanding in which Christians form a single body with Christ and to give a communitarian or corporate dimension a "more permanent and routine institutional expression."[115]

In his study of the conciliar tradition, historian Francis Oakley identifies three broad strands, distinct in origin and to some extent in subsequent history, that during this period combined into a coherent pattern.[116] The first and oldest strand, concerned with reform of the church "in head and members," looked to periodic councils acting in concert with their papal head as the necessary and effective means for that reform. This view had roots in thirteenth-century reactions to increasing Roman centralization; it was the schism that united conciliar theory with calls for church-wide reform. This strand, we shall see, was reflected in the decrees of the Council of Constance (1414–1418). With variations, the major figures of the conciliar tradition embraced this view. A second, less prominent strand looked to the cardinals as exercising a quasi-oligarchic role in the governance of the church, so giving institutional expression to the church's corporate nature. Given the cardinals' role in precipitating the schism, this view did not attract much support in the early years of the schism, but in time it won a more favorable reception. The distinguished Italian canonist Francesco Zabarella was a strong advocate of this position. He held, for example, that the expression "apostolic see" referred to the pope and cardinals who together form a single body whose head was the pope and whose members were the cardinals. A third strand and one that endured in one way or another in the centuries to follow was "the strict conciliar theory."[117] The many formulations of this strand, reflecting different political, diplomatic, and ecclesiastical circumstances, had in common the view that the pope, though holding a divinely constituted office, was a constitutional ruler having a ministerial authority delegated to him by the community of the faithful (the *congregatio fidelium*) for the good of the whole church. The church in turn could exercise its power through

---

[115] Ibid., 65.
[116] Ibid., 66–81.
[117] Ibid., 71–76.

its representatives assembled in a general council and, in certain cases, even against the wishes of the pope.

Arguments in support of the conciliar view were drawn from the Scriptures—Matthew 18:20, for example, telling of Jesus' presence where two or three are gathered in his name—and from the fathers of the church who, like Leo I, affirmed that "he who is to preside over all is to be chosen by all" or from Innocent III's use of the Roman legal maxim: "For what affects all must consistently be dealt with by all or by representatives of all."[118] Much was made of the synodal and conciliar traditions of the early church and of the important role of synods in the reform movements of the preceding centuries. Monastic traditions and contemporary "corporate" models of self-government in medieval cities, the guilds, universities, and in some of the new religious orders, also provided precedent. Democratic and representative theses inspired by the *Politics* of Aristotle were applied to the church by John of Paris or used in speculation concerning the role of cardinals. The breadth of this background is significant; conciliar theory was not invented simply to deal with the schism; its background attests to a long conciliar tradition in the church.

In November 1414, under pressure from the German "king of the Romans," a council of almost nine hundred participants gathered at Constance in southern Germany. The council opened with three goals: to end the schism and restore church unity; to deal with the writings of John Wyclif in England and Jan Hus in Bohemia (on whom, more presently); and to reform the church "in head and members." Influenced by Pierre D'Ailly and Jean Gerson, both of the University of Paris, and Francesco Zabarella—all of whom took a moderate position—the council passed three decrees representing basic conciliar thought.[119] The first, *Haec Sancta* (*Sacrosancta* in some manuscripts; April 6, 1415),

---

[118] Cited in Brian Tierney, "Roots of Western Constitutionalism in the Church's Own Tradition: The Significance of the Council of Constance," in *We, the People of God: A Study of Constitutional Government for the Church*, ed. James A. Coriden (Huntington, IN: Our Sunday Visitor, 1968), 117, and Avis, *Beyond the Reformation?*, 74.

[119] On the three named, see Avis, *Beyond the Reformation?*, 77–82, 84–87, and Oakley, *The Conciliarist Tradition*, 76–81.

asserted the council's legitimacy as an assembly gathered in the Spirit and called for everyone in the church, including the pope, to submit to the council to bring an end to the schism and to reform the church of God in head and members.[120] The second and third paragraphs of the decree move to the principle of the superiority of a general council over the pope. The second decree, *Frequens* (October 9, 1417), called for regularly held general councils, always including the pope, to promote reform and growth in the church and to weave into its ongoing life a structure of governance complementary to that of the pope.[121] A third text, on the same date, was an oath for future popes to bind themselves to the previous ecumenical councils and the medieval general councils, to ensure "the constitutional checks on the papacy that the council envisioned."[122] Though Constance is generally recognized as an ecumenical council in the Western church, the binding value of the three decrees has been much debated, given the singular circumstances in which the decrees were issued. Scholars today hold that good reasons support seeing these decrees as authentic acts of a legitimate council.[123] In 1417, a conclave elected a new pope, Martin V (d. 1431), and the schism was brought to an end.

In addition to condemning the teachings and writings of Wyclif, the council also dealt with teachings and writings of Jan Hus (ca. 1372–1415), from the Bohemian village of Husinek, who was seen as propagating the teachings of the English theologian. The latter's epistemological writings introduced him as a bold thinker to Czech professors in the 1390s. Wyclif's theological ideas, brought to Bohemia in the early fifteenth century by students returning home from studies in Oxford, received a ready acceptance in a reform movement already well underway in Prague. Czech reformers, concerned with both church reform and Bohemian nationalist aspirations, were

---

[120] Text in Tanner, *Councils of the Church*, 66.
[121] Ibid., 67.
[122] Ibid., 67–68.
[123] Ibid., 69–71. Tanner recognizes that *Haec sancta* stands in tension with the decrees of Vatican I. "But it is more correct to leave the various statements alongside each other, in a certain healthy tension, than to seek a consistency that does not exist." It may be for the church to work through this at a later time. See also Oakley, *The Conciliarist Tradition*, 81–99.

Medieval Understandings of Church 223

attracted by Wyclif's stress on a Christianity renewed on the model of the apostolic age and his ideas about a territorial church supported and regulated by local lords. In the early years of the fifteenth century, leadership of these reform efforts increasingly fell to Hus, elected in 1402 to the important preaching post at the Bethlehem Chapel in Prague and, in 1409–1410, named rector of the University of Prague.[124] While not doing so indiscriminately, Hus drew from Wyclif in his preaching and writing. Hus spoke against the corruption of the clergy and the simoniacal practices of the popes and advocated the restoration of the chalice to the laity and the use of the vernacular in worship. The abiding ideal of Hus's call for reform was a church "without a spot or wrinkle."[125] As opposition to Wyclif's writings and to himself increased, Hus adopted more radical views regarding both reform and the very understanding of church.[126]

Hus wrote his *De ecclesia* (*On the Church*) after his excommunications in 1411 and 1412. Much like Wyclif before him, he distinguished two meanings of the term "church." The first, the "most essential sense according to Augustine,"[127] is the church of the predestined known only to God, present in the one church, in heaven, on earth, and in purgatory. This church, of which Christ alone is the head, is universal and definitive, the body and spouse of Christ, to be gathered together by Christ at the last day. A second meaning refers to the church militant, the church on earth, having within it both the predestined and the "foreknown," those who will not persevere in grace and who will be separated from the former on the Day of Judgment. Hus invoked the biblical parables of the field with the wheat and the weeds (Matt 13:24-30) and of the net catching fish both good and bad (Matt 13:47). It is church in this second sense in which the pope and the cardinals have a role, though only if they live well can

---

[124] Madigan, *Medieval Christianity*, 395–402.

[125] Matthew Spinka, *John Hus' Concept of the Church* (Princeton, NJ: Princeton University Press, 1966), 256.

[126] Congar, *L'Eglise*, 302–3; Avis, *Beyond Reformation?*, 59–61, 67–70; Spinka, *John Hus' Concept of the Church*, chap. 8.

[127] From Hus's own defense at the Council of Constance, cited in Matthew Spinka, *John Hus at the Council of Constance* (New York: Columbia University Press, 1965), 260.

they hope to be part of the holy catholic church, the bride of Christ. The pope is head only of the visible church, not of the universal church of the predestined as Hus distinguishes the two. The Church of Rome is one particular church among others living under the rule of their own bishops. Only when the pope imitates the virtues of Peter's humility and poverty is he his vicar; only then can he make a claim of primacy (of honor) or exercise true authority. As the papal schism wore on, Hus concluded that the final authority in the church is the Bible, though he allowed a place for the early church fathers; to the Bible all owe obedience and by it all Christians are judged.

Hus was attracted to Wyclif's criticism of excessive wealth and his emphasis on predestination, though he did not accept Wyclif's teaching about the Eucharist or his arguments that the sacramental acts of priest or bishop in sin were invalid. Hus accepted the church-state relationship proposed by Wyclif as well as his denial of the divine institution of the papacy. With a promise of safe conduct, the emperor invited Hus to the Council of Constance to present his views, though he was placed under arrest not long after he arrived. Of the thirty charges against him, all of which Hus insisted were erroneously formulated, twenty-five concerned the church, twelve of that number concerning the papacy.[128] His judges saw traces of Wyclif in all of them. Hus refused to recant them, insisting he never held them as they were presented. He was then burned at the stake on July 6, 1415.[129] Speaking of Wyclif or Hus as the "morning stars" of the Reformation is qualified in current scholarship. Both Wyclif and Hus stressed the authority of the Bible and sought to restore Christianity to its earlier form, but neither promoted the doctrine on justification or "Scripture alone" as they were understood by the sixteenth-century reformers.[130] Wyclif and Hus did deal with issues that would be taken

---

[128] The charges, with Hus's comments, are published in ibid., 260–64.

[129] In 1999, Pope John Paul II expressed "deep regret for the cruel death inflicted on Jan Hus." Cited in Christopher M. Bellitto, *The General Councils: A History of the Twenty-One Councils from Nicaea to Vatican II* (New York: Paulist Press, 2002), 87.

[130] Madigan, *Medieval Christianity*, 401–2.

up by both Catholic and Protestant reflection on the church in the centuries that followed.

In keeping with the prescriptions of *Frequens*, another council was set for Basel, in northern Switzerland, in 1431.[131] Relations between the council and Martin's successor, Eugenius IV (1431–1447), were antagonistic and soon after its opening the pope dissolved the council, though he was pressured to rescind his decision and recognize the conciliar declarations issued during his absence. The early years at Basel were chiefly given to a restatement and hardening of the decrees of Constance, attempting to make the decrees drawn in the midst of the schism the doctrine of the church. In 1437, Eugenius, with a minority of the participants, moved the council to the Italian city of Ferrara, where it held its first session in 1438, with a later move to Florence. The pope did this both to assert his authority and to accommodate the Byzantine emperor and Eastern church representatives willing to explore the possibility of reunion with the church of the West in hopes of obtaining Western aid to ward off advances of the Ottoman Turks. A decree of reunion, containing the first conciliar definition of the Roman primacy, with "full power of tending, ruling and governing the whole church," was signed in July 1439,[132] though it was soon rejected by the Orthodox populace at large. The decree's strong statement on papal primacy in many ways signaled the end of the radical conciliarists, represented in the later years by the increasingly discredited Council of Basel.[133] Conciliar thought has continued in various forms even to the present, as we shall see.[134] We shall have a further word on the Council of Florence presently.

Elements of conciliar thought appeared in one way or another in the works of two notable fifteenth-century authors. The German theologian and canonist Nicholas of Cusa (Cusanus) (1401–1464) did not write a treatise specifically on the church, but his *De Concordantia Catholica* (On Catholic Concordance), written in the early years of the

---

[131] Joseph F. Kelly, *The Ecumenical Councils of the Catholic Church* (Collegeville, MN: Liturgical Press, 2009), 113–19.

[132] Text in Tanner, *Decrees of the Ecumenical Councils*, 1:523–28, at 528.

[133] Avis, *Beyond the Reformation*, chap. 8.

[134] Ibid., chaps. 9–13. See also Oakley, *Conciliarist Tradition*, chaps. 3–6.

council of Basel, at which he was a leader of the conciliarists, offers a vision for the reform of both the church and the empire.[135] In Cusanus's view, the church is Christ's mystical body and spouse, composed of angels and human beings, continuing Christ's saving mission. Its model is the triune God in its unity of persons, whose life the church lives. Cusanus's work seeks to address the apparent contradiction between the theory of conciliar supremacy (Council of Constance) and the many enunciations of papal supremacy in the church. The harmony (*concordantia*) in the triune God and in the created universe (Dionysius the Areopagite) are invoked to support Cusanus's conviction that an intermediate position (*medium concordantiae*) can be found. From the Scriptures and the writings of holy fathers, it "finally comes to this, that the power of the Roman pontiff as to preeminence, priority, and rulership, is from God by way of man and the councils; namely by elective consent."[136] The supreme law of the church is *concordantia*, harmony or unanimity, which resides in the one and the many, a favorite theme in Cusanus's philosophical reflections. He holds in tension notions of sacred hierarchy found in Denys the Areopagite with Aristotelian ideas of participation and consent. Both papal and conciliar authority depend on consent, not in the sense of a democratic populism but seen as "the harmonious acceptance of God's will as revealed by the Holy Spirit."[137] The notion of a world harmony was characteristic of medieval thought, but Cusanus's work is said to be "the first system of thought to make 'catholic concordance' a theme that ran through the life of the church, the unfolding of human history, the structure of the universe, and the very nature of God. The church's own existence was dependent on 'concordance.'"[138]

In 1437, as the Council of Basel became more radical and in his desire to promote potential union with the East, Nicholas of Cusa

---

[135] Nicholas of Cusa, *The Catholic Concordance*, ed. and trans. Paul E. Sigmund (Cambridge: Cambridge University Press, 1991). See Congar, *L'Eglise*, 330–34, 336–37; Avis, *Beyond the Reformation?*, 92–96; and Pelikan, *Reformation and Church Dogma*, 98–110.

[136] Cusa, *Catholic Concordance*, book 2, para. 249.

[137] Avis, *Beyond the Reformation?*, 94.

[138] Pelikan, *Reformation of Church and Dogma*, 98–99.

left Basel and gave his support to the pope. Yet Cusanus maintained his basic stance in another work in 1440, *On the Supremacy of General Councils in Church and Empire*. Here, he held that "all the other apostles were similarly foundation stones of the church" and "equal in authority with Peter" and recalled that "at the beginning of the Church there was only one general episcopate, diffused throughout the whole world."[139]

On the opposite side of the debate was the influential *Summa de ecclesia*, published posthumously in 1489, of the Spanish Dominican Juan de Torquemada (d. 1468).[140] The four books of the *Summa* deal with the nature of the church, its structures of government, especially the pope and the council, and with schism and heresy. Torquemada strongly defended papal primacy and sought to discredit conciliar thought by associating it with Ockham and Marsilius of Padua, though he retained the idea that the council was "the Church's last refuge in all her great needs."[141] In his view the college of cardinals succeeded the apostolic college and, as part of the pope's very body (*pars corporis Papae*), shared in the exercise of his supreme authority.[142] Typical of the theology of the schools of the time, he uses the four causes in his theological reflection. The principal efficient cause of the church is Christ; the sacraments are the instrumental efficient cause; the material cause is the faithful; the final cause is participation in the glory of God; the formal cause (that which makes the church what it is) is unity with Christ by faith. Torquemada incorporates ideas from the work of Aquinas but puts far more emphasis on the church's visible, external features. He gives prominence to the church as the congregation of the faithful but sees church unity in terms of a "rigorous subordination of all the members to a single head." This contrasts with the stress on "the corporate association of the members

---

[139] Text in Barry, *Readings in Church History*, 506–10, at 507.

[140] Congar, *L'Eglise*, 340–44; Jay, *Church*, 1:139–41; Bernard P. Prusak, *The Church Unfinished: Ecclesiology Through the Centuries* (New York: Paulist Press, 2004), 239–41. See also Roger Haight, *Historical Ecclesiology*, vol. 1 of *Christian Community in History* (New York: Continuum, 2004), 390–94.

[141] Cited in Hubert Jedin, *A History of the Council of Trent*, vol. 1: *The Struggle for the Council*, trans. Dom Ernest Graf (St. Louis: B. Herder Book Co., 1957), 29.

[142] Ibid.

of a Church as the true principle of ecclesiastical unity" that found expression in D'Ailly, Gerson, and Nicholas of Cusa.[143] Torquemada's work would have a strong influence on later Western theology of the church. As with many of the writings of the conciliar period, he made constitutional questions, earlier the preserve of the canonists, fundamental to his reflection on the church.[144]

The Church in the East

During roughly the same time frame as that of this chapter, the church in the East experienced great changes: the Arab conquests in the eighth century; the Christianization of the Kievan Rus in the late tenth century; the fourth crusade's sack of Constantinople in 1204 with its disastrous consequences for relations with the West; the overcoming of Kievan Russia by the Mongols in 1237; the failed efforts at reunion with the West at the Second Council of Lyons (1274) and the Council of Florence; the fall of Constantinople to Muslim Turks in the fifteenth century (1453), followed by the increasing prominence of the Russian Orthodox Church.[145] While differences in the East and in the West regarding the church had been developing for centuries, events in the thirteenth to fifteenth centuries sharpened those differences so that on the eve of modern times, the East and West had two quite different visions of the church.[146]

In the middle of the fourteenth century, during the Avignon papacy in the West, the Eastern church in Russia was beginning what would be a two-hundred-year golden age in spirituality, missionary zeal, and religious art. The most prominent leader in this revival was a monk, Sergius of Radonezh (c. 1314–1392). The Monastery of the Holy Trinity he helped to found in the forests north of Moscow spearheaded

---

[143] Tierney, *Foundations*, 240, and Oakley, *Western Church*, 164.
[144] Congar, *L'Eglise*, 337.
[145] MacCulloch, *Christianity*, chaps. 14 and 15. See also Tanner, *Church in the Later Middle Ages*, chap. 6.
[146] John Meyendorff, "Two Visions of the Church: East and West on the Eve of Modern Times," in *Christian Spirituality: High Middle Ages and Reformation*, ed. Jill Raitt, in collaboration with Bernard McGinn and John Meyendorff (New York: Crossroad, 1987), chap. 10.

Medieval Understandings of Church 229

a monastic revival in late medieval Russia. Sergius encouraged resistance to the Mongol Tartars (defeated by the Russians in the Battle of Kulikovo, 1380), encouraged close collaboration between church and state, and strove to maintain a balance between the spiritual and social in monastic life.

Roughly contemporary with these developments in Russia, Eastern Christians in Greece were engaged in debate over the nature of mystical prayer and its relationship to the liturgy and sacraments of the church. The roots of the debate lay in two centuries-old trends in Eastern mystical theology.[147] One trend, the apophatic (Greek for "negative") tradition, stressed the utter transcendence and incomprehensibility of God, though not to the exclusion of union with God through prayer. In the second trend, thirteenth-century hesychasts (from Greek *hesychia*, "quietude" or "silence") linked "prayer of the heart," stripped of images and discursive thinking, with certain physical techniques (breathing, bodily posture), with a view to experiencing the Divine Light as the disciples did at the transfiguration. A major figure in this tradition, Simeon the "New Theologian" (d. ca. 1022), intimately associated theology, mysticism, and the church and its sacraments. Presupposed in Simeon's mystical theology was his understanding the church as the body of Christ. Even more important than monastic profession was "spiritual regeneration through divine baptism" by which all could be "partakers of the divine nature."[148]

The Greek-Italian philosopher, Barlaam of Calabria (d. 1348), denounced what he thought was the grossly materialist form of prayer of the hesychasts.[149] At one point in the debate, Barlaam's

---

[147] Timothy Ware, *The Orthodox Church*, new ed. (London: Penguin Books, 1997), 62–70; Jaroslav Pelikan, *The Spirit of Eastern Christendom (600–1700)*, vol. 2 of *The Christian Tradition: A History of the Development of Doctrine* (Chicago: University of Chicago Press, 1974), 254–70; and Aristeides Papadakis in collaboration with John Meyendorff, *The Christian East and the Rise of the Papacy: The Church AD 1071–1453*, vol. 4 of *The Church in History* (Crestwood, NY: St Vladimir's Seminary Press, 1994), chap. 7.

[148] From Simeon's writings, cited by Pelikan, *Spirit of Eastern Christendom*, 256.

[149] See John Meyendorff's introduction in Gregory Palamas, *The Triads*, trans. Nicholas Gendle (New York: Paulist Press, 1983), 1–22.

"Against the Messalians" accused the hesychasts of holding the condemned Messalian doctrine that, in prayer, one could contemplate the very essence of God with material eyes. Gregory of Palamas (d. 1359), in his early years a monk on Mount Athos and later (1347) archbishop of Thessalonica, responded to Barlaam and defended the hesychast position. Palamas argued that the whole person, body and soul, can be engaged in prayer and, importantly, that the goal of the hesychast monks, deification (*theosis*) in Christ, is integral to Christian faith and is offered to all the baptized. Palamas distinguished the unknowable essence of God from the deifying divine energies that enable the baptized to enter into communion with the Unknowable. Local councils in Constantinople confirmed Gregory's teaching. A follower of Palamas, the lay theologian Nicholas Cabasilas (fl. 1345–1365), helped solidify the Orthodox conviction that mystical life always preserves its links with the sacraments and the institutional life of the church. His *Life in Jesus Christ* is really a treatise on the sacraments, underscoring his support of a mysticism that is Christocentric, sacramental, and ecclesial.[150] Western theologians had no part in this debate, a reflection of the growing distance between Christians of the East and those of the West. Western theology had its own agenda to deal with and used a scholastic method and categories of thought foreign to the Eastern mind. Eastern Christians sought to remain faithful to the tradition of the fathers even if, as in the case of Palamas, there was development and greater systematization.

The Council of Ferrara–Florence: Two Understandings of Church

No one event marks what has come to be called the schism between the Eastern and Western parts of the Christian church. Over the centuries, many factors—political, cultural, and theological—led to an increasing sense of estrangement, aggravated by mistrust and ignorance, between Latins and Greeks.[151] In Congar's view, it was the mutual acceptance of this estrangement, symbolically so at the end

---

[150] Ware, *The Orthodox Church*, 70.

[151] Yves Congar, *After Nine Hundred Years: The Background of the Schism between the Eastern and Western Churches* (New York: Fordham University Press, 1959).

Medieval Understandings of Church   231

of the eleventh century in the West, that constitutes the schism.[152] Efforts to heal that schism were a major concern of the Council of Ferrara–Florence in 1438 and 1439.[153] The Greeks and the Latins who assembled at Ferrara–Florence wanted union, though they were not united on what that union might mean. For the Latins, union meant submission to the authority of Rome; for the Greeks, it meant accepting the authentic faith preserved in the East and recognizing the authority vested in the Pentarchy regarding affairs of the church. It is also true that other agendas were at play. Uppermost in the mind of Pope Eugenius was his desire irrevocably to check the conciliarists at Basel. The emperor's desire for union was inseparable from his hope for Western military aid against the advancing Turks. The final statement of the definition regarding the papacy, "that the Roman pontiff holds the primacy over the whole world" and that to him has been "committed in blessed Peter the full power of tending, ruling and governing the whole church,"[154] is a strong endorsement of the Western view of the pope's position in the church. The Latins wanted it said that this power was grounded "in the sacred Scripture and the words of the saints";[155] the Greeks insisted on "as is contained also in the acts of ecumenical councils and in the sacred canons." That statement, and another, not strictly a part of the solemn definition, that the historical ordering of the patriarchs (Rome first, then Constantinople, followed by Alexandria, Antioch, and Jerusalem) be renewed "without prejudice to all their privileges and rights," could be interpreted differently by either side. The council's statement about the pope is not situated in a general vision of church, nor is there any reference to the statement of Constance on the role of a council and its having its power immediately from Christ. (Only with Vatican II was the teaching about the pope placed in the context of the teaching about the church and the college of bishops in an ecumenical council, though without mention of Constance.) The Greeks accepted the

---

[152] Ibid., 76 and 89.
[153] A. Edward Siecienski, *The Filioque*, chap. 8, and *The Papacy and the Orthodox: Sources and History of a Debate* (Oxford: Oxford University Press, 2017), 328–36.
[154] Tanner, *Decrees of the Ecumenical Councils*, 1:528.
[155] Siecienski, *The Papacy and the Orthodox*, 334.

filioque as a licit addition to the creed but were not required to adopt it themselves. That Florence allowed the Latin use of unleavened bread and the Greek use of leavened bread is its sole affirmation of acceptable pluralism in the church.[156] With the notable exception of the metropolitan of Ephesus, the decree of union was affirmed, the pope and the emperor doing so each with his own reasons. At the pontifical Latin rite liturgy at which the decree was promulgated, not a single Greek accepted the consecrated host.

Though the council produced a decree of union signed by both parties, the council itself and its almost immediate rejection by the vast majority of Eastern Christians strongly supports the idea that by this time the two sides had come to have different visions of the church, each believing that its understanding was faithful to the will of Christ.[157] Both Greeks and Latins affirmed that the church was of Christ; that it was united by the Spirit and held a faith in the triune God and the incarnate Word; that God's life was communicated through the sacraments, especially baptism and Eucharist; and that the church was endowed with a hierarchical structure willed by God. Yet within this framework there were serious and, for some, ultimately insurmountable differences. For *some* Easterners at the council, the *filioque* in the Latin version of the creed remained a betrayal of the faith of the fathers. Acceptance of the addition of the term in the creed by bishops of Rome suggested to Eastern minds that the pope assumed that Petrine authority permitted modification of an ecumenical creed apart from a decision of a council, so totally at odds with Eastern understanding of authority in the church. There were also differences in the theological methods used for explaining or defending the faith: generally, the Latins approached questions philosophically and dialectically; the Greeks, biblically and in the style of the fathers. No longer was it the case, as it was in the patristic age,

---

[156] Giuseppe Alberigo, "The Unity of Christians," in *Christian Unity: The Council of Ferrara–Florence 1438/39–1989*, ed. Giuseppe Alberigo (Leuven, Belgium: University Press, 1991), 7–9.

[157] Gillian R. Evans, "The Council of Florence and the Problem of Ecclesial Identity," in Alberigo, *Christian Unity*, 177–85.

Medieval Understandings of Church 233

that "Latins and Greeks recognized each other as orthodox and equally authentic members of the same Church communion."[158]

Orthodox theologian John Meyendorff describes the two visions of church after Florence and the collapse of the empire after the fall of Constantinople in 1453: "Beyond the political and cultural clashes of the times, two perceptions of the church emerged: in the one, the church was a God-sanctioned custodian of order and truth, demanding obedience to a visible head; in the other, order and visible unity, which earlier had been sanctioned by the obviously fallible but practically useful power of the Christian emperors, now, with the collapse of the empire, were seen more as a communion within which sacramental order and doctrinal integrity could be secured, as in the early centuries of Christianity, only through a consensus involving both the episcopate and the people."[159]

These political and ecclesiastical events led some to adopt the ideology of Moscow as the "Third Rome," the first Rome having been overtaken, in this view, by heresies, the second Rome, Constantinople, having fallen to the Turks.[160] A further development, emerging in the Russian Church Council of 1503, has a bearing on the understanding of church. It came in a debate between two conflicting views regarding the church's liturgy and monastic life, and the relation of the church to the state.[161] One side was represented by the Russian monk and mystic Nil Sorsky (d. 1508), who spoke forcefully against monastic ownership of land when monasteries owned about a third of the land in Russia. Ownership, these "Non-Possessors" argued, compromised the duty of the monks to pray for and be an example to the wider church. This position drew a sharp line between church and state, arguing that the church on earth is always on pilgrimage and needs the prophetic and other-worldly witness that monastic poverty should provide. Adherents of this view also emphasized the inner

---

[158] Chadwick, *East and West: The Making of a Rift in the Church*, 266.

[159] Meyendorff, "Two Visions of the Church," 447–48.

[160] Emmanuel Lanne, "The Three Romes," in *The Holy Russian Church and Western Christianity*, ed. Giuseppe Alberigo and Oscar Beozzo with Georgy Zyablitsev (London: SCM Press, 1996), 15–18.

[161] Ware, *The Orthodox Church*, 104–7.

personal relationship between God and the soul in mystical prayer rather than in liturgical prayer. Atypical of Russian spirituality, they cautioned lest the beauty of art or music impede one's worship.

Abbot Joseph (d. 1515) of the important monastery of Volokalamsk articulated the view of the "Possessors." The abbot argued that monasteries had an obligation to care for the sick and poor, to offer hospitality, to teach, and to educate "learned monks" for office in the church. The Possessors supported the idea of Moscow as the Third Rome and held to a close alliance between the church and the state, even to invoking civil authority against heretics. They emphasized the beauty of the liturgy and the importance of corporate worship. When Non-Possessors reproached Tsar Basil III in 1525–1526 for unjustly divorcing his wife, he imprisoned their leaders and closed their hermitages. Eventually the Russian Church canonized both Joseph and Nil, but the suppression of Nil's disciples contributed to an imbalance in the development of the spiritual tradition of Russian Orthodoxy.

In the next chapter, we turn to understandings of church in what has come to be called Early Modern Catholicism.

CHAPTER EIGHT

The Reformation Era and Early Modern Catholicism (1500–1800)

The sixteenth and early seventeenth centuries have a special place in the story of the church's self-understanding. In the context of the Early Modern Age, the period in many ways set parameters that would last until the mid-twentieth century, as we shall see in this chapter and in the next two.[1] At the same time, developments in this period stand in relationship to the total history of attempts to express the nature and mission of the church. A quick summary of its more immediate antecedents might take its cue from the opening words of the famous statement of Boniface VIII in *Unam Sanctam* (1302), that we are obliged to believe and to hold that there is one, holy, catholic, and apostolic church.[2] The fourteenth and, especially, fifteenth centuries were peppered with studies of the church focusing on one or another of these four traditional marks (notes) of the church, some of which were mentioned in the preceding chapter.[3]

How are we to understand church unity in the face of schism between a papacy at Rome and another at Avignon? Of the separation of the church represented at the Council of Constance with the followers of Hus among the Czechs? Or of the division between East

---

[1] See John W. O'Malley, *Trent and All That: Renaming Catholicism in the Early Modern Era* (Cambridge, MA: Harvard University Press, 2000), 5, 8–9, 140–43.

[2] Brian Tierney, *The Crisis of Church and State, 1050–1300* (Englewood Cliffs, NJ: Prentice-Hall, 1964), 188.

[3] Jaroslav Pelikan, *Reformation of Church and Dogma (1300–1700)*, vol. 4 of *The Christian Tradition: A History of the Development of Doctrine* (Chicago: University of Chicago Press, 1984), 71–126. This next section will draw heavily on Pelikan's treatment.

and West? Unity was variously seen as dependent on the Holy Spirit, on union with the pope, or on a church gathered in council. How are we to understand unity and variety in the church? James of Viterbo distinguished between "unity," which excluded multiplicity, and "union," which allowed it, and so argued that the oneness of the church is more properly found in the latter. Reformer Jean Gerson, chancellor of the University of Paris, recognized that the church is one but is distinguished by "a multiple and beautiful variety," a work of the Spirit.[4] Champions of papal authority argued that the church's oneness depended on apostolic authority coming solely through Peter's mediation and that apart from Peter there was no grace or forgiveness of sins. Proponents of conciliar authority attributed the church's unity and life to the Spirit of Christ and invoked Augustine to say the power of the keys was given to the general council as representing the church's unity. The issue of the church's holiness was brought to the fore by scandals rising from the church divisions just mentioned. In his book *The Holy Church*, ardent Hussite Peter Chelčický related the church's holiness to seeing the church as the community of the predestined.[5] Ecclesial holiness was also the backdrop to calls for church reform, to the assertions of some who identified Christian perfection with apostolic poverty, and in discussions regarding the validity or efficacy of sacraments celebrated by priests in sin or involved in simoniacal ordinations. On this last issue, generally, though not universally, Augustine's teaching about Christ's acting in the sacraments carried the day. Debates in the sixteenth century and insistence on holiness in the church kept the issue in the fore.

The church's catholicity received prominent attention in the work of Nicholas of Cusa, as we saw in the last chapter. Drawing on the writings of Hincmar of Reims, Nicholas of Cusa defined catholicity as universality "through[out] the entire world" and "from the beginning of the world to its end,"[6] so eliminating from the church those in schism or heresy. Gerson saw the attribute of catholicity related to the sacrament of baptism, making the church "the universal

---

[4] Ibid., 79.
[5] Ibid., 85.
[6] Ibid., 99.

congregation of the faithful."⁷ Lutheran theologian Martin Chemnitz would argue that for a doctrine to be "catholic" it must be able to have the support of "either the word or the example of Christ and the apostles" as seen in the Scripture.⁸

Ultimately, understanding how the church is one, holy, or catholic was related to and dependent on how one understood the church's apostolicity, and that in turn centered on the nature and locus of authority in the church. In his treatise *In Defense of Apostolic Obedience* (1462), Gabriel Biel argued that even those who doubted the justice of a papal act were "obligated for their salvation to obey the apostolic see."⁹ With him, the Spanish theologian John of Palomar and others affirmed that the papacy was the apostolic structure to which one owed obedience. This became problematic with the papal schism, so much so that apostolic obedience might be taken to refer to the "apostolic" pope, the "apostolic" council, or the "apostolic" Scripture, alone or in conjunction with the "apostolic" tradition. Wyclif and Hus called for obedience to the apostles in Scripture. In its decree *Haec sancta*, the Council of Constance affirmed that obedience in the church meant obedience to the general council. The usual criteria for the apostolicity of the church were three: "that it be founded by the apostles, that it have been extended by the apostles throughout the world (since the apostle was one sent as a messenger), and that it be governed and administered by the apostles (through their legitimate successors)."¹⁰ Critics of the papacy questioned the legitimacy of successors who did not seem to live in a way that was thought to embody the life of the apostles. In that vein, some looked to monasticism as an exemplification of the apostolic life and used it to critique ecclesiastical leaders living in wealth or luxury. Yet it was Franciscan advocacy of the pope's position in the church that contributed to the widespread reference to Rome as "the apostolic see."

Given the prominence of the pope as Peter's successor, there were various ways of interpreting the "rock" in the famous passage about

---

[7] Ibid., 99–100.
[8] Ibid., 109–10.
[9] Ibid., 110.
[10] Ibid., 112.

Jesus building his church on the "rock" (Matt 16:18): the rock could refer to Christ, to faith, to Peter's confession, to Peter as preacher and missionary rather than prelate, to all the apostles as "rocks" (so Jerome) though to Peter "chiefly" or "especially," or to the "divine Scripture and the sacred doctrine of Christ."[11] Attention was also given to the passage two chapters later (Matt 18:17-18), where the same authority was interpreted as being given to all the apostles whose successors were the bishops, though some assigned that role to the cardinals. Humanist scholars, for their part, emphasized the authority of the primitive church, retrieved through a careful study of the biblical text. Clearly, there was no single way of understanding the church's apostolicity. That, and the considerations given to the other notes, explains why fifteenth-century Dominican theologian John of Ragusa (d. 1443) noted that the church had become the fundamental theological issue in his day, "the first and the most universal principle [*principium*] of doctrine and of the science of the faith."[12]

In addition to explicit treatments on the notes of the church, an implicit theology of the church is revealed in the widespread longing for both reform of church life and for a lay spirituality.[13] Prominent in both was the emphasis given to the Scriptures and to the early church as a model or norm for church renewal. The title of the popular *Imitation of Christ*, a key expression of the reform movement known as *devotio moderna*, indicates its desire to live the life of Christ in word and deed. Renaissance humanists, preparing critical editions of the Scriptures and translations for popular use, were guided as they were by their "essentially evangelical" spirituality[14] and their desire to see the church renewed by a return to its biblical roots. We

[11] Ibid., 115–16.
[12] Ibid., 71.
[13] John C. Olin, *The Catholic Reformation: Savonarola to Ignatius Loyola* (New York: Fordham University Press, 1992), xiii–xxiv; Norman Tanner, *The Church in the Later Middle Ages* (London: I. B. Tauris, 2008), chap. 3; Hubert Jedin, *A History of the Council of Trent*, vol. 1: *The Struggle for the Council*, trans. Ernest Graf (St. Louis: B. Herder Book Co., 1957), chap. 7.
[14] William Bouwsma, "Humanism," in *Christian Spirituality: High Middle Ages and Reformation*, ed. Jill Raitt, World Spirituality: An Encyclopedic History of the Religious Quest, vol. 17 (New York: Crossroad, 1987), 250.

see this interest in the biblical roots of Christianity exemplified in three of the very prominent figures of Catholic renewal at the end of the fifteenth and beginning of the sixteenth centuries. The Franciscan Cardinal Francisco Ximenes de Cisneros (d. 1517), archbishop of Toledo, anticipated the Council of Trent in his reform of the clergy and provided catechetical instruction to the young. He founded the University of Alcalà (site of the ancient Roman settlement of *Complutum*) whose scholars, under his direction, prepared the famous Complutensian polyglot Bible. The fiery Dominican preacher Girolamo Savonarola (d. 1498), with apocalyptic fervor, decried the difference between the church of his day and the model given by the early church. The Christian humanist Desiderius Erasmus (d. 1536) published many editions of the Greek and Latin fathers, in whose style and message he saw "the ancient and genuine" theology of the church in contrast to that of the scholastics.[15] Even more important were his biblical studies, inspired by the conviction that the Bible, especially the New Testament, was "the font from which all Christians should directly derive their religious devotion."[16] For all his sometimes very sharp critique of the church of his day, Erasmus emphasized the historical continuity of the Christian Church and saw it as a community of love under Christ, marked by unity, love, and harmony, perspectives that separated him from those whose reforming efforts led to a breach in that continuity or to division within the church.[17] The advocacy by Erasmus and those who were influenced by him in promoting a reform of theological method and Christian piety based on the Bible and the fathers anticipates, we shall see, the efforts of theologians in the half century before Vatican II and the work itself of that council.

---

[15] John W. O'Malley, *Trent: What Happened at the Council* (Cambridge, MA: Belknap Press of Harvard University Press, 2013), 42.
[16] Ibid.
[17] John W. O'Malley, "Erasmus and Luther, Continuity and Discontinuity as Key to Their Conflict," *Sixteenth Century Journal* 5, no. 2 (1974): 47–65; and Hilmar M. Pabel, "The Peaceful People of Christ: The Eirenic Ecclesiology of Erasmus of Rotterdam," in *Erasmus' Vision of the Church*, ed. Hilmar M. Pabel, vol. 33 (Kirksville, MO: Sixteenth Century Journal Publishers, 1995), 57–93, at 62 and 64.

Two other aspects of an implicit popular view of church may be mentioned. The first was the development of a piety that was individualized and turned inward, encouraged in part by dissatisfaction with the services provided in parish life in many places.[18] After the middle of the fifteenth century, the increased availability of printed materials fed the interests among educated laity in monastic and ascetic piety. The same could be said of the continued popularity of the *devotio moderna*, drawing inspiration from monasticism but appealing to both laity and clergy. In many places confraternities or sodalities, made up mostly of laity, or the associations of Third Order Dominicans, Franciscans, or other orders "provided many, perhaps most, Catholics with their true spiritual homes and were more important in their lives than the parish church."[19] A second aspect was the increasingly critical attitude in some quarters toward church officials and church structures. This especially would impact later thinking of both Catholics and Protestants. Those who sought to nourish their spiritual life in *devotio moderna*, for example, did so "in face of an ecclesiasticism that had become decadent and corrupt."[20] Two works of Erasmus, *Praise of Folly* and *Colloquies*, both biting critiques of the clergy and church ceremonies, further served to discredit persons and institutions of the church. Many people found sustenance in parish communities or in communities of vowed religious, but many did not.

An ultimately unsuccessful attempt to address some of the calls for reform took place in the Fifth Lateran Council (1512–1517), called reluctantly by Pope Julius II to offset a council called by the king of France.[21] Items from the inaugural oration, given at the request of the pope, by Giles of Viterbo (Egidio da Viterbo, d. 1532), the prior general of the Augustinian order, call for our attention.[22] At the outset of

---

[18] Richard Kieckhefer, "Major Currents in Late Medieval Devotion," in Raitt, *Christian Spirituality*, chap. 3.

[19] Olin, *Catholic Reformation*, 21.

[20] Ibid., xxi.

[21] Joseph F. Kelly, *The Ecumenical Councils of the Catholic Church: A History* (Collegeville, MN: Liturgical Press, 2009), 121–25.

[22] John W. O'Malley, "Historical Thought and the Reform Crisis of the Early Sixteenth Century," *Theological Studies* 28, no. 3 (1967): 531–48.

his address, a strong call for reform in the church, he gave his famous norm for that reform: "Men must be changed by religion, not religion by men."[23] He was one with many others of his day in the thought that "the Church was so aware of the divine origin of its doctrines, rites, and discipline and of the continuity of its traditions that the historical and contingent components of these realities received very little attention."[24] This "decidedly unhistorical" approach to history would have a long life in subsequent reflection on the church.[25] It is significant to note as well that Giles refers several times to the church as the bride of Christ—the image was not lost from people's mindfulness—and, even in face of serious papal misgivings about councils, extols the irreplaceable role of the council in restoring the church to its "ancient splendor and purity." After forbidding any interpretation of the council's work without his permission or that of the Apostolic See, the pope, now Leo X, closed the council on March 11, 1517, having, it was noted, no new business brought before it.[26] The council's reform decrees, promulgated as papal bulls, were ignored by the pope. Less than nine months later, a cry for reform was uttered that would not be ignored—with great impact on the understanding of church.

The Church in the Thought of the Reformers

Though our focus is on the theology of the church in the Catholic community, that theology was influenced by the challenges coming from the Reformers, chief among them Martin Luther and John Calvin. A look at their thinking helps us appreciate subsequent Catholic response and reaction. Luther (1483–1546),[27] an Augustinian monk, stood in a long line of clerics and lay folk concerned with their own

---

[23] Olin, *Catholic Reformation*, 44–53, at 45.

[24] John W. O'Malley, *Tradition and Transition: Historical Perspectives on Vatican II*, Theology and Life Series, vol. 26 (Wilmington, DE: Michael Glazier, 1989), 107.

[25] O'Malley, "Historical Thought and the Reform Crisis," 538.

[26] Norman P. Tanner, ed., *Decrees of the Ecumenical Councils*, 2 vols. (London: Sheed and Ward, 1990), 1:653–54.

[27] The bibliography on Luther is immense. A popular treatment is given in Martin Marty, *Martin Luther* (New York: Viking, 2004).

relationship with God and with the reform of the church. His initial focus centered on the third step of the sacrament of penance, making satisfaction for the sins forgiven (following contrition and confession) and the use of indulgences as a way of doing so. While penitential practices had long been part of the discipline associated with the sacrament, the then-current option, in some places, of remitting temporal punishment for one's sins (satisfaction) or applying such for the benefit of souls in purgatory through a monetary contribution was open to serious abuse and scandalous claims. Luther, struggling with his own perception of the demands of God's justice, challenged two aspects with regard to indulgences. Could distortions in this practice seem to be trying to manipulate the just God? Could the pope claim, as it was understood, that by the power of the keys he could draw on the "treasure" of the merits of Christ and the saints and apply them to the living and the dead, and do so for monetary offerings used to complete the building of St. Peter's in Rome and pay off the debts of the archbishop of Mainz? It was in this context that Luther enunciated the thesis: "The true treasure of the church is the most holy gospel of the glory and grace of God," the sixty-second of the ninety-five he proposed regarding indulgences. In time, he would give his own interpretations to the terms "church," "gospel," and "grace."[28] The opposition his questioning provoked led to his further challenges regarding the church as teacher of gospel truth and the authority of those who claimed to be its teachers.

Some of Luther's basic thoughts on the church appear early on in three important treatises that appeared in 1520.[29] In the first, *To the Christian Nobility of the German Nation*, he argued for the basic equality of all Christians: "All [are] consecrated priests through baptism," he says, citing 1 Peter 2:9 and Revelation 5:9-10. Bishops or priests differ from the baptized only in the office they hold "in the place and stead of the whole community, all of whom have like power." They exercise the office of preaching the Word of God and ministering the

---

[28] Pelikan, *Reformation of Church and Dogma*, 128–38, at 128.
[29] Martin Luther, *Three Treatises* (Philadelphia: Fortress Press, 1970). Taken from the American Edition of *Luther's Works*.

sacraments "on behalf of the others."[30] In this same work, he accepted the office of the pope but denied his authority in three areas: that he had spiritual power over the temporal, that he alone could interpret Scripture, and that he alone had the right to call or confirm a council. His second work, written later in the year, rejected the papacy altogether.

This second work, a theological treatise on the sacraments written in Latin, was titled *The Babylonian Captivity of the Church*. The point of the title: as once the Jews were held in Babylonian captivity, Christians are being held captive by the church's sacramental practice and have been denied the liberty of their faith in what is given in the Word of God. Two teachings are paramount. First, in keeping with his view on the supremacy of the Word, Luther accepts only three sacraments—"baptism, penance, and the bread"[31]—as having a basis in Scripture. (The conclusion of the work denies that penance is strictly a sacrament; it is, rather, a recalling of the declaration of forgiveness, so "nothing but a way and a return to baptism."[32]) Interestingly, he says according to the Scriptures one might well speak of only one sacrament, Christ (1 Tim 3:16 in the Vulgate[33]), along with three sacramental signs. Second, in accord with his doctrine of justification by faith, sacraments are signs instituted by Christ that provoke justifying faith but are not of themselves instruments of grace. The bulk of the treatise centers on the sacrament of the Lord's Supper, seen as being used by the priests to hold Christians captive in three ways: withholding the option of the use of the cup; the use of doctrine of transubstantiation, decreed by "the Thomistic—that is, the Aristotelian church" (i.e., using philosophy to speak of a mystery of faith); and seeing Mass as a "good work and a sacrifice."[34] Mass was, rather, Christ's promise of forgiveness, the Body and Blood of Christ a sign and a memorial of that promise. Preachers of the gospel, chosen by

---

[30] Ibid., 12.
[31] "The Babylonian Captivity of the Church," trans. A. T. W. Steinhäuser, rev. Frederick C. Ahrens and Abdel Ross Wentz, in Luther, *Three Treatises*, 132.
[32] Ibid., 258.
[33] Ibid., 132.
[34] Ibid., 144, 152.

a rite that was not itself a sacrament, were to administer the Lord's Supper to remind people of Christ's promise, to commend it, and to awaken their faith in it. All that had been added to the word of Christ instituting the sacrament should be put aside as obstructing the response of faith. Though Luther denies that marriage is a sacrament because, he says, it lacks a scriptural warrant, Christ and the church "can and ought to be represented in terms of marriage as a kind of outward allegory."[35] The text keeps going back to the absolute need for faith and to the Scriptures as guide for all church practices.

A third work, *The Freedom of the Christian*, intended to be more conciliatory, seeks to make the case that faith in God frees the Christian from sin yet binds him by love to serve his neighbor. In the spirit of late medieval mysticism, Luther invokes the imagery of Ephesians 5:31-32 and speaks of Christ the bridegroom taking upon himself the sins of the bride (the soul) and bestowing on her all that is his. He writes, "Surely we are named after Christ, not because he is absent from us, but because he dwells in us, that is, because we believe in him and are Christs one to another and do to our neighbors as Christ does to us."[36]

These three treatises, along with two others, *On the Papacy in Rome* and *Good Works*, also written in 1520, are considered the theological core of what was emerging as a distinctly evangelical view of the church.[37] *On the Papacy in Rome*,[38] written in response to those who attacked Luther's denial of any divine warrant for the papacy, argued that the church has no other head than Christ and has no vicar of Christ on earth. He would accept what the pope establishes and does only if he judges it in accord with the Holy Scripture. The church

---

[35] Ibid., 223.

[36] Martin Luther, "The Freedom of a Christian," trans. W. A. Lambert, rev. Harold J. Grimm, in *Luther's Works*, vol. 31: *Career of the Reformer: I*, ed. Harold J. Grimm (Philadelphia: Muhlenberg Press, 1957), 368.

[37] Scott Hendrix, "Luther," in *The Cambridge Companion to Reformation Theology*, ed. David Bagchi and David C. Steinmetz (Cambridge: Cambridge University Press, 2004), 48–49 and 54.

[38] Martin Luther, *On the Papacy in Rome, Against the Most Celebrated Romanist in Leipzig*, trans. Eric W. and Ruth C. Gritch, in *Luther's Works*, vol. 39: *Church and Ministry I*, ed. Eric W. Gritch (Philadelphia: Fortress Press, 1970), 49–104.

itself is "a spiritual, internal" reality, identified by baptism, the sacrament of the Lord's Supper, and the gospel (so not a purely spiritual church). The visible or physical assembly of the church, "man-made and external,"[39] is of decidedly secondary importance and does not belong to the "essence, life, and nature of Christendom."[40]

Luther took up the topic of the church again in his *On the Councils and the Church* (1539). The work was occasioned by Pope Paul III's call, in 1536, for a council, eventually begun at Trent in 1545. Though Luther in 1518 appealed to a council, by 1536 he came to believe that a council would only serve to condemn the Reformers and not to hear them out or make any concessions. Part 3 of *On the Councils and the Church* deals with signs of the church according to the Scriptures.[41] How can a person tell where the Christian holy people are to be found in this world? He responds by pointing to seven marks of the church. The first and principal item is the presence of the word of God "preached, believed, professed, and lived."[42] The second and third are the sacrament of baptism and the "sacrament of the altar, wherever it is rightly administered, believed, and received."[43] The fourth is the office of the keys exercised publicly, as Christ decrees in Matthew 18:15-20. The fifth: bishops, pastors, or preachers who administer the previous four items on behalf of and in the name of the church. Sixth, the holy Christian people are externally recognized by prayer, public praise, and thanksgiving to God. Finally, the church is externally recognized by "the holy possession of the sacred cross,"[44] enduring misfortune and persecution.

A brief statement on the church is also present in the *Augsburg Confession* (1530). The text was done at the urging of Emperor Charles V, desiring to promote unity among the Christians so to form a united front against the Turks. The text, drafted by Luther's collaborator

---

[39] Ibid., 70.
[40] Ibid., 65.
[41] Martin Luther, *On the Councils and the Church*, trans. Charles M. Jacobs, rev. Eric W. Gritsch, in *Luther's Works*, vol. 41: *Church and Ministry III*, ed. Eric W. Gritsch (Philadelphia: Fortress Press, 1966), 148–65.
[42] Ibid., 150.
[43] Ibid., 152.
[44] Ibid., 164.

Philip Melanchthon with Luther's final approval, was intended to represent the basic teaching of Luther and his followers and to emphasize agreements with Rome. Article 7, on the church, assumes that Lutheran churches stand in continuity with ancient and medieval Christianity, a point that will surface in both Catholic and Protestant histories later in the century. The church is described as "the assembly of saints in which the gospel is taught purely and the sacraments are administered rightly [i.e., according to the gospel]."[45] The expression "assembly of saints" raised questions in the Catholic response concerning the presence of sinners in the church. Melanchthon's *Apology of the Augsburg Confession*, accepted as an official Lutheran confession of faith in 1537, responded that the church in the proper sense is the assembly of those who believe in the Gospel of Christ and live in his Spirit, though until the final revelation, the "wicked" are mingled with the church in this life.[46] Luther's thoughts on the church are scattered in many writings and, because written in different circumstances, are not completely consistent.

Luther's contemporary, the Swiss priest Ulrich (Huldrich) Zwingli (1484–1531), was more radical than Luther in his insistence on the authority of the Bible, God's Word, over against any human word (the teachings of the fathers, the councils, or the popes), though he allowed use of the fathers, the councils, or even the schoolmen to support his interpretations of Scripture.[47] His emphasis on the sovereignty of God and Christ as God supported his conviction that "we need no mediator except Christ,"[48] that we are saved by God's election, not by faith or love or the sacraments. Holding that "no outward element or action can purify the soul,"[49] Zwingli maintained that it was election and not baptism that brought salvation. The biblical commandment forbidding graven images led to a rejection of all images in churches and a stark

---

[45] In *The Book of Concord: The Confessions of the Evangelical Lutheran Church*, ed. Robert Kolb and Timothy Wengert, trans. of Latin text (Minneapolis: Fortress Press, 2000), 43.

[46] "Apology of the Augsburg Confession," in *The Book of Concord*, 176.

[47] W. Peter Stephens, "The Theology of Zwingli," in *Cambridge Companion to Reformation Theology*, chap. 8, at 82–83.

[48] Zwingli, cited by Stephens, 84.

[49] Ibid., 88.

minimizing of the use of material objects in worship.[50] Though his later writings on the topic were more positive, he maintained the view, based on John 6:63, that "it is the spirit that gives life; the flesh is useless" and that Christ was not bodily present in the Eucharist.[51] Sacraments were seen as signs of membership in the church rather than actions of Christ for us. Zwingli held that the church is the communion of all those who believe in Christ; its visibility is known to Christ but not to us. The church is also the local congregation of Word, sacrament (as he understood them), and discipline, without hierarchical mediation. Where Luther appealed to the German princes to oversee church reform, Zwingli called on the magistrates of the Swiss city of Zurich to bring reform to the church and free it of regional and outside ecclesiastical authority. He relied on the city council to enforce the reforms he proposed.

The French-born John Calvin (1509–1564) is generally seen as the second major founder of the Protestant Reformation and the most influential figure in shaping the identity of the Reformed tradition. For many, he is seen as the reformer of the Reformation.[52] Influenced by Luther's writings, Calvin published in 1536 the first edition of his *Institutes of the Christian Religion*, dedicated to the king of France as a defense of Reformation principles and a plea for religious toleration. In his letter to the king, Calvin stated what he saw as the fundamental religious concern: "how God's glory may be kept safe on earth, how God's truth may retain its place of honour, how Christ's kingdom may be kept in good repair among us."[53] In the same letter he also spoke of the two basic errors, as he saw it, of Catholic understanding of church: that the true church is "always apparent and observable" and that the visible church is one with "the see of the

---

[50] Robert Bruce Mullin, *A Short World History of Christianity* (Louisville, KY: Westminster John Knox Press, 2008), 124.

[51] Cf. Stephens, "The Theology of Zwingli," 89–91.

[52] Carlos Eire, "Calvinism and the Reform of the Reformation," in *The Oxford Illustrated History of The Reformation*, ed. Peter Marshall (Oxford: Oxford University Press, 2015), chap. 3.

[53] John Calvin, *Institutes of the Christian Religion*, ed. John T. McNeill, trans. Ford Lewis Battles, The Library of Christian Classics, vols. 20–21 (Philadelphia: Westminster Press, 1960), 11. This translation is made from the 1559 Latin text.

Roman Church and its hierarchy."[54] In the final edition (1559) of his *Institutes*, he cites two ways in which the Scriptures speak of the church: one that refers to the church as it is actually in God's presence, visible to him alone, which includes both the true members of Christ sanctified by the Holy Spirit and all the elect from the beginning of the world, and a second, designating all those who profess to worship one God and Christ even though some have nothing of Christ but the name. Just as we must believe in the former, he writes, so we are also commanded "to revere and keep communion with the latter, which is called 'church' in respect to men [sic]."[55]

More so than Luther, Calvin assigned a great importance to the visible church. We see this in an early paragraph in book 4 of the final edition of his *Institutes*, his most extensive treatment of the church:

> Let us learn from the simple title "mother" how useful, indeed how necessary, it is that we should know her. For there is no other way to enter into life unless this mother conceive us in her womb, give us birth, nourish us at her breast, and lastly, unless she keep us under her care and guidance until, putting off mortal flesh, we become like the angels. Our weakness does not allow us to be dismissed from her school until we have been pupils all our lives. Furthermore, away from her bosom one cannot hope for any forgiveness of sins or any salvation.[56]

Calvin draws the image of church as mother from the famous expression of Cyprian of Carthage, that one cannot have God for a father apart from having the church as a mother.[57] His seeing the church as school reflects his own interest in the revival of learning, influenced as he was by classical scholars Guillaume Budé and Desiderius Erasmus. The emphasis of these scholars on seeing the meaning of classical texts in their literary context inspired Calvin to do the same in

---

[54] Ibid., 24. On Calvin's ecclesiology, see Roger Haight, *Christian Community in History*, vol. 2: *Comparative Ecclesiology* (New York: Continuum, 2005), chap. 2.

[55] Calvin, *Institutes*, 1021–22.

[56] Ibid., 1016.

[57] David C. Steinmetz, "The Theology of John Calvin," in *Cambridge Companion to Reformation Theology*, 122.

interpreting Scripture for the unlearned in the church.[58] Even though Calvin firmly believed in the doctrine of predestination with the saved known only to God, the invisible church becomes visible where the Word of God and sacraments instituted by Christ are rightly administered.

Apart from three years as pastor of a French congregation in Strasbourg, Calvin spent almost all of his life as a reformer in Geneva, working to make of that city the ideal of a Christian society. He always saw himself as a reformer of the church, cleansing it of any vestige of what he saw as false religion, rather than seeing himself as one initiating a new denomination. False religion came from human inventions not supported by the Bible and from anything that detracted from his guiding principle, *Soli Deo Gloria*, "Glory to God alone." Calvin parted with Catholic understandings of baptism, penance, Eucharist, and ministry in the church.[59] With Luther, he affirmed the priesthood of all believers and recognized no difference in kind between those selected as ministers and the baptized faithful; he substituted for the ordained ministries of deacon, priest, and bishop what to him was the biblically warranted fourfold ministry of pastors, teachers, elders, and deacons. The task of pastors and teachers was to guide Christians in their reading of the Scriptures, to restore the proper worship of God the Creator according to the Scriptures, and to assist Christians in their experience of Christ's power in their lives, so to be transformed into his image and to be united with him in eternal life.[60] Calvin vigorously opposed any idea of divinization or intimacy with God, the "entirely other" and "as different from flesh as fire is from water."[61] Calvin's *Ecclesiastical Ordinances*, influenced by reformer Martin Bucer of Strasbourg and adopted by the city council of Geneva in 1541, sought to balance ecclesiastical and civil power in their joint responsibility to uphold the moral and doctrinal

---

[58] Randall C. Zachman, "John Calvin (1509–1564)," in *The Reformation Theologians: An Introduction to Theology in the Early Modern Period*, ed. Carter Lindberg (Malden, MA: Blackwell, 2002), 184–85.
[59] Steinmetz, "The Theology of John Calvin," 124–29.
[60] Zachman, "John Calvin (1509–1564)," 189–94.
[61] Eire, "Calvinism and the Reform of the Reformation," 114.

standards of the citizens of the city.⁶² The pastors and the city government also had the authority to test and nominate candidates for pastoral positions, final consent residing in the congregation. Calvin's rejection of the papacy has a conditional note about it; his stance is based on the popes' failure in his day, as he saw it, to proclaim the Word, administer the sacraments, and exercise discipline in the church.

The Church of England was distinctive in that its development was closely related to the English monarchs, beginning with Henry VIII, during whose reign (1509–1547) the church became an autonomous church, the king becoming the head of the church as well as head of the state (1530).⁶³ Under Henry's chief minister, Thomas Cromwell (d. 1540), elements of Lutheran thought and practice were introduced, some of which were overturned in Henry's *Six Articles* in 1538. Under the direction of Thomas Cranmer, archbishop of Canterbury (1533–1556), elements from John Calvin's Geneva began to give shape to the English church during the reign of Henry's young and sickly son, Edward VI (1547–1553). The Catholic reaction during the short reign of Mary Tudor (1553–1558) came to an abrupt end with her death and, on the same day, the death of Cardinal Reginald Pole, the archbishop of Canterbury (1556–58) and a major figure of the Catholic reform. Protestant elements took firm hold under Mary's successor, Elizabeth I (1558–1603), though she sought to end England's religious upheavals with the compromise later called the "Elizabethan Settlement," described inaccurately as a *via media* between those who supported Rome and those who supported Geneva. The most accomplished defense of the Elizabethan settlement of 1559 was made by one of the English church's greatest theologians, Richard Hooker (c. 1554–1600), in part as a response to English Puritans who held that what was not explicit in the Scriptures had no part in the church. The seventeenth-century Stuart successors to Queen Elizabeth favored a very "high church" approach, including an episcopal hierarchy, sacraments,

---

⁶² Eddy van der Borght, "Reformed Ecclesiology," in *The Routledge Companion to the Christian Church*, ed. Gerard Mannion and Lewis S. Mudge (New York: Routledge, 2008), 194–98.

⁶³ Peter Marshall, "Britain's Reformations," in *The Oxford Illustrated History of the Reformation*, chap. 6; and Haight, *Comparative Ecclesiology*, 148–211.

and ceremony, in what later came to be called "Anglicanism." In time, both the Lutheran and Anglican churches developed a high church wing favoring the elements just mentioned and a low church wing wanting little or no part of the same.

The Understanding of Church in the Council of Trent (1545–1563)

An important if indirect expression of the Catholic understanding of church emerged from the Council of Trent during its three periods (1545–1547, 1551–1552, 1562–1563), each called by a different pope: Paul III (1534–1549), Julius III (1550–1555), and Pius IV (1559–1565).[64] The council was not called for many years, in part because conflicting concerns of the popes, of King Francis I of France, and of Charles V, the Holy Roman Emperor. When the council was finally called, Charles, still hoping to see a return of Luther and his followers to the Catholic fold, pressed to have the council deal with reform issues. Pope Paul III, thinking futile any hope of reconciliation with the Protestants (the name used of those resisting anti-Lutheran measures imposed by Charles at the Diet of Speyer in 1529), sought to direct the council to deal with matters of doctrine for the Catholic community. The papal legates to the council compromised by directing the council to deal with both doctrinal and reform issues. The council thus focused on doctrinal decrees aimed at giving a clear statement of Catholic teaching, so responding to what were perceived to be the erroneous teaching of the Reformers, and reform decrees intended to eliminate abuses and to promote pastoral reform in the church.[65] The council issued no explicit decree "on the church," in large part because of papal resistance to any residue of conciliarism and disagreement on the practical aspects of papal ministry in the church.

Four of Trent's teachings, however, are basic elements in the council's understanding of church.[66] The first, in its decree on Scripture

---

[64] For historical background to the council, see Michael A. Mullett, *The Catholic Reformation* (New York: Routledge, 1999), chap. 2. On the council itself, O'Malley, *Trent: What Happened at the Council.*

[65] Tanner, *Decrees of the Ecumenical Councils*, 2:660–799.

[66] David C. Steinmetz, "The Council of Trent," in *Cambridge Companion to Reformation Theology*, chap. 17.

and apostolic tradition, affirms that "the whole truth of salvation and rule of conduct . . . are contained in written books and in unwritten traditions that were received by the apostles from the mouth of Christ himself, or else have come down to us, handed on as it were from the apostles themselves at the inspiration of the holy Spirit."[67] Affirming the existence of apostolic traditions considered essential to the faith of the church was meant to counter the Reformers' insistence on Scripture alone as guide to the faith.

A second teaching, in what is generally regarded as the cornerstone of the council's work, affirms that by faith and God's self-gift and divine assistance (grace) the baptized can be truly transformed (the key word here) into God's adopted children. Trent's teaching in the decree on justification is implicitly fundamental to an understanding of both the nature and the mission of the church. Closely related to this is the third teaching, on the sacraments, basically a rejection of the teaching of Luther's *Babylonian Captivity of the Church*.[68] In its emphasis on the sacraments—seven, as distinct from Luther's recognizing only two, and containing and conferring the grace they signify—the council's teaching underscores the fundamental difference between Catholics and Reformers over the role of the church's sacraments in the economy of salvation.[69] In its decree on the sacrifice of the Mass[70] the council asserts the legitimacy of using "external aids" (incense, vestments, other rituals) in the worship of the church, so arguing against "the radical spiritualization of religion" adopted in some Protestant circles.[71] In its specific teaching on marriage,[72] Trent, as the Council of Basel before it, relates the sacrament of marriage to Christ's loving union with the church, citing Ephesians 5:32, using the Vulgate's *sacramentum* for the Greek *mysterion*. A fourth teaching, on the sacrament of orders, rejects the teaching of Luther's

---

[67] Tanner, *Decrees of the Ecumenical Councils*, 2:663.
[68] "First Decree [On the Sacraments]," in Tanner, *Decrees of the Ecumenical Councils*, 2:684–86.
[69] Mullett, *Catholic Reformation*, 51.
[70] Tanner, *Decrees of the Ecumenical Councils*, 2:734.
[71] O'Malley, *Trent: What Happened at the Council*, 191.
[72] Tanner, *Decrees of the Ecumenical Councils*, 2:754.

To the Christian Nobility of the German Nation.[73] The council affirms the role of the ordained in God's plan for the church and, reasserting a teaching long held by the church both East and West, insists on the sacramental reality of orders and its power to celebrate the Eucharist and forgive sins, contradicting Luther's functional understanding of office centered so predominantly on preaching. While the doctrinal decree on orders stresses the priest's cultic role in terms of the sacrifice of the Mass, the reform decrees outline broader pastoral responsibilities for both bishops and pastors, especially preaching, teaching, and maintaining residence; doing so gives emphasis on the presence of the church in parochial and diocesan communities.[74] As Luther's emphasis on faith alone and his stress on the individual standing before God threatened Catholic emphasis on the sacraments and clerical authority, not surprisingly these latter became major concerns of Trent's doctrinal teaching.

In its firm conviction of the need for changes in long-standing attitudes and practices adversely affecting the pastoral life of the church, the council's reform decrees and canons included clear sanctions for noncompliance. This would bring positive changes in church practice, though it would also reinforce "social disciplining" as a style of church practice.[75] In this respect, post-Tridentine Catholicism resembled developments in sixteenth- and seventeenth-century Lutheranism and Calvinism.[76] All three movements sought to strengthen the authority of their leaders and in doing so influence the lives of their congregations.[77]

---

[73] Ibid., 2:742–53, 759–73.

[74] See Joseph Cardinal Ratzinger, *Principles of Catholic Theology: Building Stones for a Fundamental Theology*, trans. Mary Frances McCarthy (San Francisco: Ignatius Press, 1987), 263–66.

[75] John W. O'Malley, "The Council of Trent: Myths, Misunderstandings, and Misinformation," in *Spirit, Style, Story: Essays Honoring John W. Padberg, SJ*, ed. Thomas M. Lucas (Chicago: Loyola Press, 2002), 216–17.

[76] Simon Ditchfield, "Catholic Reformation and Renewal," in *The Oxford Illustrated History of the Reformation*, 174–75.

[77] See Wietse de Boer, "Calvin and Borromeo: A Comparative Approach to Social Discipline," in *Early Modern Catholicism: Essays in Honour of John W.*

It is noteworthy that the chapters on justification, composed in the first segment of the council (1545–1547), make significant use of the language of the Scriptures and the fathers of the church alongside some of the technical language of the scholastics. The chapters and reform decrees on the sacraments, however, reflect a more scholastic and juridical style with "minimal awareness of the historical conditioning of norms, axioms, principles and authoritative statements."[78] In reaction to Reformers' claims that much of the church's teaching on the sacraments consisted of later accretions lacking biblical warrants, Trent insisted on continuity and changelessness in the handing on of church doctrine, so contributing again to what for a long time has been a Catholic tendency to sidestep issues of historical development in the church's tradition.[79]

The council took notable steps to deal with the reform of the bishops, priests, and lay faithful, but it never addressed the first part of the cry for reform since the time of the Great Schism, *reformatio in capite et in membris*, "reform in head and members." In all three periods of the council, the popes successfully resisted any effort to deal with "reform of the head." One aspect of proposals for reform centered on whether a bishop was required by divine law to reside in his diocese, in which case even the pope could make no dispensation, so an important limit to the exercise of his authority. Underneath that question was the yet more fundamental question: Did bishops receive their power from God through their consecration (held by those who pressed for reform) or, by their appointment, from the pope (defended by those who supported a strong papal authority)? Trent never decided the issue, though the debates at the council and the example of some leading bishops after the council contributed much to promote a residential

---

O'Malley, SJ, ed. Kathleen M. Comerford and Hilmar M. Pabel (Toronto: University of Toronto Press, 2001), 84–96.

[78] John W. O'Malley, "Trent and Vatican II: Two Styles of Church," in *From Trent to Vatican II: Historical and Theological Investigations*, ed. Raymond F. Bulman and Frederick J. Parrella (New York: Oxford University Press, 2006), 305.

[79] O'Malley, "The Council of Trent: Myths, Misunderstandings, and Misinformation," 212.

pastorate and a residential episcopacy. Pressed for time, a decree at the final session of Trent remanded to the pope the unfinished work on revision of the *Index of Prohibited Books* and on the catechism, the missal, and the breviary. Another decree, "The Reception and Observance of the Council's Decrees,"[80] charges "all princes in the Lord" to see that the decrees are faithfully observed and, influenced perhaps by the final decree of Lateran V,[81] reserves to the pope any clarifications that might be needed. That decree did not preclude future tensions between the pope, the local bishops, and the secular rulers regarding the interpretation of the council. Finally, lacking its own authority to promulgate its decrees, the council requested confirmation of its decrees by the pope. Pius IV did so at the end of January 1564.

Three years after the council's close, the *Catechism of the Council of Trent* (or *The Roman Catechism*) was promulgated by Pius V (1566–1572) to guide pastors in their instructing others in the faith.[82] Its use as a guide to the faith was recommended by popes even as recently as 1979.[83] While the introduction speaks of the need to counter "false prophets . . . practiced in all the arts of Satan"[84] who seek to lead unsuspecting minds astray, the text itself has a positive tone, concerned to help pastors "lead their flocks into a heartfelt appreciation of the gifts of God."[85] The Catechism's teaching on the church comes in the first two of its four parts: the creed, sacraments, the Decalogue, and the Lord's Prayer. The introduction to the article on the creed's teaching on the church notes Augustine's foreseeing that a greater number would be deceived regarding the church than on the mystery of the incarnation. It also notes that what is to be said about the church

---

[80] Tanner, *Decrees of the Ecumenical Councils*, 2:798.

[81] Nelson H. Minnich, "The Last Two Councils of the Catholic Reformation: The Influence of Lateran V on Trent," in *Early Modern Catholicism: Essays in Honour of John W. O'Malley*, 14–16.

[82] *The Roman Catechism*, trans. Robert I. Bradley and Eugene Kevane (Boston: St. Paul Editions, 1985). See Haight, *Comparative Ecclesiology*, 266–75.

[83] Eugene Kevane, introduction to *The Roman Catechism*, vi–vii.

[84] *The Roman Catechism*, 5.

[85] O'Malley, *Trent: What Happened at the Council*, 265.

hinges on what was said about the Holy Spirit. The church is understood as "the assemblies of the faithful, that is, of those who were called by faith to the light of truth and the knowledge of God . . . those who forsake the darkness of ignorance and error, worship the living and true God in piety and holiness, and serve him from their whole heart."[86] Unlike other societies, the church is called forth "by the interior inspiration of the Holy Spirit . . . through the external work and ministry of his pastors and evangelists."[87] Four biblical "names" for the church are specially recognized: the church as the house and edifice of God, the pillar and bulwark of the truth; the flock of Christ; the spouse of Christ; and the body of Christ. The one church has two constituent parts: the blessed in the church triumphant and the faithful on earth in the church militant, the latter possessing both the good and the bad and waging war with those "implacable enemies, the world, the flesh and the devil." Specifically excluded from the church are infidels, heretics and schismatics, and the excommunicated. The word "church" also applies to "portions of the Universal Church," such as those at Corinth, Galatia, Laodicea, and Thessalonica; to "private houses of the faithful" (e.g., the family of Priscilla and Aquila, Rom 16:4); and to "prelates and pastors." In an echo of the Reformers' definition, "The place in which the faithful assemble to hear the Word of God or for other religious purposes is also called a Church."[88]

The Catechism treats the marks of the church as supports given to show the blessings God gives to the church.[89] Exposition of the church's oneness begins with references to the Song of Songs (6:8: "But my dove is unique, mine, unique and perfect") and to the Letter to the Ephesians (4:5: "One Lord, one faith, one baptism"). Paul is invoked to assert that the church has "only one ruler and one governor," though with a visible head needed to establish and preserve the unity in the visible church. The church's unity is also marked by one and the same Spirit, one hope, and one faith. No

---

[86] *The Roman Catechism*, 98.
[87] Ibid., 99.
[88] Ibid., 103.
[89] Ibid., 104–9.

reference is made to the pope's temporal claims. Even though sinners are among her children, the church is holy because she is dedicated to God and is united to her holy head, Christ, the fountain of all holiness. The church is catholic in that she is not confined to any one country—a counter, no doubt, to the emerging national identities of the Reform churches—but embraces all races, classes, all men and women. All the faithful since the time of Adam are included. The church is apostolic, "known from her origin from the Apostles under the law of grace." Any appreciation of development is lacking in the assertion that "her teaching is neither recent nor contemporary in origin; it was handed forward by the Apostles and disseminated from them throughout the whole world." A rare polemical note sounds in comparing that teaching to "the impious opinions which heresy invents," opposed "as they are to the doctrines taught by the Church from the days of the Apostles to the present time." Guided by the Spirit, she cannot err in faith or morals. The Catechism notes the difference between believing *in* God and believing the church, distinguishing God from the benefits God gives us in the Church.

The Catechism's second article on the church deals with the "communion of saints." The term refers, first, to our fellowship with the Father and the Son (1 John 1:3) and the "society of saints" that the baptized hope to join. The term also refers to the communion of sacraments, by which one enters the assembly of the saints, and the communion of goods shared by all members of the body of Christ. Concern for others is an integral part of the ecclesial communion: "Every true Christian possesses nothing which he should not consider common to all others with himself. . . . For he that is blessed with worldly goods, and sees his brother in want, and will not assist him, is at once convicted of not having the love of God within him."[90]

The treatment of the sacraments is by far the longest section of the Catechism. Though delegates at the council called for "a revolution in theological studies under the banner of humanism,"[91] the

---

[90] Ibid., 114.
[91] Herbert Jedin, *A History of the Council of Trent*, vol. 2: *The First Sessions at Trent 1545–47*, trans. Ernest Graf (St. Louis: B. Herder, 1961), 104.

treatment was cast very much in the scholastic mode, emphasizing correct matter, form, proper minister, effects, with little attention to their liturgical celebration. The sacrament of orders[92] is given special notice: the other sacraments are said to depend on it, some "for their very existence—both as confected and as conferred." Defense of the priesthood in the face of Reformers' denial led to problematic exaggeration: "Priests and bishops are, as it were, the interpreters and messengers of God. . . . They act in the world as the very person of God. It is evident that no office greater than theirs can be imagined. Rightly have they been called angels (Mal 2:7), even gods (Ex 22:28 [Vulgate]), holding as they do among us the very name and power of the living God."[93] In continuity with the medieval tradition, the power of orders is said to refer to the Body of Christ in the Eucharist; the power of jurisdiction, to the mystical body, the church. The Catechism's teaching on an "internal priesthood" by which all the faithful are said to be priests who offer spiritual sacrifices to God on the altar of their hearts summarizes what is implicitly asserted in the decrees of Trent and what was explicitly propounded in the discussions of its general congregations.[94]

Catholicism emerging from the council was "more strongly sacramental than ever."[95] At the same time it also entered into "almost a golden age" of preaching, influenced by the council's decrees on this issue, but by other influences as well: the humanist emphasis on preaching and the preaching ministries of the revived mendicant orders and, preeminently so, of the Jesuits.

The Understanding of Church in Years after the Council of Trent

The implementation of the reform decrees of the Council of Trent reveal two implicit approaches to ecclesial understanding, one adopted by papal Rome, the other by episcopal leadership focusing

---

[92] *The Roman Catechism*, 307–26.

[93] Ibid., 308.

[94] Nelson H. Minnich, "The Priesthood of All Believers at the Council of Trent," *The Jurist* 67 (2007): 361.

[95] O'Malley, *Trent: What Happened at the Council*, 255, 257.

on the needs and the particularities of the local church. The latter found its most notable representative in the ministry of Charles Borromeo, archbishop of Milan from 1565 to 1584.[96] Inspired by his fourth-century predecessor, Ambrose of Milan, Borromeo "placed emphasis on the leadership of the local churches and on the duty of bishops to adapt, regulate, and even expand what the council had decreed."[97] Borromeo based his approach on the council's repeated insistence on the leadership role of the local bishop in what were some of its most important reform decrees. While many saw in Borromeo's personal efforts and the many synods over which he presided the key to a differentiated reception of the Tridentine decrees, his work often aroused distrust among representatives of the papal curia. When the saintly archbishop was canonized in 1610, it was his personal holiness that was accorded recognition, not his pastoral and reforming activity, though he was a major influence on diocesan reform well beyond the borders of Italy.

A second approach came from Rome. For forty years following the council, the papacy asserted itself as the principal interpreter of the council and leader of the Catholic reformation. Perhaps most prominent among the popes of this period was Pius V (1566–1572) who was largely responsible for implementing the council's recommendation that the papacy oversee the publication of missal, breviary, catechism, and *Index of Prohibited Books*. The Congregation of the Council, established in 1564 by Pius IV but expanded by Pius V, was made the official interpreter of Trent's reform decrees. The publication of the Roman Missal (sometimes called the Pian Missal) in 1570 played a major role in "the processes of relative standardization and Romanization that characterized the Catholic Reformation."[98] Several features of the missal and its development involved an implicit

---

[96] Mullett, *Catholic Reformation*, 137–41 and chap. 5.
[97] O'Malley, "The Council of Trent: Myths, Misunderstandings, and Misinformation," 222.
[98] Mullett, *Catholic Reformation*, 114.

understanding of church.[99] First, by the elimination of Marian intrusions in the Mass and reducing the sanctoral cycle of the calendar, a Christocentric focus was restored to the principal liturgical celebration of the community. Second, while the Missal of Pius V allowed some regional and national liturgical variations going back at least two hundred years (e.g., the Ambrosian Rite of Milan and the Spanish Mozarabic Rite), overall there was a loss of regional and local particulars. This was, in large part, a reaction to the chaotic situation before printed missals, when liturgical books were locally produced manuscripts with all sorts of variations. Third, the commission charged with the composition of the missal aimed, significantly, to return to "the original norm and rite laid down by the holy Fathers,"[100] though, unbeknownst to the commission, the so-called Gregorian Sacramentary on which the missal was based bore many elements added since the time of Pope Gregory the Great. Finally, most significantly but not the fault of the commission, the concept of liturgy on which the missal was based was that which emerged at the beginning of the ninth century, that the Mass was basically a clerical activity rather than the celebration of the entire Christian community characteristic of earlier centuries. The Roman Missal of 1570 and the Sacred Congregation of Rites founded in 1588, charged with preventing any changes in the Mass, led to what liturgical scholars regard as a long period of rigidity in the liturgy and an overemphasis on rubrics over community participation.

The Romanization of the Western church advanced by the liturgy was complemented by attention to the city of Rome itself.[101] Gregory XIII (pope 1572–1585), for example, used architecture to restate Rome as the "head and mother"[102] of Catholicism. Pope Sixtus V (1585–1590) sought to restore ancient Christian buildings and to convert pagan

---

[99] See ibid., 114–16, and Clifford Howell, "From Trent to Vatican II," in *The Study of Liturgy*, ed. Cheslyn Jones and others, rev. ed. (New York: Oxford University Press, 1992), 285–89.

[100] Cited in Howell, "From Trent to Vatican II," 286.

[101] Mullett, *Catholic Reformation*, 120–33.

[102] Ibid., 124.

Rome "physically and visually into Christian Rome."[103] Inspired by the influential priest reformer Filipo Neri, Clement VIII (pope 1592–1605) aimed to make Rome the model reformed diocese, a center for priestly education and the publishing capital of Catholicism. Through the dissemination of the several texts cited above, the twelve congregations of the Roman Curia set up by Sixtus V, and the agency of nuncios and apostolic visitors, the official image of the Council of Trent was that set by Rome and the papal theologians.[104] Given the council's unmistakable emphasis on the authority of the bishops in their own dioceses, contemporary scholarship recognizes a distinction between the council and its decrees, on the one hand, and, on the other, the dominant style of implementation, Roman and universalist, that prevailed from the seventeenth to the nineteenth century.[105]

It was not simply popes and bishops who helped shape the understanding of church in the second half of the sixteenth and in the seventeenth centuries. Jesuit Peter Canisius (d. 1597), author of widely used catechisms, spoke of the interior reality of the church but, with increasing emphasis, focused on its visible hierarchical structure under the authority of the pope. English theologian and controversialist Thomas Stapleton (d. 1598), in his *Defense of Ecclesiastical Authority*, argued that only in the Catholic Church and through it can one hear the voice of God. While he defined the church as the assembly of all those who adhere to Christ, he was preoccupied with the church's teaching authority, especially that of the pope, even saying, in another work, that the faithful should attend to who it is who speaks even more than to what is said.[106]

By far the most influential theologian of the Catholic reform was the Italian Jesuit Robert Bellarmine (1542–1621), whose three-volume *Disputations on the Controversies of Christian Faith Against the Heretics*

---

[103] Ibid., 126.

[104] Giuseppe Alberigo, "The Council of Trent," in *Catholicism in Early Modern History: A Guide to Research*, ed. John W. O'Malley (St. Louis: Center for Reformation Research, 1988), 219–23.

[105] Giuseppe Alberigo, "From the Council of Trent to 'Tridentinism,'" in Bulman and Parella, *Trent to Vatican II*, 19–37.

[106] Yves Congar, *L'Eglise de saint Augustin à l'époque modern* (Paris: Editions du Cerf, 1970), 371.

of Our Times (1586–1593) both examines the teachings of the Reformers and presents Catholic teaching.[107] His famous definition of the church was influential for the next 350 years. Against some of the Reformers (e.g., Calvin and, before him, Wycliff and Hus), he insists on the identity and visibility of the one church of Christ. The church is "the group of men and women brought together by the profession of the same Christian faith and by communion in the same sacraments under the governance of legitimate pastors, especially of the one vicar of Christ on earth, the Roman Pontiff."[108] From this follows who belongs to the church and who does not. By reason of the first element, infidels, heretics, and apostates are excluded; by reason of the second, catechumens and the excommunicated; by reason of the third, those who have faith and sacraments but who are not subject to the church's legitimate pastors. The church's external exclusivity is joined with "a surprising internal inclusivity," one that allows, in Bellarmine's words, room for "reprobates, the wicked, and the ungodly," so avoiding the echoes of Donatism that surfaced in some of the prior critiques of the church.[109] Unlike those who saw the essence of the church in an interiority known only to God, Bellarmine famously stresses the church's visibility: "The church is a group of men and women as visible and palpable as is the group of the Roman people or the Kingdom of France or the Republic of Venice."[110]

In considering the unity of the church, Bellarmine cites several factors: "(1) the one call of God, (2) the one ultimate end, (3) the same means: faith, sacraments, and laws, (4) the one Holy Spirit, 'the external and separate governor' of the Church." But it is "(5) the one 'internal and conjoined governor', Christ and his Vicar, and (6) the 'connection of members among themselves and especially with their

---

[107] Ibid., 371–76, and Christopher Ruddy, "*Ressourcement* and the Enduring Legacy of Post-Tridentine Theology," in *Ressourcement: A Movement for Renewal in Twentieth-Century Catholic Theology*, ed. Gabriel Flynn and Paul D. Murray, with the assistance of Patricia Kelly (Oxford: Oxford University Press, 2012), 192–93.

[108] Cited in Ruddy, "*Ressourcement*," 192.

[109] Ibid., 193.

[110] Ibid., 192.

head,'" that are most fundamentally important. Submission to authority, rather than communion in the divine life or a sacramental fellowship, is given principal place even when he speaks of *communio* in the church or of its sharing in spiritual goods (*commercium spiritual*).[111] Representing Christ the head, the pope is said to possess universal jurisdiction. By delegation from the pope, bishops share that power in the dioceses assigned to them, and, in turn, delegate such power to pastors.[112] Spiritual authority in the church, though, is to serve the church's sole purpose, to provide the means by which the faithful are brought to salvation.

For all his emphasis on the visibility of the church, Bellarmine also notes that one might belong to the soul of the church by living with the Spirit's gifts of faith, hope, and charity, without belonging to the visible body of the church. Based on the doctrine of the universal salvific will of God, he is the first to so interpret the axiom "No salvation outside the church" as to allow that there is no one who does not, at some time, receive such grace from God as would enable one to be "disposed for justification, and eventually arrive at salvation."[113] Bellarmine's work, topical rather than comprehensive, lacks treatment of the laity apart from church-state considerations. It has a minimum of polemics and, unlike his scholastic contemporaries, is sensitive to history and patristic sources. Bellarmine's theological work is complemented by a retreat he wrote for himself and as "a sort of counselor" for others occupied in the affairs of the church, *The Mind's Ascent to God by the Ladder of Created Things*.[114] The work is written in a style that seeks to arouse gratitude to God and to impart a joyful vision of life and religion. In this it has an affinity with the art and rhetoric of the Baroque, of which we shall see more soon.[115]

---

[111] Joseph A. Komonchak, "Concepts of Communion: Past and Present," *Cristianesimo nella Storia* 16 (1995): 324.

[112] Congar, *L'Eglise*, 373–74 and note 11.

[113] Citation from Bellarmine's *On Grace and Free Will* in Francis A. Sullivan, *Salvation Outside the Church? Tracing the History of the Catholic Response* (New York: Paulist Press, 1992), 90.

[114] In *Robert Bellarmine: Spiritual Writings*, trans. and ed. John Patrick Donnelly and Roland J. Teske (New York: Paulist Press, 1989), 47–230, at 50.

[115] John O'Malley, "Preface," in ibid., 8–9.

The theme of the church was a major concern of post-Tridentine theology. Given the challenges of the Reformers and the political and intellectual developments of the seventeenth, eighteenth, and nineteenth centuries, the key themes are not surprising: "The church's authority in matters religious and political, the papacy, ecclesial visibility and institutions, the necessity and distinctiveness of the ordained priesthood, the objectivity of the sacraments, a quantitative catholicity emphasizing universality in time and space, and an apologetic focus on the four notes of the church."[116] One notes in these topics a marked difference from the summary of the fathers' theology of the church given at the conclusion of chapter 6 above. In its debate with the Protestants, the postconciliar emphasis on the social dimensions of the church failed to take full advantage of Trent's most innovative element, its teaching on justification.[117]

Implicit in some of the theological reflections on the church was an understanding of the church's relationship to the New Testament and to the church of the fathers. Sixteenth-century Reformers often pointed negatively to changes in the church that, they said, departed from the apostolic faith. Catholics spoke of Protestants as "innovators" because they departed from the faith and practices the church had known for centuries. Protestant historical work, done by a team of scholars, began to appear in 1559.[118] The work, called *The Magdeburg Centuries*, attempted to describe each century in terms of sixteen categories, among which were such items as the expansion of the church, doctrine and heresies, important figures, church rituals and government, and Judaism. The work tried to show that in each age the ministry of the Word took place and that the core of the faith as they saw it, justification by faith, was maintained throughout. The teachings of the Reformers, these historians asserted, were not new but really a return to the apostolic church in the face of Catholic accretions that departed from that faith. The chief innovator of the latter, they said, was the papacy, and in each age voices spoke against

---

[116] Ruddy, "*Ressourcement*," 192.

[117] Alberigo, "From the Council of Trent to 'Tridentinism,'" 28–29.

[118] Robert L. Wilken, *The Myth of Christian Beginnings: History's Impact on Belief* (Garden City, NY: Doubleday, 1971), 107–13.

the abuses of the papacy. The Catholic response began to appear in 1588.[119] The *Annales Ecclesiastici*, undertaken by Cesare Baronius (d. 1607), tried to present the church's history year by year. Baronius saw the need "to prove that Catholicism had always been and still was the same as it had been in the beginning."[120] He sought to show that the church was a "visible monarchy" established by Christ the Lord, founded on Peter, and preserved inviolate by his successors. Baronius's own contribution suffered from his biased presuppositions, but it laid the foundations for later historical studies that so contributed to understanding the church's history and its theology.

Other voices in this period also spoke of a vision of church. Ignatius of Loyola (d. 1556) expressed his understanding of church in the "company of Jesus" (the Society of Jesus) he founded and in his distinctive apostolic spirituality. Ignatius intended that he and his companions "serve the Lord alone and the Church his spouse, under the Roman pontiff, the vicar of Christ on earth."[121] Only by making Christ the center of one's life and remaining in his company could an individual or the church itself be renewed. His *Spiritual Exercises* were written to that end. The first of his "Rules for Thinking with the Church" at the conclusion of the *Exercises* refers to the church as "the true Spouse of Jesus Christ, our Holy Mother the hierarchical Church," a phrase that has been called his "quintessential view of the Church."[122] He often speaks of the church as the mother of believers; the expression "the hierarchical Church," twice used in the *Exercises*, appears to have been original with him.[123] In what has been called Ignatius's "ecclesial mysticism there is a dynamic relationship between God,

---

[119] Ibid., 114–17.

[120] Cyriac K. Pullapilly, *Caesar Baronius: Counter-Reformation Historian* (Notre Dame, IN: University of Notre Dame Press, 1975), 145.

[121] From the "Formula of the Institute," written by Ignatius himself, cited in Avery Cardinal Dulles, *Church and Society: The Lawrence J. McGinley Lectures, 1988–2007* (New York: Fordham University Press, 2008), 498.

[122] *The Spiritual Exercises of Saint Ignatius*, trans. and commentary by George E. Ganss (Chicago: Loyola Press, 1992), 133–37, at 133, and Olin, *Catholic Reformation*, 202.

[123] Olin, *Catholic Reformation*, 369.

church, obedience, and mission.[124] While promoting the immediacy of the individual to God, he places great emphasis on the mediation of the church. The thirteenth of the rules just mentioned states the belief that "between Christ our Lord, the Bridegroom, and the Church, his Spouse, there is the one same Spirit who governs and guides us for the salvation of our souls."[125] For Ignatius, following Christ and serving the church are one. Undergirding this sense of serving the mission of Christ in the church is what has been called "a virtual sea change in spirituality": by making God's will, God's choice, the determining guide to one's fundamental choice in life or in the daily choices made in trying to serve the Lord, the classical idea of "deification" is replaced by the desire to give oneself in obedience to the will of God in the unfolding of God's plan for the salvation for the world.[126] The ministry of the Society had a counterpart in the Ursuline Sisters founded by Angela Merici (d. 1540). The world-affirming spirituality of the Jesuits would be complemented by the highly influential ministry and writings of Francis de Sales (d. 1622).[127]

Both Teresa of Avila (d. 1582) and John of the Cross (d. 1591), often recognized as the Western Church's preeminent authorities in the theology of the spiritual life,[128] saw life in the context of the church. For Teresa, the church is the indispensable mediator of God's saving work in Christ, exercised in the retelling of Scripture and through the sacraments, the latter seen as witnesses to God's abiding com-

---

[124] Dulles, *Church and Society*, 242, and Congar, *L'Eglise*, 370.

[125] Ganss, *The Spiritual Exercises*, 135.

[126] Mark A. McIntosh, *Mystical Theology: The Integrity of Spirituality and Theology*, Challenges in Contemporary Theology (Malden, MA: Blackwell Publishing, 1998), 106–7, and Hans Urs von Balthasar, *Thérèse of Lisieux: The Story of a Mission*, trans. Donald Nichol (London and New York: Sheed and Ward, 1953), 225–26.

[127] Robert Bireley, *The Refashioning of Catholicism, 1450–1700: A Reassessment of the Counter Reformation* (Washington, DC: The Catholic University of America Press, 1999), 178–81.

[128] E. W. Trueman Dicken, "Teresa of Jesus and John of the Cross," in *The Study of Spirituality*, ed. Cheslyn Jones, Geoffrey Wainwright, and Edward Yarnold (New York: Oxford University Press, 1986), 364.

mitment to the church.¹²⁹ While submitting to the authority of the church, Teresa, contemplative radical that she was, did not shrink from questioning church practice or the exercise of authority of its officeholders if she saw them at odds with what the church said and did "authoritatively." At times, she appealed to gospel accounts of Jesus and the apostles as guides for herself and for the church. In her view, the prayer of a reformed religious life was indispensable for a renewal of life in the church; religious lives lived with integrity, she maintained, were to stand as a challenge to the whole church.¹³⁰

The major works of John of the Cross, often using the imagery of the Song of Songs, regard the bride not primarily the individual Christian but "the ecclesial soul in which the Church is personified."¹³¹ In his lengthy *Romance* on the gospel text "In the beginning was the Word," John situates a consideration of creation and salvation in his vision of church. In that romance, he speaks of the church:

> He would take her
> tenderly in his arms
> and there give her his love;
> and when they were thus one,
> he would lift her to the Father
> where God's very joy
> would be her joy . . .
> for, taken wholly into God,
> she will live the life of God.¹³²

John's commentary on the final verses of his Spiritual Canticle often relates the soul-bride to the church-bride.¹³³ The commentary concludes with the bride's desire that the Son of God transfer her from

---

¹²⁹ Rowan Williams, *Teresa of Avila* (London: Continuum, 1991), 218.

¹³⁰ Mullin, *Short World History*, 140, and Williams, *Teresa of Avila*, 123.

¹³¹ Antonio Maria Sicari, "The Vision of the Church in St. John of the Cross," *Communio* 37 (Winter 2010): 701–7, at 702.

¹³² "Romances, No. 4," in *The Collected Works of John of the Cross*, trans. Kieran Kavanaugh and Otilio Rodriguez, rev. Kieran Kavanaugh (Washington, DC: ICS Publications, 1991), 60–68, at 64.

¹³³ *The Spiritual Canticle*, in *Collected Works of John of the Cross*, stanzas 29.2; 29.3; 30.7; and 36.5.

the spiritual marriage in the church militant to the glorious marriage of the church triumphant. The passage concludes with a prayer that Jesus, the Bridegroom of faithful souls, bring all who invoke his name to his heavenly marriage.[134] Both Teresa and John continue the centuries-old tradition of seeing in the nuptial imagery of the Song of Songs a symbol of the mutual love between Christ and the church.

Trent said nothing about the missionary efforts associated with Portuguese and Spanish colonial expansion that was well underway even before the council was called.[135] (With only limited success, Rome sought to remove the missions from colonial control through the founding of the *Congregatio de Propaganda Fide*, "for the propagation of the faith," in 1622.) Missionary experience contributed insights regarding church, even if they were not widely accepted at the time. A minority voice in the royal patronage system (the Spanish *patronato real* and Portuguese *padroado*), Bartolomé de Las Casas (d. 1566) sought to reenvision the church in the context of the peoples being exploited by Iberian economic and political interests.[136] In his early work, *De unico vocationis modo omnium gentium ad veram religionem* (The Only Way to Draw All People to the True Faith), Las Casas saw the church as "the body of Christ insofar as it places the poor of the world, and in them Christ, at the center of its life and concern."[137] Only if it does that will the church have the power to save. Ecclesial indifference to injustice to the powerless, Las Casas claimed, compromised the church's evangelizing mission.

In the mission to Asia, Jesuit Francis Xavier (d. 1552) tried to discern the strengths and virtues of a highly developed Japanese culture as a point of contact with the Christian message when he began a mission to Japan in 1549. Accommodations to Chinese culture were made by Italian Jesuit Matteo Ricci (d. 1610), following the directives of the

---

[134] Ibid., 40.7.

[135] R. Po-Chia Hsia, *The World of Catholic Renewal, 1540–1770*, 2nd ed. (Cambridge: Cambridge University Press, 2005), chaps. 12 and 13, and Bireley, *Refashioning of Catholicism*, chap. 7.

[136] James B. Nickoloff, "A 'Church of the Poor' in the Sixteenth Century: The Ecclesiology of Bartolomé de Las Casas' *De unico modo*," *Journal of Hispanic/Latino Theology* 2, no. 4 (1995): 26–49.

[137] Ibid., 35.

1579 *Instruction* of the Jesuit *visitador*, Alessandro Valignano, that missioners should not attempt to persuade Asian peoples to change "their customs, their habits, and their behavior" provided they were not clearly contrary to religion or morality. "What could be more absurd, indeed, than to transport France, Italy, or some other European country to the Chinese? Do not bring them our countries but the faith."[138] Even with setbacks, the Chinese mission grew until the adaptation expressed in the so-called Chinese Rites was prohibited by Pope Clement XI in 1715 and again by Benedict XIV in 1749. Efforts to adapt to the traditions of India, undertaken by Italian Jesuit Roberto de Nobili (d. 1656) made some headway, though church officials abandoned this approach after de Nobili's death.

Baroque Catholicism (1580–1720)

Even as efforts were being made in the missions to adapt to local cultures, the church in Europe was itself developing what came to be called Baroque Catholicism. The word "baroque" comes from the Middle French word for an irregularly shaped pearl. The movement began in Renaissance Rome but gradually spread to other parts of Catholic Europe and, through mendicant and Jesuit missionaries, even to the Spanish colonies overseas. Epitomized by the Jesuit church of the Gesù, built in Rome between 1568 and 1575, and later by the baldachino over the high altar and the Chair of Peter in St. Peter's in Rome by Gianlorenzo Bernini (d. 1680), the baroque extended from the end of the sixteenth century well into the twentieth century, even if it went "underground" during the Enlightenment of the eighteenth century. Inspired by the reform orders of the Jesuits, the followers of Philip Neri (d. 1595), and the priestly order of the Theatines, founded in 1524, the baroque reflected a restored Catholic self-confidence. Two features of the baroque are important indicators of its approach to the church. The first is evident in its architecture

---

[138] Hsia, *The World of Catholic Renewal*, 210. J.-M.-R. Tillard, *Church of Churches: The Ecclesiology of Communion*, trans. R. C. De Peaux (Collegeville, MN: Liturgical Press, 1992), 258, attributes the same text to the Congregation of the Propagation of the Faith, 1659.

and art. The Gesù and the countless churches it influenced eliminated the choir space and any altar screens hindering the congregation's view of the altar and, in the process, permitting women to be part of the choir. Emphasis on preaching led to prominence given to the pulpit, though the focal point of the church was the altar and, prominently above it, a tabernacle and a place for a monstrance to expose the sacred host. Lavish decorations replete with representations of angels and saints were designed to celebrate a church triumphant after the trials of the Reformation. "Everything in both piety and architecture focused on the splendor, the power, the majesty, the glory of God reigning in heaven but also present in that segment of earthly space enclosed by the church building," itself "a heavenly throne room set on earth."[139] Through the church came God's grace helping people to avoid sin and live prayerful Christian lives. A second feature was the liturgy itself. If barriers were removed to give the congregation clear sight of the altar, what happened at the altar was very much the affair of the priest and his assistants rather than that of the congregation: "Forced into the background [was] any notion that the faithful had a part to play in the prayer of the priest or that they should co-offer in closer union with him."[140] The faithful in the congregation made use of prayer books with meditations on parts of the Mass or various expressions of popular piety, though they were more spectators than participants. Yet even with limits, Baroque Catholicism preserved and nourished the faith, the devotion, and the prayer of generations. The restored confidence of the baroque architectural style, combined with the Catholic revival in Italy and the Iberian Peninsula, give cause to speak now of a *Roman Catholicism* "that recognizably differed from the earlier western Catholic heritage" and from the emerging Protestant churches.[141] It is this situation in which

---

[139] James F. White, *Roman Catholic Worship: Trent to Today* (New York: Paulist Press, 1995), 28.

[140] Joseph A. Jungmann, *The Mass of the Roman Rite: Its Origins and Development (Missarum Sollemnia)*, trans. Francis A. Brunner, 2 vols. (New York: Benziger Brothers, 1950), 1:142.

[141] Robert Bruce Mullin, *Short World History*, 140. We shall see in the next chapter that Joseph Komonchak uses the term "Roman Catholicism" to describe

Roman Catholicism, Lutheranism, and the Reform tradition (Calvin) came to have more clearly distinct and settled identities in what some historians today speak of as the "Confessional Age."

The Jansenist View of the Church

The name Jansenism comes from the Flemish Cornelius Jansen (d. 1638), director of a college at the University of Louvain and later bishop of Ypres (in modern Belgium). Early French Jansenists were also much influenced by Jansen's friend and collaborator, Jean Duvergier de Hauranne, abbé de Saint-Cyran (d. 1643). Jansen's work, *Augustinus*, published in 1640, shared the fear that Catholic critiques of Protestant reliance on Augustine's views on grace and predestination might contribute to a Catholic denial of the bishop of Hippo's thought. Not only did the *Augustinus* give an exaggeratedly pessimistic outlook on the nature of original sin and human freedom, it proposed that Augustine's teaching was the doctrine of the church to which the authority of the church was subordinate.[142] Jansen's work was condemned the year after its publication, though its rigorous tenets found a reception among devout French and Dutch Catholics, and eventually among some in Austria, Spain, and Italy. In their desire to renew the church, Jansenists (they preferred to be called "Friends of the Truth" or "Disciples of St. Augustine") raised issues involving the life and understanding of the church, several of which were seen as challenging papal authority. Jansenists promoted vernacular translations of the Hebrew and Greek biblical texts (Trent insisted on the Latin Vulgate) and of most of the liturgy, using both as a means of promoting lay participation, especially among women, in the life of the church. Texts of the fathers, especially those of Augustine, and of the ancient councils were invoked as the authoritative guides for Catholic life and as giving support to the collegial role and

---

the specific social form of the Catholic Church in the nineteenth and the first half of the twentieth centuries.

[142] Gemma Simmonds, "Jansenism: An Early Ressourcement Movement?," in *Ressourcement: A Movement for Renewal in Twentieth-Century Catholic Theology*, ed. Gabriel Flynn and Paul D. Murray (Oxford: Oxford University Press, 2012), 23–35, at 31.

teaching authority of the bishops. Arguing that the five propositions of Jansenist thought condemned in 1653 were not in fact to be found in Jansen's book, supporters defended the rights of the individual conscience against external authority. Much of this ran counter to post-Tridentine official thinking, though debates between the Jansenists and papal authority lasted well into the eighteenth century. Elements of Jansenist reform—lay participation in the liturgy, the promotion of Bible reading by the laity, appreciation of the writings of the fathers of the church, the collegial responsibility of the bishops—would eventually be adopted by the church, but at the time they were caught up in a radical Augustinianism that hindered their implementation in the wider church.

The Church as "Perfect Society"

Alongside the development of Baroque Catholicism there also emerged the juridical and canonical view of church as "perfect society."[143] Three notes by way of background: First, the unity of the medieval Christian commonwealth, the *respublica christiana*, had gradually broken down as autonomous states and nations asserted their independence in the fourteenth and fifteenth centuries. Prior to that, for almost a thousand years, church and state were parts of a unified whole, admittedly with sometimes strong differences regarding the exercise of authority by either one or the other. Second, in Protestant parts of Europe, "state churches" were being established whereby the church was seen as a *collegium* within the state, giving the government a role in ecclesial affairs. Third, nationalist movements in the seventeenth and eighteenth centuries sought to restrict Roman authority in the local church and to allow for greater power of civil officials in church matters. The most prominent of such took place in France, in part as a response to Rome's condemnation of Jansenism.

---

[143] Patrick Granfield, "The Rise and Fall of *Societas Perfecta*," in *May Church Ministers Be Politicians?* Concilium 157, ed. Peter Huizing and Knut Walf (New York: Seabury Press, 1982), 3–8.

French bishops sympathetic to Jansenist ideas challenged the role of the pope in the church in France in what became a revived French version of conciliarism. The Four Gallican Articles of 1682, adopted by the Assembly of the Clergy of France during the reign of Louis XIV (1643–1715), the "Sun King," (1) recognized the authority of the pope but held to a complete independence of the French king from Roman control in temporal matters; (2) affirmed the superiority of a general council over the pope; (3) demanded papal respect of the rights and customs of the church in France; and (4) taught that the supreme teaching authority of the pope was irreformable only on the consent of the universal church.[144] Though condemned repeatedly by the popes, Gallican theses were upheld by bishops, priests, and laity in France throughout much of the eighteenth century.

Variations of the Gallican outlook were proposed in Germany and Austria in the latter part of the eighteenth century. In Germany, this took the name of Febronianism, from the pseudonym, Febronius, of a suffragan bishop of Trier who advocated the creation of a national German Church subject to local rulers. The full title of this work, published in Latin in 1763 and soon translated into German, French, Italian, Spanish, and Portuguese, reveals its irenic interest: *On the Constitution of the Church and the Legitimate Power of the Pope, a Book Composed for the Purpose of Reuniting in Religion Separated Christians.*[145] The Austrian version became known as Josephism (or Josephinism), after Emperor Joseph II (Holy Roman Emperor 1765–1790), who sought to subject the church to the power of the sovereign. Government opposition to the church grew with the French Revolution and the policies of Napoleon (emperor of the French 1804–1815) and, toward the end of the nineteenth century, with the *Kulturkampf* (1871–1890) of German Chancellor Otto von Bismark.

One official response to these conflicts—the use of concordats was another—relied on the concept of the church as *societas perfecta*, the

---

[144] Text published in Klaus Schatz, *Papal Primacy From Its Origins to the Present*, trans. John A. Otto and Linda M. Maloney (Collegeville, MN: Liturgical Press, 1996), 188–89.

[145] Francis Oakley, *The Conciliarist Tradition: Constitutionalism in the Catholic Church, 1300–1870* (New York: Oxford University Press, 2003), 184.

church as "perfect society." The term, first used by an Austrian canonist in the late eighteenth century and later developed by other canonists, refers to a society, distinct from others, having its own proper end and the means necessary to achieve that end and not subject to or part of any other society. The notion was a deliberate counterpart to Protestant jurists who held that the church was not a perfect society but, as mentioned, a *collegium* within the state. Catholic use of the term lasted through the nineteenth century and up to the mid-twentieth century. The idea of church as perfect society underscores the visible societal nature of the church possessing the God-given means needed to achieve its ends. It also affirms both the church's independence from the state and its freedom to engage in its mission, but it afforded little room for a theology of the local church and reinforced a juridical approach to ecclesial understanding. Since true church and perfect society were equated, neither did the term allow any recognition of church in other Christian communities. Jesuit theologian Henri de Lubac noted that up to the mid-twentieth century, the treatise on the church "in its regular form has been built up in two major stages: one in opposition to the imperial and royal jurists [in the early fourteenth century], the other in opposition to Gallican and Protestant doctrines."[146] Official preoccupation with the church's external and hierarchical elements over these years is understandable, given the challenges of the times, but the church as mystery and community of worship was inevitably sidelined.[147] As we have seen, though, and shall see again, there were simultaneously many other understandings of the church as well.

The notion of church as perfect society became a mainstay in defending Catholic identity during the eighteenth-century "Enlightenment" (in England, the "Age of Reason"), generally considered the dawn of the modern era.[148] Influenced by seventeenth-century astronomers

---

[146] Henri de Lubac, *Catholicism: Christ and the Common Destiny of Man*, trans. Lancelot C. Sheppard and Elizabeth Englund (San Francisco: Ignatius Press, 1988), 314.

[147] Granfield, "Rise and Fall of *Societas Perfecta*," 6.

[148] Diarmaid MacCullogh, *Christianity: The First Three Thousand Years* (New York: Viking, 2009), chap. 21, and John Vidmar, *The Catholic Church Through the*

Johannes Kepler (d. 1630) and Galileo Galilei (d. 1642) and French mathematician and philosopher René Descartes (d. 1650), and somewhat later from John Locke (d. 1704) and Isaac Newton (d. 1727), the Enlightenment came to full flower in the eighteenth century, a combination of scientific, philosophical, and political movements that made the period quite distinctive from what had gone before. Characteristics of the age were the general adoption of the scientific method as a path to truth, an optimistic outlook regarding the world and human nature, its confidence in the power of reason to improve the lot of humankind, its rejection of revelation and extrinsic authority, and, in Protestant countries, its antisacramentalism; these characteristics posed serious challenges for the church. The Catholic notion of an ecclesial and hierarchical mediation of the sacred was rejected. In the culture of the age, there was no room for a church sacramentally continuing the mission of the Son and the Spirit. Rather, Christians stood alone before God and were individually responsible for their personal commitment to Christ.[149] Many of these Enlightenment ideas inspired the political and social goals of the French Revolution of 1789 and the years following. The revolution and the increasing radicalization that followed it not only attacked the notion of a hierarchical society with which the official church was closely aligned but challenged the very existence of Christianity. While Napoleon restored a measure of political order and recognized the importance of the church, his own rule severely restricted the church in many ways. The restoration of both the European monarchs and the papacy in the Congress of Vienna in 1815 gave new impetus to reflecting on the church in itself and in its relations to society at large. To these we shall turn in the next chapter.

Ages, 2nd ed. (New York: Paulist Press, 2014), 258–66.

[149] Matthew L. Lamb and Matthew Levering, "Introduction," in *Vatican II: Renewal within Tradition*, ed. Matthew L. Lamb and Matthew Levering (New York: Oxford University Press, 2008), 6. The authors draw on the work of Canadian philosopher Charles Taylor.

CHAPTER NINE

Theologies of the Church: 1815 to the Eve of Vatican II

The near century and a half from 1815 to the opening of the Second Vatican Council in 1962 was marked by distinctive developments in understanding the church. This chapter will discuss these by way of three considerations. We look first at the social construct of "Modern Roman Catholicism," extending from 1815 to the eve of the council. A second segment examines alternative efforts to understand the church during the nineteenth century. A third section reflects on the theology of the church in the twentieth century prior to the council. This strategy is admittedly somewhat artificial as there is an overlap of time between the sections and some figures deserve to be considered in more than one area. Hopefully, though, this approach will introduce us to the rich complexity of these years.

The Development of Modern Roman Catholicism

The events of the French Revolution (1789) and the Napoleonic era (1799–1815) left the church in Europe in near shambles. In France and in the many areas of Europe that had come under Napoleon's control, many of the structures of the church were seriously damaged: dioceses had no bishops; church property was confiscated; seminaries were closed; communication with Rome was destroyed; one pope, Pius VI (pope 1775–1799), died in exile as a prisoner of the Revolutionary army, and another, Pius VII (pope 1800–1823), was held prisoner by Napoleon from 1809 until March 1814. Only after Napoleon's final defeat in 1814 and the Congress of Vienna in that year and the next were the pope and papal sovereignty restored.[1] In many ways the church on the local level recovered from the trauma of these years. But official Catholicism, led largely by the popes themselves, set about constructing a sociological form of Catholicism that differed from both its medieval and baroque predecessors. The church was put forward as a "counter-society, legitimated by a counter-culture," an alternative to the social, political, and economic world inspired by the Enlightenment and values of the French Revolution.[2] Officials in the church sought to give authoritative certainty to those shaken by such scientific works as Charles Lyell's *Principles of Geology* (1830–1833) and Charles Darwin's *Origin of Species* (1859), both of which challenged accepted religious understandings.[3]

This official construct, with its monarchical view of the papacy, is often designated as Modern Roman Catholicism. The understanding of church in this construct merits attention in itself but also because of the role it plays in understanding the Second Vatican Council. This official Catholicism was most pronounced from 1815 to the death of Pius X (1914), though its influence continued through the first half of the twentieth century. Other efforts to articulate a theology of the church, minority voices in the nineteenth century but prominent in the 1930s to 1950s, are the subject of the other two segments of this chapter.

A fundamental characteristic of Rome's theological construct, especially in the nineteenth century, was its negative stance vis-à-vis the so-called modern world inspired by Enlightenment and Revolutionary principles. This negativity was anticipated in the 1775 encyclical of Pius VI, *Inscrutabile Divinae Sapientiae*, issued in the first year of his pontificate. The encyclical was "a categorical denunciation of

---

[1] See Stephen Schloesser, "Reproach vs. *Rapprochement*: Historical Preconditions of a Paradigm Shift in the Reform of Vatican II," in *50 Years On: Probing the Riches of Vatican II*, ed. David G. Schultenover (Collegeville, MN: Liturgical Press, 2015), xi–l.

[2] Joseph A. Komonchak, "Modernity and the Construction of Roman Catholicism," *Cristianesimo nella Storia* 18 (1997): 353–85, at 356. Komonchak "builds upon the work of several European scholars" (ibid.).

[3] T. Howland Sanks, "Co-operation, Co-optation, Condemnation: Theologians and the Magisterium, 1870–1978," *Chicago Studies* 17, no. 2 (1978): 245.

the ideas associated with the Enlightenment . . . an official declaration of war from on high for a conflict that had been raging in the trenches for decades."[4] The church in this view stood opposed to four ideas: Luther's teaching on private judgment; the Enlightenment's insistence on critical reason and its repudiation of external authority and tradition; the political idea of democratic popular sovereignty; and either the individualism of emerging *laissez-faire* capitalism or its opposites in socialism or communism. Modern Roman Catholicism was deliberately constructed as an alternative to these views. To speak of the construction of a social form of church reminds us of the need to make the sometimes difficult distinction between the church in its theological definition, a gift of God, and the social form of its embodiment in a particular cultural, social, and political milieu.[5] The church is both theological reality and social and historical construct, the latter embodied in a human response to the divine givens. Notable examples of changes in the social reality of the church came with the rule of Constantine, growing differences between the East and the West, and again in the medieval church of feudal Europe and the Gregorian Reform.

After the restoration of 1815, church officials looked to an idealized view of medieval Christendom as the norm for understanding the church. A state-recognized Catholicism would be the basis of political and social unity and stability. Church law would guide civil law, and the church would oversee education and institutions and programs of social assistance. The state, for its part, would protect and support the church and encourage citizens in their religious responsibilities. Where the ideal of a Catholic state was not possible, other forms of church-state relationships would be tolerable. State protection of religious rights was called for when Catholics were a minority. This Catholic outlook was not exceptional: The Peace of Augsburg (1555), recognizing both Lutheranism and Catholicism in Germany, and the Peace of Westphalia (1648), ending the Thirty Years' War, allowed for

---

[4] John W. O'Malley, *A History of the Popes: From Peter to the Present* (Lanham, MD: Rowman & Littlefield, 2010), 227.

[5] Komonchak, "Modernity and the Construction of Roman Catholicism," 357.

established churches, both treaties accepting the principle of *cuius regio, eius religio* (whose region, his religion) that subjects should adhere to the religion of their ruler.

A further articulation of what would become the official view of church came in the 1799 publication by the Camaldolese monk Mauro Cappellari (1765–1846), *The Triumph of the Holy See and the Church over the Attacks of Innovators, Who Are Rejected and Fought with Their Own Weapons*.[6] Written at a time when the papacy was at very low ebb, the book was a response to a 1784 work promoting conciliarist and Gallican ideas, along with the notion of popular sovereignty. Two ideas in Cappellari's work are especially important. First, the work saw no reason to study the testimonies of tradition; the church, it asserted, received from Christ a form of government that remained unchanged over the centuries. The author simply dismissed the practice of theologians of the first millennium who sought to respect the authority of tradition in new situations. What was in the present was always so. Bypassing tradition also meant there was no longer any way to test the legitimacy of any papal activity. Second, in an analogy between church and state, Cappellari applied the concept of sovereignty to the pope's plenitude of power, which included legislative, judicial, and executive authority and called for unqualified obedience on the part of all. Papal infallibility was a necessary condition of papal sovereignty. When Cappellari was elected pope as Gregory XVI in 1831, his book was translated into several languages and became a guide to practical implementation.

Cappellari's views were supported in the treatise *Du Pape* (1819) by the Sardinian ambassador to St. Petersburg, Count Joseph de Maistre (d. 1821).[7] The work argued for the absolute necessity of an infallible papal sovereignty and its union with the monarchy as the only bulwark against the social and political rebellions against legitimate authority inspired by the Reformation and the French Revolution. A

---

[6] Hermann J. Pottmeyer, *Towards a Papacy in Communion: Perspectives from Vatican Councils I and II*, trans. Matthew J. O'Connell (New York: Crossroad, 1998), 51–53.

[7] See a summary of *Du Pape* in Wilfrid Ward, *William George Ward and the Catholic Revival* (London: Macmillan and Co., 1893), 88–92.

famous sentence from a letter written in 1814 expresses the kernel of de Maistre's thought: "Christianity rests entirely on the pope. . . . There can be no European religion without Christianity; there can be no Christianity without Catholicism; there can be no Catholicism without the pope; there can be no pope without the sovereignty that belongs to him."[8] While political in motivation, de Maistre's work had a powerful influence on theological developments leading to the First Vatican Council (1869–1870). His work has been called the "gospel of modern Ultramontanism."[9]

The ultramontane movement referred to those who, from the viewpoint of France or Germany, looked "beyond the mountains" (the Alps) to Rome and to the pope for direction and guidance. The term "new" or "modern" was added to distinguish the nineteenth-century movement from the earlier papal ecclesiology of Robert Bellarmine. The notion of papal primacy in terms of sovereignty became its dominant idea. The movement gained strength especially in France, but also in Germany, Spain, England, and, in its own way, the United States. The reasons for this development vary. In France, some, believing that acceptance of liberal and democratic ideas was the best means to promote a Catholic revival, looked to a strong papacy to offset the autocracy of the restored French monarchy. Others regarded a strengthened papacy as the principal bulwark against the liberal ideas that, they believed, threatened the established order of a Christian Europe. German Catholics promoted ultramontanism as a way to combat secularism and rationalism. Members of the Society of Jesus, fully restored in 1814 after their suppression in 1773, were generally ultramontane in outlook. Instructed by the pope, the Jesuits founded the journal *La Civiltà Cattolica* ("Catholic Civilization") in 1850 "with the expressed purpose of restoring in the modern world the role played by the church in medieval christendom."[10]

---

[8] Letter to Count von Blacas, May 22, 1814, cited by Pottmeyer, *Towards a Papacy in Communion*, 53–54.

[9] Ward, *William George Ward*, 88.

[10] James Hennesey, "Leo XIII's Thomistic Revival: A Political and Philosophical Event," *The Journal of Religion* 58 Suppl. (1978): S191.

Gregory XVI's thought is further indicated in his response to the influential French liberal priest, Felicité Robert de Lammenais (d. 1854). The latter was among those who looked to the papacy as a means of opposing the French monarchy and supporting liberties inspired by the French Revolution, notably freedom of the church from state control. Gregory responded in his encyclical *Mirari vos* (1832), a scathing denunciation of liberal Catholicism. The encyclical dismissed outright any thought of possible church renewal: "It is obviously absurd and injurious [*absurdus ac maxime . . . iniurosus*] to propose a certain 'restoration and regeneration' for her as though necessary for her safety and growth, as if she could be considered subject to defect or obscuration or other misfortune." The same letter attacked the idea of religious liberty: "[The] shameful font of indifferentism gives rise to that absurd and erroneous proposition which claims the *liberty of conscience* must be maintained for everyone,"[11] an idea he "thoroughly condemned" in a second encyclical, *Singulari nos* (1834).[12] The notion of religious liberty at that time could imply the idea of religious indifference, though not necessarily. Many of the notions rejected in the two encyclicals had recently been incorporated in the state constitutions of Belgium (1831), in several Latin American countries after revolutions led by Simon Bolívar and Bernardo O'Higgins, and, earlier, in the Constitution of the United States (1789). *Mirari vos* was "a landmark document," setting "to some extent the agenda for the key utterances of his successor, Pius IX."[13]

Pius IX, *Pio Nono* (pope 1846–1878), began his pontificate with some genuinely liberal gestures. But increasing Italian nationalism and the murder of the papal prime minister two years later led Pius to embrace the policies of Gregory XVI. As with his recent predecessors, Pius IX shared the religious conviction that the role of the pope was inseparably dependent on his remaining ruler of the Papal States.

---

[11] www.papalencyclicals.net/greg16/g16mirar.htm, nos. 10 and 14 (accessed November 20, 2015).
[12] www.papalencyclicals.net/greg16/g16singu.htm, no. 3 (accessed November 20, 2015).
[13] Eamon Duffy, *Saints and Sinners: A History of the Popes* (New Haven, CT: Yale University Press in association with S4C, 1997), 220.

His encyclical *Quanta cura* and, even more, the *Syllabus of Errors* appended to it give a summary of Pius IX's views.[14] The *Syllabus* lists eighty propositions taken from various documents of his pontificate. The section on religion and society rejects the idea of separation of church and state and the idea that the church was not a "true and perfect society, entirely free." Proposition 77 rejects the notion that "it is no longer expedient that the Catholic religion should be held as the only religion of the State, to the exclusion of all other forms of worship." The final statement rejects the thesis that the pope should reconcile himself with "progress, liberalism, and modern civilization." The text from which this last statement came sought to counter the aggressively secularist policies of the Piedmont and is properly understood only in that context; taken out of this setting it fed the idea of the church's opposition to modern society. The *Syllabus* as a whole was "not entirely off the point," given that many ideas of nineteenth-century "modernity" were inimical to Catholicism and "out of touch with the deep religious sentiments of most of the people."[15] But it reinforced a very specific image of the church.

Pius IX and his successors adopted a triad of strategies that served to promote an official vision of church with a highly centralized papal authority and a negative stance toward the social, political, and economic world of the nineteenth century. One strategy involved encouraging or even promoting a "counter-revolutionary mysticism"[16] involving Marian piety and devotion to Christ the King and his Sacred Heart. Mary's immaculate conception was often given a counter-revolutionary and even apocalyptic interpretation. Pius IX chose December 8, the solemnity of the Immaculate Conception, to mark important events of his pontificate and looked to Mary, "Aid of Christians," to protect himself and his See as she was credited with protecting Pius V in battle with the Turks at the Battle of Lepanto (1571). He had considered linking the condemnation of modern errors with the definition of the dogma of the immaculate conception (1854);

---

[14] www.ewtn.com/library/papaldoc/p9syll.htm (accessed March 13, 2014).
[15] O'Malley, *A History of the Popes*, 245–46.
[16] Komonchak, "Modernity and the Construction of Roman Catholicism," 363–69.

it was promulgated instead on the definition's tenth anniversary. Pope Leo XIII (1878–1903) issued sixteen major documents on the rosary, appealing at times to the role attributed to the Virgin at Lepanto and in the struggle with the Albigensians, seen as precursors of modern socialists and Freemasons. Leo's encyclical (1899) dedicating the human race to Christ the King under the symbol of the Sacred Heart encouraged seeing Christ's heart as a sign of hope as once Constantine saw the cross as a sign of ultimate victory.

A second strategy consisted in papal efforts to direct Catholic intellectual life.[17] In the first two decades of the pontificate of Pius IX the works of several scholars were placed on the *Index* or authors were required to submit to propositions drafted by Roman congregations.[18] German scholarship's announced desire to understand Protestant thought and to engage in dialogue with contemporary philosophy and historical studies provoked grave misgivings among scholastics with close ties to Rome. Overt opposition followed a congress of German philosophers, theologians, and historians at Munich in the fall of 1863. The keynote by priest-historian Ignaz von Döllinger (d. 1890) argued that scholastic method ought to study the revealed given in its organic whole, attentive to its historical development. There was to be no ecclesiastical interference in intellectual inquiry unless it contradicted church dogma, allowing scholarship itself to correct its own exaggerations or errors. In a publicized letter to Munich's archbishop, Pius IX rejected any implicit critique of scholasticism, lamented that an assembly of theologians would meet without hierarchical mandate, and insisted that it belonged to ecclesiastical authority to oversee and direct theological activity.[19] The *Syllabus of Errors* was published the following year.

Pope Leo XIII made notable attempts to guide intellectual life in the church and promoted independent scholarship by opening the

---

[17] Ibid., 373–76.

[18] Gerald A. McCool, *Catholic Theology in the Nineteenth Century: The Quest for a Unitary Method* (New York: Seabury Press, 1977), 129–35.

[19] R. Aubert, *Le pontificat de Pie IX (1846–1878)*, new ed., Histoire de l'Eglise depuis les origines jusqua'à nos jours, vol. 21 (Bloud & Gay, 1963), 205–9.

Vatican archives.[20] Though he shared the critical stance of his predecessors to what he regarded as the social and political evils of the day,[21] he proposed a positive means to meet the challenges facing the church. This he did authoritatively in his encyclical *Aeterni Patris* (1888), promoting the study of the philosophy and theology of Thomas Aquinas—the greatest mind of medieval Christendom.[22] He saw in the Thomistic synthesis a sure means of interpreting and responding to the ills caused by "the fatal disjunctions of reason from faith and of society from religion."[23] His directive also sought to keep modern philosophy, especially German Romanticism, out of Catholicism.[24] As political as it was philosophical, the encyclical was meant to provide the underpinnings for the unrealized ultramontane goal of Pius IX, that the church would be the guardian of an immutable social order.[25] Leo XIII also exemplified the new papal teaching role assumed in the mid-nineteenth century. Earlier popes "taught" principally by condemning doctrinal error; the teaching role was largely left to professional theologians in the universities. In the eighty-one years following 1775 the popes issued sixteen encyclicals; in twenty-five years, Leo issued eighty-eight, many of them doctrinal statements.[26] Some of them, we shall see, had an important bearing on the theology of the church.

The most notable exercise of authoritative teaching in the early twentieth century came in the so-called modernist crisis.[27] The term was used to identify varied attempts to incorporate into Catholic thinking

---

[20] See O'Malley, *History of the Popes*, chap. 25: "Leo XIII: Searching for Solutions," 251–60.

[21] See Pope Leo XIII's first encyclical, *Inscrutabili Dei consilio*, April 28, 1878. Available at www.papalencyclicals.net/.

[22] McCool, *Catholic Theology*, 226–40.

[23] Komonchak, "Modernity and the Construction of Roman Catholicism," 375.

[24] Fergus Kerr, *Twentieth-Century Catholic Theologians: From Scholasticism to Nuptial Mysticism* (Malden, MA: Blackwell, 2007), 2.

[25] Hennesey, "Leo XIII's Thomistic Revival," S190.

[26] www.papalencyclicals.net/Leo13 (accessed April 4, 2014).

[27] C. J. T. Talar, "'The Synthesis of All Heresies'—100 Years On," *Theological Studies* 68 (2007): 491–514.

current developments in biblical studies, theological understanding, or social and political theory. The use of historical criticism in biblical studies and in the history of dogmas and the exploration of the subjective element in human knowing, especially when done with little nuance, aroused concern not only in those sympathetic to these efforts but especially in those who saw them as serious threats to officially accepted understandings. An insight into one aspect of the modernist approach appears in the famous sentence by the French Catholic priest Alfred Loisy (d. 1940). No institution on earth or in history could be questioned, he wrote, if one held the principle that nothing may exist except in its original form. "Such a principle is contrary to the law of life, which is movement and a continual effort of adaptation to conditions always new and perpetually changing."[28] Pius X (pope 1903–1914) reacted swiftly and severely. Under his direction, in 1907 the Office of the Roman and Universal Inquisition (its name was changed in 1908 to the Holy Office and changed again in 1965 to the Congregation for the Doctrine of the Faith) issued a Syllabus (*Lamentabili Sane*) of sixty-five statements drawn from Loisy's writings. The encyclical *Pascendi* two months later drew a composite of ideas of the modernist heresy. Between 1905 and 1915 the Biblical Commission, founded in 1902 by Leo XIII to give cautious but constructive guidance to Catholic biblical studies, issued a series of directives that promoted a very uncritical view of the church's beginnings (see appendix 1). Three years later an oath against modernism reinforced opposition to any of these scholarly developments, affecting Catholic scholarship for several decades. In 1950 a further effort to direct the church's intellectual life came in the encyclical *Humani Generis* of Pius XII, which we will treat in the last part of this chapter.

A third strategy of modern Roman Catholicism was the official promotion of Catholic associations meant to counter the political and social agenda of nineteenth-century liberalism, to immunize Catholics from their influence, and to defend the church's claims.[29] While

---

[28] Alfred Loisy, *The Gospel and the Church*, ed. Bernard B. Scott, Lives of Jesus Series, ed. Leander Keck (Philadelphia: Fortress Press, 1976), 166.

[29] Komonchak, "Modernity and the Construction of Roman Catholicism," 369–71.

involved in a wide range of activities, the symbolic context for many of these associations was that of warfare, defending the church against "[forces] destructive of all religion and of all civilization," so said an article in *La Civiltà Cattolica* in 1871.[30] These associations contributed to the formation of the Catholic subculture we have been describing. Some decades later many associations came to be included under the umbrella of Catholic Action, a movement of Catholic lay activity, promoted especially by Pius XI (pope 1922–1939). His encyclical *Non abbiamo bisogno* of 1931 affirmed that such Catholic groups participated in the apostolate of the hierarchy. While under strict ecclesiastical control, the efforts of one group, at least, Young Christian Workers, was seen as a sign that the church was abandoning "the state of siege."[31]

The First Vatican Council (1869–1870)

A "culminating moment" in the development of modern Roman Catholicism came in the First Vatican Council, reckoned as the twentieth council of the church, the first since the Council of Trent.[32] Pius IX called for the council in 1867 in reaction to antidogmatic movements of the day and to focus Catholic life on the basic elements of revelation. In reality, the council was in many ways a continuation of the church's battle with the Enlightenment and the principles of the French Revolution and a deliberate effort to promote papal authority in the church and in society. Of the fifty-one draft documents (schemas) prepared for the council, only six were discussed; only two were promulgated, both "central to the drama of the century."[33] The first, the Dogmatic Constitution on the Catholic Faith,

---

[30] Cited in ibid., 370.

[31] Joseph A. Komonchak, "Returning from Exile: Catholic Theology in the 1930s," in *The Twentieth Century: A Theological Overview*, ed. Gregory Baum (Maryknoll, NY: Orbis Books, 1999), 39.

[32] Komonchak, "Modernity and the Construction of Roman Catholicism," 376–77. See Roger Aubert, "The Vatican Council," in Roger Aubert and others, *The Church in the Age of Liberalism*, trans. Peter Becker, History of the Church, vol. 8, ed. Hubert Jedin and John Dolan (New York: Crossroad, 1981), 315–30.

[33] Komonchak, "Modernity and the Construction of Roman Catholicism," 376.

addressed such issues as revelation and Scripture, the nature and necessity of faith, and the relationship between faith and reason. The constitution's statement on revelation (chap. 2) includes the notion of God's self-revelation but places primary emphasis on revelation as divinely revealed truth, the "deposit of faith" spoken of in the second of the two constitutions. The argument for the credibility of the church reflects a line of nineteenth-century apologetics, which puts emphasis on exterior facts to argue for the divine origin of the church: "The church herself by reason of her astonishing propagation, her outstanding holiness and her inexhaustible fertility in every kind of goodness, by her catholic unity and her *unconquerable stability*, is a kind of great and perpetual motive of credibility and an incontrovertible evidence of her own divine mission."[34] The assertion (chap. 4) that our understanding of the mysteries of faith is helped by seeing their connection with one another would be taken up by later theological reflection on the church.

The first draft of the text on the church, composed by professors at the Roman universities, generally reflects official thinking about the church at the time. To the fifteen chapters of the text there were added twenty-one canons and seventy lengthy notes explaining the text, indicating the opposing errors, and giving supporting sources.[35] The opening chapter on the mystical body, with a plea that this idea be "deeply and firmly rooted" in the minds of the faithful, was a significant shift from the heavy emphasis on the visible and sociological approach prominent since Bellarmine. Five reasons were given for the use of the term: its frequency in Scripture; its expressing the divine essence of the church; its use in countering Protestant claims

---

[34] Norman P. Tanner, ed., *Decrees of the Ecumenical Councils*, vol. 2: *Trent to Vatican II* (London: Sheed and Ward, 1990), 807–8; emphasis added. Henry Edward Manning, archbishop of Westminster, spoke of "the beauty of inflexibility." Duffy, *Saints and Sinners*, 275.

[35] Henri Rondet, *Vatican I: Le Concile de Pie IX; La préparation; Les méthods de travail; Les schémas restés en suspens*, Collection "Théologie, Pastorale et Spiritualité: Recherches et Synthèses" (Paris: P. Lethielleux, 1962), 118. English translation of the first ten chapters in Josef Neuner and Heinrich Roos, *The Teaching of the Catholic Church as Contained in Her Documents*, ed. Karl Rahner (Staten Island, NY: Alba House, 1967), 211–20.

that Catholic thinking considered only the external dimensions of the church; the balance it provides for the external and internal elements of the church; and its value in countering the materialism of the age.[36] Use of this metaphor reflects developments to be described in the latter parts of this chapter. Much of the rest of the schema was defensive, more sociological than theological, with a distinctly anti-Protestant tone.[37] The church as a true society, perfect, visible, and absolutely necessary for salvation, was the "controlling idea" of the schema.[38] Emphasis on the philosophical notion of society allowed no room for historical sensitivity. Though the draft's lengthy treatment of the papacy comes only after ten chapters on the church in general, bishops receive very scant attention, reflecting continuing Roman nervousness about anything reminiscent of Gallican or conciliar ideas. The final four chapters of the schema deal with papal temporal sovereignty as the providential guarantor of independence for the pope's ministry, rejection of the separation of church and state, and the necessity of governments to take into account Christian morality, and the precepts of the church.

While the draft never came to the floor for council discussion, written observations of the council members showed dissatisfaction on several points.[39] Some opposed the metaphor of the mystical body as too vague or too abstract and mystical. Others regretted a lack of greater attention to the church's foundation by Christ or its place in the economy of salvation and its relation to the people of God in the Old Testament. Some regretted the heavy reliance on the philosophical notion of society or the schema's lack of historical perspective. Major criticism centered on the lack of treatment of the role of bishops in the church and the theocratic views of the final chapters.

[36] Patrick Granfield, "The Church as *Societas Perfecta* in the Schemata of Vatican I," *Church History* 48 (1979): 434.

[37] Roger Aubert, *Vatican I*, ed. Gervais Dumeige, Histoire des conciles oecuméniques, vol. 12 (Paris: Editions de l'Orante, 1964), 151.

[38] Granfield, "Church as *Societas Perfecta*," 435.

[39] Roger Aubert, "L'ecclésiologie au concile du Vatican," in B. Botte and others, *Le concile et les conciles: Contribution à l'histoire de la vie conciliare de l'Eglise* (Paris: Editions du Cerf, 1960), 252–57.

A second draft, incorporating the council members' written observations on the first draft, was composed by Jesuit theologian Joseph Kleutgen.[40] Though the text, a revision of the first ten chapters of the original, was never distributed, it is another indication of thinking about the church at the time.[41] Three terms—*corpus* (body), *coetus* (assembly), and *regnum* (kingdom)—were used to describe the church, though all were given a sociological understanding. Mention was made of the church as the body of Christ to indicate the divine and supernatural element of the church as well, though the theme was not consistently maintained; the church as true and perfect society remained central to the exposition.[42] The Scriptures are referred to, especially in the opening chapters on Christ's institution of the church, but there is little indication that they much inspired the rest of the text. Only rarely is the Holy Spirit mentioned. The role of bishops in their own dioceses and in the universal church is recognized, though far more attention is given to the rights of the Roman pontiff. What is said of bishops is exclusively juridical. No attention is given to the role of the lay faithful. Sixteen canons rejected errors.

The draft text on the missions was largely disciplinary in its focus, though it did call for respect for Eastern rites and recognition of local customs.

The original draft on the church contained no mention of papal infallibility, though in the months before the council there was much agitation for and against the council's dealing with that issue. A month after the council began, some five hundred bishops petitioned that the topic be placed on the council's agenda. One hundred thirty-six bishops opposed such a move, either because they thought that papal infallibility could not be defined or that such a definition was unnecessary or inopportune. The majority carried the day. The minority group of bishops played an important part in tempering the sometimes excessive proposals of a small group of the majority.

---

[40] A French translation of the text is given in Rondet, *Vatican I*, 191–207.
[41] Aubert, "L'ecclésiologie au concile du Vatican," 257–62.
[42] Granfield, "Church as *Societas Perfecta*," 443–44.

Vatican I: The First Dogmatic Constitution on the Church of Christ

Chapter 11 on the papacy in the original draft was excised from the rest of the schema and to it was joined an added text on papal infallibility. This revised text was presented in four chapters: on the institution of the primacy in Peter (drawing on Matt 16:16-19 and John 21:15-17); on the permanence of that primacy in the bishop of Rome; on the nature and power of the primacy; and on the pope's infallible teaching authority. Since the rest of the schema on the church was to be dealt with at a later time, this text was called the First Dogmatic Constitution on the Church of Christ. After nearly two months of sometimes impassioned debates, the text was solemnly approved on July 18, 1870.[43]

The preamble to the text describes the pope's role as the permanent principle and visible foundation of the church's twofold unity, that of faith and that of communion. The third chapter describes the pope's primacy of jurisdiction: it is supreme (subject to no one) and universal (no exemptions). It is *ordinary* (belongs to his office), truly *episcopal* (the same as every bishop in his own diocese), and *immediate* (allows of no civil or ecclesiastical intermediaries). The decree notes that papal authority does not detract from the ordinary and immediate power of episcopal jurisdiction coming to bishops as successors of the apostles and by appointment of the Holy Spirit. This advances the teaching of Trent, though it makes no mention of their authority as members of the episcopal college with the pope as head of the college.[44] The text cites the words of Gregory I, that the pope is honored when rightful honor is given to the entire church and when due honor is not denied to his brother bishops.

The chapter on the pope's teaching authority is very carefully crafted.[45] The pope's charism of infallibility is a divine assistance from

---

[43] Tanner, *Decrees of the Ecumenical Councils*, 2:811–16.

[44] Gilles Langevin, "Synthèse de la tradition doctrinale sur la primauté du successeur de Pierre durant le second millénaire," in *Il primate del successore di Pietro: Atti del simposio teologico, Roma, dicembre 1996* (Vatican City: Liberia editrice Vaticana, 1998), 164.

[45] Pottmeyer, *Towards a Papacy in Communion*, chap. 5.

error in carefully delineated circumstances: when, *ex cathedra* (Latin for "from the chair"), that is, with his supreme apostolic authority, he defines a doctrine concerning faith or morals to be held by the whole church. In this instance, he possesses the same infallibility Christ willed for his church. In the historical preamble to the actual definition, mention of the pope's use of ecumenical councils or his "consulting the opinion of the churches (*sententia ecclesiae*) scattered throughout the world"[46] served to relate the papal magisterium to the Scriptures and apostolic tradition and to void any idea that the pope might propose some "new doctrine." A final sentence—added to quash any lingering Gallican sentiment—that papal definitions are irreformable of themselves and not by the consent of the church (*non autem ex consensu ecclesiae*) deals with a juridical consideration that, if not understood correctly, could seem to support a papal infallibility independent of the faith of the church.

The outbreak of the Franco-Prussian War the day after the solemn promulgation of the constitution led to the eventual suspension of the council with the result that it never returned to the topics in the original schema on the church or in Kleutgen's revision. The council was never officially reconvened. Within the following year, Victor Emmanuel II (d. 1878), king of Sardinia-Piedmont, and the Italian nationalists invaded the Papal States, and Rome was declared the capital of a united Italy. The pope was accorded the rights and honors of a sovereign for what became the Vatican City State. Pius IX saw himself as "prisoner of the Vatican"; only with Pius XI in 1929 were papal claims to the earthly sovereignty of the Papal States relinquished.

While in the popular mind Vatican I is often associated with the teaching on papal infallibility, and then too often without the nuances in the council itself, it is the teaching on papal primacy of jurisdiction that is the more important of the two teachings, though both had an enormous impact on the life and understanding of the church. In its statements about papal authority, conceived as absolute sovereignty, official Catholicism was strengthening the hand of its leader in the church's battle with modernity and secular liberalism. The council's

---

[46] Tanner, *Decrees of the Ecumenical Councils*, 2:815–16.

historical setting must be taken into account in understanding the development of its teaching.[47]

Nineteenth-Century Alternative Efforts to Understand the Church

Concurrent with the developments described above, other quite different approaches were underway seeking to express the nature and mission of the church. We look at four examples: the Catholic faculty at Tübingen; Jesuit theologian Johann Baptist Franzelin; German professor Matthias Joseph Scheeben; and England's John Henry Newman.

At the beginning of the nineteenth century, Catholic Germany faced two competing worldviews, each with its own understanding of the church and its mission.[48] The first, described as *Aufklärung* Catholicism, drew on themes prominent in the eighteenth-century German Enlightenment. Sharing the latter's interest in religious matters, it saw the church primarily as a school of moral teaching, the liturgy as an educative tool, and church structure largely in terms of the Febronian episcopal ideas mentioned in the previous chapter. It emphasized the local church, use of the vernacular in liturgy, and the importance of freedom and of the individual, all as a way to promote Protestant respect for Catholicism. The second worldview was that of Catholic romanticism, influenced by early German romanticism, one of whose principal representatives was Friedrich Schleiermacher (d. 1834), commonly seen as the father of modern Protestant theology.[49] Reacting against Enlightenment rationalism and attracted to an earlier Pietist evangelism and devotion, Schleiermacher defended a "sense and taste for the Infinite" as the essence of religion. If there is religion at all, he insisted, it must be social, a consequence of the

---

[47] Walter Kasper, "Introduction to the Theme and Catholic Hermeneutics of the Dogmas of the First Vatican Council," in *The Petrine Ministry: Catholics and Orthodox in Dialogue*, ed. Walter Kasper (New York: Paulist Press, 2006), 19.

[48] Michael J. Himes, *Ongoing Incarnation: Johann Adam Möhler and the Beginnings of Modern Ecclesiology* (New York: Crossroad, 1997), 1–42.

[49] See Roger Haight, *Comparative Ecclesiology*, Christian Community in History, vol. 2 (New York: Continuum, 2005), 311–36.

nature of being human and the human desire to communicate. Representatives of Catholic romanticism, for their part, emphasized the role of the Holy Spirit as the "soul" in the life of the church and preferred to see the church in terms of community rather than an organized society. Yet its most prominent representative, Johann Michael Sailer (d. 1832), theologian and later bishop of Regensburg, drawing on the writings of Thomas à Kempis, John of the Cross, and Teresa of Avila, so emphasized the need for personal experience in the life of the individual Christian that the community was given little attention.

Many of these ideas were considered by the Catholic faculty of theology at the state university at Tübingen.[50] Johann Sebastian Drey (d. 1853), often considered the founder of Catholic Tübingen, stood at the beginning of what has been called the "romantic-idealist renaissance of German Catholicism."[51] He sought to construct a theology "that combined fidelity to the breadth and depth of the Catholic tradition with an engagement of contemporary philosophical movements."[52] In his view, the church is the Spirit-guided historical community living in fidelity to Christ and continuing to be a living witness to the story of salvation. Drey's insights were taken up and developed by his pupil, his later colleague and Tübingen's most famous representative, Johann Adam Möhler (1796–1838).[53] Influenced by the thinking of Schleiermacher and, more so, by Protestant church historian Johann August Neander, Möhler came to appreciate the importance of history as a study of "the life beneath the institutions and the spirit beneath the doctrines."[54] The encounter with romantic "concern for community and the primacy of life over

[50] Grant Kaplan, *Answering the Enlightenment: The Catholic Recovery of Historical Revelation* (New York: Crossroad, 2006), chap. 6, and Himes, *Ongoing Incarnation*, 28–42.

[51] Thomas F. O'Meara, "Revelation and History: Schelling, Möhler and Congar," *Irish Theological Quarterly* 53, no.1 (1987): 26.

[52] Kaplan, *Answering the Enlightenment*, 99.

[53] Haight, *Comparative Ecclesiology*, 336–55, and Himes, *Ongoing Incarnation*.

[54] Hervé Savon, *Johann Adam Möhler: The Father of Modern Theology*, trans. Charles McGrath (Glen Rock, NJ: Deus Books/Paulist Press, 1966), 22.

thought" and with idealist interest in subjectivity and the organic nature of community had an abiding influence on his thought.[55]

The young scholar's early teaching of canon law reflected the generally accepted juridical and sociological approach to understanding the church. But other courses on patristics and church history and articles and reviews he published in Tübingen's newly founded *Theologische Quartalschrift* indicate his attraction to a Spirit-centered understanding of church. Möhler sought to resolve the tension between these two approaches in his first major work, *Einheit in der Kirche* (1825), whose full title in English reads *Unity in the Church, or the Principle of Catholicism Expounded in the Spirit of the Fathers of the Church of the First Three Centuries*. Here, Möhler argues that Christianity experiences its truest self as a "matter of life, of communal life."[56] Unity in the church comes from the divine Spirit and is maintained "by the loving interaction of the faithful."[57] The conception of church in *Einheit* is distinctly theological or, more precisely, pneumatocentric and communitarian. We experience Christ only in the church, and the more we accept the divine life flowing in her, the more we shall live in her and she in us.[58] The first part of *Einheit* deals with the role of the church in the individual's relationship with the Spirit of God; the second, with the tension between this Spirit-formed unity and the historical and hierarchically ordered structures of the church.[59] Desiring, however, that emphasis on the Spirit not lead to a neglect of the role of Christ in the church's institution and in her offices led him to further reflection.

That reflection continued in the several editions of his *Symbolik*, the title referring to the symbols or creeds held by Catholics and

---

[55] Christopher Ruddy, *The Local Church: Tillard and the Future of Catholic Ecclesiology* (New York: Crossroad, 2006), 33.

[56] *Unity in the Church or the Principle of Catholicism, Presented in the Spirit of the Church Fathers of the First Three Centuries*, ed. and trans. Peter C. Erb (Washington, DC: The Catholic University of America Press, 1996), 5, 90, cited by Kaplan, *Answering the Enlightenment*, 103.

[57] *Unity* 7, 93, in Kaplan, *Answering the Enlightenment*, 104.

[58] *Unity* 7, 94, in Kaplan, *Answering the Enlightenment*, 104.

[59] Himes, *Ongoing Incarnation*, chaps. 2 and 3.

Protestants.[60] He sought to relate the church more clearly to the mysteries of the Trinity and the incarnation and to the divine-human relationship generally. Without denying the role of the Spirit, the pneumatocentric approach of *Einheit* cedes to the Christocentric view of his later work. In this context, Möhler writes that "the visible church is the Son of God appearing within mankind in human form in a continuous fashion, constantly renewed, eternally rejuvenated, his ongoing incarnation, just as the faithful are also called in holy scripture the body of Christ."[61] Analogously, he uses the Chalcedonian formula concerning Christ to help explain the church's divine and human elements.[62] Möhler's early death cut short his continuing revision on what would have been the fifth edition of his *Symbolik*.

Möhler is a major figure in the development of the theology of the church.[63] Though his Spirit-centered approach of *Einheit* was largely neglected in the nineteenth century, it would receive much greater recognition in the century that followed. His incarnation-centered theology helped to restore the notion of the church as the body of Christ; this in turn also helped lay the foundations for the later renewal of the church's liturgy.[64] Möhler's seeing the church in relationship to Christ and the mystery of grace led later theology to see the church itself as part of the mystery of faith, not simply as the bearer of that mystery.

---

[60] Johann Adam Möhler, *Symbolism: Exposition of the Doctrinal Differences between Catholics and Protestants as Evidenced by Their Symbolical Writings*, trans. James Burton Robertson, intro. Michael J. Himes (New York: Crossroad, 1997).

[61] Cited in Himes, *Ongoing Incarnation*, 259.

[62] J. R. Geiselman, "Les variations de la définition de l'Eglise chez Joh. Adam Möhler, particulièrement en ce qui concerne les relations entre l'Episcopat et le Primat," trans. M. L. Steinhauser, in *L'Ecclésiologie au XIXe Siecle*, ed. M. Nédoncelle and others (Paris: Editions du Cerf, 1960), 167–69.

[63] Michael J. Himes, "The Development of Ecclesiology: Modernity to the Twentieth Century," in *The Gift of the Church: A Textbook on Ecclesiology in Honor of Patrick Granfield, O.S.B.*, ed. Peter C. Phan (Collegeville, MN: Liturgical Press, 2000), 58–59.

[64] Keith Pecklers, "*Ressourcement* and the Renewal of Catholic Liturgy: On Celebrating the New Rite," in *Ressourcement: A Movement for Renewal in Twentieth-Century Catholic Theology*, ed. Gabriel Flynn and Paul D. Murray with assistance of Patricia Kelly (Oxford: Oxford University Press, 2012), 321.

In the latter part of the nineteenth century, theologians of the Jesuit School of Theology in Rome, generally advocates of Roman scholasticism, came to imitate both Möhler's use of the body of Christ metaphor to speak of the church and his practice of incorporating patristic insights into his theology. A prominent member of this school was Johann Baptist Franzelin (d. 1886), whose manual on the church stands as a major effort to incorporate a greater theological dimension in his reflections. Exploring various aspects of Christ's relation to the church (with references to 1 Cor 1:9 and 1 John 1:3), he was led to see the church as the supernatural society in which all the just from the beginning of the world to its end constituted what the creed speaks of as the communion of saints.[65] The just, he says, are joined as "members with Christ the Head, in Christ with God the Sanctifier, in Christ and God with one another."[66] Using the analogy of the incarnation, Franzelin spoke of the church's inmost constitution expressed through an external element, human and visible, and an internal element that is divine and invisible. Yet when he came to specifically address the questions of visibility and membership, he remained in the constraints set centuries before by Robert Bellarmine. The external bonds alone were said to constitute the church as a visible society; the internal bonds, utterly spiritual and the goal of the church, were not essential to that visibility. So strong was Bellarmine's influence still that Franzelin was unable successfully to integrate the two basic dimensions of the church.

Perhaps the most important nineteenth-century heir to Möhler's thought was the Rome-educated German theologian Matthias Joseph Scheeben (1835–1888). His conviction concerning the homogeneity between the mystery of Christ and the church guided his understanding of the latter.[67] The inner nature of the church is as supernatural as is the inner nature of the God-man. This explains, he says, why the church is hidden and mysterious. It conforms to other human

---

[65] Joseph A. Komonchak, "Concepts of Communion: Past and Present," *Cristianesimo nella Storia* 16 (1995): 326–29.

[66] Franzelin, cited in Komonchak, "Concepts of Communion," 327.

[67] Stanislas Jaki, *Les Tendances nouvelles de l'Ecclésiologie* (Rome: Casa Editrice Herder, 1957), 208 and 212.

societies in its being visible and in matters of organization, but it differs essentially from them in its innermost character.[68] The church continues the work of Christ as Christ continually forms his body by the activity of the Spirit. In and through the baptized, Christ continues his twofold priestly task of giving worship to the Father in the name of all people and bringing to them his redeeming grace.[69] Scheeben sees in the church the full fruition of the union of Christ with the entire human race that took place at the incarnation. And another way of seeing this, he says, citing Ephesians 5:22-33, is seeing the church in terms of its mystical marriage with the God-man.[70]

The fourth voice we consider is that of John Henry Newman (1801–1890). His importance in our study is twofold: he gives important reflections on the theology of the church, and he does so with the desire to lead others to commit themselves to Christ's church and to what that might mean for their lives. His ideas about church developed in the course of his own spiritual journey from Calvinistic Evangelicalism to High-Church Anglicanism and ultimately to his acceptance of Roman Catholicism.[71] Three interconnected principles undergird his approach to the church: the testimony of our conscience concerning the existence of a moral sovereign; the conviction that this moral sovereign provides a guiding revelation concerning right and wrong; and the principle of sacramentality by which God acts in our world, this last coming from his appreciation of the thought of Clement of Alexandria and Origen.[72] Newman sees revelation unfolding first in nature, then in historical events such as the exodus, and finally in Jesus Christ and continuing after him in the sacraments and structures of the church. Newman never tried to "prove" the church; he held that one comes to give a *real* (not simply *notional*)

---

[68] Matthias Joseph Scheeben, *The Mysteries of Christianity*, trans. Cyril Vollert (St. Louis: B. Herder, 1946), 540.

[69] Kevin McNamara, "The Ecclesiological Movement in Germany in the Twentieth Century," *Irish Ecclesiastical Record* 102 (1964): 350.

[70] Scheeben, *The Mysteries of Christianity*, 543.

[71] See the brief description in Avery Cardinal Dulles, *Newman*, ed. Brian Davies, Outstanding Christian Thinkers (London: Continuum, 2002), chap. 1.

[72] Edward Jeremy Miller, *John Henry Newman on the Idea of Church* (Shepherdstown, WV: Patmos Press, 1987), 12–20.

assent to Christ present and acting in the church when the cumulative probabilities lead one to make such a commitment.

Resolution of the two difficulties that once kept Newman from embracing Catholicism led to important insights regarding the church. He wondered, first, if recent church teachings (e.g., transubstantiation, papal infallibility, the immaculate conception) corrupted the ancient faith. His response came in his *Essay on the Development of Christian Doctrine*, published in 1845, the year of his entering the church. Newman makes no claim to prove the details of development; there is always room for the exercise of faith. The essay, though, makes the point that "an historic thing, if it remains alive in history, will not remain the same as it was when it first saw the light of day."[73] As the Tübingen School did before him, Newman sees that an understanding of church necessarily involves a sensitivity to its historical development. The second difficulty centered on corruptions in the church or what seemed like unwarranted excesses of one type or another. This he addressed in 1877, in the lengthy preface to the third edition of *Lectures on the Prophetical Office of the Church*, the first of two volumes of *The Via Media of the Anglican Church*. Newman observes three functions at play in the church, corresponding to the three offices of Christ: priest, prophet, and king. The church's priestly function is concerned with worship; the prophetic, with truth; the kingly, with leading the church in the name of the Lord. Each function has an essential role in the church and can and must support the others. Imbalance or abuse comes when one function dominates or acts apart from the others. Isolated, the priestly function could tend to "superstition and enthusiasm"; the prophetic or theological function, to "rationalism"; the governing function, "to ambition and tyranny." In practice, the functions are not infrequently in tension one with another; a vitally interacting church cannot expect otherwise. As revelation is "the initial and essential idea of Christianity," it must be the guide for all the functions. Since revelation is the basic concern of the theological function, Newman accords to it the "fundamental and regulating principle of the whole Church system," while recognizing

---

[73] Gustave Weigel's foreword in John Henry Cardinal Newman, *An Essay on the Development of Christian Doctrine* (Garden City, NY: Image Books, 1960), 11.

that theology itself cannot function apart from worship and the governing function.[74] In a letter to a father whose son he had received into the church, Newman offers a guide to the effective exercise of teaching authority in the church: where leaders inspire "admiration, trust, and love" for Christ and the church, appeals to merely formal authority are not needed; where they have not done that, it is ineffective.[75]

Reflections on the three functions in the church became rather standard after the work of John Calvin, though nineteenth-century Catholic theologians and canon lawyers restricted all three offices to the pope and bishops.[76] That Newman would ascribe them to the entire church and to all individuals within the church is consistent with his emphasis on the lay faithful in the theology and life of the church.[77] This emphasis appears most notably, perhaps, in his 1859 essay, "On Consulting the Faithful in Matters of Doctrine," even if more recent scholarship challenges his use of some of the evidence.[78] Newman saw the laity as having a unique and specific responsibility in the mission of the church as the historical bearer of God's message. To prepare a well-instructed laity lay behind his efforts at a Catholic university in Ireland, in his promoting, unsuccessfully, Catholic attendance at Oxford and Cambridge, and in his support of a lay journal for lay readers.

Newman's understanding of church, drawing from his study of patristic sources, is thoroughly sacramental: the church is a visible sign and instrument of the invisible.[79] As the sermon "The Visible

---

[74] John Henry Cardinal Newman, *The Via Media of the Anglican Church: Illustrated in Lectures, Letters, and Tracts Written between 1830 and 1841*, new ed. (London: Longmans, Green and Co., 1918), xlvii.

[75] Joseph A. Komonchak, "Authority and Its Exercise," in *Church Authority in American Culture: The Second Cardinal Bernardin Conference*, intro. Phillip J. Murnion (New York: Crossroad, 1998), 37–38.

[76] Dulles, *Newman*, 112.

[77] H. F. Davies, "Le rôle et l'apostolat de la hiérarchie et du laïcat dans la théologie de l'Eglise chez Newman," trans. J. Leblond, in *L'ecclésiologie au XIXe siècle*, chap. 12.

[78] John Henry Newman, "On Consulting the Faithful in Matters of Doctrine," printed in *CrossCurrents* 2 (1954), 69–97. See Dulles, *Newman*, 106.

[79] Miller, *Newman*, 130–41.

Temple" puts it: The church is a spiritual temple on earth, made of living stones, a "Temple with God for its Light, and Christ for the High Priest, with wings of Angels for its arches, with Saints and Teachers for its pillars, and with worshippers for its pavement; such a temple has been on earth ever since the Gospel was first preached."[80]

Before turning to the final section of this chapter, we note the pivotal pontificate of Pope Leo XIII (1878–1903). We have seen that Popes Gregory XVI and Pius IX had a major hand in shaping the official view of church so prominent in the nineteenth century. Their successors, from Leo XIII to Pius XII, continued to try to influence the church's self-understanding, sometimes reinforcing the earlier view, but also at times tempering it or giving it a new direction.[81] While Leo XIII's advocacy of the study of Aquinas, mentioned above, was a conservative measure, it influenced Catholic research in ways that would have a direct bearing on the theological understanding of the church. Several of his encyclicals continued to see the church as society, yet Leo moved from a juridical emphasis to underlining the church's holiness and spiritual perfection.[82] A monarchist himself who promoted the centralization of the church in the papacy, he wrote in praise of the ninth-century efforts of Cyril and Methodius to respect and adapt to local culture, though he condemned "Americanism" in the impression—unfounded, in the view of Cardinal Gibbons of Baltimore—that the church in the United States was adapting basics to win converts. Leo's landmark 1891 encyclical *Rerum Novarum*, addressing the plight of the working poor in industrial society, moved the papacy and the official church "away from the ecclesial entrenchment and social detachment and negligence that had extended from

---

[80] John Henry Newman, *Parochial and Plain Sermons* (San Francisco: Ignatius Press, 1987), 1350.

[81] For this and the popes from Leo XIII to Pius XII, see Duffy, *Saints and Sinners*, 235–68. See also Michael J. Lacey, "Leo's Church and Our Own," in *The Crisis of Authority in Catholic Modernity*, ed. Michael J. Lacey and Francis Oakley (New York: Oxford University Press, 2011), chap. 2.

[82] Rembert Weakland, "Images of the Church: From 'Perfect Society' to 'God's People on Pilgrimage,'" in *Unfinished Journey: The Church 40 Years after Vatican II; Essays for John Wilkins*, ed. Austen Iverleigh (New York: Continuum, 2003), 80–81.

the French Revolution (1789) to the death of Pius IX."[83] The encyclical follows the earlier efforts of many others, laypersons and clerics, for whom the "social question" had become a major concern. *Providentissimus Deus* (1893) cautiously promoted Catholic biblical studies; the Pontifical Biblical Commission, founded in 1902, was to promote the study of God's word, even if it also sought to shield that study "not only from every breath of error but even from every rash opinion."[84] The roles of Leo's successors will be mentioned in the next section.

The *Ressourcement* Movement and the Theology of the Church

We conclude this chapter by looking at the remarkable developments that took place in the twentieth century, especially in the 1930s, 1940s, and 1950s. Of this period, Cardinal Ratzinger noted, "More than one observer has remarked that . . . [these decades were] a period of intense and fruitful development, almost unparalleled in the history of the Church, which culminated in the Second Vatican Council."[85] The century opened, recall, with the so-called modernist crisis and the strong reaction of Pius X against what he termed the "synthesis of all heresies." Catholic scholarship in the early decades of the century was largely influenced by Leo XIII's promotion of Thomism and Pius X's condemnation of modernism. Directives from Pius X and the Code of 1917 led to the "strict-observance Thomism" of the Roman schools.[86] At the same time, other scholars tried to deal with the intellectual and spiritual challenges of the time, trying to

---

[83] Stephen J. Pope, "*Rerum Novarum*," in *The New Dictionary of Catholic Social Thought*, ed. Judith A. Dwyer (Collegeville, MN: Liturgical Press, 1994), 828–44, at 843.

[84] Cited in John W. O'Malley, *What Happened at Vatican II* (Cambridge, MA: Belknap Press of Harvard University Press, 2008), 68.

[85] Joseph Cardinal Ratzinger, "*Deus locutus est nobis in Filio*: Some Reflections on Subjectivity, Christology, and the Church," in *Proclaiming the Truth of Jesus Christ: Papers from the Vallombrosa Meeting* [1999] (Washington, DC: United States Catholic Conference, 2000), 13.

[86] Jürgen Mettepenningen and Ward De Pril, "Thomism and the Renewal of Theology: Chenu, Charlier, and Their *Ressourcement*," *Horizons* 39, no. 1 (2012): 53.

avoid anti-modernist censure and what were perceived as the limitations of the regnant neoscholasticism. Several of these efforts would have a direct bearing on an understanding of church.

One of the earliest areas of theological renewal concerned the liturgy.[87] The twentieth-century liturgical movement began in a sense with decrees from Pius X mandating the restoration of Gregorian chant in the liturgy, replacing the operatic music that hindered congregational participation (1903), and advocating the faithful's communicating at each Mass they attended (1905). The pope looked to the liturgy as an indispensable source of the true Christian spirit and sought to promote the "active participation" of all the faithful.[88] Yet in Pius's 1906 encyclical, *Vehementer Nos*, responding to France's unilateral abrogation of the concordat and assigning supervision of worship to an association of laymen, he notes that the church, mystical body of Christ, is "essentially an *unequal* society, a society comprising two categories of persons." Only the pastors have "the right and authority for promoting the end of society and directing all its members towards that end; the one duty of the multitude is to allow themselves to be led, and, like a docile flock, to follow the pastors."[89] The Benedictine Lambert Beauduin (d. 1960) agreed that liturgy is the central act of the church, but he also saw it as a basic guide to the theology of the laity.[90] Romano Guardini (d. 1968) sought to give the theological underpinnings for liturgical renewal in his *The Spirit of the Liturgy* (1918) and *The Church and the Catholic* (1921).[91] Odo Casel (d. 1948) of the German Benedictine abbey of Maria Laach argued for an understanding of Christianity as a mystery made present by the liturgy. These twentieth-century liturgical scholars benefited from the earlier work of the Tübingen School, with its emphasis on the church as the body of Christ and on the power of the church's wor-

---

[87] Pecklers, "*Ressourcement* and the Renewal of Catholic Liturgy," 318–26.
[88] Cited in ibid., 323.
[89] http://www.vatican.va/holy_father/pius_x/encyclicals/documents/hf_p-x_enc_11021906_vehementer-nos_en.html. Italics in the original.
[90] In his *La Piété de l'Eglise* (1914). E.T.: *Liturgy the Life of the Church* (1926).
[91] Romano Guardini, *The Church and the Catholic and the Spirit of the Liturgy*, trans. Ada Lane (New York: Sheed and Ward, 1953).

ship to form the faithful into a single community sharing the divine life. Cautious blessing of the liturgical movement came in the 1947 encyclical of Pius XII (1939–1958), *Mediator Dei*, recognizing the movement's importance in the life of the church. A few years later, the same pope issued decrees that modified the liturgies for the Sacred Triduum and moved them to the times we know them to have today, so restoring awareness of the paschal mystery as the church's principal liturgical celebration. The preconciliar liturgical movement is credited with being "the true breeding ground" for many of the ideas about church taken up by the Second Vatican Council.[92]

After working in the shadow of the anti-modernist directives in the early decades of the century, Catholic biblical studies revived in the 1930s. The publication in 1942 of *The Theology of the Church according to St. Paul* by Louvain professor Lucien Cerfaux reminded Catholics of the breadth of the Pauline ideas of the church, as body of Christ and people of God, as local assembly and cosmic reality. Biblical studies received major support in the 1943 encyclical of Pius XII, *Divino Afflante Spiritu*. The encyclical importantly recognized the diversity of literary genres in which the Scriptures were written and the place of the historical-critical method in biblical interpretation. Scholarly works and the publication of the *Bible de Jérusalem* promoted use of the Bible in theology and in popular piety.

The liturgical and biblical renewals, both in scholarly circles and in popular piety, were part of a broader *ressourcement* in which Dominican and Jesuit scholars had a major role.[93] The term is meant to connote "a fountain or a spring, a source of living water" rather than a retreat motivated by "antiquarian concerns or theological nostalgia."[94] Broadly speaking, the movement had three characteristic features: relating theology to human experience and growth in

---

[92] Joseph Cardinal Ratzinger, "The Ecclesiology of the Second Vatican Council," *Communio* 13 (1986): 245.

[93] The essays in Flynn and Murray, *Ressourcement*, are an excellent resource for a study of this development.

[94] A. N. Williams, "The Future of the Past: The Contemporary Significance of the *Nouvelle Théologie*," *International Journal of Systematic Theology* 7, no. 4 (2005): 353.

the life of the Spirit; seeing its principal resources in the Bible, the liturgy, and the fathers; and being concerned with the apostolate and missionary challenges facing the church. This last reflected the pontificates beginning with Leo XIII that began to supplement concern regarding church-state relations with a desire to influence the world in which the church lived. The forerunners to this effort were Dominicans Marie-Dominique Chenu (1895–1990) and Yves Congar (1904–95), both associated at the time with the Parisian Dominican house of studies, Le Saulchoir. (The school's name comes from the small village near Tournai in southern Belgium where it was located during the anticlerical period in France at the beginning of the century.) In 1935 both published articles calling for a theology deliberately related to the faith and life of ordinary folk and mindful of its historical roots. On the latter point, the faculty at Le Saulchoir studied Aquinas's thought in its historical, literary, and cultural context, using the method of historical criticism applied to the study of Scripture. In 1937, Chenu's privately circulated little book, *Une école de théologie: le Saulchoir*, described the approach used at Le Saulchoir, critically contrasting it to the ahistorical, systematized, and deductive methods practiced elsewhere (that is, in Rome). In 1942 Chenu's book and an article written in the same vein by Louis Charlier (1898–1981), a professor at the Dominican theologate in Louvain, Belgium, were placed on the *Index of Prohibited Books*. An article in *L'Osservatore Romano*, referring derogatorily to the works as *la nouvelle théologie* (the new theology), justified the condemnation because the works "brought neo-scholasticism into discredit with their (exaggerated) interest in the subject, experience, religious commitment, and the notion of development,"[95] charges reminiscent of those made against modernism.

In 1935, Congar launched the *Unam Sanctam* series of monographs on various aspects of the theology of the church, designed, he said, "to recover for ecclesiology the inspiration and the resources of an older and deeper Tradition than the juridical and purely hierarchological schemas that prevailed in first anti-conciliar polemic, then

---

[95] Jürgen Mettepenningen, *Nouvelle Théologie—New Theology: Inheritor of Modernism, Precursor of Vatican II* (London: T & T Clark, 2010), 33.

anti-Protestant, and lastly during the revival under the pontificates of Gregory XVI and Pius IX." The church, he said, "would no longer appear as merely *societas perfecta* or *societas inaequalis, hierarchica* but as the Body of Christ wholly and intimately inspired by his life."[96] Translation difficulties prevented Congar from beginning the series with Johan Adam Möhler's *Unity in the Church*, chosen "to provide the spirit of the series."[97] (It became the series' second volume.) Congar acknowledged the importance of and his indebtedness to the Tübingen theologian in a major article published in 1938, the hundredth anniversary of Möhler's death. In the article, Congar described the theological vision Möhler inspired: "To live *in the church* is to be a living part of an organic totality of which the Holy Spirit is the interior principle, a principle continuing the Incarnation of Christ and incorporating itself in dogma, worship and the social or hierarchical institutions."[98] The first volume of the *Unam Sanctam* series was Congar's own *Chrétiens Désunis: Principes d'un 'eocuménisme' catholique* (1937), influenced, in part, by his conviction that ecumenism is not a specialty added to a treatment on the church but rather belongs to its very life. The work reviewed Protestant, Orthodox, and Anglican notions of the church and its unity and looked for a way Catholics might engage in ecumenism.

In 1950 Congar published his singularly important *Vraie et fausse réforme dans l'Église (True and False Reform in the Church)*.[99] He explained that the work was done in the context of the church of that day in the hope of "liberating the Gospel from more or less outmoded sociological, pastoral, and liturgical forms so as to give it the best possible success in a world calling for new forms, new

---

[96] Yves Congar, "My Path-Findings in the Theology of Laity and Ministries," *The Jurist* 32, no. 2 (1972): 170.

[97] Yves Congar, *Une vie pour la vérité: Jean Puyo interroge le Pére Congar*, ed. Jean Puyo (Paris: Centurion, 1975), 48, cited by Hans Boersma, *Nouvelle Théologie and Sacramental Ontology: A Return to Mystery* (Oxford: Oxford University Press, 2009), 42.

[98] O'Meara, "Revelation and History: 29.

[99] Yves Congar, *True and False Reform in the Church*, trans. with intro. Paul Philibert (Collegeville, MN: Liturgical Press, 2011). The translation is that of the "second and revised edition" of 1967.

expressions, and new structures."[100] Part 2 of the work lists four conditions for reform without schism: holding to the primacy of charity; remaining in communion with the whole church; having patience with delays; undertaking renewal by a return to the fundamental principles of Catholicism. He sought to use a method "that integrates history and theological reflection," so as to be applicable beyond the time of his writing.[101] Three years later, another major work, *Jalons pour une théologie du laïcat* (*Lay People in the Church*),[102] sought to give a theological grounding for the role of the laity in the church by basing that role on baptism and a participation in Christ's threefold office as priest, prophet, and king. A few years earlier American Jesuit John Courtney Murray (d. 1967) published two articles (1944) in the newly founded *Theological Studies* on theology *for* the laity, looking to a theological preparation to help prepare the lay faithful for their proper mission.[103] Like Newman before them, both Murray and Congar saw the laity as primary agents in "transforming," Murray would say, "the total milieu of modern life." Both theologians drew on and advanced the teaching of Pius XI, who wrote, we have seen, of lay participation in the apostolate of the hierarchy.

Jesuit scholars at Fourvière, the Society's theologate for the Provinces of Lyon and Paris, and at the *Institut Catholique* in Paris also contributed to theological and patristic *ressourcement*. Most prominent in this effort were Jean Daniélou (1905–1974) and Henri de Lubac (1896–1991), both asking about the theological task and how best to understand the theology of the church. Daniélou identified three challenges facing theology: as the study of God, it must be permeated with a religious spirit; it must be intelligible to the con-

---

[100] Ibid., 2. From Congar's preface to the second edition.

[101] Ibid., 6.

[102] Yves Congar, *Lay People in the Church: A Study for a Theology of Laity*, trans. Donald Attwater (Westminster, MD: Newman Press, 1957).

[103] See the summary of Murray's argument in Joseph A. Komonchak, "The Future of Theology in the Church," in *New Horizons in Theology*, ed. Terrence W. Tilley, Publication of Catholic Theology Society 50 (2004) (Maryknoll, NY: Orbis Books, 2005), 23–26.

temporary mind; and, more than an intellectual exercise, it must engage the whole of life.[104] To meet these challenges, theology must return to its threefold source: the Bible, the fathers of the church, and the liturgy. Daniélou saw the three sources linked in the fathers: their theology was in large part commentary on the Scriptures and their exegesis intimately related to the liturgy. Led by Daniélou and de Lubac, the French Jesuits in 1943 began publication of bilingual translations of the fathers in the series, *Sources chrétiennes*. The early volumes were largely from the Eastern tradition (and appreciated by Orthodox theologians, émigrés expelled from Russia in the early 1920s, who were themselves engaged in *ressourcement*). Jesuits also inaugurated in 1946 a series of monographs, *Théologie*, many of which would be written from a history-of-doctrine perspective. These efforts and the trajectory they suggested drew criticism for what was interpreted as disdain for the more objectivist and ahistorical world of neo-Thomism.

The scholarly work just mentioned was complemented by the important *History of the Council of Trent*, published in four volumes between 1949 and 1975, by Hubert Jedin (d. 1980). The work is considered one of the most important works of church history in the twentieth century in its embrace of the historical-critical method, championed earlier by other German scholars, as a means of understanding the church as a historical subject.[105] At the same time, in speaking of *church* reform, Jedin held to the framework of Catholic thought so prominent since the sixteenth century, which defined the church largely in terms of the three public offices of pope, bishops, and pastors.[106]

---

[104] Brian Daley, "The *Nouvelle Théologie* and the Patristic Revival: Sources, Symbols and the Science of Theology," *International Journal of Systematic Theology* 7, no. 4 (2005): 363.

[105] Massimo Faggioli, "Hubert Jedin Changed the Paradigm for Church Historians," https://www.ncronline.org/blogs/ncr-today/hubert-jedin-changed-paradigm-church-historians (accessed September 26, 2016).

[106] John W. O'Malley, *Trent and All That: Renaming Catholicism in the Early Modern Era* (Cambridge: Harvard University Press, 2000), 56–57.

Church in the Works of Henri de Lubac

During these same years Henri de Lubac published three major works, each bearing directly on a theological understanding of the church. The first volume (1938), the third of the *Unam Sanctam* series, was his programmatic *Catholicisme: Les aspects sociaux du dogme*.[107] Among others, Congar, von Balthasar, Wojtyla (later John Paul II), and Ratzinger regarded it as "the key book of twentieth-century Catholic theology, the one indispensable text."[108] The work "not only helped restore the idea of the church as sacrament but also pivoted around the notions of an original unity created by God, splintered by sin and destined to be restored in Christ." This vision, de Lubac argued, "could overcome the idea that Christianity was a religion for the comforting of individuals alienated from the wider course of history."[109] De Lubac saw human solidarity in creation and redemption and the church's insertion in time and history as the two ideas fundamental to understanding Catholicism. This essentially social perspective has its roots in Judaism.[110] The Jesuit scholar sees Catholicism as all embracing; it rejects any antithesis between "rites or morals, authority or liberty, faith or works, nature or grace, prayer or sacrifice, Bible or pope, Christ the Savior or Christ the judge, sacraments or the religion of the spirit, mysticism or prophecy."[111] He lamented the practical neglect of the church's spiritual unity in the fourteenth-century treatises on the church and, in the sixteenth and seventeenth centuries, in official teaching opposing Protestantism and Gallicanism. He appreciated the earlier efforts of the Tübingen School toward a renewed vision of church and saw in a prospectus of their *Theologische Quartalshrift* (1819) an important expression of

---

[107] Henri de Lubac, *Catholicism: Christ and the Common Destiny of Man*, trans. Lancelot C. Sheppard and Elizabeth Englund (San Francisco: Ignatius Press, 1988). An earlier trans.: *Catholicism: A Study of the Corporate Destiny of Mankind*, trans. Lancelot C. Sheppard (New York: Sheed and Ward, 1950).

[108] Kerr, *Twentieth-Century Catholic Theologians*, 71.

[109] Joseph Komonchak, "Ecclesiology of Vatican II," *Origins* 28, no. 44 (April 22, 1999): 766.

[110] De Lubac, *Catholicism: Christ and the Common Destiny of Man*, 15 and 156.

[111] Ibid., 315.

the spirit and essence of Catholicism: "The central fact is the revelation of the plan realized by God in humanity: this plan is an organic whole with progressive development in history."[112] This conviction stands behind de Lubac's appreciation of the biblical exegesis of the fathers who, mindful of God's revelation in history, sought the spiritual meaning in the events described in the Bible.

De Lubac's second major work was *Corpus Mysticum: L'Eucharistie et l'Eglise au moyen age: Etude historique* (1944), the third volume of the *Théologie* series.[113] It was this study of the patristic and early medieval periods that showed, as we saw above, that the term mystical body (*corpus mysticum*), long applied to the Eucharist, came to be applied to the church, while the term, the true body of Christ (*corpus verum*), formerly applied to the church, the people of God and community of believers, came to be used for the Eucharist. The transposition of the terms helped prepare the way for fourteenth-century views of church in a more sociological and juridical perspective. Rethinking the relationship between the Eucharist and the church, de Lubac thought, would lead to a theology of the church much more reflective of the church's rich tradition: "Literally speaking . . . the Eucharist makes the Church. It makes of it an inner reality."[114] Highlighting the Eucharist-church interconnectedness would also contribute to a greater theological appreciation of the local church, of the diocese, and also of the local parish community. Dominican scholar Ian Kerr joins others in seeing in Congar's study of the laity and de Lubac's *Corpus Mysticum* the value of historical research in renewing theology and, where needed, reforming church structures.[115]

The third major work was *Surnaturel: Etudes historiques* (1946). The study looked to patristic and medieval Catholic doctrine, including

---

[112] Ibid., 320.

[113] Henri de Lubac, *Corpus Mysticum: The Eucharist and the Church in the Middle Ages*, trans. Gemma Simmonds, with Richard Price and Christopher Stephens, ed. Laurence Paul Hemming and Susan Frank Parsons (Notre Dame, IN: University of Notre Dame Press, 2006).

[114] Ibid., 88.

[115] Fergus Kerr, "French Theology: Yves Congar and Henri de Lubac," in *The Modern Theologians: An Introduction to Christian Theology in the Twentieth Century*, ed. David Ford, 2nd ed. (Malden, MA: Blackwell, 1997), 107 and 110.

the teachings of Augustine and Aquinas, to make the case that, made in the image of God, all human beings are open to supernatural communion with God. Not without controversy, de Lubac challenged the hypothesis, developed in the sixteenth and seventeenth centuries and held by the neo-Thomists of his time, that there could have been a "state of pure nature" that could have enjoyed a purely natural happiness. The thesis of *Surnaturel*, already introduced in *Catholicisme* ("the vision of God is a free gift, and yet the desire for it is at the root of every soul"[116]) would have a bearing on the understanding of the church and the salvation of nonbelievers and non-Christian religions. *Surnaturel* gives the basic *anthropological* context for de Lubac's theological understanding of the church.[117]

In his *Méditations sur l'Eglise*[118] de Lubac attempted to enter "into the very heart" of the mystery of the church.[119] Described as "the spirituality for the theology of *Catholicisme*,"[120] the work explores the paradox (a favorite notion in de Lubac's thinking) of the one church that is visible and invisible, human and divine, both body and bride of Christ. The heart of the church, he says, is the Eucharist; the two are so related that each stands as cause to the other. The titles of the first and final chapters of this work would be virtually the same as the first and final chapters of Vatican II's Dogmatic Constitution on the Church.

The Church as Body of Christ

The 1920s through the 1940s also witnessed a great interest in the notion of the church as the (mystical) body of Christ. Contributing to this was the continuing influence of Johan Adam Möhler and by the wide popularity, through multiple translations, of *The Spirit of*

---

[116] De Lubac, *Catholicism: Christ and the Common Destiny of Man*, 327.

[117] Paul McPartlan, *The Eucharist Makes the Church: Henri de Lubac and John Zizioulas in Dialogue* (Edinburgh: T & T Clark, 1993), 9 and chap. 2.

[118] Henri de Lubac, *The Splendour of the Church*, trans. by Michael Mason (New York: Sheed and Ward, 1956).

[119] De Lubac, *Splendour*, ix.

[120] Hans Urs von Balthasar, *The Theology of Henri de Lubac: An Overview* (San Francisco: Ignatius Press, 1991), 107.

Catholicism (1924) by Karl Adam (d. 1966), a professor at Tübingen from 1919 to 1949. Two prominent works dealt with this theme: in 1933, *The Whole Christ: The Historical Development of the Doctrine of the Mystical Body in Scripture and Tradition* by the Belgian Jesuit Emile Mersch (d. 1940) and the 1937 work of the Dutch Jesuit Sebastian Tromp (d. 1975), *Corpus Christi quod est Ecclesia* (The Body of Christ which is the Church). The popularity of the theme led to some exaggerations that either paid little attention to the structural aspects of the church or spoke of a mysticism that seemed to eliminate any difference between the human and the divine. German theologian M. D. Koster in 1940 was severely critical of the attention given to the mystical body theme, a mere figure or metaphor, in his view. He argued instead for the use of the term "the people of God" to underscore the continuity between the two testaments.[121] Koster saw the new chosen people as "the assembly called together to hear the Word of God and to enter with God into a new alliance of mercy and love."[122]

To counter exaggerations in the use of the term "mystical body," Pius XII issued his encyclical *Mystici Corporis* (1943), in which he taught that in defining the church of Christ, identified with the Roman Catholic Church, "we shall find nothing more noble, more sublime, or more divine than the expression 'the Mystical Body of Jesus Christ'—an expression which springs from and is, as it were, the fair flowering of the repeated teaching of the Sacred Scriptures and the Holy Fathers."[123] The pope pointedly includes grace and charism in his understanding of church, so challenging the view of the prominent Jesuit neo-Thomist philosopher and theologian, Louis Billot (d. 1931). The latter's treatise on the church (1898; third edition, 1909) regarded grace and charisms as conceptually distinct from the basic understanding of church as a "society which is a collection of members under a hierarchy set up with a twofold power [jurisdiction and

---

[121] Jerome Hamer, *The Church Is a Communion*, trans. Ronald Matthews (New York: Sheed and Ward, 1964), 18–20.
[122] McNamara, "The Ecclesiological Movement in Germany," 351.
[123] w2.vatican.va/content/pius-xii/en/encyclicals/documents/hf_p-xii _enc_29061943_mystici-corporis-christi-html, no. 13 (accessed November 27, 2015).

order]."¹²⁴ Pius XII was able to challenge Billot by acceding to the request of the respected Jesuit philosopher-theologian Erich Przywara (d. 1972) "not to define the Church in terms of the mystical Body, but rather to define the mystical Body in terms of the Church, that is, in terms of a society."¹²⁵ The notion of church as society led the encyclical to identify membership in the church by the same three criteria used by Robert Bellarmine, though it also recognized that those who are not members of the church may have "a certain relationship" through "an unconscious desire and longing."¹²⁶ The encyclical, even with what in hindsight might be called its limitations, represents a major step in the official understanding of the theology of the church.

The mystical body of Christ was also the primary image of the church in the only formal systematic treatment of the church in the twentieth century, *Church of the Word Incarnate*, by Swiss theologian, seminary professor, and professed Thomist Charles Journet (d. 1975).¹²⁷ In the 1939 introduction to his work, he described his approach: In Augustine and Aquinas "I have found a theology of the Church more living, more far-reaching and more liberating than that which our manuals commonly contain. In them we feel the active presence of a vision of the Mystery of the Church understood as an extension of the Incarnation."¹²⁸ As in some manuals of the time, Journet used the four causes of Aristotle to speak of the church. The manuals generally saw the hierarchy as the formal cause of the church, along with sacraments and defined dogmas, and the laity as the material cause, so depicting the church as formally a hierarchical organization. Journet saw the formal cause of the church—that which makes the church to be what it is—as the Holy Spirit. In doing so, he overturned "the juridically based notion of the Church while maintaining an essential role for the hierarchy within the Church." The

---

¹²⁴ Cited by Yves Congar, "Moving Towards a Pilgrim Church," in *Vatican II Revisited by Those Who Were There*, ed. Alberic Stacpoole (Minneapolis, MN: Winston Press, 1986), 131.

¹²⁵ Ibid. Congar's words refer to a 1940 article by Erich Przywara.

¹²⁶ No. 103 (see note 123 above.)

¹²⁷ Dennis M. Doyle, *Communion Ecclesiology: Vision and Versions* (Maryknoll, NY: Orbis Books, 2000), 38–45.

¹²⁸ Cited by Doyle, *Communion Ecclesiology*, 41.

Theologies of the Church: 1815 to the Eve of Vatican II   313

hierarchy he regarded as "most fundamentally a service to help bring about the [Church's] mystical communion."[129] Though Journet differed in method from that used by the *ressourcement* theologians mentioned earlier, with them he looked at the church not only as something to be studied but, analogously, as a person, "*someone* to be recognized and loved."[130]

Differences in method had long simmered between *ressourcement* theologians and Thomists at Rome's Dominican-led Angelicum and at the studium of the Dominican province of Toulouse. Ultimately, Pius XII himself became involved.[131] We noted earlier the criticisms of the writings of Chenu, Congar, and Charlier and the published justification for the condemnations of some of their writings. In 1947 an article by Réginald Garrigou-Lagrange (d. 1964), longtime professor at Rome's University of St. Thomas (the Angelicum) and adviser to the Holy Office, charged that the "new theology" was heading to skepticism and heresy, a return to modernism. Congar, de Lubac, and some of their colleagues were removed from their teaching positions. John Courtney Murray, trying to make the case for Catholic acceptance of constitutionally protected religious liberty, was asked by his superiors to refrain from further writings on the topic.

In mid-1950, Pius XII published his encyclical *Humani Generis*. An attempt to correct what were perceived as errors in the revival of Catholic theology in the previous two decades, the letter complained that the "nature and constitution of the Church" as expounded in papal encyclicals was habitually neglected in favor of "a certain vague notion which [theologians] profess to have found in the ancient Fathers, especially the Greeks."[132] The letter objected to the use of ancient sources to explain the teaching of "recent constitutions and decrees" and insisted, citing Pius IX, that "the most noble office of

---

[129] Ibid., 43.

[130] John Saward, "*L'Eglise a ravi son coeur*: Charles Journet and the Theologians of *Ressourcement* on the Personality of the Church," in Flynn and Murray, *Ressourcement*, 125–37, at 125.

[131] Joseph A. Komonchak, "*Humani Generis* and *Nouvelle Théologie*," in Flynn and Murray, *Ressourcement*, chap. 9.

[132] Pius XII, "*Humani Generis*: Encyclical Letter of Pope Pius XII" (Washington, DC: National Catholic Welfare Conference [1950]), art. 18.

theology is to show how a doctrine defined by the Church is contained in the sources of revelation."[133] The encyclical condemned no individuals and was far more moderate in tone than Pius X's *Pascendi* against the modernists, though its dogmatic style was intended to end debate. The letter "was one of the last efforts to hold back a tide that was calling into question the near-monopoly in theology enjoyed by scholastic method, language, principles, and concepts."[134]

While some of the preparatory documents for the Second Vatican Council sought to continue in the spirit of the encyclical, the next chapter will show that the council largely took another direction in what it said about the church and in the way in which that was expressed.

---

[133] Ibid., art. 21.
[134] Komonchak, "*Humani Generis* and *Nouvelle Théologie*," 155.

CHAPTER TEN

The Second Vatican Council (1962–1965)

Yesterday, the theme of the Church seemed to be confined to the power of the Pope. Today it is extended to the episcopate, the religious, the laity and the whole body of the Church. Yesterday, we spoke of the rights of the Church by transferring the constitutive elements of civil society to the definition of a perfect society. Today, we have discovered other realities in the Church—the charisms of grace and holiness, for example—which cannot be defined by purely juridical ideas. Yesterday, we were above all interested in the external history of the Church. Today, we are equally concerned with its inner life, brought to life by the hidden presence of Christ in it.[1]

In reality the profound intention of the Second Vatican Council was clearly to insert the discourse on the church within and subordinate to the discourse on God, therefore proposing an ecclesiology which is truly theo-logical.[2]

These two citations, the first from Cardinal Montini of Milan at the end of the first session of Vatican II, the second from a commentary of the Congregation for the Doctrine of the Faith, introduce us to the theology of the church as articulated by the Second Vatican Council and remind us of the deliberate and significant development that theology represents. This chapter begins with a historical overview

---

[1] Cardinal Giovanni Battista Montini, December 7, 1962, cited by Yves Congar, "Moving Towards a Pilgrim Church," in *Vatican II Revisited by Those Who Were There*, ed. Alberic Stacpoole (Minneapolis, MN: Winston Press, 1986), 135.
[2] Congregation for the Doctrine of the Faith, "Commentary on Doctrinal Congregation Document," *Origins* 37, no. 9 (July 19, 2007): 137.

of the "event" of the council, its preparation, and the four sessions that gave birth to its theology. The council must be seen in light of the past as we have seen it up until now, but, as "event," the council also involved a "rupture" in the sense of a "break from routine" and "initiating a new routine,"[3] a new stage in the effort to articulate a theological understanding of church.[4] It helps to keep in mind three major projects of Vatican II: balancing Vatican I's teaching on the papacy with an understanding of the role of the bishops; incorporating the riches of the church's tradition in articulating a more adequate doctrine of the church; considering anew the relationship and role of the church in the world of the present day. The second part of the chapter will present an overview of the council's vision of church.

Pope John XXIII (1958–1963) announced his intent to call the council in January 1959, three months after his election. In his opening address to the council he asked that it show the validity of the church's teaching rather than make condemnations, that it be "predominantly pastoral in character," and that it bring the church "up to date [*aggiornamento*] where required" to better enable the church to serve her apostolic mission.[5] Prior to the council's opening, three and a half years were given to consultation regarding proposals for the agenda of the council and the preparation of some seventy documents, largely done under the supervision of the various Roman congregations, headed by what was then called the Supreme Con-

---

[3] Joseph A. Komonchak, "Vatican II as an 'Event,'" in John W. O'Malley and others, *Vatican II: Did Anything Happen?* ed. David G. Schultenover (New York: Continuum, 2007), 24–51, at 27.

[4] Three studies may be mentioned. The shortest (141 pages) is Giuseppe Alberigo, *A Brief History of Vatican II*, trans. Matthew Sherry (Maryknoll, NY: Orbis Books, 2006). John W. O'Malley, *What Happened at Vatican II* (Cambridge, MA: Belknap Press of Harvard University Press, 2008) deals with both the history and meaning of the council (380 pages). The most extensive study is that edited by Giuseppe Alberigo, English version edited by Joseph A. Komonchak, *History of Vatican II*, 5 vols. (Maryknoll, NY: Orbis Books, 1995–2006), henceforth Alberigo/Komonchak.

[5] O'Malley, *What Happened at Vatican II*, 95. Full text in Floyd Anderson, ed., *Council Daybook, Vatican II: Session 1, Oct. 11 to Dec. 8, 1962; Session 2, Sept. 29 to Dec. 4, 1963* (Washington, DC: National Catholic Welfare Conference, 1965–1966), 25–29.

gregation of the Holy Office. The many documents were combined into twenty-two schemata (draft texts). The council met for four sessions, in the fall months of each year from 1962 to 1965. Valuable work was done by various commissions on individual texts during the intersessions. The members of the council were bishops of the Latin Rite, of the Eastern Catholic Churches, and major superiors of religious orders of men. There were 168 congregations over the four years; public sessions were held at the beginning of each of the four periods of the council and when texts approved by the pope and the council were solemnly promulgated. The work of the council is often spoken of in terms of two words: *aggiornamento*, updating, and *ressourcement*, a return to the basic fonts of the church's tradition, very especially but not exclusively the Scriptures and the early centuries of the church.

The first session of the council, in the fall of 1962, had three important developments regarding the theology of the church. First, the session began with a consideration of the liturgy, seen as providing a programmatic statement for the council as a whole: that the council give new vigor to Christian life, that it adapt changeable structures to better meet current needs, that it contribute to the union of all Christians, and that it promote the growth of the church. The second development regarded the schema "On the Sources of Revelation."[6] The draft text reflected anti-modernist concerns, showed minimal interest in the current methods of biblical study, and viewed revelation primarily as a "deposit" of faith, the basis for the church's dogmas and doctrines.[7] Where Trent applied the term "source" to the gospels, the draft text applied the term to both Scripture and tradition as two sources of revelation. At issue in this instance was the stance of the church: would it continue "the old policy of exclusiveness, condemnation and defense leading to an almost neurotic denial of all that was new" or "would the Church, after it had taken all the necessary precautions to protect the faith, turn over a new leaf and move on into a new and positive encounter with its own origins, with

---

[6] Giuseppe Ruggieri, "The First Doctrinal Clash," in Alberigo/Komonchak, vol. 2: *The Formation of the Council's Identity, First Period and Intersession, October 1962–1963*, 235.

[7] O'Malley, *What Happened at Vatican II*, 141–52.

its brothers [sic] and with the world of today?"[8] A preliminary vote on the draft text on November 20 fell short of the number needed to begin anew, but Pope John intervened and called for a new schema to be prepared. Many participants saw this as a turning point of the council.

The third development concerned the much-awaited proposed draft on the church.[9] The text's eleven chapters continued the largely institutional emphasis set by Robert Bellarmine, with some elements from Pius XII's encyclical on the Mystical Body.[10] Many bishops were critical of the schema and looked to a different approach to understanding the church. The draft text represented only the scholastic tradition of preceding centuries and did not take into account the breadth of the church's tradition in the early Latin fathers and those of the Greek tradition; it was cast in predominantly juridical terms and preoccupied with the question of authority; it was faulted for its focus on the church as the body of Christ to the neglect of the theology of the people of God; and it stood at odds with the spirit of Pope John's address at the outset of the council.[11] Two speeches in the discussion that followed the introduction of the draft text to the council are especially noteworthy. Cardinal Léon-Josef Suenens of Malines, Belgium, proposed that the topic of the church be the central topic of the council, both the church's inner life and its relationship with the world.[12] Cardinal Giacomo Lercaro of Bologna proposed that "the Church of the poor" be the dominant idea of the council's vision of the church and of the council itself—its "synthesizing idea, the point that gives light and coherence to all the subjects thus far

---

[8] Joseph Ratzinger, *Theological Highlights of Vatican II* (New York: Paulist Press, 2009), 44. Original published in 1966.

[9] Giuseppi Rugieri, "Beyond an Ecclesiology of Polemics: The Debate on the Church," in Alberigo/Komonchak, vol. 2, 285–98.

[10] Hubert Jedin, "The Second Vatican Council," in Gabriel Adrianyi and others, *The Church in the Modern Age*, trans. Anselm Biggs, vol. 10, *History of the Church*, ed. Hubert Jedin, Konrad Repgen, and John Dolan (New York: Crossroad, 1980), 113.

[11] Ruggieri, "Beyond an Ecclesiology of Polemics," 330–46.

[12] Leon-Josef Cardinal Suenens, "A Plan for the Whole Council," in Stacpoole, *Vatican II Revisited*, 97.

discussed and of all the work that we must undertake."[13] Soon after the council opened, Suenens commissioned Gérard Philips of the University of Louvain to compose an alternate draft text on the church. The first version of Philips's text gave the lion's share of attention to the topic of bishops, reflecting the widely shared desire to bring balance to Vatican I's teaching on the papacy. The day before the first session concluded, Cardinal Montini of Milan, anticipating the direction of the council, made the remarks in the first of the epigraphs above.

The intersession in 1963 saw the draft text on the church reduced to four chapters: (1) "On the Mystery of the Church," (2) the episcopacy, (3) the laity, and (4) religious orders. The title of the first chapter is the same as the first chapter of Henri de Lubac's *The Splendour of the Church*, an early indication of the impact the *ressourcement* movement would have not only on the conciliar teaching but also on the use of the rhetorical and sometimes poetic style of the early fathers of the church that became a hallmark of many texts of the council.[14] To expedite the council's work, the council's Coordinating Commission reduced the many draft texts before the council to seventeen, the last of which (later to become "Schema 13") concerned the church in the modern world.

The work of the council was interrupted by the death of Pope John in June 1963, though his last encyclical, *Pacem in Terris*, would help the council by its focus on the dignity of the human person and the right to honor God according to one's conscience. Later that month Giovanni Battista Montini was elected pope, took the name of Paul VI, and announced his intent to have the council continue. His opening address at the second session of Vatican II in late September 1963 proposed four objectives for the council: (1) a "more thorough definition" of the church as "a reality imbued with the divine presence"; (2) the renewal of the church, honoring tradition but "stripping it of what is unworthy or defective"; (3) promoting the unity of the church while allowing for "a great variety of verbal expressions, movements, lawful institutions, and preference with regard to modes of acting"; and (4) building a "bridge toward the contemporary world."[15]

---

[13] Cited by Ruggieri, "Beyond an Ecclesiology of Polemics," 345–46.
[14] O'Malley, *What Happened at Vatican II*, 163.
[15] Anderson, *Council Daybook: Sessions 1 and 2*, 143–50.

The second session of the council, in the fall of 1963, began with a yet further revised schema on the church, largely the work of Msgr. Philips.[16] The text had four chapters: (1) the mystery of the church; (2) the hierarchical constitution of the church, especially the bishops; (3) the people of God, especially the laity; (4) the call to holiness. The opening words were to be *Lumen gentium* ("light to the nations"), applied now to Christ and not, as had been proposed earlier, to the church. The new chapter 4, on the call to holiness, was a novelty: it affirmed the call to holiness given to all the baptized before turning to professed religious. The chapter on the episcopate gave much more attention to the role of bishops, even if it gave repeated affirmations of the papal prerogatives defined at Vatican I. The new text differed from the original schema in using a style of rhetoric reminiscent of the Bible and the fathers of the church. In the discussion, motions were made to place the chapter on the people of God before that on the hierarchy and to recognize that all baptized persons belong in some way to the mystical body of Christ, even if they do not belong to the visible Catholic Church.[17] Quite different views emerged in the discussions regarding the episcopacy and whether to include a treatment of Mary in the schema on the church or in a separate schema. Votes at the end of October narrowly placed Mary within the schema on the church and, a day later, showed widespread support for a sacramental view of the episcopacy and its responsibility as a college, of which the pope is the head, in exercising a governing authority in the church. Discussion of the schema on the bishops revealed an eagerness to have collegiality implemented in a practical way. Debate on the schema on ecumenism revealed two approaches. Some council fathers saw a need for a common Christian witness and sought to recognize the common elements between Catholics and other Christians. Others expressed concern about ecumenism's potential danger to the faith and looked only to the return of other Christians to the one true church. Discussion of the same schema's fourth and fifth chapters, on the church's attitude toward other religions, especially

---

[16] O'Malley, *What Happened at Vatican II*, 173–77.
[17] Jedin, "The Second Vatican Council," 117.

the Jews, and on religious freedom, both very sensitive issues, was put off until later. At the end of the second session, the Constitution on the Sacred Liturgy was promulgated by Pope Paul "in union with the venerable fathers," a formula chosen by the pope to recognize the heightened collegial consciousness that emerged during the session.[18]

The period between the second and third sessions was marked by the pope's unprecedented visit to the Holy Land and his meeting with Orthodox Patriarch Athenagoras, the first meeting between pope and patriarch since the Council of Florence in the fifteenth century.

Gestures such as this—or when in 1996 John Paul II invited the archbishop of Canterbury, in miter and cope and with the pope's gift of a gold pectoral cross, to process with him at Vespers celebrating the fourteen hundredth anniversary of Gregory the Great's sending Augustine and his fellow monks to England, or when he invited both the archbishop and a representative of the Orthodox Church to assist him in opening the Holy Door in the Year of Jubilee 2000—have their own contribution to make in a developing understanding of church. Massimo Faggioli points out that Yves Congar faulted Paul VI for not articulating a theology implicit in such gestures. The ecumenist Fr. Pierre Duprey responded: "The pope must be left to make such gestures and messages. . . . The gestures will create a familiarity and when that has been done, one day, the formulas will be able to be accepted."[19]

Conciliar commissions continued their work, especially on the delicate issue of the relationship between the college of bishops and its head and on a text on Mary that would become the final chapter of the Constitution on the Church. In early August, Pope Paul issued his first encyclical, *Ecclesiam Suam*. The letter spoke of three concerns:

---

[18] Claude Soetens, "The Ecumenical Commitment of the Catholic Church," in Alberigo/Komonchak, vol. 3: *The Mature Council, Second Period and Intersession, September 1963–September 1964*, 328–29.

[19] Massimo Faggioli, "Off Script: What to Expect from Synod 2015," *Commonweal* 142, no.16 (October 9, 2015): 12.

(1) the church's duty "to deepen the awareness that she must have of herself" regarding her origin, her nature, her mission, and her ultimate destiny; (2) the collaboration of the council in finding "greater courage to undertake the necessary reforms"; and (3) the need to explore "the relationships which the Church of today should establish with the world which surrounds it and in which it lives and labors."[20] The emphasis on dialogue in the encyclical would influence the final conciliar text on ecumenism and, especially so, the text on the church in the modern world.

The third session in the fall of 1964 began with Pope Paul's highlighting the council's need to deal with the nature and function of the episcopacy as successors of the apostles even as it confirmed the "sovereign prerogatives regarding the primacy and infallibility" defined at Vatican I. This, he said, was "the weightiest and most delicate" issue facing the council, one that would distinguish Vatican II in the memory of future ages.[21] The pope was expressing his own view but also trying to win over those who held to the conviction that an affirmation of episcopal collegiality would be a denial of past church teaching.

This third session witnessed intense debates that took place on what were the fourth and fifth chapters of the original schema on ecumenism, now treated as independent texts: one on religious freedom, the other on non-Christian religions.[22] The first was problematic on two counts: the classical Catholic position, maintained even in the 1950s, held that only truth had the right to freedom and that the state should support the truth given in Catholic faith, though for prudential reasons Catholics could tolerate separation of church and state and religious tolerance; second, that teaching was presupposed in various concordats between 1929 and 1954. At issue too was the fact that support for religious freedom ran counter to vigorous official

---

[20] Pope Paul VI, *His Church*: Ecclesiam Suam (Boston: St. Paul Editions [1964]).
[21] Text in Floyd Anderson, ed., *Council Daybook: Vatican II, Session 3* (Washington, DC: National Catholic Welfare Conference, 1965), 6–10, at 8.
[22] Giovanni Miccoli, "Two Sensitive Issues: Religious Freedom and the Jews," in Alberigo/Komonchak, vol. 4: *Church as Communion, Third Period and Intersession, September 1964–September 1965*, 95–193.

opposition to two dramatic movements of the nineteenth century.[23] The first was the movement from a sacral to a secular conception of society and state, a process by which the political functions of the secular rule were becoming separate from religious functions governed by church authority. Because this process in continental Europe was tainted by rationalist or atheist inspiration, it was totally opposed by Pius IX, though Leo XIII took steps toward a development of the notion of two distinct societies and two distinct powers. The second movement was the developing appreciation of the historicity of truth and human progress in understanding what is true. Entanglement of this development with modernist exaggerations provoked, we have seen, strong official opposition. American Jesuit John Courtney Murray had been making the case for a revision of the classical position regarding religious freedom in the light of the current political reality, quite different from that of the nineteenth century. While some council fathers rejected the text because it appeared to contradict papal condemnations of the previous century, bishops from the United States and from communist-controlled countries gave it strong support. Debate continued as well on the text on the Jews, now including mention of Islam. Some speakers wanted a stronger rejection of the charge of deicide, sometimes used in the past by Christian polemicists. Bishops from the Middle East continued to fear that the text would complicate the situation for Christian minorities in their countries.

On October 20, debate began on schema 13, now called On the Church in the Modern World.[24] The title contrasts with the ninth chapter of the original draft on the church that used the categories of church and state and religious tolerance. The new text would one day begin with the famous "The joys and the hopes, the grief and anguish of the people of our time, especially of those who are poor or afflicted," which are the special concern of the followers of Christ.

---

[23] John Courtney Murray, "The Declaration on Religious Freedom," *Concilium* 5, no. 2 (1966): 3–10.

[24] Analysis of the text in Henri Fesquet, *The Drama of Vatican II: The Ecumenical Council, June, 1962–December, 1965*, trans. Bernard Murchland (New York: Random House, 1967), 403–12.

Responsible for "reading the signs of the times," the text adopts a "historically conscious" method that contrasts with a classicist approach that might have settled for a statement about the nature of the world.[25] Speakers clearly moved away from the siege mentality and negative stance vis-à-vis modernity and the world characteristic of the official stance taken in the nineteenth and early twentieth centuries.[26] Cardinal Ratzinger would later say that the final version of this schema, along with those on religious freedom and world religions, was "a kind of countersyllabus" to the "one-sidedness of the position adopted by the Church under Pius IX and Pius X."[27] Encyclicals from Leo XIII to John XXIII had, of course, already been moving the church toward engagement with modern social issues. The schema already contained some of the basic themes appearing in the final version: an emphasis on human dignity, human solidarity, and human activity directed to the common good of all. The text spoke of the church's servant role in the world even as it learned from the world.

The final week of the third session showed the complexity of the council's working out what it wanted to say about the church.[28] Tensions still surfaced regarding the schema on religious freedom, though the Declaration on the Relation of the Church to Non-Christian Religions passed with a wide margin. The day before a final vote was to be taken on the Decree on Ecumenism, the assembly learned of nineteen "kind suggestions authoritatively expressed" regarding the proposed decree. Though it is not clear who proposed the changes, it was clear that the pope wanted them made. Many were stylistic, but some thought they saw possible doctrinal concerns in three of

---

[25] Frederick J. Cwiekowski, "Vatican Council II," in *New Dictionary of Catholic Social Thought*, ed. Judith A. Dwyer (Collegeville, MN: Liturgical Press, 1994), 965–66.

[26] For the debates in the third session, see Norman Tanner, "The Church in the World (*Ecclesia ad Extra*)," in Alberigo/Komonchak, vol. 4, 269–328.

[27] Joseph Cardinal Ratzinger, *Principles of Catholic Theology: Building Stones for a Fundamental Theology*, trans. Mary Francis McCarthy (San Francisco: Ignatius Press, 1987), 381. German original published in 1982.

[28] See Luis Antonio G. Tagle, "The 'Black Week' of Vatican II (November 14–21, 1964)," in Alberigo/Komonchak, vol. 4, 387–452.

them: the "right and duty" of the Eastern Churches to preserve their own traditions was changed to their having the "faculty" to do so; that non-Catholic Christians "find" God in the Scriptures was changed to their "seeking" him; that the non-Catholic "churches and ecclesial communities" of the West did not retain the "full reality of the eucharistic mystery" was changed to "they have not preserved the proper reality of the eucharistic mystery in its fullness."[29] It is important to note that the text does *not* say there is *nothing* of the Eucharist present in non-Catholic churches or ecclesial communities.

On November 17, "on higher authority" (generally understood to be Pope Paul), a "Preliminary Explanatory Note" was distributed to the council fathers. It was intended to be an interpretive guide to address lingering concerns about the council's statements on bishops and the relationship between the college of bishops and the pope. The text had four points: (1) The structure and authority of the college comes from revelation; the college is not a strictly juridical group of equals entrusting authority to its head. (2) One becomes a member of the college by episcopal consecration and hierarchical communion; only in that communion can one exercise the triple functions (*munera*) received in ordination, those of teaching, sanctifying, and governing. (3) The college, presupposing the head and never without it, has "supreme and full power in the universal church," but the head preserves unhindered his function as Christ's vicar and pastor of the universal church; he can use "his own discretion in arranging, promoting and approving the exercise of collegial activity." (4) The pope as supreme pastor of the church can exercise his office as he wills. The college requires the head's consent, though understood as a feature of communion and not coming from something extrinsic to the college. The note reflects the concern to preserve the prerogatives of the papacy in an attempt to secure as wide an acceptance as possible of the conciliar teaching; it also underscores seeing the role of the bishops in a sacramental, so theological, perspective.[30] The

---

[29] *Unitatis Redintegratio* (Decree on Ecumenism) 22, in *Vatican Council II: The Basic Sixteen Documents*, ed. Austin Flannery (Collegeville, MN: Liturgical Press, 2014), 520. Unless otherwise noted, translations of conciliar texts come from this edition.

[30] Ratzinger, *Theological Highlights*, 185–90.

explanatory note is now appended to the constitution but was never voted on by the council.

The third session concluded with the solemn promulgation of the Dogmatic Constitution on the Church, the Decree on Ecumenism, and the Decree on the Catholic Eastern Churches. Pope Paul's address at the public session is itself a lesson in the sometimes difficult process of arriving at the council's vision of church. The pope notes that the "doctrinal task" of Vatican I had now been completed, indebted as it was to the "advance of theological studies in modern times." The assertion that the "best commentary" of the constitution on the church is that "nothing in traditional doctrine is really changed" would certainly have been understood in different ways by the council participants. Considerable attention is given to the papal prerogatives even as he acknowledges the increase of a communion of co-responsibility and collaboration. Mention of "the monarchical and hierarchical character" of the church is surprising in that the word "monarchical" does not appear in the constitution. Almost half of the address is given to the proclamation of Mary as Mother of the Church. The title was much discussed in the preparation of the text but was not finally included.[31] Was the pope's proclamation simply a response to his wish and that of "very many of the Fathers," as he mentions in his address, or an assertion of his primacy?

During the intersession prior to the opening of the fourth and last session, the commissions had before them eleven texts, some needing only final votes, others requiring discussion or a response to proposed amendments.[32] The remaining questions showed the magnitude of the task before the council. Regarding the schema on revelation: How to reconcile the proposed text with what some interpreted as the teaching of Trent and Vatican I? On the church in the modern world: How best to proceed in what was in many ways new territory? The text on non-Christian religions: How to affirm belief that the Jewish people were not a "deicide people" without provoking Arab reaction

---

[31] Joseph A. Komonchak, "Toward an Ecclesiology of Communion," in Alberigo/Komonchak, vol. 4, 52–62.

[32] Riccardo Burigana and Giovanni Turbanti, "The Intersession: Preparing the Conclusion of the Council," in Alberigo/Komonchak, vol. 4, 505–606.

or the opposition of the Vatican Secretariat of State fearing such a reaction? How to reject the judgment against all the Jews of Jesus' day and of Jews in the present when some within the council believed that the New Testament (e.g., Acts 3:15) and the early church fathers supported the idea that Jews were guilty of rejecting the Son of God? Congar was not alone in thinking: "Twenty years after Auschwitz it is impossible for the Council to say nothing."[33] And regarding the text on religious freedom, the pope made it clear that the schema was not to be seen as a charter for freedom *within* the church or with regard to the church.[34] When the council resumed, four of the remaining eleven texts had serious issues to be dealt with.

On September 14, 1965, the fourth and last session of the council opened with an address by Paul VI in which he announced the formation of a synod of bishops "in accordance with the wishes of the council."[35] The *motu proprio* ("on his own initiative") by which he established the synod shows, however, that his doing so was a primatial act with no reference to the council, making the synod "directly and immediately subject to the authority of the Roman Pontiff." The council began its work by discussing the new schema On Religious Liberty.[36] There were arguments for and against, not least of which was the belief of some, noted above, that papal teaching from Pius IX to Pius XII condemned the idea. But more than the issue of religious freedom, the underlying issue was that of development of doctrine. Debate also continued regarding the schema on the church in the world. There were two major approaches to the introduction and the doctrinal part of the schema. The German school, with others, influenced by the recent tragic history of war in Europe, sought to heighten the distinction between the natural and the supernatural. This view would see the church in a more adversarial relationship

---

[33] Cited in ibid., 555.
[34] Ibid., 542.
[35] Floyd Anderson, ed., *Council Daybook: Session 4, Sept. 14, 1965 to Dec. 8, 1965* (Washington, DC: National Catholic Welfare Conference, 1966), 4–7, at 7. Text of *motu proprio* in ibid., 13–14.
[36] Gilles Routhier, "Finishing the Work Begun: The Trying Experience of the Fourth Period," in Alberigo/Komonchak, vol. 5: *The Council and the Transition, The Fourth Period and the End of the Council, September 1965–December 1965*, 63–122.

to the world. Others, more optimistic regarding the world's progress and development, emphasized links between the natural and the supernatural, between creation and redemption. In this view, the church would have a more cooperative role. The first group might be called more Augustinian in outlook; the second, drawing on what was considered a more Thomistic approach, received strong support in an extraconciliar lecture by M.-D. Chenu.[37] A third position, proposed by Giuseppe Dossetti, chief adviser to Cardinal Lercaro of Bologna, tried unsuccessfully to promote the idea that only a call to the radical conversion of the Gospel would satisfy the vision of John XXIII. The Germans came to accept that what was in their view a flawed statement was better than none at all. Would the document be a letter or message, or a constitution? The Polish bishops argued that it be called a pastoral constitution: as the Constitution on the Church contained the "law of belief," so a pastoral constitution would contain the church's "law of action."

Further attention to the schema on the pastoral office of bishops revealed continuing tensions regarding collegiality in the church. The working text's stated desire for a permanent group of bishops to collaborate with the pope in church governance was preempted by the pope's creation of the synod of bishops. At one point in the preliminary voting on the text Pope Paul sent a correction stating that bishops were members of the college insofar as they received jurisdiction.[38] This would have countered the assertion that bishops become members of the college by virtue of their ordination. The commission declined to make any change, and in early October the schema passed by an overwhelmingly positive vote. This final text was important for its practical application of the doctrine on bishops, its emphasis on the local church, and its promoting a collaborative style of ministry for the bishop and those with whom he ministers. A rewritten schema on the church's missionary activity surfaced differences over two issues: should mission be understood in terms

---

[37] Joseph Komonchak, "Augustine, Aquinas or the Gospel *sine glossa*?," in *Unfinished Journey: The Church 40 Years after Vatican II; Essays for John Wilkins*, ed. Austen Ivereigh (New York: Continuum, 2003).

[38] Routhier, "Finishing the Work Begun," 179.

of the church's territorial expansion into new territories under Roman jurisdiction, or should it embrace a developing theology of mission that recognized a sense of mission in all the church's activity, including rechristianization to counter the secularization of society?[39] The council's teaching on the priesthood and the lay apostolate will be mentioned in the next section of this chapter. Historically it is worth mentioning that lay observers assisted in the drafting of the text on the lay apostolate, and the discussion on the floor of the council included the first address by a layman. (A month later the suggestion that a woman address the council on the topic of world poverty was turned down; it would be "premature," it was said, for a woman to address the council.[40])

The public session on December 7 promulgated the last of the council's documents. The Decree on Missionary Activity and the Decree on the Ministry and Life of Priests passed with virtual unanimity. Voting on the Declaration on Religious Liberty and the Pastoral Constitution on the Church in the Modern World (*Gaudium et Spes*; the Latin reads: "The Church in the World of Our Times") showed a persistent disquiet on the part of a small minority. The session also included a reading of the Joint Declaration of Paul VI and Patriarch Athenagoras of Constantinople withdrawing the mutual excommunications of 1054 and pledging to work for full communion between the two churches.

The Theology of the Church of the Second Vatican Council

As we turn to the council's theology of the church, it helps to keep several points in mind. First, what Vatican II says about the church can be fully appreciated only in light of the *entirety* of the church's ecclesial tradition. This explains the council's indebtedness to the *ressourcement* movements in the decades prior to the council. It also explains the differences between Vatican II's vision of church and much of the official teaching about the church of the previous century

---

[39] See Peter Hünermann, "The Final Weeks of the Council," in Alberigo/Komonchak, vol. 5, 427–51.

[40] Tanner, "The Church in the World (*Ecclesia ad Extra*)," 318.

and a half. The ecclesial tradition that is also background to Vatican II includes, for example, the understanding of the church in the sixteenth and seventeenth centuries, the treatises on the church in the fourteenth century, the works of Thomas and Bonaventure, the Gregorian Reform of the eleventh century, and ultimately the vision of church in the patristic and New Testament periods. Second, Vatican II identifies many elements that enter into a theological understanding of church, though it does not give a comprehensive systematic theology. The latter is simply not the work of a council. Further, the council followed the longstanding practice of trying to reach a consensus among the participants, so several times placing ideas side-by-side in tension with each other, creating a "both-and" situation, rather than providing a worked-out synthesis. Third, the four constitutions of the council—we shall say something about each—are basic to the council's theology of the church. The decrees and the declarations have significant doctrinal elements, though in most cases they are satellites to the constitutions. It is helpful to think of the council saying, in effect: the four constitutions tell us what we believe are constitutive of the church.

Finally, it is very important to keep in mind the rhetoric generally used by the council. The literary genre used in many of the documents of Vatican II, most especially in the four constitutions, differs from that used in previous councils.[41] For one, faithful to John XXIII's opening discourse at the first session, the juridical form of the canon (e.g., "If anyone says . . . let him be anathema") was not used at all. Even more important, rather than use a style deliberately geared to clarifying doctrine or giving definitions, as was the case in most prior councils, Vatican II used a rhetorical style reminiscent of the early church fathers, a panegyric, "the painting of an idealized portrait in order to excite admiration and appropriation."[42] The council portrays Christ's church as an ideal, meant to evoke wonder and admiration or, as the fathers would have it, spiritual conversion. A theology worthy of its name should be doing just that. Using the insights of one of the great voices in contemporary interpretive theory, Paul

---

[41] O'Malley, "Vatican II: Did Anything Happen?" 67–83.
[42] Ibid., 74.

Ricoeur, one could say that interpreting the theological vision of Vatican II "involves entering into the proposed world unfolded by the text" so that one becomes "transformed by the vision the text offers."[43] It is in seeing the teaching of Vatican II as a theological effort calling for conversion on the part of everyone in the church that we best appreciate its contribution.[44]

The Dogmatic Constitution on Divine Revelation (*Dei Verbum* [DV]) was promulgated in the fourth session of the council, but what it says about revelation is fundamental because of what it says about God and what it says about the church. The God who reveals himself in Christ is God who invites and calls all people to union and friendship with himself, Father, Son, and Holy Spirit, and to share in the very life of God. Revelation leads to the formulation of doctrine, certainly, but that only follows God's self-communication, in love and mercy. While revelation is fulfilled in the person of Christ, by his will that revelation is passed on in the preaching of the apostles and their successors and in the doctrine, worship, and life of the entire people of God. By the help of the Holy Spirit, this living, passed-on revelation, this tradition that comes from the apostles, makes progress in the church as the church advances toward the plenitude of truth. Walter Kasper, for many years professor of theology at the University of Tübingen, speaks of the witness of faith in the community of believers as "an essential element in revelation itself. Only in and through the church does the revelation in Christ arrive at its goal."[45]

To the entire church, sacred tradition and sacred Scripture have been entrusted as a single deposit of the word of God (DV 10). By God's will and with the help of the Spirit, the authoritative interpretation of that word of God is entrusted to the teaching office of the church, the magisterium, which, as its servant, listens to it devotedly,

---

[43] Peter Feldmeier, "Seeking the Meaning of Vatican II," *Chicago Studies* 52, no. 2 (2013): 54–69, at 58.

[44] For more details than can be given here, see Gerald O'Collins, *The Second Vatican Council: Message and Meaning* (Collegeville, MN: Liturgical Press, 2014) and Richard R. Gaillardetz and Catherine E. Clifford, *Keys to the Council: Unlocking the Teaching of Vatican II* (Collegeville, MN: Liturgical Press, 2012).

[45] Walter Kasper, *Theology and Church*, trans. Margaret Kohl (New York: Crossroad, 1989), 139.

guards it, and explains it. The Scriptures are accorded as venerable a place in the life of the church as the body of Christ in the Eucharist (DV 21), so extending "a concept of the Church that had been structured in an over-exclusively sacramental way."[46] The constitution confidently asserts that all the church's preaching, as the Christian religion itself, must be "nourished and regulated" (*nutriatur et regatur*) by the sacred Scripture (DV 21).

The first constitution promulgated (1963) was the Constitution on the Sacred Liturgy (*Sacrosanctum Concilium* [SC]).[47] It was also the first discussed, in part because the draft was well prepared, though providentially, one might say, the choice of liturgy was also "a profession of faith in the true source of the Church's life, and the proper point of departure for all renewal."[48] The constitution opens (SC 1) with a programmatic statement for the council as a whole, as noted above. The final text gives at least four basic and interconnected ideas central to understanding the church.[49] First, the church's public worship, most especially the Eucharist, is the principal means of expressing to ourselves and manifesting to others the mystery of Christ and the nature of the church (SC 2). The same article gives a foundational statement regarding the church itself: "The church is both human and divine, visible but endowed with invisible realities, zealous in action and dedicated to contemplation, present in the world, yet a migrant, so constituted that in it the human is directed toward and subordinated to the divine, the visible to the invisible, action to contemplation, and this present world to that city yet to come, the object of our quest." Second, implicit in this statement and explicit later in the constitution is a sacramental view of the church, the visible as a sign and instrument of the invisible, a theme developed in the preconciliar theology of Congar, de Lubac, and others. Related to this is the affirmation of the fourfold presence of Christ in

---

[46] Joseph Ratzinger, "Sacred Scripture in the Life of the Church," in *Commentary on the Documents of Vatican II*, ed. Herbert Vorgrimler, vol. 3 (New York: Herder and Herder, 1969), 265.

[47] *Vatican Council II: The Basic Sixteen Documents*, 117–61.

[48] Ratzinger, *Theological Highlights*, 31.

[49] See Massimo Faggioli, *True Reform: Liturgy and Ecclesiology in* Sacrosanctum Concilium (Collegeville, MN: Liturgical Press, 2012), esp. chap. 3.

the Eucharist: in the Scriptures proclaimed and listened to by the congregation, in the sacred species, in the person of the minister, and in the community gathered in prayer and song (SC 5 and 7).

Third, the church's worship is the summit of its activity and the source of its power. By its very nature worship demands the "full, conscious, and active" participation of all the faithful (SC 10). What is said of the liturgy would later be said of the church itself, with important implications for understanding the lay faithful. Finally, emphasis on the church's manifestation of itself in worship leads to a heightened theological assessment of the local church in diocese and parish (SC 41–42), an important complement to the strong emphasis since Trent on the universal church. The inseparable connection between Eucharist and church present in all these observations was a hallmark, we recall, of the theology of the church in the early centuries; it was also a major concern of the exiled Russian Orthodox theologians whose work influenced Catholic *ressourcement* efforts in the decades before the council. Two other points deserve mention. While the practical norms of the constitution concern only the Roman Rite, the council speaks of the equal honor in which it held the self-governing Eastern Catholic Churches (twenty-one in number), a recognition of liturgical and canonical plurality in the church (SC 4). The constitution also recognizes the need for revising the church's rites according to "sound tradition" to meet current circumstances and needs. Local church authorities may make adaptations to the liturgy that would reflect the temperament and traditions of the people (SC 22, 37–40). The council's role in the development of the constitution, along with openness to liturgical adaptation and other recommended changes—a richer use of the Scriptures, for example, and some use, at least, of the vernacular (SC 36 and 51)—along with the authority given to local groups of bishops in the liturgy, exemplifies an "ecclesiology-in-act," whereby the church, through the council, was engaged in articulating its own self-understanding.[50] The text itself "implied an entire ecclesiology

---

[50] Joseph A. Komonchak, "The Significance of Vatican II for Ecclesiology," in *The Gift of the Church: A Textbook on Ecclesiology in Honor of Patrick Granfield, O.S.B.*, ed. Peter C. Phan (Collegeville, MN: Liturgical Press, 2000), 70, 74.

and thus anticipated (in a degree that cannot be too highly appreciated) the main theme of the entire Council—its teaching on the Church."[51] By linking the church so closely with the liturgy, the church was freeing itself from the "hierarchical narrowness" of the previous several hundred years and returning to its sacramental origins.[52] This constitution and that on revelation make the important point, briefly put but with depth of meaning, that the church is both the "community of the body of Christ" and the "community of the Logos."[53]

The Dogmatic Constitution on the Church (*Lumen Gentium* [LG]), we saw above, had a sometimes difficult gestation, but its final form is one of the major achievements of the council.[54] Its first two chapters are the foundation to all that is said subsequently. The very first words of the constitution, *Lumen gentium cum sit Christus*, "Christ is the light of nations," evokes the vision of a church called "to bring to all humanity that light of Christ which is resplendent on the face of the church" (LG 1). The first chapter's title, "The Mystery of the Church," reminds us that we are dealing with something of God; it encourages us to approach the church as part of the unfolding of God's plan. The church is called into being by the Father; brought into being by Christ, in his proclamation of the kingdom of God and most especially in his paschal mystery; and guided and unified by the gift of the Spirit (LG 2, 3, and 4). The first chapter sees the church "in its great span from before creation in the plan of God until its fulfillment in heaven"; the second chapter discusses "the same mystery in the time between the ascension and the Parousia, that time during which it lives by faith until it is perfected in the blessed vision."[55] Three biblical images are especially prominent in the council's vision and continue its

---

[51] Ratzinger, *Theological Highlights*, 31.

[52] Ibid., 31–32.

[53] Ratzinger, "Sacred Scripture in the Life of the Church," 262–63.

[54] The remainder of this section draws much from Joseph Komonchak, "Ecclesiology of Vatican II," *Origins* 28, no. 44 (April 22, 1999): 763–68. See also Cardinal Joseph Ratzinger, "The Ecclesiology of the Second Vatican Council," in *Church, Ecumenism and Politics: New Essays in Ecclesiology*, trans. Robert Nowell (New York: Crossroad, 1988), 3–20.

[55] Komonchak, "Ecclesiology of Vatican II," 764.

trinitarian emphasis. One image is the Pauline and deutero-Pauline metaphor, the body of Christ: we, though many, are one with him and, in him, members of one another, with Christ as our life-giving head (LG 7). To preserve the necessary distinction within the unity of Christ and the church, the body image is joined to the image of the church as Christ's bride, loved by him, united to him by "an unbreakable covenant" (LG 6). A second image of the church is the temple of the Holy Spirit, who, dwelling within us, bears witness that we are God's adopted children and who endows and directs the church with hierarchic and charismatic gifts (LG 4).

The principal image, dependent always on what the council says about the church's relationship to Christ, is the church as the people of God: a messianic people with Christ as its head, possessing dignity and freedom as sons and daughters of God, bound by the law to love as Christ loved us, and called to serve the kingdom of God that will be brought to perfection only when Christ comes again (LG 9). Attention to this image reminds us of the church's rootedness in the Old Testament, its historical character as a pilgrim people, its openness to renewal, and its provisional character before its final consummation at the completion of God's saving plan. The term "people of God" refers to the lay faithful and clergy alike and calls us to consider what is common to all the baptized before considering any differentiation of roles. The people image also lends itself to recognizing various possible ways of being joined or related to the church, even beyond its visible confines. The image reminds us as well that the church can never be seen solely as a sociological or political reality, though insights from such studies can and do contribute to an integral understanding of church. The church of Christ is at once a community of faith, hope, and charity and a visible society, a mystical union with Christ and a structured community. As a complex reality with divine and human elements, the church is compared, with good reason, to the mystery of the incarnate Word (LG 8). For these same reasons, the church, in Christ, is likened to a sacrament, a sign and an instrument of God's desire to unite all people to himself and to bring about the unity of the whole human race (LG 1).

Recognizing that divine elements building up and giving life to the church (e.g., the written Word of God, baptismal incorporation into Christ, the life of grace, the gifts of the Spirit) exist outside the visible boundaries of the Catholic Church, the council says that the church of Christ *subsists in* the Roman Catholic Church rather than that the two are simply identified (LG 8). Vatican II's Decree on Ecumenism (*Unitatis Redintegratio* [UR]) affirms the fullness of the means of salvation in the Catholic Church, though it also recognizes the significance and importance of other churches and communities in the mystery of salvation (UR 3). The same reasoning explains the absence of the language of membership when speaking of belonging to the church; the council prefers the language of incorporation (LG 14) and communion (UR 3), though the latter is regarded as imperfect when referring to other Christians. The council uses the term "separated sisters and brothers" when referring to other Christians (UR 3), though Pope John Paul II, in his 1995 encyclical That All May Be One (*Ut Unum Sint* 42), suggests that term be replaced by expressions (e.g., "other Christians") that better respect the link formed by baptism in spite of historical and canonical divisions. Besides speaking of bonds of communion between Catholics and other Christians, chapter 2 of *Lumen Gentium* also speaks of the church's relatedness to the first people of God, the Jews, then also to Muslims, and to others who seek God or to those who, without explicit knowledge of God, seek to live a good life (LG 16).

While Vatican II generally speaks of the church in a universalist perspective, there are instances where the council makes a major contribution regarding the theological importance of the local church, understood as the diocese, the church in a given area, or the parish. *Lumen Gentium*, for example, speaks of the particular church (the diocese in this instance) being fashioned after the model of the universal church by reason of its having the same spiritual and sacramental elements that constitute and animate the church generally. The same sentence goes on to say that it is in and from such churches that the one and only Catholic Church comes into being (LG 23).[56] The late Italian canonist Eugenio Corecco regarded this statement as

---

[56] Ibid., 764–65.

"the most important ecclesiological formula of the council"[57] in that it sees the universal church as a "communion of [local] churches." We shall see more of this in the next chapter. The relationship between the local churches and the universal church would become a major topic of discussion in postconciliar theology. The council itself, especially in the Decree on the Church's Missionary Activity (*Ad Gentes* [AG]), gives several indications of various factors that make a local church *local*: being rooted in the social life of the people, for example, or incorporating elements of local culture (AG 19); also, borrowing from local customs and tradition or using the wisdom of the people to explain the faith (AG 22).

This greater appreciation of local churches in the communion of churches is at one with the council's understanding of the church's catholicity. The variety of local churches sharing a common life is seen as a major factor of the one church's catholicity (LG 23). As gift and task, the church's catholicity is "a gift from the Lord himself whereby the catholic church ceaselessly and effectively strives to recapitulate the whole of humanity and all its riches under Christ the Head in the unity of his Spirit. In virtue of this catholicity, each part contributes its own gifts to other parts and to the entire church, so that the whole and each of its parts are strengthened by the common sharing of all things and by the common effort to achieve fullness in unity" (LG 13). By attending to the particular, the church is most faithful to its catholicity. Implementing this will be another challenge in the postconciliar church.

Lumen Gentium's vision of church emphasizes the universal call to holiness among all the baptized, laity and hierarchy alike. The entirety of chapter 5, "perhaps the most remarkable aspect of *Lumen Gentium*," is devoted to this theme, "one of the great themes running through the council." This emphasis makes the documents of Vatican II "religious documents in a way notably different from those of previous councils."[58] In the past it was common to apply "states of perfection"

---

[57] Eugenio Corecco, "Aspects of the Reception of Vatican II in the Code of Canon Law," in *The Reception of Vatican II*, ed. Giuseppe Alberigo, Jean-Pierre Jossua, and Joseph A. Komonchak, trans. Matthew J. O'Connell (Washington, DC: The Catholic University of America Press, 1987), 274.

[58] O'Malley, *What Happened at Vatican II*, 50–51.

to vowed religious; the council resolutely affirms that all the faithful are called to the perfect holiness by which the Father is holy, an allusion to Matthew 5:48 (LG 11). The council recognizes the particular manner in which the spiritual life is lived according to the evangelical councils, though such a life is not restricted to any one group.[59] Whatever one's state of life, all are called to the perfection of love, that is, loving God with one's whole heart, soul, and understanding and loving one another as Christ loved us (LG 32, 39, and 40). A subset of the universal call to holiness is the life lived by vowed religious (LG chap. 6).

In our historical overview, we have seen the major concern to give a more complete teaching about bishops. The final teaching of the council stressed the sacramental reality of the bishop as the fullness of orders; the basis in their ordination of their threefold doctrinal, sanctifying, and governing ministry (designated by the biblical term *diakonia*); their collegial responsibility for the universal church; and their individual role as vicar of Christ, visible source and foundation of unity in their local church (LG 21–27). Most notable in the council's teaching about priests (the council favors the biblical term "presbyter") is its seeing the priest in his threefold functions, grounded in ordination, as minister of the word, as minister of the sacraments, and as pastor, so expanding the narrower Tridentine emphasis (in its dogmatic decree) on priesthood and sacrifice. It also sees priests as cooperators of the episcopal college and forming, with the bishop at its head, the presbyterate of the diocese (LG 28). The Decree on the Ministry and Life of Priests (*Presbyterorum Ordinis* [PO]) affirms that the sanctity of priests, acting as servants of Christ the head of the church, comes through the performance of their ministry in union with the bishop and their fellow priests (PO 12). In what the council says about bishops and priests, three notions are preeminent: their roles as servants, their collegial relationships, and the close link between the exercise of their ministry and their own sanctification.

Perhaps ultimately more consequential than what the council teaches about bishops, as important as that is, is what it teaches about

---

[59] Gustave Thils, "The Universal Call to Holiness in the Church," *Communio* 17 (1990): 494–503, at 498–99.

the lay faithful.[60] What was said earlier concerning the vision of church in the constitutions on the liturgy and revelation speak of the entire church, so implicitly they speak also of the lay faithful. In the Constitution on the Church, placing consideration of the entire people of God before looking to any differentiation within the church and speaking of the fundamental equality and dignity given by baptism and the common vocation to perfection (LG 32) are monumentally significant. The council deals explicitly with the lay faithful in three places. The Constitution on the Church, chapter 4, speaks of the lay faithful's participation, by baptism, in the threefold ministry of Christ, prophet, priest, and king (LG 33–36). They exercise their part in the mission of the whole Christian people in the church and in the world (LG 31). Laity participate in the last by their being witnesses and servants of Christ's kingdom of truth and life, of holiness and grace, of justice, love, and peace (LG 36). By reason of their knowledge or competence, laity are permitted and sometimes obliged to express their views on church issues (LG 37). As did the women and men who helped the apostle Paul (Rom 16:3ff.), laypeople can also assist the hierarchy in some ecclesiastical offices. The Decree on the Apostolate of Lay People (*Apostolican Actuositatem* [AA]) speaks of the laity's assignment to the apostolate by the Lord himself and of their right and duty to exercise in the church and in the world the charisms given them by the Spirit (AA 3). Theirs is an apostolate of evangelization and sanctification by which they draw people to faith and to God (AA 6) and an apostolate to renew the temporal order, in such areas as family life, for example, or the economic and political orders, the arts and sciences, and even matters regarding international relations (AA 7). The Decree on the Church's Missionary Activity is very direct: "The church is not truly established and does not fully live, nor is a perfect sign of Christ unless there is a genuine laity existing and working alongside the hierarchy" (AG 21).

Vatican II spells out the work of the church—its mission—in both the Constitution on the Church (LG) and in the Pastoral Constitution on the Church in the Modern World (GS). The first of these, we have noted earlier, sees the church likened to a sacrament, a sign, and, by

---

[60] See Komonchak, "The Ecclesiology of Vatican II," 765–76.

the power of the Spirit, an instrument of bringing about people's unity with God and unity among themselves (LG 1). This theme is taken up again when the constitution speaks of the church as a messianic community, which, even if it appears as a small flock, is "a most certain seed of unity, hope and salvation for the whole human race." As a "communion of life, love and truth," Christ uses the church as "the instrument for the salvation of all," sent into the world as "the light of the world and the salt of the earth" (LG 9, cf. Matt 5:13-16). This vision is very reminiscent of de Lubac's *Catholicism*, described in the previous chapter. De Lubac saw the church in the context of God's creation of an original unity, splintered by sin but destined to be restored in Christ. The council sees this restoration of all in Christ as both universal and cosmic and ultimately doxological. "Thus the church both prays and works so that the fullness of the whole world may move into the people of God, the body of the Lord and the temple of the holy Spirit, and that in Christ, the head of all things, all honor and glory may be rendered to the Creator, the Father of the universe" (LG 17).[61] This cosmic vision is background to the entire seventh chapter of *Lumen Gentium*, "The Eschatological Nature of the Pilgrim Church and Its Union with the Church in Heaven."[62] The constitution's final chapter, on Mary in the mystery of Christ and the church, sees in Mary "the image and beginning of the church as it is to be perfected in the world to come" (LG 68). The church looks to her intercession for the day when "all the families of people, whether they are honored with the title of Christian or whether they still do not know the Saviour, may be happily gathered together in peace and harmony into one people of God, for the glory of the most holy and undivided Trinity" (LG 69).

Explicitly presupposing the teaching of the Constitution on the Church (GS 2 and 40), the Pastoral Constitution on the Church in the Modern World seeks to describe the presence and the activity of the church in the world.[63] The constitution describes the *world* as the

---

[61] See Christopher Ruddy, "'In My End Is My Beginning': *Lumen Gentium* and the Priority of Doxology," *Irish Theological Quarterly* 79, no. 2 (2014): 144–64.

[62] Regrettably, the translation we are using has an abbreviated "The Pilgrim Church."

[63] Komonchak, "The Ecclesiology of Vatican II," 766–67.

"theater of human history" shaped by human activity, by social and cultural transformations, by industrialization and urbanization, and by new ways of thinking and acting (GS 2 and 54). Joined with the council's emphasis on what it describes as the birth of a *new humanism* in which humankind is defined by its responsibility to one another and to history (GS 55), perhaps it is better, Komonchak suggests, to see the world less as a theater of human history than as the "drama of human history," which relates God's gifts embodied in the church to "the larger drama of the collective and historical self-responsibility" of humankind.[64] The council itself describes the church's role in a programmatic statement:

> Proceeding from the love of the eternal Father, the church was founded by Christ in time and gathered into one by the holy Spirit. It has a saving and eschatological purpose which can be fully attained only in the next life. But it is now present here on earth and is composed of women and men; they, the members of the earthly city, are called to form the family of the children of God even in this present history of humankind and to increase it continually until the Lord comes. . . . Thus the church, at once "a visible organization and a spiritual community" [LG 8], travels the same journey as all of humanity and shares the same earthly lot with the world: it is to be a leaven and, as it were, the soul of human society in its renewal by Christ and transformation into the family of God.
>
> That the earthly and the heavenly city penetrate one another is a fact open only to the eyes of faith; moreover, it will remain the mystery of human history, which will be harassed by sin until the perfect revelation of the splendor of the children of God. In pursuing its own salvific purpose not only does the church communicate divine life to humanity but in a certain sense it casts the reflected light of that divine life over all the earth, notably in the way it heals and elevates the dignity of the human person, in the way it consolidates society, and endows people's daily activity with a deeper sense and meaning. The church, then, believes that through each of its members and its community as a whole it can help to make the human family and its history still more human. (GS 40)

---

[64] Ibid., 766.

The saving purpose mentioned in the second paragraph of the citation is at one with the goals of the church's role in the very first article of *Lumen Gentium*, that the church is a sign and instrument of the unity with God and the unity of the whole human race. The christological affirmation at the conclusion of the first part of *Gaudium et Spes*, that "The Lord [Jesus] is the goal of human history, the focal point of the desires of history and civilization, the center of humanity, the joy of all hearts, and the fulfillment of all aspirations" (GS 45, with a reference to Eph 1:10), reminds us of the very opening words of *Lumen Gentium*, that the church is called to bring the light of Christ to all peoples, a light visible on the countenance of the church. The two texts form christological bookends for the council's two constitutions on the church.

Because *Gaudium et Spes* represents a major reassessment of the church's attitude to the world, its teaching is understandably related to two of the council's declarations, that on non-Christian religions and that on religious freedom. The first of these, originally the fourth chapter of the schema on ecumenism, builds on the recognition of non-Christian religions in *Lumen Gentium*, article 16. Vatican II broke new ground in its formal recognition of the various ways in which the Catholic Church is related to Judaism and Islam and to those who seek God in different ways. The Declaration on the Relation of the Church to Non-Christian Religions (*Nostra Aetate*) recognized elements of truth and holiness in other religions and acknowledged its high regard for Muslims and the church's spiritual ties to Judaism and affirmed its belief that God does not withdraw the gifts he bestowed on the Jewish people.[65]

The Declaration on Religious Liberty (*Dignitatis Humanae*, originally the fifth chapter of the schema on ecumenism) is important for several reasons. It reflected the council's willingness to interface the doctrinal heritage of the church with the reality of a world where the church could no longer live as it did in a single unified empire, the old model of Christendom.[66] As mentioned earlier, it also dealt directly with the issue that lay below many of the debates of the

---

[65] See O'Collins, *The Second Vatican Council*, chap. 5.
[66] Gaillardetz and Clifford, *Keys to the Council*, 142.

council, the issue of development of church doctrine. The doctrinal teaching of the declaration is threefold: "the ethical doctrine of religious freedom as a human right (personal and collective); a political doctrine with regard to the functions and limits of government in matters religious; and the theological doctrine of the freedom of the church as the fundamental principle in what concerns the relations between the church and the socio-political order."[67] The declaration did not deal with a related issue: the theological meaning of Christian freedom within the church. The declaration is widely seen as the most important test of the council's ecumenical sincerity.[68]

We conclude this chapter by noting again the two words often used to summarize the council's work and its theological achievement. The council sought to articulate an understanding of church faithful to its truest self but addressing the present—mindful, Pope John said, of "the new conditions and new forms of life introduced into the modern world which have opened new avenues to the Catholic apostolate."[69] In this, the council undertook *aggiornamento*. It did that by drawing on the riches of the church's tradition, especially as that had been studied in the decades before the council, a *ressourcement* put to the service of the church. In the light of the latter, the council came to see many aspects of church in a new light, in terms of new relationships, with a new openness—the first of the epigraphs of this chapter. In the process, it came to appreciate more fully that discourse about the church must be grounded always in discourse about God, triune, incarnate, living in us through the gift of the Spirit—both of the epigraphs. Finally, and perhaps most important, the council's vision of church is just that, a vision into which believers are invited to respond and to accept their place and their role.

---

[67] John Courtney Murray, "Religious Freedom," in *The Documents of Vatican II*, ed. Walter M. Abbott, trans. ed. Joseph Gallagher (New York: America Press, 1966), 672–73.

[68] Robert McAfee Brown, "Introduction" to the discussion on religious freedom in *Vatican II: An Interfaith Appraisal*, ed. John H. Miller (Notre Dame, IN: University of Notre Dame Press, 1966), 564.

[69] John XXIII, Opening Address to the Council, Anderson, ed., *Council Daybook, Vatican II: Session 1*, 27.

CHAPTER ELEVEN

From Vatican II to Pope Francis

This final chapter will look at some of the principal developments in theological reflection on the church in the postconciliar period. Much of that reflection continues to explore the contribution of Vatican II, oftentimes exploring its directional inspirations[1] or being challenged to apply to new questions the methods used by the council.[2] We turn first to three efforts by bishops and theologians who, though not major voices at Vatican II, drew on the council's teaching as it might apply to their own local situations. The three efforts continue to be very much works in progress.

Understanding Church in Latin America, Africa, and Asia

The first such effort took place in Latin America.[3] Even before the council concluded, officials of the *Consejo Episcopal Latinoamericana* (CELAM) saw the need for an assembly to consider the reception of the council and to deal with concerns specific to their situation. In 1968, the bishops met at Medellín, Colombia, the second such meeting after the group was founded in 1955. In preparation for the meeting, the bishops drew on Vatican II's attention to the historical dimension of the church and, from the Constitution on the Church

---

[1] See the comment of Yves Congar, cited in Massimo Faggioli, *A Council for the Global Church: Receiving Vatican II in History* (Minneapolis: Fortress Press, 2015), 166.

[2] See Gilles Routhier, "Vatican II: Relevance and Future," in *50 Years On: Probing the Riches of Vatican II*, ed. David G. Schultenover (Collegeville, MN: Liturgical Press, 2015), 419–438.

[3] O. Ernesto Valiente, "The Reception of Vatican II in Latin America," *Theological Studies* 73, no. 4 (2012): 795–823.

in the Modern World, its concern for the poor and the afflicted and the need to discern the signs of the times in coming to understand the church's mission on the continent. Prominent in this preparation was Pope Paul VI's 1967 encyclical, On the Development of Peoples (*Populorum Progressio*), with its focus on the suffering and poverty caused, in part at least, by elements of the current economic system. The Latin American bishops also wanted to explore how Christ's saving work encompasses the many dimensions of human history and how this relates to the church. The title of Medellín's final document indicates the bishops' intent: "The Church in the Transformation of Latin America in the Light of the Council." While sections of the text seek to promote transformation in the lives of people, so resulting in a more just society, the section titled "Peace" confronts the "sinful situation" that leads to the misery of marginalized sectors of society. The bishops align the church with the plight of the poor and see that concern "directed to the fulfillment of the redeeming mission to which it is committed by Christ."[4] They propose "that the Church in Latin America should be manifested, in an increasingly clear manner, as truly poor, missionary and paschal, separate from all temporal power and courageously committed to the liberation of each and every man [sic]."[5] Calling the church to be "separate from all temporal power" marked a clear change from the previously close ties between many of the Latin American churches and the colonial rulers and local oligarchies. This is also the first time, it is noted, that the word and theme of "liberation" appears in an official church document.[6] Seeking to encourage broad participation in the church's mission, the conference saw the Christian base community (*communidad ecclesial de base* or CEB) as

---

[4] Second General Conference of Latin American Bishops, *The Church in the Present-Day Transformation of Latin America in the Light of the Council*, II Conclusions, 2nd ed. (Washington, DC: Division for Latin America—USCC, 1973), 191.

[5] Ibid, 97.

[6] Segundo Galilea, "Latin America in the Medellín and Puebla Conferences: An Example of Selective and Creative Reception of Vatican II," in *The Reception of Vatican II*, ed. Giuseppe Alberigo, Jean-Pierre Jossua, and Joseph A. Komonchak, trans. Matthew J. O'Connell (Washington, DC: The Catholic University of America Press, 1987), 64.

"the first and fundamental ecclesiastical nucleus . . . the focus of evangelization . . . the most important source of human advancement and development."[7] Begun as a catechetical experiment in Brazil in 1956, CEBs after Medellín became widespread in Latin America; often lay directed, they were regarded as a new structure for the church. While not all bishops equally supported Medellín and its implementation was uneven, "the Medellín Conference will go down in history not only for having given broad and official recognition to the 'local' characteristics of the Latin American Church, but also for having drawn the conclusions for pastoral practice and Christian life that this recognition implies."[8] Both the vision of Vatican II, especially the Constitution on the Church in the Modern World, and Medellín were very much inspirations for the three-year ministry of Oscar Romero as archbishop of San Salvador before his assassination in 1980. His beatification in 2015 recognizes the inseparability of the church's mission to evangelize and its work for justice.

Building on Medellín and drawing now on Pope Paul's 1975 apostolic exhortation, On Evangelization in the Modern World (*Evangelii Nuntiandi*) following the 1974 Synod of Bishops dedicated to that topic, CELAM's next general conference at Puebla, Mexico, in 1979 looked to "The Present and Future Evangelization of America." While some thought that increasing secularism and the weakening of the faith were the major challenges facing the Latin American church, Puebla's final document identified the situation of poverty and oppression as the church's principal concern. The conference explicitly spoke of the "preferential option for the poor," relating their situation to impoverishing economic and social factors. Puebla also reaffirmed the value of the CEBs and credited them with promoting a more evangelical life, embodying "the Church's preferential love for the common people," and working "committedly for the transformation of the world." The bishops lamented, though, that some groups had become "ideological radicals . . . in the process of losing

---

[7] Second General Conference of Latin American Bishops, *The Church in the Present-Day Transformation of Latin America*, 201.

[8] Galilea, "Latin America in the Medellín and Puebla Conferences," 66.

From Vatican II to Pope Francis 347

any authentic feel for the Church."⁹ Further conferences have been held at Santo Domingo, Dominican Republic (1992), on the "New Evangelization" and at Aparecida, Brazil (2007), on "Missionary Disciples of Jesus Christ: That Our Peoples May Have Life in Him." With some variations, running through these conferences since Medellín and serving to give the Latin American understanding of church its distinctive character are three interrelated principles: reading the signs of the times, giving preferential option to the poor, and seeing church as communion expressed in parishes and, especially on the periphery of the large cities and in the countryside, by the CEBs. The bishops at Aparecida placed great emphasis on the church's being a community of missionary disciples, called to see the option for the poor rooted in one's relationship of friendship with Christ. The option applies to the church as well: "That it is [a] preferential [option] means that it should permeate all our pastoral structures and priorities. The Latin American church is called to be sacrament of love, solidarity, and justice within our peoples."¹⁰ Focus on the preferential option for the poor has been named the Latin American church's most important contribution to the universal church.¹¹ Redaction of the final document of Aparecida was directed by Argentinian Cardinal Jorge Mario Bergoglio, elected Pope Francis in 2013.

A second notable attempt to articulate a vision of church after Vatican II concerned the church in Africa. Still a vision yet to be realized, the heart of this vision was expressed by Pope Paul VI during his 1969 visit to Africa: "You may, and you must, have an African Christianity."¹² The pope was referring to the task of "inculturation," the process by which the church seeks to be

---

⁹ "The Final Document," published in *Puebla and Beyond: Documentation and Commentary*, ed. John Eagleson and Philip Scharper, trans. John Drury (Maryknoll, NY: Orbis Books, 1979), 211–13.

¹⁰ V General Conference of the Bishops of Latin America and the Caribbean, *The Aparecida Document/Concluding Document* (Middletown, DE: no publisher listed, 2015), no. 396, p. 125.

¹¹ Valiente, "Reception of Vatican II," 823.

¹² Adrian Hastings, "The Council Came to Africa," in *Vatican II Revisited by Those Who Were There*, ed. Alberic Stacpoole (Minneapolis, MN: Winston Press, 1986), 321.

embodied in the culture of a given area. That call, along with a theological appreciation of the local church and the desire for the church to be engaged with contemporary society, were important legacies from Vatican II. The adjustment was not easy. The church in Africa in the early 1960s was still very much an outpost of the European Church in its leadership and its self-understanding;[13] some saw fidelity to Rome as "the guarantee of orthodoxy and clear identity."[14] By the mid-1970s, however, thanks to the efforts of the Symposium of Episcopal Conferences of Africa and Madagascar (SECAM)—formed the same year as the pope's visit—and with the help of others, the translation of the Scriptures in local languages was becoming a major influence in promoting an African Christianity. The Synod for Africa in 1994 and John Paul II's 1995 exhortation *Ecclesia in Africa* gave further impetus to African reflection on the church and its mission, though preparation for the event raised tensions between eagerness to implement inculturation for the church in Africa and worried concerns lest that impinge on a universalist perspective.[15] The 1995 exhortation subsumes the theme of inculturation within the theme of evangelization, while recognizing the proposition coming from the synod that "inculturation is a movement toward full evangelization."[16]

The synod and local theological reflection make much of the idea of the church as God's family with its emphasis on "care for others, solidarity, warmth in human relationships, acceptance, dialogue and trust."[17] An important feature of this understanding of church is the small Christian community, abbreviated SCC to distinguish it from

---

[13] Agbonkhianmeghe E. Orobator, "'After All, Africa Is Largely a Nonliterate Continent': The Reception of Vatican II in Africa," *Theological Studies* 74, no. 2 (2013): 284–301, at 289.

[14] Patrick A. Kililombe, "The Effect of the Council on World Catholicism: Africa," in *Modern Catholicism: Vatican II and After*, ed. Adrian Hastings (London: SPCK, 1991), 312.

[15] Joseph G. Donders, "Ambiguity about Africa: From Council to Synod," *America* 170, no. 2 (January 15, 1994): 10–12.

[16] John Paul II, "Apostolic Exhortation *Ecclesia in Africa*," *Origins* 25, no. 16 (October 5, 1995): no. 62.

[17] Ibid., no. 63.

the small communities in Latin America (CEB). Already in 1976 the Association of Member Episcopal Conferences in East Africa (AMECEA) gave strong endorsement to such communities as the basic unit of the church and an important means of developing African Christianity.[18] The parish is seen as a community of small communities; the diocese, a communion of parishes. This vision stands in practical tension, though, with a view of church that strongly emphasizes hierarchical structures of governance.[19] Vatican II's more positive appreciation of goodness and truth in other religions has prompted instances of concerned respect for indigenous African religion and openness to dialogue. Sensitivity to indigenous religious culture by colonial missionaries had earlier helped the church become more at home in African religious culture.[20] Liturgy provides an important area of inculturation. While its use and assessments of its significance vary, the use of the drum "was the great symbol of post-Vatican II liturgy—a symbol at once of cultural pluralism and popular participation, the arrival of an active laity, but still more the arrival of Africa in all its vibrant, populist, rhythmic vitality as a major reality within Catholicism."[21]

Asia provides a third instance of efforts to forge a vision of a local church that seeks to develop in its own cultural and religious context. To speak of Asia is to refer to nearly two-thirds of the world's population, an immense territory, a multitude of languages and dialects, several ancient apostolic churches, many non-Christian Asian religions, and varied histories and cultures in many countries. "Asia" is conventionally divided into five regions: the countries of the Middle East; Central Asia (e.g., Republics of Kazakhstan, Kyrgyzstan, etc.); East Asia (mainly China, Japan, Korea, and Taiwan); South Asia (mainly India, Pakistan, Bangladesh, Myanmar); and Southeast Asia (e.g., Indonesia, Vietnam, Cambodia, Philippines). The Middle East

---

[18] Joseph Healey and Donald Sybertz, *Towards an African Narrative Theology* (Maryknoll, NY: Orbis Books, 1996), 137–53.

[19] Orobator, "After All," 300.

[20] Richard Gray, *Christianity, the Papacy, and Mission in Africa*, ed. with intro. by Lamin Sanneh (Maryknoll, NY: Orbis Books, 2012), 155.

[21] Hastings, "The Council Came to Africa," 320.

is home to seven ancient patriarchal churches; India has three communities of churches, Latin, Syro-Malabar, and Syro-Malankara.[22] With the exception of the Philippines, in all Asian countries Catholics are a very small or even miniscule portion of the population.[23] The first steps toward implementing Vatican II consisted of translations of conciliar texts and liturgical books to local Asian languages, no mean task since a basic Christian vocabulary was not immediately available for some Asian languages.[24] A vernacular liturgy and small changes in liturgical practice allowed for greater participation and at least some local liturgical inculturation. A new sense of corporate identity rose when 180 bishops of Asia met in Manilla in 1970 for a pastoral visit by Pope Paul. From that came the formation of the Federation of Asian Bishops Conferences (FABC) from all but the first of the regions mentioned above.[25] (The churches of the Middle East have their own Council of Catholic Patriarchs.) FABC's mission sought to receive Vatican II and apply it to the Asian context, implementing three conciliar principles: "episcopal collegiality, ecclesial communion, and dialogue as the mode of being church."[26] The dialogue itself is threefold: with Asian cultures, with Asian religions, and with the Asian peoples, many of whom are very poor. This dialogical way of being church is expressed in a fourfold presence: sharing life's joys and sorrows with others in an open and neighborly way (dialogue of life); collaboration with others in promoting the development and liberation of people (dialogue of action); working toward a deepened understanding of one's own religious heritage and an appreciation of the spiritual values in others (dialogue of theological exchange); and, rooted in one's own religious tradition, sharing such spiritual riches as prayer and contemplation (dialogue

---

[22] Peter C. Phan, "Reception of and Trajectories for Vatican II in Asia," *Theological Studies* 74, no. 2 (2013): 305.

[23] See ibid, 307.

[24] Peter C. Phan, "'Reception' or 'Subversion' of Vatican II by the Asian Churches? A New Way of Being Church in Asia," in *Vatican II: Forty Years Later*, ed. William Madges, Annual Publication of the College Theology Society 2005 (Maryknoll, NY: Orbis Books, 2006), 33.

[25] See its website: http://www.fabc.org.

[26] Phan, "Reception and Trajectories," 312.

of religious experience).²⁷ FABC documents in 1992 and 1997 speak of this as "a new way of being church," with special emphasis on seeing the church as a sign and servant of the kingdom of God.²⁸

Major efforts to express an understanding of church in Asia came in the 1998 Special Assembly for Asia of the Synod of Bishops.²⁹ Perceptions of how best to proceed as proposed by the general secretariat of the Synod of Bishops in Rome differed at times from those of the various Asian episcopal conferences. The Outline (*Lineamenta*) prepared by the Roman offices recognized Asian efforts to present Christ in a way most suitable to the Asian situation but insisted on presenting "Jesus Christ as the one and only Savior as well as the universality of salvation in Him."³⁰ Several responses from Asian conferences of bishops looked for some recognition as well of a salvific significance of the great ancient religions of Asia. Only by dialogue with these religious traditions, the bishops asserted, could the church proclaim the Gospel of Jesus Christ. The Catholic bishops of India held that a "dialogical model is the new Asian way of being Church, promoting mutual understanding, harmony and collaboration."³¹ The bishops of Japan called for a study of people's religiosity, as the fathers of the early church studied the Greco-Roman culture, to discover a way to present Jesus Christ as an answer to their needs.³² Taking up these responses, the Working Document (*Instrumentum laboris*) kept the basic title of the Outline but changed the focus from Christology to "how the Church must carry out the mission of Jesus in Asia today."³³

Three themes especially received attention in the synod: the importance of the three areas of dialogue, a plea for a legitimate autonomy

---

[27] Peter C. Phan, "The Church in Asian Perspective," in *The Routledge Companion to the Christian Church*, ed. Gerard Mannion and Lewis S. Mudge (New York: Routledge, 2008), 280.

[28] Phan, "'Reception' or 'Subversion,'" 36–37.

[29] Peter C. Phan, ed., *The Asian Synod: Texts and Commentaries* (Maryknoll, NY: Orbis Books, 2002).

[30] Cited in ibid., 15.

[31] Ibid., 18–23, at 21.

[32] Ibid., 27–32, at 30.

[33] Ibid., 73; analysis of the text, 73–82.

of the local churches, and the need to expand the roles of the laity, especially women, in the life of the church. A Japanese bishop asked that a "principle of graduality" be applied to the relationship between the local churches of Asia and authorities in Rome, that those authorities give Asian churches responsibility to grow and that churches in other areas respect and support these local efforts.[34] To win a hearing in Indian/Asian minds and hearts, a bishop of the Syro-Malabar Church in India noted, there is urgent need for the leadership style of the church "to become more and more spiritual, free from institutional authoritarianism." We have to develop, he said, "a new way of being Church . . . a kenosis ecclesiology" that follows the self-emptying of the cross.[35]

Pope John Paul's exhortation *Ecclesia in Asia* (1999) cites many of the synod's propositions[36] but is less a summary of the synod's discussions than the pope's own exhortation to the church in Asia on the eve of the third millennium.[37] The exhortation begins with a focus on Christ as the one mediator and sole redeemer, to be clearly distinguished from the founders of other great religions, and ends with the prayer that all the peoples of Asia may come to know Jesus Christ, "the only savior of the world."[38] The key issue for the church, in the exhortation, is its proclamation of the Gospel; dialogue, witness, and service are to be directed to that end. A summary of Taiwanese Cardinal Paul Shan's commentary on the papal exhortation holds that the major issue is "not *why* the local churches in Asia have to proclaim the Christian Gospel, but *how* best to carry out this task within the diversity and plurality of Asia's religions, cultures, and the poor."[39] In fact, the pope took a similar tack when he spoke to leaders of other

---

[34] Berard T. Oshikawa, "Pastoral Life in Asia and 'The Principle of Graduality,'" in Phan, *The Asian Synod*, 104–5.

[35] Gratian Mundaban, "Leadership in the Church in Asia," in Phan, *The Asian Synod*, 111.

[36] Phan, *The Asian Synod*, 140–65.

[37] John Paul II, "Post Synodal Apostolic Exhortation *Ecclesia in Asia*," published in Phan, *The Asian Synod*, 286–340.

[38] John Paul II, *Ecclesia in Asia*, nos. 2 and 51.

[39] Vu Kim Chinh, "Inculturation of Christianity into Asia: Reflections on the Asian Synod," in Phan, *The Asian Synod*, 268.

religions the day after signing his exhortation: "Religious leaders in particular have the duty to do everything possible to ensure that religion is what God intends it to be, a source of goodness, respect, harmony, and peace! . . . Dialogue . . . does not mean that we abandon our own convictions. What it means is that, holding firmly to what we believe, we listen respectfully to others, seeking to discern all that is good and holy, all that favors peace and cooperation."[40] FABC documents and Asian theologians see in the kingdom proclaimed and inaugurated in the person and ministry of Jesus the basic guide for the mission of the church. As "sign, sacrament, and servant of the Kingdom" the church continues the mission of Christ. By its presence in the lives of the Asian peoples, in a "Christian discipleship lived in servanthood, in a kenosis and self-sacrificing love shorn of all triumphalism, and in the triple dialogue . . . the Church learns to be itself, as Church in Asia and a Church of Asia."[41] The FABC recognizes the challenge of keeping these several elements in harmony, avoiding any reduction of the church's role to one or another aspect.[42]

The Extraordinary Synod of 1985

In 1985 Pope John Paul II called an extraordinary synod to assess the reception of Vatican II twenty years after the council's close.[43] A few months before the synod, Cardinal Joseph Ratzinger, the head of the Congregation for the Doctrine of the Faith (CDF), published an interview, *The Ratzinger Report*, which gave a very critical assessment of ecclesiological developments of the previous twenty years.[44]

---

[40] Cited in Michael Amaladoss, "Mission in Asia: A Reflection on *Ecclesia in Asia*," in Phan, *The Asian Synod*, 232.

[41] Soosai Arokiasamy, "Synod for Asia: An Ecclesial Event of Communion and Shared Witness of Faith," in Phan, *The Asian Synod*, 181–88, at 186–87.

[42] James Thoppil, *Towards an Asian Ecclesiology: The Understanding of the Church in the Documents of the FABC (1970–2000)* (Shillong, India: Oriens Publications, 2005), 297.

[43] See Massimo Faggioli, *Vatican II: The Battle for Meaning* (New York: Paulist Press, 2012).

[44] Joseph Cardinal Ratzinger with Vittorio Messori, *The Ratzinger Report: An Exclusive Interview on the State of the Church*, trans. Salvator Attanasio and Graham Harrison (San Francisco: Ignatius Press, 1985), chaps. 2 and 3.

Mindful also of the coming synod, the International Theological Commission (ITC) in 1984 gave its reflections on the reception of the council's Dogmatic Constitution on the Church.[45] The synod's work, along with these other two texts just mentioned, constitutes an important indication of theological reflection on the church twenty years after the council ended.[46] There were basically two schools of thought in approaching the concerns of the synod.[47] One group, led largely by Cardinal Ratzinger and other German cardinals, was very critical in its evaluation of contemporary culture and opposed what appeared to be excessive postconciliar preoccupation with ecclesial structures. This group emphasized the need to present the church as mystery, urging it to "take a sharper stance against the world and seek to arouse the sense of God's holy mystery."[48] A second group, represented by Cardinal Basil Hume of England and the heads of episcopal conferences in Canada and in the United States, looked to the concept of *communio* for its pastoral value and its implications for implementing collegial and synodal structures that would promote greater exercise of responsibility and wider participation in the life of the church. Other bishops accepted the need for the development of synodal structures but were more concerned to see the church address the needs of the poor and the oppressed.

The synod issued a Final Report,[49] best understood in the context of the various synod documents and discussions.[50] The report refers

---

[45] "Select Themes of Ecclesiology on the Occasion of the Eighth [*sic*. Should read Twentieth] Anniversary of the Closing of the Second Vatican Council," in *International Theological Commission, Texts and Documents 1969–1985*, ed. Michael Sharkey (San Francisco: Ignatius Press, 1989), chap. 13.

[46] Joseph Komonchak, "The Theological Debate," in *Concilium*, no. 188, *Synod 1985—An Evaluation*, ed. Giuseppe Alberigo, James Provost, and English Language ed. Marcus Lefébure (Edinburgh: T & T Clark, 1986), 52–63.

[47] Hermann Pottmeyer, "The Church as Mystery and as Institution," in *Concilium*, 188, *Synod 1985—An Evaluation*, 99–109, at 100–101.

[48] Avery Dulles, "The Reception of Vatican II at the Extraordinary Synod of 1985," in *The Reception of Vatican II*, 354.

[49] *Origins* 15, no. 27 (December 19, 1985).

[50] Joseph A. Komonchak, "Introduction," in *Synode extraordinaire: Célébration de Vatican II* (Paris: Editions du Cerf, 1986), 9–32.

to Vatican II as the Magna Carta for the church's future (II.D.7), though the text gives greater attention to the "shadows" in the council's reception than to the benefits it brought to the church (I.3 and 4). Particular concerns are a loss of a sense of transcendence and worry that a "partial reading of the council" led to "speaking too much of the renewal of the church's external structures and too little of God and of Christ." Principles of interpretation of the council documents, meant to promote a "deeper reception" of the council, stress the harmony between the different conciliar texts, minimizing tensions between them or between Vatican II and previous church teaching, no doubt to counter interpretations that underscored such tensions. In dealing with particular themes of Vatican II's theology of the church, minimal attention is given to the term "people of God." Many pre-synodal reports recognized the value of that image in speaking of the church, though several lamented the neglect of attention to the church as the body of Christ and temple of the Spirit. The term "people" had also been read, at times, in an ideological sense, identifying it as a social or economic class or set in opposition to the hierarchical church.[51]

The synod's Final Report emphasizes instead the church as mystery and the church as communion. The first was chosen to offset what was perceived as a growing secularist anthropology that neglected or denied the dimension of mystery and to respond to "signs of a return to the sacred" in some quarters (II.A.1). While emphasizing that the church's importance comes from her connection with Christ, the same section of the report cautions against replacing a one-sided hierarchical understanding of church with a new sociological conception. This caution may reflect the German-language group's distinction between "the Church we 'receive' and the Church we 'make,'" implying that the first is theological and the second 'purely sociological.'"[52] Against such an implication theologians point out that, at least in the Thomist tradition, the church is at once the *Ecclesia de*

---

[51] Joseph A. Komonchak, "The Synod of 1985 and the Notion of the Church," *Chicago Studies* 26, no. 3 (1987): 330–45, at 335. The following paragraphs draw from this article.
[52] Ibid., 335.

Trinitate and the *Ecclesia de hominibus*, the first pointing to the transcendent dimension, the second, to the fact that the church created by God's word and grace only exists as a community freely receiving and actively appropriating God's gift. The Final Report identifies the sources of life for the church in the word of God and the liturgy.

The report identifies the church as communion as the "central and fundamental idea" of Vatican II and describes it as "a matter of communion with God through Jesus Christ in the sacraments" (II.C.1). Again, the synod cautions lest the theology of church as communion be reduced to purely organizational questions, though it affirms communion as the foundation for order in the church. The report goes on to say that "the ecclesiology of communion provides the sacramental foundation for collegiality," making a distinction between collegial action in the strict sense (the activity of the whole college, together with its head) and "diverse partial realizations" of the collegial spirit (the Synod of Bishops, episcopal conferences, the Roman Curia, the *ad limina* visit of bishops, etc.; see II.C.4). The comment could appear to relativize the oft-expressed desire for appropriate structures in the church—what a Spanish-language group during the synod called the "horizontal dimension of communion"—which would support a more collegial way of exercising responsibility in the church. English-speaking bishops made the same appeal. A statement that communion requires "participation and co-responsibility at all her levels" (II.C.6) gives examples of those called to such responsibility but offers no specifics on structures and omits any reference to collegiality as it might affect the pope.

A last section of the Final Report reaffirms the importance of the Constitution on the Church in the Modern World and recognizes that since the council the church has become "more aware of her mission in the service of the poor, the oppressed and the outcast." The report says that "the church must prophetically denounce every form of poverty and oppression" and that the spiritual mission "involves human promotion even in its temporal aspects," rejecting any opposition between the church's spiritual mission and service for the world (II.D.6). It mentions *aggiornamento* and inculturation only as referring to the church in its mission *ad extra*, outside of itself, and not, as Vatican II had it, affecting the church itself. The Final Report tried to represent the concerns of the various groups at the synod. Its guarded endorsement of Vatican II reflects the second week of the synod, which focused on errors or abuses after the council; the report failed to give adequate attention to the first week, which celebrated the accomplishments of the council. The synod points to two major challenges in realizing ecclesial communion in "a genuinely and concretely catholic Church," one cultural, the other structural.[53] The first: how to reconcile unity and plurality in a global church after centuries of European cultural dominance. The second: how to realize local churches, responsible for themselves and in communion with other churches, after centuries of Roman centralization. Though the synod did not address these issues head on, it is a reminder that the theology of the church is both theoretical and practical; neither can be neglected, even if the church must live with the tension of trying to honor both.

In contrast to the Final Report's preference for the idea of church as mystery, the statement of the International Theological Commission recognized the "pride of place" given to the image of the church as "people of God" at Vatican II.[54] As the commission sees it, the fathers of Vatican II gave preference to the "people" image over others because it had the advantage of better respecting the sacramental reality shared by all the baptized, the source of their dignity in the church and the basis of their responsibility in the world. The image also underlines both the communitarian nature of the church and its historical dimension. As people *of God*, it implies a constitutive reference to Jesus Christ and the Spirit. As *people* it points to the church's identity as "historic subject" in a given time and place, living a corporate life, engaged in Christ's mission, aware that she is always "on the way." In this perspective, the mystery constitutes the historic subject and the historic subject discloses the mystery.[55] The church as a whole needs to be attentive to the specific situations in Asia, Africa, Oceania, and North and South America. While not offering complete reflection on the topic, the Theological Commission notes the need

---

[53] Komonchak, "The Theological Debate," 61–62.
[54] International Theological Commission, "Select Themes," 271–78.
[55] Ibid, 274.

for inculturation, one aspect of which would be a correspondence between the concrete forms of institutions and the positive values of a given culture.[56] The text also points to the need for theological discernment, based on scientific analysis, to address local and worldwide injustice. We leave until later the commission's comments on the local church and the universal church.

Both the revised *Code of Canon Law* for the Latin Church (1983) and the *Catechism of the Catholic Church* (1992) are seen to show a certain reserve in receiving Vatican II. The Code makes the people of God one of its principal themes, and in promulgating it, Pope John Paul expected the Code would help the church "progress in conformity with the spirit" of the council.[57] The rights of all the baptized listed in council are included in the canons, though they omit mention of the right and the duty of each believer to exercise one's charisms in the church and in the world (Decree on the Apostolate of Lay People 3),[58] *pace* the promulgating constitution's saying the Code is to promote an order "assigning the primacy to love, grace and charisms." Scholars can point to places where the Code improves on the council and places where it falls short but credits it as a transitional stage in that it introduces theology as an essential element in the development of church law.[59]

A legal system operates, of course, in a social context. Scholars point to a tension between the church's legal system and what Charles Taylor calls the "social imaginary" operative at least in much of the West. The latter term describes "the ways people imagine their social existence, how they fit together with others, how things go on between themselves and their fellows, the expectations that are normally met, and the deeper normative notions and images that underlie these

---

[56] Ibid, 280–81.

[57] John Paul II, "Apostolic Constitution *Sacrae disciplinae leges*," in *Code of Canon Law*, Latin-English Edition (Washington, DC: Canon Law Society of America, 1998), xxx–xxxi.

[58] Joseph A. Komonchak, "The Significance of Vatican Council II for Ecclesiology," in *The Gift of the Church: A Textbook on Ecclesiology in Honor of Patrick Granfield*, ed. Peter Phan (Collegeville, MN: Liturgical Press, 2000), 84n18.

[59] Eugenio Corecco, "Aspects of the Reception of Vatican II in the Code of Canon Law," in *The Reception of Vatican II*, 249–96, at 295.

expectations."[60] Canon 208 speaks of "a true equality regarding dignity and action by which [all the baptized] cooperate in the building up of the Body of Christ according to each one's own condition and function,"[61] but the Code's lack of mechanisms for ensuring participation in decision-making processes and the discretion it gives to church authorities regarding the rights of the lay faithful contribute to the view of some, at least, that church law represents a paternalistic social imaginary in tension with one in which active participation and responsible cooperation are given an important place.[62]

The *Catechism of the Catholic Church* was first promulgated by John Paul II in 1992, a definitive edition promulgated five years later. A "provisional text" drafted by a papal commission of cardinals and bishops was sent to the bishops of the world in November 1989. To assist the study of the draft text, scholars at the Woodstock Center at Georgetown University found that "certain teachings" of the council were included, but "many of its concerns, such as *aggiornamento*, the reformability of the church, the importance of the Word of God, the structures of collegiality, the active role of the laity, the value of religious life, regional diversification, and ecumenism, are skirted or suppressed."[63] A much-improved treatment of the church in the final text was "generally faithful to the vision rediscovered by Vatican II of the Church-as-communion," though it showed a decided preference for the universal aspect of communion rather than with what that might mean for the local level.[64]

---

[60] Charles Taylor, *Modern Social Imaginaries* (Durham, NC: Duke University Press, 2004), 23.

[61] *Code of Canon Law*, 62.

[62] John P. Beal, "Something There Is That Doesn't Love a Law," in *The Crisis of Authority in Catholic Modernity*, ed. Michael J. Lacey and Francis Oakley (Oxford: Oxford University Press, 2011), 144–54.

[63] Avery Dulles, "The Church in the Catechism," in *The Universal Catechism Reader: Reflections and Responses*, ed. Thomas J. Reese (New York: HarperSanFrancisco, 1990), 92.

[64] J.-M.-R. Tillard, "The Church," in *Commentary on the Catechism of the Catholic Church*, ed. Michael J. Walsh (Collegeville, MN: Liturgical Press, 1994), 178–204, at 203–4.

The Church as Communion and the Local Church

A major development in Roman Catholic theology of the church, especially since the synod of 1985, has been reflection on the church as communion, an interest shared with Orthodox and Protestant theologians. Catholics find the notion appealing because, with Vatican II, it shifts emphasis from the heavily juridical and institutional stress of previous understandings. A study of the many versions of communion theology by University of Dayton professor Dennis Doyle points to four constant elements: a return to the vision characteristic of the undivided church of the first millennium; an explicit recognition of our communion with God and with others in God; the need for visible unity expressed in and brought about by Eucharist; and a dynamic interplay between unity and diversity and between the church universal and local churches.[65] The particular versions of communion theology discussed in Doyle's study differ from one another in what they emphasize, though each can contribute to an understanding of the church, faithful to and developing the insights of Vatican II. The issues at play in communion reflections are important: the transcendent dimension of the church and its historical concreteness; the relationship between the universal church and the local churches; the relation of the Catholic Church to other Christian communities, to other religious traditions, and to the community of humankind generally; and, finally, within the church, the place of sacraments, ministries, charisms, and, importantly, the papal ministry itself. The CDF in 1992 issued a Letter to the Bishops of the Catholic Church on Some Aspects of the Church Understood as Communion,[66] which reflects its particular concerns at the time, that in the development of this thinking there be no underplay of the universal church, of its transcendent dimensions, of the distinctive identity of the Catholic Church, and of its internal structures. The congregation's letter shows less concern with attention to local churches, the church's

---

[65] Dennis M. Doyle, *Communion Ecclesiology: Visions and Versions* (Maryknoll, NY: Orbis Books, 2000), 13.

[66] www.vatican.va/roman_curia/congregations/cfaith/documents/rc_con _cfaith_doc_28051992_communionis-notio_en.html (accessed January 16, 2017). Also in *Origins* 22, no. 7 (June 25, 1992).

historical concreteness, ecumenical relations, or the church's interrelatedness with the world.[67]

One major issue in this discussion is the relationship between local churches and the church universal.[68] Vatican II's Dogmatic Constitution on the Church (LG 23) makes two points: (1) particular (local) churches image the universal church and (2) the one Catholic Church exists only in and out of the particular churches. Several other passages of the council recognize the reality of church "in all legitimate local congregations . . . united with their pastors" (LG 26). The 1992 text of the congregation speaks of the "mutual interiority between the universal Church and particular Church" but goes further to state that the universal church is "a reality *ontologically and temporally* prior to every *individual* particular Church" (no. 9; italics in original). The text cites passages of the fathers that speak of the church-mystery preceding creation to support an ontological priority and the church at Pentecost, seen as universal church, to support a temporal priority. Theological criticism of what seemed to be an assertion of the existence of an invisible church existing apart from historically existing churches led to a clarification in *L'Osservatore Romano* a year later, which ruled out any idea of an abstract reality of church opposed to the concrete reality of particular churches, though it held to the ontological and historical priority of the universal church.[69] Jean-Marie Roger Tillard thinks it more accurate to see the Jerusalem church as simultaneously universal and particular. He sees the Church of God as a communion of churches that are at once universal and local, universal because they share the same divine constitutive principles, local because always realized in concrete historical situations.[70] A quite public debate between Cardinal Ratzinger of the CDF and Bishop Walter Kasper, shortly thereafter appointed

---

[67] Doyle, *Communion Ecclesiology*, 127–30.

[68] Joseph A. Komonchak, "The Theology of the Local Church: State of the Question," in *The Multicultural Church: A New Landscape in U.S. Theologies*, ed. William Cenkner (New York: Paulist Press, 1995), 35–49, at 38.

[69] Christopher Ruddy, *The Local Church: Tillard and the Future of Catholic Ecclesiology* (New York: Crossroad, 2006), 106.

[70] Ibid, 99–109, at 106–7.

president of the Pontifical Council for Promoting Christian Unity, pointed to different understandings on the issue, the former emphasizing the priority of the universal church, the latter arguing that such a stance weakens the balance between the universal church and the local churches.[71]

A further question: How are we to understand the theological significance of the human, historical reception of the God-given constitutive principles of the church? One approach sees elements that serve to differentiate local churches or groupings of churches as "simply human" factors, belonging to a "socio-cultural order," geographical perhaps, and useful or even indispensable for the good of the church but not properly theological principles.[72] Other studies, several by Catholic University of America professor Joseph A. Komonchak, insist that the divine gifts that constitute the church do not and cannot be found apart from their being received, under the Spirit's guidance, by historical human beings, in a specific cultural, social, political, and economic context. In this view, one can speak of a "humanly subjective pole" as part of the very being of the church.[73] A properly theological understanding of church involves both the divine gifts and the women and men who, accepting these gifts in faith and love, become a local realization of the people of God, the body of Christ, and the temple of the Spirit.

German theologian Hermann Pottmeyer points out that both Vatican I and Vatican II reflect the church's growing awareness of itself as "the historical subject of its own self-realization," understood, always, as receiving the divine gifts mentioned above.[74] Vatican I asserted the church's right to self-determination "as a carefully constructed Catholic 'world,' independent and self-sufficient," with its

---

[71] Kilian McDonnell, "The Ratzinger/Kasper Debate: The Universal Church and Local Churches," *Theological Studies* 63 (2002): 227–49.

[72] Joseph A. Komonchak, "The Local Church and the Church Catholic: The Contemporary Theological Problematic," *The Jurist* 52 (1992): 435 and note 47.

[73] Joseph A. Komonchak, "The Epistemology of Reception," *The Jurist* 57 (1997): 186. See bibliography in Ruddy, *The Local Church*, 246.

[74] Joseph A. Komonchak, "Ministry and the Local Church," in *Catholic Theology Society of America Proceedings*, vol. 36 (1981), ed. Luke Salm (Bronx, NY: Manhattan College, 1981), 62–64, 71–73.

life centered on the symbol and ministry of the pope.[75] Vatican II affirmed that all the members of the church are active subjects responsible for the self-realization of the church in their local situations. No longer, in theory, are the clergy the principal agents, the lay faithful active only in their own obedience. The council saw secular concerns as the special though not exclusive concern of the lay faithful, though the secular role was presented as a "typological" description, not an ontological definition.[76] Pope John Paul II, however, in his 1988 exhortation on the laity, *Christifideles Laici*, speaks of the laity's role *in the world* as "not only an anthropological and sociological reality, but in a specific way, a theological and ecclesiological reality as well."[77] If what canon lawyers see in this instance as a misinterpretation of the council—a narrowing of the role of the laity—is regarded as the official interpretation, this would impact the role of the lay faithful as active subjects in the life of the church.[78]

Accepting the theological reality of the subjective pole of the church and what was said above about the social imaginary invites reflection on the exercise of authority in the church.[79] An instance of such reflection is the important study by the International Theological Commission, " 'Sensus Fidei' in the Life of the Church" (2014).[80] The text points out that Vatican II banished "the caricature" of an active hierarchy and a passive laity, particularly the notion of a strict separation between the teaching church and the learning church. While giving many instances of hierarchical-lay cooperation in the past, the text points to the need for an effective means of consulting the faithful.

---

[75] Ibid., 71–72.

[76] Joseph A. Komonchak, "Clergy, Laity, and the Church's Mission in the World," *The Jurist* 41 (1981): 429.

[77] *Christifideles Laici* (December 30, 1988), in *Origins* 18, no. 35 (February 9, 1989): no. 15.

[78] Beale, "Something There Is That Doesn't Love a Law," 142 and note 35.

[79] Joseph A. Komonchak, "Authority and Conversion or: The Limits of Authority," *Cristianesimo nella Storia* 21 (2000): 207–29, online at https://jakomonchak.wordpress.com/2010/07/24/authority-and-conversion/ (accessed February 8, 2015). See also Bernard Hoose, ed., *Authority in the Roman Catholic Church: Theory and Practice* (Burlington, VT: Ashgate, 2002).

[80] *Origins* 44, no. 9 (July 3, 2014): 133–55.

(A dramatic instance of an effort at such consulting—even with its limitations—came in the preparation for the Extraordinary Synod of Bishops in the fall of 2014. More on this below.) Related also to the role of the lay faithful in the church, scandals involving clergy are prompting historical and theological considerations regarding governance and accountability in the church.[81]

The Church in Contemporary Culture

We note three other developments in theological reflection on the church in the decades since the council. The first concerns the notion and mission of the church in what has been called "liberation theology," begun in Latin America but spread to Africa and Asia as well.[82] The theme of liberation, we have seen above, entered into the deliberations of the Latin American bishops as they looked to the mission of the church in their local situation. Liberation theology seeks to reflect on the meaning of faith based on the commitment to abolish injustice and to verify that reflection in actual practice. The CDF's "Instruction on Certain Aspects of the 'Theology of Liberation'" (1984)[83] distinguishes an "authentic theology of liberation" resting on the truth about Jesus Christ, the church, and humankind (V.8) and those theologies of liberation (unnamed) marked by an uncritical borrowing from Marxist social analysis (VI.9; VII.1) and its understanding of history and truth. A second text, the "Instruction on Christian Freedom and Liberation" (1986),[84] makes the point that human freedom receives its meaning from God and our relationship to him and to others. Because we are created as social beings, our

---

[81] See Christopher Ruddy, "Ecclesiological Issues Behind the Sexual Abuse Crisis," *Origins* 37, no. 8 (July 5, 2007): 119–26, and Francis Oakley and Bruce Russett, eds., *Governance, Accountability, and the Future of the Catholic Church* (New York: Continuum, 2004).

[82] Gerard Mannion, "Liberation Ecclesiology," in Mannion and Mudge, *The Routledge Companion to the Christian Church*, 421–42.

[83] Congregation for the Doctrine of the Faith, "Instruction on Certain Aspects of the 'Theology of Liberation,'" *Origins* 14, no. 13 (September 13, 1984).

[84] Congregation for the Doctrine of the Faith, "Instruction on Christian Freedom and Liberation," *Origins* 15, no. 44 (April 17, 1986).

human freedom calls us to act in ways that promote love, justice, and peace (no. 63), so contributing to the liberating mission of the church. The instruction uses the expression "love of preference for the poor" in addition to "special option for the poor," probably to underscore the Christian motive for the option.[85] This second instruction, with all of its caveats, has been seen as "a formal Vatican endorsement . . . of the liberation approach" for the universal church.[86] Shortly before the instruction was released, Pope John Paul told the bishops of Brazil that liberation theology, shorn of adulterating elements, is "not only orthodox but necessary."[87]

A second development is represented by the declaration of the CDF in 2000, *Dominus Iesus* (On the Unicity and Salvific Universality of Jesus Christ and the Church), signed by Cardinal Ratzinger.[88] The declaration builds on the ITC's 1997 document, "Christianity and the World Religions,"[89] and the 1990 encyclical letter of John Paul II, Mission of the Redeemer (*Redemptoris Missio*).[90] The declaration is meant to guide bishops, theologians, and the faithful generally in their theological reflection. After recalling the fullness and definitiveness of revelation in Christ and the unicity and universality of Christ's salvific meditation in God's single plan of salvation, the text turns to the need to affirm the unicity and universality of the church. With Vatican II, the text recognizes the presence of elements of sanctification and truth in other churches and ecclesial communities, even as it affirms that the church of Christ exists fully only in the Catholic Church. The final section of the text looks to the church and other religions in relation to salvation; it insists that one must keep together two truths: the real possibility of salvation

---

[85] Alfred T. Hennelly, "The Red-Hot Issue: Liberation Theology," *America* (May 24, 1986): 426.

[86] Ibid., 425.

[87] Ibid., 428.

[88] www.vatican.va/roman_curia/congregations/cfaith/documents/rc_con _faith_doc_20000806_dominus-iesus_en.html.

[89] International Theological Commission, *Christianity and the World Religions*, trans. Michael Ledwith, in *Origins* 27, no. 10 (August 14, 1997).

[90] w2.vatican.va/content/john-paul-ii/en/encyclicals/documents/hf_jp-ii _enc_07121990_redemptoris-missio.htlm.

in Christ for all humankind and the necessity of the church for this salvation. It rejects the idea that the church is one way alongside other ways of salvation. The introduction to the declaration refers to the danger to truths of the faith coming from "relativistic theories" that seek to justify religious pluralism, "not only *de facto* but also *de iure* (or in principle)." The text can be seen as another effort to guide interpretation of Vatican II. For Irish Catholic lay theologian Gerard Mannion, the declaration "illustrates a great number of the most pressing ecclesiological issues of concern today." It serves, he says, as an excellent case study regarding the church's place and future in "the postmodern context."[91] Some of these issues surfaced in our look at Asian reflections on the church.

Reflection on the church in the era of "postmodernity" is yet another line of thought. Mannion sees in postmodernity the increasing rejection of any "overarching explanatory hypotheses" for the world, for humankind, or for society. "The 'grand narratives' such as religion, political ideologies and even science itself are no longer seen to have 'all the answers' to humanity's questions. The postmodern era is thus marked by a shift from belief in certainties and truth claims to more localized and piecemeal factors. The individual is seen as creating his or her own meaning to a certain extent, rather than receiving it from without."[92] Though not easily categorized, the major concerns of an approach to church in this postmodern context include an emphasis on the relation between theology and culture, a wariness of anything that hints of exclusion (differing, thus, with the emphasis of *Dominus Iesus*), and insistence that dialogue, as the "true legacy of Vatican II," is "the most positive way to negotiate the challenges of a postmodern age."[93] Combined with stress on dialogue, Mannion

---

[91] Gerard Mannion, *Ecclesiology and Postmodernity: Questions for the Church in Our Time* (Collegeville, MN: Liturgical Press, 2007), 75–101, at 98.

[92] Ibid., 4, citing his "A Virtuous Community—The Self-Identity, Vision and Future of the Diocesan Church," in *Diocesan Dispositions and Parish Voices in the Roman Catholic Church*, ed. Noel Timms (Chelmsford, UK: Matthew James, 2001), 125.

[93] Gerard Mannion, "Response: Ecclesiology and the Humility of God; Embracing the Risk of Loving the World," in *Ecclesiology and Exclusion: Boundaries of Being and Belonging in Postmodern Times*, ed. Dennis M. Doyle, Timothy J. Furry, and Pascal D. Bazzell (Maryknoll, NY: Orbis Books, 2012), 37–38.

proposes seeing the church as sacramental, a sign and mediation of God's loving self-communication to the world, helping to effect, by the power of the Spirit, God's reign of justice and righteousness. He speaks of this as a "virtue ecclesiology" for our time.[94]

Final Reflections

We conclude this overview of postconciliar developments by looking at two prominent theologians and three very gifted popes. Further remarks on theologian Joseph Ratzinger will be considered when we look at Pope Benedict. From German Jesuit Karl Rahner (d. 1984) we note two items. The first is his thesis that Vatican II represents "the beginning of a tentative approach by the Church to the discovery and official realization of itself as *world*-Church."[95] He sees the council as an initial transition from a Western church to a world-church analogous to the transition that occurred when the assembly at Jerusalem opened the Jewish-Christian community to becoming the church of the Gentiles. Whether this second transition really takes hold, he said in 1979, would depend on the unfolding of the church in the years and decades to come. A second theme (common to others but in Rahner's thought part of his theological vision of God's self-communication to all in the humanity of Jesus) is his emphasis on the church as sacrament, "the saving presence of Christ visibly embodied within human history."[96] God's self-gift is offered to every human being and insofar as it is accepted, even without explicit reference to Christ or the church, one is linked to the embodiment of that offer in Christ and the church. The church, in short, is the "basic sacrament of salvation for the world."[97] The church's preaching and mission is born of its awareness of the

---

[94] Mannion, *Ecclesiology and Postmodernity*, 192–236. See also *A Church with Open Doors: Catholic Ecclesiology for the Third Millennium*, ed. Richard R. Gaillardetz and Edward P. Hahnenberg (Collegeville, MN: Liturgical Press, 2015).

[95] Karl Rahner, *Concern for the Church*, Theological Investigations 20, trans. Edward Quinn (New York: Crossroad, 1981), 77–89, at 78 (italics in the original).

[96] Nicholas M. Healy, "The Church in Modern Theology," in Mannion and Mudge, *The Routledge Companion to the Christian Church*, 119.

[97] Karl Rahner, *Writings of 1965–67 2*, Theological Investigations 10 (New York: Herder and Herder, 1973), 14.

reality of God revealed in Christ and of its call to proclaim that to others.[98]

Rahner's contemporary, Swiss theologian Hans Urs von Balthasar (d. 1988), is "widely regarded as the greatest Catholic theologian of the century."[99] His programmatic essay *Razing the Bastions* (1952), written after the horror of World War II, called for the church to take its part in a new epoch of world history, to engage lovingly in an openness to the world by directing our lives to God and to all others.[100] Balthasar's understanding of church is situated in the context of his vision of the divine *drama* of God's creating and redeeming love revealed by the incarnate Son, Jesus Christ, unfolding in our world, to which all are invited. By the gift of the Spirit the church is given the power to express Christ, not merely as a historical effect of his coming but rather as his "fullness" and his "bridal body." "Beneath the double servant form of a Church that is herself truly sinful and is darkened by sinners there shines the glory of Christ's love."[101] Concerned that the image of the church as people of God is too easily given to a sociological interpretation, he prefers to see the church as the body of Christ, the source of the being and unity of the church. The church "is, and cannot be other than, an extension, a communication, a partaking of the personality of Christ."[102] The Body of Christ in the Eucharist serves to underscore the bodiliness of the risen Christ and of the church. The complementary images of church as bride and mother serve to distinguish Christ and the church. In both of these latter images, Mary is the archetype. She is already the immaculate

---

[98] See Michael A. Fahey, "On Being Christian—Together," in *A World of Grace: An Introduction to the Themes and Foundations of Karl Rahner's Theology*, ed. Leo J. O'Donovan (New York: Seabury Press, 1980), 120–37.

[99] Fergus Kerr, *Twentieth-Century Catholic Theologians: From Neoscholasticism to Nuptial Mysticism* (Malden, MA: Blackwell, 2007), 121.

[100] Hans Urs von Balthasar, *Razing the Bastions*, trans. Brian McNeil (San Francisco: Ignatius Press, 1993).

[101] Hans Urs von Balthasar, *The Glory of the Lord: A Theological Aesthetics*, vol. 1: *Seeing the Form*, trans. Erasmo Leiva-Merikakis, ed. Joseph Fessio and John Riches (San Francisco: Ignatius Press, 1983), 603–4.

[102] Hans Urs von Balthasar, "Who Is the Church?," in *Explorations in Theology 2: Spouse of the Word* (San Francisco: Ignatius Press, 1991), 145.

one, the bride (Eph 5:27), and she is the mother, made so by Christ's words on the cross (John 19:27).

Balthasar's distinctive approach to understanding the church may be summarized in three adjectives: the church is feminine, nuptial, and Marian. Feminine, because of the church's basic receptivity before Christ, giving birth to what she receives from Christ;[103] nuptial, because in the incarnate Christ the images of nuptiality between God and humanity foreshadowed in the old covenant give way before the bodiliness of both sides of the relationship (Eph 5:32);[104] Marian, because Mary's *fiat* (Luke 1:38), "in its truly *unlimited* availability, is, by grace, the bridal womb, *matrix* and *mater*, through which the Son of God becomes man, and thus it is by this *fiat* that he also forms the truly universal Church."[105] Reflecting on the institutional aspects of church, Balthasar notes in four biblical figures prototypes that determine the church's shape and vitality: Peter, representing the pastoral office; James, tradition and law; Paul, freedom in the Holy Spirit; and John, the love that "abides." The missions represented by the four are exercised within the unity of the body of Christ and, essentially, are premised by the acceptance of Christ's word and grace, so within Marian consent.[106] Balthasar's development of these thoughts and his use of gender complementarity in speaking of the Christ-church relationship and of office in the church are warmly endorsed by some but debated by others.[107]

The present Pope Francis and his two immediate predecessors offer distinctive approaches to the understanding of church, each of them doing so while interpreting and implementing Vatican II. Karol Wojtyla, archbishop of Kraków, was elected Pope John Paul II in 1978 and held the post until his death in 2005. In his work written for the archdiocese

---

[103] Hans Urs von Balthasar, *New Elucidations*, trans. Mary Theresilde Skerry (San Francisco: Ignatius Press, 1986), 210.

[104] Hans Urs von Balthasar, *The Glory of the Lord: A Theological Aesthetics*, vol. 7: *Theology: The New Covenant*, trans. Brian McNeil, ed. John Riches (San Francisco: Ignatius Press, 1989), 470–84, at 472, and *Spouse of the Word*, 184–91.

[105] Hans Urs von Balthasar, *The Office of Peter and the Structure of the Church*, trans. Andrée Emery (San Francisco: Ignatius Press, 1986), 206–7.

[106] Balthasar, *The Office of Peter*, 308–10.

[107] Kerr, *Twentieth-Century Catholic Theologians*, 138–41.

in 1972, *Sources of Renewal: The Implementation of Vatican II*, the future pope saw the renewal set by the council as "a historical stage in the self-realization of the Church."[108] His first papal encyclical, The Redeemer of Man (*Redemptor Hominis*, 1979), described the church in the light of the council as "the social subject of responsibility for divine truth,"[109] a theme recurring in many of his other writings and in the documents published by the CDF on his authority. At the heart of John Paul's understanding of church, based on his reading of the council, is his seeing church as a communion (*communio*) on mission.[110] He sees communion as the integrating and central content of the "mystery," the divine plan for the salvation of humanity.[111] By *communio* he means our sharing in the self-giving of the triune God and the giving of ourselves to others by means of mutual services "in different ways and in various relationships."[112] The idea of personal loving relationships stands behind the pope's emphasis on the church as God's household, God's family, and people of God.[113] This communion is nourished and sustained by the gift of the Eucharist and by the church's hierarchical structure. In his encyclical Church of the Eucharist (*Ecclesia de Eucharistia*, 2003), he makes his own the statement of Henri de Lubac: "The eucharist builds the church and the church makes the eucharist."[114]

Other notes as well enter into the pope's vision of the church. His 1995 encyclical That All May be One (*Ut Unum Sint*) speaks of the church's need to "breathe with her two lungs," that of the East and that of the West.[115] The same letter situates the "office of the bishop

---

[108] Karol Wojtyla, *Sources of Renewal: The Implementation of Vatican II*, trans. P. S. Falla (San Francisco: Harper & Row, 1980), 11.

[109] John Paul II, *Redemptor Hominis*, Origins 8, no. 40 (March 22, 1979): 19.

[110] See James Voiss, "Understanding John Paul II's Vision of the Church," in *The Vision of John Paul II: Assessing His Thought and Influence*, ed. Gerard Mannion (Collegeville, MN: Liturgical Press, 2008), 62–77. Other essays in the same volume give other elements of John Paul's teaching on the church.

[111] John Paul II, *Christifideles Laici*, Origins 18, no. 35 (February 9, 1989): 19.

[112] Wojtyla, *Sources of Renewal*, 120–21.

[113] Avery Dulles, *The Splendor of Faith: The Theological Vision of Pope John Paul II* (New York: Crossroad, 1999), 46–48.

[114] John Paul II, *Ecclesia de Eucharistia*, Origins 32, no. 46 (May 1, 2003): 26.

[115] John Paul II, *Ut Unum Sint*, Origins 25, no. 4 (June 8, 1995): 54.

of Rome" in the context of the mission entrusted to the whole body of bishops; the bishop of Rome is "a member of the 'college,' and the bishops are his brothers in the ministry." Remarkably, he invites church leaders and theologians from other Christian communities to help find a way of exercising the primacy that might better serve the plea of the Lord that all may be one.[116] Ten years earlier, his 1985 encyclical Apostles of the Slavs (*Slavorum Apostoli*) named the evangelizing efforts of Cyril and Methodius "a model of what today is called *inculturation*."[117] Reflecting Balthasar's thinking, the pope's Wednesday catechetical talks between 1979 and 1984 on the theology of the body included reflection on the nuptial relationship between Christ and the church.[118] The same theme is taken up again in his 1988 apostolic letter, *Mulieris Dignitatem*, with added attention to the Eucharist as specially expressing the redemptive act of Christ the bridegroom and its implications for a male priesthood.[119] As part of his vision of a church called to renewal, his Service Requesting Pardon on the First Sunday of Lent in the Jubilee Year 2000 sought forgiveness for sins committed by members of the church in the service of truth, against the people of Israel, against the rights of peoples and respect for cultures and religions, against the dignity of women, and sins related to the fundamental rights of persons.[120]

The vision of church in John Paul's writings over his long pontificate stands in tension with the "operative vision of the church" seen in the actual practice of his leadership.[121] This is most evident, perhaps, in his consistent emphasis on the universal church, in the constraints placed on the synods of bishops or the special synods for

[116] Ibid., art. 95–96. See John R. Quinn, *The Reform of the Papacy: The Costly Call to Christian Unity* (New York: Crossroad, 1999).

[117] John Paul II, *Slavorum Apostoli, Origins* 15, no. 8 (July 18, 1985): 21.

[118] John Paul II, *Man and Woman He Created Them: A Theology of the Body*, trans. and intro. by Michael Waldstein (Boston: Pauline Books and Media, 2006), 465–529.

[119] John Paul II, "On the Dignity and Vocation of Women," *Origins* 18, no. 17 (October 6, 1988): 23–27.

[120] John Paul II, "Service Requesting Pardon," *Origins* 29, no. 40 (March 23, 2000): 645, 647–48.

[121] Voiss, "Understanding John Paul II's Vision of the Church," 69–77.

various regions of the world, especially those of Africa and Asia, and in the letter, issued on his authority, on episcopal conferences.[122] At the same time John Paul's penchant for symbolic gestures went beyond what was expected at the time, good examples of which were noted in the previous chapter.

When Cardinal Joseph Ratzinger followed John Paul II to become Pope Benedict XVI in 2005, he came as a major theologian, a university professor from 1959 to 1977, and prefect of the CDF from 1981 to 2005, all but three years of his predecessor's pontificate. We have encountered him several times already in our review of Vatican II and in the works issued by the CDF when he was prefect. Many of his writings deal with the theme of the church and, with some variations in his views (notably regarding the teaching and governing role of the Synod of Bishops and of national episcopal conferences), do so with a basic continuity of thought.[123] Two texts twenty years apart give insight to his approach to understanding the church and its mission. In the interviews that were published in the 1985 *The Ratzinger Report*, he speaks of his impression that "the authentically Catholic meaning of the reality 'Church' is tacitly disappearing, without being expressly rejected. Many no longer believe that what is at issue is a reality willed by the Lord himself."[124] In his inauguration homily as pope, Benedict said the church as a whole and all her pastors must lead people out of the many deserts in which so many people live, or out of the "salt waters of suffering and death," "a sea of darkness without light" onto "the land of life, into the light of God."[125]

---

[122] Paul Lakeland, "John Paul II and Collegiality," in Mannion, *The Vision of John Paul II: Assessing His Thought and Influence*, 191–99. See also Joseph Komonchak, "On the Authority of Bishops' Conferences," *America* (September 12, 1988): 7–10.

[123] Gerard Mannion, "Understanding the Church: Fundamental Ecclesiology," in *The Ratzinger Reader: Mapping a Theological Journey*, ed. Lieven Boeve and Gerard Mannion (London: T & T Clark, 2010), 81–118, at 81.

[124] Ratzinger, *The Ratzinger Report*, 45.

[125] Benedict XVI, "The Inauguration Homily," *Origins* 34, no. 46 (May 5, 2005): 736. See also Joseph A. Komonchak, "The Church in Crisis: Pope Benedict's Theological Vision," *Commonweal* (June 3, 2005): 11–14.

The church, Ratzinger insists, is founded on belief in the claim "that Jesus of Nazareth is the center and fullness of revelation, the only mediator between God and the human race, in whom all truth is found." As "spouse of the Word" listening to the Word and being formed by the Word, especially in the liturgy, the church is a "truly new subject called into being by the Word and in the Holy Spirit."[126] Ratzinger sees Christ and the church in the light of what has been called the heart of his theology, the notion of "vicarious representation," where Christ stands for or in the place of humankind yet involves us in his own paschal mystery.[127] Ratzinger sees Christ's entire being as a being for others, a "pro-existence" to serve and save the many.[128] He sees the church—making the words of Yves Congar his own—as a *pars pro toto*, a part for the whole, a "minority in the service of the majority."[129] As the church's identity and saving mission flow from Jesus' identity and mission, so the church exists as a sacrament of salvation, called to serve and save others by participating in Jesus' own vicarious representation. She does this by her missionary activity, by the example of love that Christians show to one another and respond to the claim on Christian love from those in need, and, in some cases, by accepting suffering by the side of the Lord.[130] In this understanding, Ratzinger affirms God's universal salvific will, the absolute character of Christianity with respect to other religions, Christ's unique and universal saving role, and, in

---

[126] Joseph Cardinal Ratzinger, "*Deus Locutus Est Nobis in Filio*: Some Reflections on Subjectivity, Christology, and the Church," in *Proclaiming the Truth of Jesus Christ: Papers from the Vallombrosa Meeting* (Washington, DC: United States Catholic Conference, 2000), 21–23.

[127] Joseph Ratzinger/Pope Benedict XVI, "Vicarious Representation," trans. Jared Wicks, *Letter and Spirit* 7 (2011): 209–20, and Christopher Ruddy, " 'For the Many': The Vicarious-Representative Heart of Joseph Ratzinger's Theology," *Theological Studies* 75, no. 3 (2014): 564–84.

[128] Joseph Ratzinger/Pope Benedict XVI, *Jesus of Nazareth, Part 2: Holy Week; From the Entrance into Jerusalem to the Resurrection*, trans. Philip Whitmore (San Francisco: Ignatius Press, 2011), 134.

[129] Yves Congar, *The Wide World My Parish: Salvation and Its Problems*, trans. Donald Attwater (Baltimore: Helicon Press, 1961), 8–26, at 12.

[130] Joseph Cardinal Ratzinger, *The Meaning of Christian Brotherhood* (San Francisco: Ignatius Press, 1993), 81–84. German original, 1960.

him, the church's mediating role in God's saving plan. It is this thinking that stands behind the declaration *Dominus Iesus* mentioned above.

As prefect of the CDF Ratzinger promoted communion theology of the church as normative and official. His emphasis on the church as communion focuses on both the lived spiritual life of the church and on such matters as the relationship of primacy and collegiality. In line with the thinking of Johann Adam Möhler and Henri de Lubac, Ratzinger sees that "being a Christian [in the church] is in reality nothing other than sharing in the mystery of the Incarnation, or as St. Paul puts it: the Church, insofar as she is the Church, is the 'Body of Christ' (i.e., a participation on the part of men [sic] in that communion between man and God which is the Incarnation of the Word)."[131] In what he sees as the core of both eucharistic spirituality and the spirituality of the church, Christ "performs the 'alchemy' which melts down human nature and infuses it into the being of God."[132] Perhaps the key to Pope Benedict's vision of church, Christopher Ruddy suggests, is Galatians 2:20, "It is no longer I who live, but it is Christ who lives in me. And the life I now live in the flesh I live by faith in the Son of God who loved me and gave himself for me."[133] To highlight the church's dependence on Christ, Ratzinger is fond of the moon symbolism of the church fathers. The church, like the moon, "is darkness and light both at once. In itself it is darkness, but it sends out light from another whose light is transmitted through it."[134] The same dependence on Christ is present in his linking Eucharist, the cross, and church. Drawing on another image of the fathers—Eve's coming forth from the side of Adam, prefiguring the new Eve, the church, coming forth from the pierced side of Christ—Benedict speaks, as did John Paul, of the causal influence of the

---

[131] Joseph Cardinal Ratzinger, *Behold the Pierced One: An Approach to a Spiritual Christology*, trans. Graham Harrison (San Francisco: Ignatius Press, 1986), 88.

[132] Ibid., 90.

[133] Christopher Ruddy, "No Restorationist: Ratzinger's Theological Journey," *Commonweal* (June 3, 2005): 16.

[134] Joseph Ratzinger, "Why I Am Still in the Church," in Hans Urs von Balthasar and Joseph Ratzinger, *Two Say Why*, trans. John Griffiths (Chicago: Franciscan Herald Press, 1971), 77.

Eucharist at the church's very origins. The Eucharist, he says, is "constitutive of the church's being and activity."[135] Union in the life of Christ and maturity in faith and in the knowledge of the Son of God, as condition and content of unity in the body of Christ, have a constant presence in his view of church. In his homily at the opening of the conclave that elected him, Ratzinger put it very succinctly: Doing the truth in love, he said, is the basic formula of Christian existence. Also part of his communion theology of church are his understanding of the human element in the church and his insistence on the priority of the universal church, both of which have been considered earlier in this chapter.

Ratzinger's thoughts in the 1980s on the church and the world were influenced by what he saw as the exaggerated openness to the world's culture in postconciliar interpretations of the Pastoral Constitution on the Church in the World.[136] We examined his position in our consideration of the synod of 1985. The pastoral constitution, he had insisted a few years earlier, should be read within the framework of the Constitution on the Church and not the other way around. Even more, it should be read in the context of the whole of the council's teaching.[137] Indications of Pope Benedict's thoughts on the role of the church in the world appear in his encyclicals. In his first encyclical (2005), God Is Love (*Deus Caritas Est*), Benedict says the church is "duty bound to offer, through the purification of reason and through ethical formation, her own specific contribution toward understanding the requirements of justice and achieving them politically. The church cannot and must not take upon herself the political battle to bring about the most just society possible."[138] This comes from the second part of the encyclical, which reworks themes inherited from

---

[135] Benedict XVI, "*Sacramentum Caritatis*: Apostolic Exhortation," *Origins* 36, no. 40 (March 22, 2007): 14–15.

[136] Lieven Boeve, "Christian Faith, Church and World," in Boeve and Mannion, *Ratzinger Reader*, 119–38.

[137] Joseph Cardinal Ratzinger, *Principles of Catholic Theology: Building Stones for a Fundamental Theology*, trans. Mary Frances McCarthy (San Francisco: Ignatius Press, 1987), 390.

[138] Benedict XVI, "*Deus Caritas Est*: Encyclical," in *Origins* 35, no. 33 (February 2, 2006): 28.

his predecessor. Perhaps closer to Benedict's own convictions are the views expressed in his third encyclical, Charity in Truth (*Caritas in Veritate*), published in 2009 and developing the teaching of the 1967 encyclical of Paul VI, On the Development of Peoples. Here, Benedict invokes the teaching of Vatican II that "the church, being at God's service, is at the service of the world in terms of love and truth." The church "in all her being and acting," in proclamation, celebration, and performing works of charity, is called to promote "integral human development," which concerns "the whole of the person in every single dimension." Charity is at the heart of the church's social doctrine, he maintains, a charity linked with truth. The charity exercised in the truth of God's revelation has its source in God, who is "eternal Love and absolute Truth."[139]

In the first year of his pontificate, forty years after the conclusion of the council, Benedict addressed the issue of the interpretation of Vatican II in a talk to the Roman Curia. The correct key to the interpretation and implementation of the council, he maintains, is a "hermeneutic of reform," of "renewal in the continuity of the one subject-church."[140] He dismisses what he calls "a hermeneutic of discontinuity and rupture" that implies a split between the preconciliar church and the postconciliar church. He also criticizes the assertion that the conciliar texts, because they reflect a compromise between differing outlooks, do not express the true spirit of the council, which is to be found instead in "the impulses towards the new that are contained in the texts." He admits, though, to a combination of continuity and discontinuity involved in a true reform in the church. The pope's remarks seem to be intended for those who continued to believe that Vatican II, on such issues as religious freedom, the relation of the church to modernity, and the relationship between

---

[139] Benedict XVI, "*Caritas in Veritate*: Encyclical," in *Origins* 39, no. 9 (July 16, 2009): nos. 11 and 1.

[140] Pope Benedict XVI, "Interpreting Vatican II," in *Origins* 35, no. 32 (January 26, 2006): 536–39, at 536. Though referring to this 2005 address to the Curia, his apostolic exhortation *Sacramentum Caritatis* (February 22, 2007) speaks of the need of a "hermeneutic of continuity" for the correct interpretation of the liturgical changes called for by Vatican II. *Origins* 36, no. 40 (March 22, 2007): no. 3 and note 6.

Christian faith and the world religions, represented a revolutionary discontinuity in official church doctrine. He seeks to make the point, as he sees it, that the council's teaching represents the application of enduring principles to new circumstances.[141]

Much more could be said about Ratzinger/Benedict XVI's understanding of the church.[142] We make three concluding remarks. We can safely assume that the second epigraph in the preceding chapter, published by the CDF in the second year of Benedict's pontificate, represents his thought about the intention of the Second Vatican Council. It seems similarly true to say that it represents the overriding concern of most, perhaps all, of his many writings that concern the church and of his desire that our understanding of the church be truly theological. A second comment: In his introduction to the theology of Joseph Ratzinger, Dominican scholar Aidan Nichols suggests that the theology of Ratzinger and Pope Benedict must be judged in terms of systematic theology's twofold project of exploring how the meaning of tradition may be received anew in response to the concerns of the present and, second, challenging, complementing, and transforming the concerns of the present day with the divine power of the tradition.[143] And finally, in the Catholic Church where symbolic gestures and the papacy figure so significantly in our understanding of church, the pope's dramatic resignation may justly be seen as a final contribution.

As Cardinal Ratzinger/Pope Benedict had distinctive features in his theological reflections on the church, the same is true of his successor, the Argentinian Jesuit Jorge Mario Bergoglio, who became Pope Francis in the election of March 2013. He brought with him experience as a Jesuit provincial and rector and, for twenty-one years, auxiliary, vicar general, and archbishop of Buenos Aires, positions

---

[141] See Joseph A. Komonchak, "Benedict XVI and the Interpretation of Vatican II," in Lacey and Oakley, *Crisis of Authority in Catholic Modernity*, 96–110.

[142] See the lengthy study by Maximilian Heinrich Heim, *Joseph Ratzinger: Life in the Church and Living Theology: Fundamentals of Ecclesiology with Reference to Lumen Gentium*, trans. Michael J. Miller (San Francisco: Ignatius Press, 2007).

[143] Aidan Nichols, *The Thought of Pope Benedict XVI: An Introduction to the Theology of Joseph Ratzinger*, new ed. (London: T & T Clark, 2007), 240.

marked by a concern for the poor. Important indications of Cardinal Bergoglio's vision of church were given in his pre-conclave remarks and, we shall see presently, in the final document of the conference at Aparecida some years earlier. To the cardinals assembled for the conclave, he recalled that the church's reason for being is evangelization, which "implies in the Church the *parrhesia* [apostolic courage] to come out from itself. The Church is called to come out from itself and to go to the peripheries, not just the geographical but also the existential peripheries: those of the mystery of sin, of suffering, of injustice, of ignorance and lack of religion, those of thought and those of every kind of misery."[144] The next pope, he said, citing Paul VI, should help the church "to be the fruitful mother who lives from 'the sweet and comforting joy of evangelizing.'"[145] Cardinal Bergoglio chose the name Francis in large part because of the saint of Assisi's acceptance of poverty in his own life and his concern for the poor. To journalists a few days after his election, the new pope added: "How I would like a Church which is poor and for the poor!"[146] In this he was picking up on a theme expressed by John XXIII at the outset of the council and in two speeches of Cardinal Lercaro of Bologna: one at the first session, when he asked that this very theme be the synthesizing idea of the council, and another in the debate on schema 13, asking that the church let go of unnecessary cultural baggage that burdens a pilgrim community.[147] There were also some voices at the synod of 1985 who called for greater attention to the poor.

Eight months after his election, the pope spelled out his views on the church in his apostolic exhortation, The Joy of the Gospel (*Evangelii Gaudium* [EG]).[148] The text opens with repeated mention of the importance of our encounter with Jesus (EG 1 and 3), an encounter

---

[144] Austen Ivereigh, *The Great Reformer: Francis and the Making of a Radical Pope* (New York: Henry Holt and Company, 2014), 357–58.

[145] Ibid., 359.

[146] http://w2.vatican.va/content/francesco/en/speeches/2013/march/documents/papa-francesco_20130316rappresentanti-medial.html (accessed September 15, 2015).

[147] Faggioli, *A Council for the Global Church*, 169.

[148] Pope Francis, "*Evangelii Gaudium*: Apostolic Exhortation," in *Origins* 43, no. 27 (December 5, 2013) and *Origins* 43, no. 28 (December 12, 2013).

that liberates us from our narrowness and self-absorption (EG 8). Further on he writes that the church "that 'goes forth' is a church whose doors are open . . . going out to others to meet the fringes of humanity. . . . At times we have to be like the father of the prodigal son, who always keeps his door open so that when the son returns, he can readily pass through it" (EG 46). The church is "not a tollhouse; it is the house of the Father, where there is a place for everyone, with all their problems" (EG 47). The church grows not by proselytizing but "by attraction" (EG 14), a reference to Pope Benedict's homily at the Fifth General Conference of CELAM at Aparecida. The Eucharist, the fullness of the sacramental life, Pope Francis says, is "not a prize for the perfect but powerful medicine and nourishment for the weak" (EG 47). There are other important themes in the exhortation: (1) that the church is the people of God "advancing on its pilgrim way toward God," rooted in the Trinity yet concretely existing in history as pilgrims and evangelizers (EG 111); (2) that all the baptized are missionary disciples (EG 120); (3) that the poor have a special place among God's people and that the church's option for them is a theological reality, rather than one that derives from sociological or political considerations (EG 198); and (4), citing the final document of Aparecida, that popular piety is "a spirituality incarnated in the culture of the lowly" (EG 124).

Evangelii Gaudium draws heavily on the Aparecida document whose final redaction was directed by Cardinal Bergoglio; his ideas very much influenced its vision.[149] Biographer Austen Ivereigh describes the insights of the Aparecida text: "A Church of and for the poor, rooted in the Second Vatican Council, geared to mission, focused on the margins, centered on God's holy faithful people, in confident dialogue with culture yet bold in denouncing what harmed the poor. It presented a Church that was tender and maternal, a big, borderless lazaretto of healing and love."[150] Pope Francis often speaks of the church, in homilies on solemn occasions and at weekday liturgies, in addresses to various groups, and in interviews. In his interview with

---

[149] V General Conference of the Bishops of Latin America and the Caribbean, *The Aparecida Document*.

[150] Ivereigh, *The Great Reformer*, 211.

Jesuit Antonio Spadaro for several Jesuit journals, the pope spoke of his liking the image of the church as "the holy, faithful people of God" [*santo pueblo fiel de Dios*], of the church "as a field hospital after battle," a "church that is a mother and shepherdess" whose ministers must accompany people "like the good Samaritan, who washes, cleans and raises up his neighbor."[151] In his encyclical *Laudato Sí*, Pope Francis takes up themes from his previous writings and from Pope Benedict's major encyclicals and offers a "genuinely ecclesial vision," concerned with "the unbreakable links between contemplation, eucharist, justice, and social transformation."[152]

Ecclesiologist and historian Massimo Faggioli sees in the pontificate of Pope Francis a change of paradigm in the way the papacy interprets Vatican II, as a pivotal event in church history not to be overshadowed by the issues involved in its interpretation during the previous fifty years.[153] In a similar vein, Walter Kasper sees Francis initiating a "prophetic interpretation of the council" and inaugurating "a new phase of its reception."[154] The pope's identifying himself primarily as the bishop of Rome, his setting up of a group of cardinal consultors to assist him, his seeing a need to promote a sound decentralization (EG 16), his endorsement of the authority of individual bishops and episcopal conferences, his calling an extraordinary synod in the fall of 2014 and an ordinary synod in 2015, involving a broad consultation beforehand—these are so many indications of his desire to implement the council's call for a more collegial exercise of the Petrine ministry

---

[151] "Pope Francis' Interview with Jesuit Magazines," in *Origins* 43, no. 19 (October 10, 2013): 298 and 300.

[152] Rowan Williams, "Embracing Our Limits: The Lessons of *Laudato Si?*," *Commonweal* 142, no. 16 (October 9, 2015): 15.

[153] Massimo Faggioli, "The Ecclesiology of Vatican II as a New Framework for Consecrated Life," in *Origins* 45, no. 15 (September 10, 2015): 256. See also Massimo Faggioli, *Pope Francis: Tradition in Transition* (New York: Paulist Press, 2015) and his essay, "The New Beginning of the Second Vatican Council," in *Origins* 45, no. 35 (February 4, 2016).

[154] John Thavis blog, April 11, 2013: http://www.johnthavis.com/cardinal-kasper-pope-francis-has-launched-new-phase-on-vatican-ii#wionyewng70 (accessed September 16, 2015).

and a more synodal understanding of church.[155] These actions receive explicit endorsement in his address on the fiftieth anniversary of the institution of the Synod of Bishops.[156] The address speaks of the "path of synodality" as the path of the church in the third millennium, to be manifested at the levels of the particular church, regional churches, and the universal church. The *sensus fidei* of the whole people of God gives the church, he says, an "instinctive ability to discern the new ways that the Lord is revealing to the Church" and he invokes the patristic adage dear to the church of the first millennium: *Quod omnes tangit ab omnibus tractari debet* ("What involves every one ought to be decided by everyone"). Two sentences from that address say much about the pope's view of the primacy and of the pope: "I am persuaded that in a synodal Church, greater light can be shed on the exercise of the Petrine primacy. The Pope is not, by himself, above the Church; but within it as one of the baptized, and within the College of Bishops as a Bishop among Bishops, called at the same time—as successor of Peter—to lead the Church of Rome which presides in charity over all the Churches."[157] In the interview with the Jesuit magazines, he had said that he looks to learn from the Orthodox about the meaning of episcopal collegiality and the tradition of synodality.[158]

Underlying all of this, Francis has a vision of a church that embodies the loving and forgiving mercy of God. In The Face of Mercy (*Misericordiae Vultus*), proclaiming the Holy Year of Mercy (2015–2016), the pope said that wherever the church is present, it should be seen as "an oasis of mercy," whose credibility rests on how she lives and testifies to God's mercy."[159] A couple of sentences from that text

---

[155] *Evangelii Gaudium*, nos. 16 and 32.

[156] w2.vatican.va/content/francesco/en/speeches/2015/october/documents/papa-francesco_20151017_50-anniversario-synodo.html (accessed October 30, 2015).

[157] The final phrase comes from Ignatius of Antioch, proemium to the Letter to the Romans.

[158] "Pope Francis' Interview with Jesuit Magazines," 301. See also Richard R. Gaillardetz, *An Unfinished Council: Vatican II, Pope Francis, and the Renewal of Catholicism* (Collegeville, MN: Liturgical Press, 2015).

[159] Pope Francis, "*Misericordiae Vultus*: Bull of Indiction for Holy Year of Mercy," in *Origins* 44, no. 46 (April 23, 2015): no. 12.

provide a summary of his vision of church and its agenda: "The time has come for the church to take up the joyful call to mercy once more. It is time to return to the basics and to bear the weaknesses and struggles of our brothers and sisters. Mercy is the force that reawakens us to new life and instills in us the courage to look to the future with hope" (no. 10).[160]

Epilogue

Reflection on the theology of the church will continue; no final word can be spoken or written. When the unfolding of God's plan is complete, no word will be needed. The church, we have seen, is a living mystery of God who calls and of people who respond to that call, in different times and places and circumstances. The human mind can never be finished reflecting on the riches and wisdom and knowledge of God, nor can it give a definitive word on how God's call and gifts might elicit the response of believers to those gifts. We may consider ourselves blessed for many of the insights that have come to the fore of our attention in the recent past, though we cannot fully appreciate those insights apart from all that has gone before, beginning with the people of the covenant described in the Pentateuch and the life and ministry of Jesus. At the same time, we should not be surprised if from the treasure of the church's tradition we see afresh what might be applied to new questions and new challenges. Hopefully an awareness of the church's history helps us better appreciate the mystery that is the church and, even more, helps us to be the community of disciples—missionaries of all the Lord's love and mercy and justice—that the church is called to be.

> May the God of peace, who brought back from the dead our Lord Jesus, the great shepherd of the sheep, by the blood of the eternal covenant, make [us] complete in everything good so that [we] may do his will, working among us that which is pleasing in his sight, through Jesus Christ, to whom be the glory forever and ever. Amen. (Heb 13:20-21)

---

[160] See Walter Kasper, *Pope Francis' Revolution of Tenderness and Love: Theological and Pastoral Perspectives*, trans. William Madges (New York: Paulist Press, 2015).

APPENDIX 1

Contemporary Biblical Scholarship

Our principal sources for knowledge about Jesus' first followers are the four gospels. The New Testament as a whole serves the same function for our knowledge of the first-century church. In the Catholic community, methods of studying these biblical texts have undergone profound changes during the last century and a quarter. This appendix may assist those who would be helped by a review of this development.[1]

In the eighteenth and nineteenth centuries, scholars applied newly developed historical-critical methods to the study of the Bible. Besides working to establish an authoritative text from existing manuscripts, scholars focused on the historical value of the New Testament texts and their theological meaning. In particular, they studied the sources used by the evangelists and the manner in which the actual texts were composed. At times, the newer critical methods were used with an anti-dogmatic and even anti-Catholic bias: they were used to discredit dogmas, structures, and sacraments that were part of Catholic self-understanding. Not surprisingly, these critical biblical methods were regarded with suspicion by church authorities.

Toward the end of the nineteenth century, as these methods became more refined and more balanced, they came to be viewed more positively. In his 1893 encyclical *Providentissimus Deus*, Pope Leo XIII gave guarded endorsement to the use of these methods in the Catholic community. In 1902, he established a Pontifical Biblical Commission to monitor developments in biblical studies. Some Catholics, how-

---

[1] See a more extensive treatment in Frederick J. Cwiekowski, *The Beginnings of the Church* (New York: Paulist Press, 1988), chap. 1.

ever, using the new methods, came to conclusions that could be seen only as extravagant and unwarranted. This, in turn, provoked a reaction. Under Leo's successor, Pope Pius X, the Pontifical Biblical Commission issued a series of guidelines that insisted on a literal approach to the historical interpretation of the gospel texts.

Two examples illustrate the approach mandated by these directives, which were widely used for the next several decades in Catholic studies. The Gospel according to Matthew was, we were told (1911), written by one of the Twelve, an eyewitness to the events recorded in the gospel. Specifically, Matthew 16, the scene at Caesarea Philippi where Jesus gives Peter the keys of the kingdom, "referring to the primacy," was to be regarded as literally historical. The scene in Matthew 14:22-33 was interpreted as describing "the apostles' profession of faith in Jesus' divinity" during the public ministry. Jesus' commission to the disciples in Matthew 28:19-20, where Jesus gives the apostles the triadic baptismal formula and the universal mission, was to be regarded as an eyewitness account.

The Fourth Gospel was also said (1907) to have been written by one of the Twelve. The discourses of Jesus in that gospel, frequently speaking of Jesus' exalted self-understanding and his opposition to and separation from the Jewish religion of his day, were to be regarded as historical. These directives, and others like them, encouraged and even mandated a strictly historical reading of the gospel texts.

A Precritical View of the Beginnings of the Church

Adhering to the approach implicit in these early directives had a profound effect on one's understanding of the ministry of Jesus and the beginnings of the church. In this perspective, Jesus, clearly aware of his own divinity and therefore knowing all things, came to preach the advent of the reign of God and to set up a new community, distinct from Judaism, which was the beginning of the Christian Church. Among his disciples he selected a group of twelve to be the future leaders of the church and its teaching authority. Jesus was also understood to have set up the basic elements of the sacramental system, most especially the sacraments of baptism, in the command in

Matthew 28, and Eucharist and priesthood, at the Last Supper. In effect, Jesus was seen to have given his followers a type of "blueprint" for the establishment of the church with a new religious identity distinct from Judaism.

If one adopts such an understanding of Jesus and the beginnings of the church, one encounters notable difficulties. A few examples will show this. If Jesus, very soon after the resurrection, gave so explicit a directive concerning the triadic baptismal formula (Matt 28:19), how do we account for baptism in the name of Jesus, which we find so frequently in the Acts of the Apostles (2:38; 8:16; 10:48; 19:5)? If Matthew and John were both eyewitnesses of the events they record, how do we account for the very marked differences between the two gospels? How do we account for Luke's omission of any reference to the important commission given to Peter in Matthew 16, especially since Peter is such an important figure in Luke's second volume, Acts of the Apostles? If Jesus gave so clear a mission to evangelize all nations, why did the church have such serious debate about admitting Gentiles to their number? Finally, if Jesus clearly set up a new religion apart from Judaism, why does the book of Acts portray the early believers frequenting the temple and participating in its worship?

Three Stages of the Gospel Tradition

Attention to questions such as these led Catholic biblical scholars to press for the application of historical-critical methods to a study of the New Testament texts. These studies received a very important endorsement in the 1943 encyclical letter, *Divino Afflante Spiritu*, of Pope Pius XII (1939–1958). The encyclical's most important contribution is to relate the truth of the Scriptures, above all historical truth, to the literary genre of the biblical writings. In effect, one properly interprets the truth of the texts by taking into account the genre of the writing in which the truth is expressed. The book of Jonah, for example, contains the truth that God's mercy has no boundaries; it does not provide historical truth about "a large fish."

Specific attention to the literary form of the gospels was given in the 1964 statement of the Pontifical Biblical Commission, "On the

Historical Truth of the Gospels."[2] While the term "historical truth" was used in the title, the statement insists that we cannot understand the gospels correctly if we do not take into account the *three stages* in which the gospels developed.

The first stage of the gospel tradition consists of what Jesus said and did during his public ministry. The second stage, following Jesus' resurrection, consists of the oral tradition and possibly some written form of that tradition, reflecting now the new insights and new clarity that came with the experience of the risen Jesus and the gift of his Spirit. Memories of what Jesus said and did, seen now with a heightened awareness of their meaning after the resurrection, were passed from community to community by the disciples of Jesus. These memories were preserved as testimonies of faith and as guides to prayer, preaching, and living as disciples of the risen Lord, not immediately to transmit a strictly historical record.

The gospel texts we have today are the third and final stage of the gospel tradition. These are our principal sources for our knowledge of Jesus. The evangelists selected material from the post-resurrection traditions, synthesized it, and edited it as they addressed the needs of the communities for which they were writing. In the process, they also incorporated the fruits of their own theological insights on the meaning of Jesus and his message. This understanding of gospel formation is a characteristic of contemporary biblical scholarship.

A précis of the Pontifical Commission's 1964 statement, drafted to assist the bishops in the course of the Second Vatican Council, was included in the council's 1965 Dogmatic Constitution on Divine Revelation, article 19. In 1993 the Pontifical Biblical Commission published another statement, "On Interpreting the Bible in the Church," in which approbation is again given to the use of historical-critical methods in the study and use of the Bible.[3] The first two chapters of this

---

[2] Complete text in Joseph A. Fitzmyer, *A Christological Catechism: New Testament Answers*, rev. ed. (New York: Paulist Press, 1991), 153–62. Fitzmyer's commentary on the text appears on pages 119–52. Not all biblical scholars using this method apply it to one or another text in the same way.

[3] Printed in *Origins* 23, no. 29 (January 6, 1994): 497, 499–524.

book are a summary of the results obtained by use of this method. As the 1993 statement points out, the historical-critical method is not the only method used to interpret the biblical texts, though it is "the indispensable method for the scientific study of the meaning of ancient texts."[4]

---

[4] Ibid., 500.

APPENDIX 2

Our Understanding of Jesus

Implicit in both a critical and a precritical understanding of Jesus' ministry as it pertains to the foundations of the church is an understanding of Jesus himself. On this issue also the difference between the two approaches is quite pronounced. A few observations concerning our understanding of Jesus as we look upon him during his ministry may help.[1]

Using the historical-critical method of study, we see Jesus as an eschatological prophet, an itinerant preacher and teacher convinced of his unique relationship to the God of Israel and of the mission God gave him. This sense of mission is presupposed in the description given in chapter 1. During his ministry, Jesus revealed his sense of identity only indirectly or implicitly, in the ways he spoke of God and the kingdom of God or in the ways he exercised his mission as an agent of God. Scholars discuss how Jesus might have referred to himself as "Son of Man" or "Son," though more as means of evoking questions in the minds of others than explicitly teaching about himself. Using the canons of historical criticism, we nowhere find Jesus during his public ministry proclaiming his divinity or teaching others of his divinity. Nor do we find, as we have seen, his giving explicit directives on founding a new religious entity apart from Judaism.

A precritical approach to understanding Jesus during his public ministry was wont to emphasize his unlimited knowledge, his teaching his disciples of his divinity, and his setting up at least the basic outlines of the church as a new religion. Such an understanding found support in a historical reading of Matthew and John, assuming that

---

[1] See the helpful summary in Fitzmyer, *Christological Catechism*, 97–102.

Our Understanding of Jesus 389

the evangelists were members of the Twelve, writing as eyewitnesses and intent on preserving historical accuracy. Those suppositions, we have seen, are challenged by modern biblical studies using methods that have received official church approval.

A second reason why some persons believed that Jesus in his public ministry possessed a divine knowledge and therefore foresaw and provided for the church was the assumption that such knowledge flows from Jesus' divinity. He is, after all, God incarnate, the Second Person of the Blessed Trinity. It is also a basic tenet of Christian faith, defined at the Council of Chalcedon (AD 451), that Jesus of Nazareth, born of Mary, was fully and completely a human being, like us in all things but sin (Heb 4:15). This says something that should not be denied or minimized. During Jesus' public ministry, some of his contemporaries thought he was a good man, a holy man, one in whom God's Spirit was present and at work, and so they placed their trust in him. There were others, though, who thought he was in league with the devil (Mark 3:22) or guilty of blasphemy (Mark 2:7; 14:64). Yet others, perhaps reacting to his radical teaching and his strange ways, said of him, "He has gone out of his mind" (Mark 3:21), which caused members of his family to seek to restrain him. And in his crucifixion, he seemed totally abandoned by the God whose reign, he claimed, was being inaugurated through him.

As devout Jews, Jesus' disciples were fiercely monotheistic. Further, they believed that only God could raise one from the dead. When Jesus was raised, his disciples came to see him in new ways and with a new depth of understanding. The 1964 instruction of the Pontifical Biblical Commission referred to in appendix 1 underscored this development. Assuming that the early sermons of Acts recall at least elements of early Christian preaching, we see Jesus being proclaimed in ways that emphasize the closeness of his relationship with God and the unique role he had as agent of God. Paul's letters speak of God's presence in Christ and of the risen Christ being the functional equivalent of God.[2] Gradually the early believers applied to Christ,

---

[2] Joseph A. Fitzmyer, "Pauline Theology," in *The New Jerome Biblical Commentary*, ed. Raymond E. Brown, Joseph A. Fitzmyer, and Roland E. Murphy (Englewood Cliffs, NJ: Prentice-Hall, 1990), 82:54.

as God's agent, functions which until then were attributed only to God. In this they drew on the Jewish Scriptures and Second Temple Jewish monotheism mentioned in the text, whereby the personifications of God's Wisdom and Word, intrinsic to the divine identity, were used to speak of God's relations to the world and to human history. Toward the end of the New Testament period, in some few places, Jesus is called "God" (see John 1:1; 20:28; Heb 1:8).[3]

Second- and third-century Christians struggled with the many ways the New Testament writings speak of Jesus, especially with the belief that Jesus of Nazareth was fully human and at the same time one with God (John 10:30; but see John 14:28). During this same period, some groups, despairing of reconciling the two affirmations, held to one and rejected the other. Such solutions the church as a whole rejected as inadequate. In the fourth and fifth centuries, church councils met to settle disputes concerning the proper understanding of Jesus. These councils drew up guidelines for expressing Christian belief in Jesus: that, though one individual, he was, in a way that is and always will be beyond our ability to comprehend, fully human and fully divine. In some of the language of the fourth of these councils, that at Chalcedon (AD 451), Jesus was spoken of as having a human nature and a divine nature. Neither the humanity nor the divinity of Christ was to be compromised or separated. The Council of Chalcedon taught also that the humanity and divinity of Jesus were united in a single person (in Greek: *hypostasis*). The word "person" was an ontological concept (concerned with the being of something), used to express the belief that Jesus, who was human and divine, was one individual and not two. Human attributes, such as emotions, knowledge, and the various capacities that enable one to reflect, to remember, to make choices and decisions, and to plan for the future were ascribed to Jesus because of his human nature. Divine qualities, such as being eternally one with the Father, having the power to forgive sins, or being an agent in creation, were ascribed to Jesus because of his divine nature.

After the Second Council of Constantinople (AD 553), the person of Jesus was explicitly spoken of as the one *divine* person, the Word,

---

[3] Fitzmyer, *Christological Catechism*, 102–10, and Raymond E. Brown, *Jesus: God and Man* (Milwaukee: Bruce, 1967), chap. 1.

the *Logos*, the Second Person of the Blessed Trinity. It was the person of the Word that grounded, as it were, both the divine nature and the human nature in Jesus. Debates concerning the human will of Jesus continued well into the seventh century. Only with the work of Maximus the Confessor and the Third Council of Constantinople in 680 was the affirmation of the human will of Christ firmly set in place. In time, Jesus' human knowledge and human self-consciousness were no longer understood in terms of his human nature, as in the teaching of Chalcedon, but were seen in light of his divine person. Difficulties arose when the term "person" lost its classical *metaphysical* meaning and came to have a modern *psychological* meaning as the center of consciousness, reflection, and will. This very important change of meaning led to the understanding that Jesus in his human knowledge knew and foresaw all that God knew and foresaw. Accepting that Jesus' discourses in the Fourth Gospel were reminiscences of an eyewitness reinforced this tendency. Today, biblical scholarship and sound contemporary Christology hold that Jesus' human knowledge was truly human and hence limited. Recognition of this limitation does not imply that Jesus was not divine; limitations in his human knowledge were fully a part of his being human.[4]

---

[4] See Brown, *Jesus: God and Man*, chap. 2.

Index of Names

Abraham, 2, 169
Adam, Karl, 311
Alexander the Great, 4
Ambrose of Milan, 128, 130, 151, 166–68, 174, 259
Andrew (apostle), 8
Anicetus (pope ca. 155–ca. 166), 144
Antiochus IV (king), 21
Antony of Egypt, 160
Aristotle, 209, 211, 218, 221, 312
Arius, 152
Athanasius of Alexandria, 160
Athenagoras, Patriarch, 321, 329
Augustine of Hippo, 116, 118, 128, 131–32, 140, 151, 154, 159, 162–63, 167–74, 187, 208–9, 217, 223, 236, 255, 271–72, 310, 312, 333

Balthasar, Hans Urs von, 131, 308, 368–69, 371
Barlaam of Calabria, 229–30
Barnabas, 47, 48–49, 84, 134
Baronius, Cesare, 265
Beauduin, Lambert, 302
Bellarmine, Robert, 261–63, 280, 287, 296, 312, 318
Benedict of Nursia, 161
Benedict XIV (pope 1740–58), 269
Benedict XVI (pope 2005–13. Joseph Ratzinger), 161, 174, 197, 199, 301, 308, 324, 353–54, 361, 365, 367, 372–77, 379–80
Bergoglio, Jorge Mario. *See* Francis (pope)
Bernard of Clairvaux, 195, 198–99, 209
Bernini, Gianlorenzo, 269
Biel, Gabriel, 237
Billot, Louis, 311–12
Bismark, Otto von, 273
Bolívar, Simon, 281
Bonaventure, ix, 207–11, 213, 330
Boniface VIII (pope 1294–1303), 212–13, 235
Borromeo, Charles, 259

Cabasilas, Nicholas, 230
Caelestius, 171
Calvin, John, 241, 247–50, 262, 271, 299
Canisius, Peter, 261
Cappellari, Mauro. *See* Gregory XVI (pope)
Casel, Odo, 302
Catherine of Siena, 218
Cerfaux, Lucien, 303
Charlemagne, 182–84, 212
Charles V (emperor), 245, 251
Charlier, Louis, 304, 313
Chelčický, Peter, 236
Chemnitz, Martin, 237

393

Chenu, Marie-Dominique, 210, 304, 313, 328
Clement of Alexandria, 127, 130, 132, 297
Clement of Rome, 138, 190
Clement VIII (pope 1592–1605), 261
Clement XI (pope 1700–21), 269
Clovis, 181
Congar, Yves, x, 179, 193, 201, 230, 304–6, 308–9, 313, 321, 327, 332, 373
Constantine (emperor), 116, 147–54, 156, 181–82, 195, 278, 283
Corecco, Eugenio, 336
Cranmer, Thomas, 250
Cromwell, Thomas, 250
Cyprian of Carthage, 116, 123–24, 140–45, 169–70, 174, 248
Cyril and Methodius, 186, 189, 300, 371
Cyril of Alexandria, 162–64
Cyril of Jerusalem, 118, 162, 164

D'Ailly, Pierre, 221, 228
Damasus (pope 366–84), 155–57, 190
Danielou, Jean, 306–7
Dante, 198, 206
David (king), 3, 22, 76, 109
Denys the Areopagite, 128, 174–78, 209, 226
Diocletian, 147, 152, 169
Döllinger, Ignaz von, 283
Dominic de Guzman, 205–6
Donatus, 169
Dossetti, Giuseppe, 328
Doyle, Denis, 360
Drey, Johann Sebastian, 293
Dunn, James D. G., 6
Duprey, Pierre, 321

Elijah, 5

Elizabeth I, 250
Ephrem the Syrian, 162
Erasmus, Desiderius, 239–40, 248, 260
Eugenius IV (pope 1431–47), 225, 231
Eusebius of Caesarea, 65, 154, 173

Faggioli, Massimo, 321, 380
Francis (pope 2013–. Jorge Mario Bergoglio), 347, 369, 377–81
Francis de Sales, 266
Francis I (king of France), 263
Francis of Assisi, 205–9, 378
Francis Xavier, 268
Franzelin, Johann Baptist, 292, 296

Garrigou-Lagrange, Réginald, 313
Gelasius (pope 492–96), 158, 167, 193, 214
Gerson, Jean, 221, 228, 236
Gibbons, James Cardinal, 300
Giles of Rome, 213
Giles of Viterbo (Egidio da Viterbo), 240, 241
Gregory I (pope 590–604), 159–60, 174, 189, 192, 260, 290, 321
Gregory of Nyssa, 128, 162, 164, 177, 189
Gregory of Palamas, 230
Gregory VII (Hildebrand, pope 1073–85), 189, 191, 192–94, 209, 214
Gregory XI (pope 1370–78), 218
Gregory XIII (pope 1572–85), 260
Gregory XVI (pope 1831–46), 279, 281, 300, 305
Guardini, Romano, 302

Harrington, Daniel J., 13
Hauranne, Jean Duvergier de, 271

Index of Names 395

Henry III (king), 190
Henry of Langenstein, 219
Henry VIII (king), 250
Hildebrand, 191. *See also* Gregory VII (pope)
Hildegard of Bingen, 199
Hincmar of Reims, 187, 188, 236
Hippolytus, 123, 130, 133
Hooker, Richard, 250
Hugh of St. Victor, 200
Humbert (cardinal), 191–92
Hume, George Basil, 354
Hus, Jan, 221–24, 235, 237, 251, 262

Ignatius of Antioch, 121–22, 125, 133–34, 137–38, 143, 150
Ignatius of Loyola, 265–66
Innocent III (pope 1198–1216), 295–96, 212, 221
Irenaeus of Lyons, 122–24, 126, 129, 138–39, 145
Isidore of Seville, 174, 188
Ivereigh, Austen, 379

James (brother of the Lord), 30, 44, 47–51, 62, 65, 71, 77, 84, 91, 369
James (son of Zebedee), 47, 69
James of Viterbo, 213, 236
Jansen, Cornelius, 271–72
Jedin, Hubert, 307
Jerome, 150, 156, 238
Jesus of Nazareth, chaps. 1–4 passim, 115, 121–26, 133–36, 138, 140, 152, 156, 158, 165, 205, 208, 221, 238, 265, 267–68, 297, 311, 327, 342, 347, 351–53, 356–57, 364–65, 367–68, 373, 378, 382–86, 388–91
Joachim of Fiore, 207, 208
John Chrysostom, 151, 162, 165
John Damascene, 177–78, 184

John Gratian, 194
John of Palomar, 237
John of Paris, 214–15, 221
John of Ragusa, 238
John of the Cross, 266–68, 293
John Paul II (pope 1978–2005. Karol Wojtyla), 186, 308, 321, 336, 348, 352–53, 358–59, 363, 365, 369–72, 374
John, son of Zebedee, 69
John the Baptist, 7, 8, 11, 14, 16, 57, 84
John, the evangelist, 94
John XXII (pope 1316–34), 216
John XXIII (pope 1958–63), 316, 318–19, 324, 328, 330, 343, 378
Joseph II (emperor), 273
Joseph of Volokalamsk, 234
Journet, Charles, 312–13
Judas (apostle), 17, 33, 80, 85
Julian (emperor 361–63), 151
Julius II (pope 1503–13), 240
Julius III (pope 1550–55), 251
Justin Martyr, 118, 122, 134, 135
Justinian (emperor 527–65), 149, 176, 181, 195

Kasper, Walter, 331, 373, 380
Kerr, Ian, 309
Kleutgen, Joseph, 289, 291
Komonchak, Joseph A., x, 341, 362
Koster, M. D., 311

Lammenais, Felicité Robert de, 281
Las Casas, Bartolomé de, 268
Leander of Seville, 174
Leo I (pope 440–61), 153, 157–59, 162, 188, 190, 221
Leo III (emperor 717–41), 177
Leo III (pope 795–816), 182
Leo IX (pope 1049–54), 191, 193

Leo X (pope 1513–21), 241
Leo XIII (pope 1878–1903), 283–85, 300–301, 304, 323–24, 383–84
Lercaro, Giacomo, 318, 328, 378
Loisy, Alfred, 285
Louis the Pius, 183, 187
Louis XIV (king of France), 273
Lubac, Henri de, x, 274, 306–10, 313, 319, 332, 340, 370, 374
Luther, Martin, 241–49, 251–53, 278

Maistre, Joseph de, 279, 280
Mannion, Gerard, 366
Marsilius of Padua, 215, 227
Martel, Charles, 181
Martin V (pope 1417–31), 222, 225
Mary Tudor, 250
Matthias (apostle), 17, 33
Maximus Confessor, 176, 177, 391
Maximus of Turin, 132
Meier, John P., 15, 17, 26, 29
Melanchthon, Philip, 246
Melito of Sardis, 135
Merici, Angela, 266
Mersch, Emile, 311
Methodius of Olympus, 131
Methodius of Thessalonica. *See* Cyril and Methodius
Meyendorff, John, 233
Möhler, Johann Adam, 293–96, 305, 310, 374
Montini, Giovanni Battista. *See* Paul VI (pope)
Moses, 3, 50, 105, 211, 215
Muhammad, 181
Murray, John Courtney, 306, 313, 323

Napoleon, 273, 275–76
Neri, Philip, 261, 269

Newman, John Henry, 292, 297–99, 306
Nicholas I (pope 858–67), 189
Nicholas of Cusa, 225–26, 228, 236
Nichols, Aidan, 174, 377
Nil Sorsky, 233–34
Nobili, Roberto de, 269

O'Higgins, Bernardo, 281
O'Malley, John W., 147
Oakley, Francis, 229
Optatus of Milevis, 170, 174
Origen, 124, 127–28, 130–33, 143, 176–77, 198, 297

Paul (apostle), 17, 25, 30–32, 35–36, 38–39, 40, 44, 46–56, 58–63, 65, 70–71, 77–78, 81, 83–84, 89–91, 94, 96, 100, 104, 113, 115, 116, 122, 125–26, 134, 136, 139, 142–45, 155, 157, 162–63, 166, 174, 190, 196, 256, 303, 339, 369, 374, 401
Paul III (pope 1534–49), 245, 251
Paul VI (pope 1963–78. Giovanni Battista Montini), 315, 319, 321–22, 325–29, 345–47, 350, 376, 378
Pelagius, 169, 171
Peter (apostle), 8, 18–20, 24, 27, 30, 32, 34, 46, 47–49, 51, 62–63, 65, 68, 71, 74–77, 83–84, 87, 96, 100–102, 113, 139–41, 143–45, 155–59, 166, 182–83, 188–90, 193, 195, 212, 224, 227, 231, 236–38, 265, 290, 369, 381, 384–85
Peter Damian, 191, 195
Peter Lombard, 200, 210
Peter Waldo, 204
Philip IV (king of France), 212
Philips, Gérard, x, 319–20

Index of Names 397

Pippin III, 181–82
Pius IV (pope 1559–65), 251, 255, 259
Pius V (pope 1566–72), 255, 259–60, 282
Pius VI (pope 1775–99), 276–77
Pius VII (pope 1800–1823), 276
Pius IX (pope 1846–78), 281–84, 286, 291, 300–301, 305, 313, 323–24, 327
Pius X (pope 1903–14), 277, 285, 301–2, 314, 324, 384
Pius XI (pope 1922–39), 286, 291, 306
Pius XII (pope 1939–58), 300, 303, 311–13, 318, 327, 385
Pole, Reginald, 250
Pottmeyer, Hermann, 362
Przywara, Erich, 312

Rahner, Karl, 367–68
Ratzinger, Joseph. *See* Benedict XVI (pope)
Ricci, Matteo, 269
Ricoeur, Paul, 331
Romero, Oscar, 346
Ruddy, Christopher, 374

Sailer, Johann Michael, 293
Saul (king), 3
Saul. *See* Paul (apostle)
Savonarola, Girolamo, 239
Scheeben, Matthias Joseph, 292, 296–97
Schleiermacher, Friedrich, 292–93
Schmemann, Alexander, 150
Sergius of Radonezh, 228–29
Shan, Paul (cardinal), 352
Simeon the New Theologian, 229
Siricius (pope 384–99), 157

Sixtus V (pope 1585–90), 260–61
Solomon, 3, 22
Spadaro, Antonio, 380
Stapleton, Thomas, 261
Stephen (protomartyr), 43, 45, 49, 84, 113
Stephen (pope 254–57), 145
Stephen II (pope 752–57), 181
Suenens, Léon-Josef, 318–19

Taylor, Charles, 358
Teresa of Avila, 266–68, 293
Tertullian, 130, 133, 169, 174
Theodosius (emperor), 148, 167, 172
Theodulph, 183–84
Thomas à Kempis, 293
Thomas Aquinas, ix, 170, 207, 209–11, 213, 284, 330
Tillard, J.-M.-R., 102, 361
Torquemada, Juan de, 227–28
Tromp, Sebastian, 311

Valignano, Alessandro, 269
Victor Emmanuel II, 291
Victor I (pope ca. 189–ca. 198), 145
Vladimir, Prince, 186

William Durandus, 203
William of Ockham, 216, 227
William of St. Thiery, 200
Wojtyla, Karol. *See* John Paul II (pope)

Xavier, Francis, 268
Ximénez de Cisneros, Francisco, 239

Zabarella, Francesco, 220–21
Zwingli, Ulrich, 246–47

Index of Subjects

abbā, 10, 13–14, 41
Acts of the Apostles, 18, 30, 33–34, 36–39, 42, 46–49, 51, 81–88, 160, 190, 385, 389
Africa, church in, 140, 145–46, 152, 171, 347–49, 357, 364, 372
Agape-Eucharist, 120
aggiornamento, 316–17, 343, 356, 359
Albigensians, 283
allegory, 79, 198, 244
alter Christus, 184
Ambrosian Rite, 167, 260
AMECEA, 349
Americanism, 300
Anglicanism, 251, 297
Annales Ecclesiastici (Baronius), 265
Antioch, 36, 45–51, 65, 70, 121, 125, 144, 146, 151, 154, 181
Antioch, patriarchate, 231
Antioch, school at, 128
Aparecida, conference, 347, 378–79
apocalyptic, 6, 11, 64, 107, 109, 208–9, 239, 282
apophatic tradition, 29
apostle, 18, 50, 56, 58, 60, 62, 65, 81, 87, 93, 95–96, 108, 136, 138–39, 141, 143–44, 148, 150, 178, 190, 205, 211, 215–16, 227, 237–38, 252, 257, 267, 290, 322, 331, 384
Apostles' Creed, 59, 129, 210
Apostles of the Slavs (John Paul II), 186, 371

apostolic period, 30, 202
apostolic see, 144, 146, 157, 170, 189, 206, 220, 237, 241
apostolic succession, 135, 138–39
apostolic tradition, 65, 123, 128, 138–39, 146, 237, 252, 291
Apostolic Tradition, The, 123, 138
apostolicity (of the church), 138, 164, 203–4, 237–38
ascension of Christ, 33, 85, 89, 163, 218, 334
Asia, church in, 268–69, 349–53, 357, 364, 366, 372
Aufklärung Catholicism, 292
Augsburg Confession, 245–46
Augsburg, Peace of, 278
authority in the church, 24, 37, 58, 77, 79–80, 90, 101–3, 113, 138, 140–41, 143, 145, 150–51, 153, 155, 158, 180, 187, 193–94, 204, 211–12, 214–16, 224, 227, 232, 237–38, 242, 246–47, 264, 267, 271, 282, 302, 318, 323, 333, 363
authority, civil, 104, 111, 151–53, 157, 174, 186, 214–15, 234, 250, 253, 263
authority, collegial, 290, 320, 325
authority, conciliar, 153, 215, 226, 236, 255
authority, episcopal, 138, 140, 145, 150, 158–59, 163, 166, 214, 238, 261, 272, 290, 380

authority, imperial, 152–53, 158, 193
authority of the Pentarchy, 231
authority, papal, 145, 155, 157, 159, 188–89, 191–92, 194, 204, 209, 211–12, 214–15, 217, 220, 224–27, 231–32, 236, 243, 254, 261, 271–73, 279, 282, 286, 290–91, 325, 327, 372
Avignon, 215–16, 218, 228, 235

Babylonian Captivity of the Church (Luther), 243, 252
baptism of Jesus, 7, 83
baptism of John, 7, 36
baptism, 28, 36–37, 52–53, 57, 69, 78, 80, 95, 102, 117–20, 124, 126, 128, 130–32, 140, 145–46, 149, 155, 160–63, 169, 172, 175, 184, 187, 195–96, 229, 232, 236, 242–43, 245–46, 249, 256, 306, 335–36, 339, 384–85, 397
baptismal creed, 129
Baroque Catholicism, 263, 269–70, 272, 277
Basel, Council of, 225–27, 231, 252
basilica, 148–49, 160, 205
Beloved Disciple, 8, 27, 94–95
Bible de Jérusalem, 303
biblical interpretation, 2, 303
binding and loosing, 77, 188
bishop, 90, 121–22, 129, 133, 136–46, 148–55, 157–62, 169–71, 175, 186–89, 192, 196–97, 201, 214–15, 217–18, 224, 238, 242, 245, 253–55, 258–59, 261, 263, 272, 276, 288–90, 299, 307, 316, 319–20, 325, 327–28, 333, 338, 356, 359–60, 365, 371, 381, 386
bishop of Rome, 133, 144–45, 152, 154–55, 157–59, 166, 181, 187–90, 232, 290, 371, 380. *See also* pope

body of Christ (church), 38, 40, 53–57, 98, 117, 129, 161–64, 166–68, 184, 187, 196–97, 200–201, 208, 210, 229, 256–57, 268, 289, 295–96, 302–3, 305, 310–12, 318, 320, 322, 334–35, 359, 362, 368–69, 374–75
Body of Christ (Eucharist), 196–97, 200–201, 210, 258, 309, 368
Books of the Sentences (Peter Lombard), 200, 210
bread of life discourse, 25, 95
breaking of bread, 37, 39–40
breviary, 255, 259
bridegroom, 11, 57, 109, 130, 168, 198, 244, 266, 268, 371. *See also* nuptial imagery
brothers (early Christian designation), 35, 61
Byzantine Christianity, 186
Byzantium. *See* Constantinople, city of

Calvinism, 253
canon law, 157, 194–95, 204, 294, 299, 358, 363
Canterbury, archbishop of, 250, 321
Carolingian period, 180, 184, 186–87, 195, 203
Catechism of the Catholic Church (1992), 358–59
Catechism of the Council of Trent, 255–59
catechumens, 150, 175, 262
Cathari, 204–5
cathedral schools, 199–200
Catholic Action, 286
Catholic Romanticism, 292–93
Catholicisme (de Lubac), 308, 310

catholicity (of the church), 164, 170, 203, 236, 264, 337
CELAM, 344, 346, 379
Celestial Hierarchy (Denys Areopagite), 175
Chalcedon, Council of, 153–55, 157, 295, 389–91
charisms, 59, 89, 95, 311, 315, 339, 358, 360
Charity in Truth (Benedict XVI), 376
Chrétiens Désunis (Congar), 305
Christ the King, 282–83
Christendom, 245, 278, 280, 284, 342
Christian base community (CEB), 345–47, 349
Christian Nobility of the German Nation, To the (Luther), 242, 253
Christianity and the World Religions (ITC), 365
Christians (first time used), 36, 46
Christifideles Laici (John Paul II), 363
church and state, 214, 229, 233, 272, 279, 282, 288, 322–23
church as bride, 57–58, 196, 199, 224, 241, 310
church as *collegium*, 272, 274
church as communion, 38, 43, 49, 53, 55, 77, 99, 113, 145–46, 163, 170, 187, 233, 247–48, 257, 262–63, 290, 306, 313, 325, 329, 336, 340, 347, 349–50, 355–57, 359–61, 370, 374–75
church as God's family, 348, 370
church as mother, 117, 129–30, 142, 149, 169, 184, 192, 199, 207, 217, 248, 260, 265, 368–69, 378, 380
church as mystery, ix, 57, 128, 177, 200, 210, 274, 295–96, 310, 312, 319–20, 334, 340, 354–55, 357, 361, 382
church as spouse, 11, 130, 189, 206, 217, 223, 226, 256, 265–66, 373
church as virgin, 117, 130
church, local, 59, 90, 113, 121, 133, 140, 158, 166, 259, 272, 274, 292, 309, 328, 333, 336–38, 348–49, 352, 357, 360–62
church militant, 198, 217, 223, 256, 268
Church of England, 250
church of the poor, 318
church triumphant, 198, 217, 256, 268
church, universal, 55, 59, 157, 159, 166, 170, 183, 211, 215, 219, 224, 256, 273, 289, 325, 333, 336–38, 347, 358, 360–62, 365, 369, 371, 375, 381
church "without spot or wrinkle," 57, 132, 170, 223
circumcision, 13, 46, 48–51
City of God (Augustine), 172–73, 209, 213
Clement, First Letter of, 131, 136–38, 144
Clement, Second Letter of, 131
Clericis laicos (Boniface VIII), 212
Cluny, 190
Code of Canon Law (1983), 358
college of bishops, 146, 231, 321, 325, 381
college of cardinals, 219, 227
collegiality, 320, 322, 328, 350, 356, 359, 374, 381
Colossians, Letter to, 52, 55–56, 58–59, 110
communion of local churches, 113, 146, 337, 357, 361

communion of saints, 257, 296
communion with God, 201, 230, 310, 356, 360
conciliar theory, 219–21
conciliarism, 251, 273
concordat, 274, 302, 322
Concordia Discordantium Canonum (Gratian), 194
concubinage, 190
Confessional Age, 271
congregatio (church as), 24, 52–53, 122, 149, 166, 216, 227, 237, 247, 270, 361
Congregations (Roman), 261, 283, 316
Congregation for the Doctrine of the Faith (CDF), 285, 315, 353, 360–61, 364–65, 370, 372, 374, 377
Congregation for the Propagation of the Faith, 268
Congregation of Rites, 260
Congregation of the Council, 259
Congress of Vienna, 375–76
Constance, Council of, 220–22, 224–26, 231, 235, 237
Constantinople, city of (formerly Byzantium), 149, 151–52, 157, 166, 176, 181, 189, 206, 228, 233
Constantinople, First Council of (381), 153–55, 164
Constantinople, Second Council of (553), 390
Constantinople, Third Council of (680), 391
Constantinople, patriarch of, 181, 189, 191, 329
Constantinople, See of, 154–56, 177, 189, 230–31
convocation (church as), 52
Corinth, community at, 39, 51

corpus Christi mysticum, 196, 309
corpus Christi verum, 196, 309
Corpus Mysticum (de Lubac), 309
counter-revolutionary mysticism, 282
covenant, 2–3, 7, 12, 25–26, 34, 38, 40, 48, 50, 52, 54, 83, 105–6, 108, 117, 126, 134, 141, 156, 335, 369, 382
cuius regio, eius religio, 279
Curia (Roman), 194–95, 218, 259, 261, 356

Daniel, book of, 5, 6, 197
De Concordantia Catholica (Cusa), 225
De Ecclesia (Hus), 223
De Ecclesia (Wyclif), 217
deacons, 90–91, 122, 133, 136–38, 150, 175, 192, 249
Decretists, 194
Decretum Gratiani, 194
Defensor Pacis (Marsilius of Padua), 215–16
deification, 164, 175, 230, 266
democracy in the church, 211
deutero-Pauline texts, 52, 54–55, 58, 122, 335
development of doctrine, 327
devotio moderna, 238, 240
diakonoi, 90, 136
dialogue, 283, 322, 348–53, 366, 379
Dialogue (Catherine of Siena), 218
Dialogue with Trypho (Justin Martyr), 134
Diaspora, 4, 20, 42, 45
Dictatus Papae, 192
Didache, 118, 120, 136
Diet of Speyer, 251
diocese, 140, 154–55, 192, 211, 215, 254, 261, 263, 276, 289–90, 309, 333, 336, 338, 349

402 The Church

Diognetus, Letter to, 118–19, 134
disciples of Jesus, chaps. 1–3
    passim, 93–98, 100–102, 104, 109,
    111, 159, 229, 347, 353, 379, 382,
    384, 386, 388–89
disciples of John the Baptist, 7–8
Disputations on the Controversies of
    Christian Faith (Bellarmine), 261
divinization, 175, 249
Divino Afflante Spiritu (Pius XII),
    303, 385
Dogmatic Constitution on the
    Catholic Faith (Vatican I), 286
Dominus Iesus (CDF), 365–66, 374
Donation of Constantine, 181
Donatists, 169–71, 217
drum, use in liturgy, 349
Du Pape (de Maistre), 279

Easter, 24, 30, 33, 35, 40, 112, 117,
    129, 135, 144–45, 161, 206
Eastern Christianity, 152, 154, 159,
    162, 166–67, 174, 176–77, 179,
    181–84, 188, 191, 206–7, 225, 228–
    30, 232, 289, 307, 317, 325–26, 333
Eastern (Roman) Empire, 147, 149,
    151, 157, 166, 181–82, 225
Eastern Orthodoxy, 174, 228, 229,
    307
Ebionites, 125
Ecclesia de Eucharistia (John Paul II),
    370
Ecclesia de hominibus, 356
Ecclesia de Trinitate, 356
Ecclesia in Africa (John Paul II), 348
Ecclesia in Asia (John Paul II), 352
Ecclesiastical Hierarchy (Denys
    Areopagite), 175
Ecclesiastical Ordinances (Calvin),
    249

ecumenical council, 153, 222, 231,
    291
ecumenism, 59, 305, 320, 322, 324,
    326, 336, 342, 359
Einheit in der Kirche (Möhler), 294–
    95
ekklēsia (church), 51–53
elders, 44, 50, 84, 103–4, 136–37,
    211, 215, 249
elect (early Christian designation),
    35
Elizabethan Settlement, 250
Emmaus, 32, 88
end time, 5, 15, 17, 23–24, 28, 32–34,
    42, 55
Enlightenment, 269, 274–75, 277–
    78, 286, 292
eparchy, 154
Ephesians, Letter to, 52, 55–61, 110,
    130, 244, 252, 256, 297
Ephesus, Council of, 153
epieikeia, 219
episcopal conferences, 348–49, 351,
    354, 356, 372
episkopos, 90, 150
eschaton, 5
Essay on the Development of Christian
    Doctrine (Newman), 298
Essenes, 21
Eucharist, 25, 32, 39–40, 54, 60, 71,
    88, 94–95, 113–14, 117–18, 120–
    24, 128, 134–38, 140–41, 146, 148,
    150, 155, 160–61, 163, 166, 168,
    174–75, 185, 187, 196–97, 200–
    201, 210, 224, 232, 247, 249, 253,
    258, 309–10, 325, 332–33, 360,
    368, 370–71, 374–75, 379–80, 385
eucharistic ecclesiology, 124, 166,
    197
evangelization, 49, 339, 346–48, 378

Index of Subjects   403

Evangelization in the Modern World (Paul VI), 346
ex cathedra, 291
exile (Babylonian), 4, 36, 109
exodus (from Egypt), 4, 40, 102–3, 135, 295
Exodus, book of, 26, 102–3, 178, 311
Explanation of the Divine Liturgy (William Durandus), 203
Exposition on the Creed (Aquinas), 210
Ezekiel, book of, 26, 57, 107

FABC (Federation of Asian Bishops Conferences), 350–51, 353
Face of Mercy (*Misericordiae Vultus*; Pope Francis), 381
False Decretals, 188–89
fasting, 11, 22, 28, 167
Febronianism, 273
fellowship meals, 40
Ferrara-Florence, Council of, 225, 228, 230–33, 321
feudal system, 180, 186–87, 192, 278
filioque, 184, 232
Final Report (Synod of 1985), 354–57
First Dogmatic Constitution on the Church of Christ (Vatican I), 290–91
First Vatican Council, 286–92, 319–20, 322, 326, 362
Fourth Gospel. *See* John (Gospel)
Fourvière, 306
freedom in the church, 216, 327, 335, 343, 369
Freedom of the Christian (Luther), 244
Freemasons, 283
French Revolution, 273, 275–77, 279, 281, 286, 301

Frequens (Council of Constance), 222, 225

Gallican Articles, 273
Gallicanism, 308
Gaul, 66, 144, 146, 180
Genesis, 2, 12
Gentiles, 23–24, 29, 45–48, 50, 54–55, 76, 89, 102–3, 118, 143, 210, 367, 385
German bishops at Synod of 1985, 354–55
German bishops at Vatican II, 328
German Romanticism, 284, 292
Gesù, 269
Gnostics, 100, 122, 125, 132, 144
God Is Love (*Deus Caritas Est*; Benedict XVI), 375
God-fearers, 46–48
Gothic cathedrals, 201–2
government in the church, 211, 213, 215, 227, 264, 272, 279
grace, 84, 108, 123, 128, 172, 199–201, 209–11, 217, 223, 236, 242–43, 252, 257, 263, 270–71, 295, 297, 308, 311, 315, 336, 339, 356, 358, 369
graduality, principle of, 352
Great Western Schism, 218
Greek East, 101, 155, 162, 164, 166–67, 174–79
Gregorian Reform, 193–94, 278, 330

Haec Sancta (Council of Constance), 221, 237
Hagia Sophia, 175, 191
harlot, symbol of church, 131
Hebrew Christians, 42–43, 45
Hebrews, Letter to the, 49, 104–6, 112, 126

404   The Church

Hellenists, 42–47, 49, 51, 71, 77, 84, 105
hermeneutic of reform (Benedict XVI), 376
hermeneutic of rupture, 378
hesychasts, 229–30
hierarchical church, 265
hierarchy, 175, 177, 195, 226, 248, 250, 286, 306, 311–13, 320, 325, 337, 339, 363
historical consciousness, 189, 254, 288, 324
historical criticism, 285, 303–4, 307, 383, 385–88
historical development, 31, 193, 241, 254, 283–94, 298, 311
holiness (of the church), 59, 103, 119, 123, 132, 164, 203, 236, 257, 287, 300
holiness, call to, 320, 337–38
Holy Church (Chelčický), 236
Holy Office, 285, 313, 317
Holy See, 139, 279
Holy Spirit, 50, 54, 81, 83, 89–90, 99, 112, 117, 119, 123, 129, 142, 163–64, 169, 171, 199, 208–9, 211, 226, 236, 248, 252, 256, 262, 289–90, 293, 305, 312, 331, 335, 340–41, 369, 373
homoousios, 153
Hosea, book of, 57, 102
household codes, 58
Humani Generis (Pius XII), 285, 313

icon, 177–78, 183, 188
iconoclasm, 177–78
Imitation of Christ, 238
immaculate conception, 282, 298
imperium, 212
incarnate Word, 94, 232, 335

incarnation, x, 89, 98, 105, 123, 169, 177, 186, 199, 210, 255, 295–97, 305, 312, 374
inculturation, 186, 347–50, 356, 358, 371
Index of Prohibited Books, 255, 259, 304
indulgences, 242
infallibility of the church, 291
infallibility of the pope, 279, 289–91, 298, 322
in solidum (Cyprian), 141
Institutes of the Christian Religion (Calvin), 247–48
Instruction on Certain Aspects of the "Theology of Liberation" (CDF), 364
Instruction on Christian Freedom and Liberation (CDF), 364
International Theological Commission, 354, 357, 363
intersessions (Vatican II), 317, 319, 326
investiture, 190, 192
Islam, 176, 178, 181, 183, 323, 342

James, leader of Jerusalem community, 30, 44, 47–51, 62, 65, 71, 77, 84, 91
James, Letter of, 62, 65, 91–92, 112
Jamnia, 64, 77, 98, 114
Jansenism, 271, 273
Jerusalem (city), 3–4, 19, 22, 25, 30, 34, 39, 42, 45, 47, 63, 79, 81, 82, 113, 149, 151, 176–77
Jerusalem (Christian community at), 37, 39, 43–45, 47–48, 50, 62, 65, 82, 84, 91, 361
Jerusalem conference, 49–51, 82–83, 367

Jerusalem (heavenly), 108, 111
Jerusalem patriarchate, 155, 181, 231
Jesuit order. *See* Society of Jesus
Jesuit School of Theology (Rome), 296
Jesus movement, 1–2, 13–14, 20, 27–28
Jesus, understanding of, 388–91
Jesus' meals, 14, 21, 28, 32
Jewish revolt, 62–63, 65–66, 114
Job, book of, 198
Johannine community, 8, 94, 98–100
Johannine School, 94, 101
John (Gospel), 8, 18, 23, 25, 27, 32–33, 44, 49, 57, 65, 91–98, 100–101
John (Letters), 98–100
Joint Declaration (Paul VI and Patriarch Athenagoras; 1965), 329
Josephism, 273
Journey of the Mind into God (Bonaventure), 207
Joy of the Gospel (*Evangelii Gaudium*; Pope Francis), 378
Judaism, 4, 6, 12, 20–22, 28, 30, 35, 37, 40, 42–43, 46, 49, 62, 64–65, 70, 78–82, 84, 103, 105, 110, 112–14, 134–35, 151, 207, 264, 308, 342, 384–85, 388. *See also* Second Temple Judaism *and* post-Jamnia Judaism
Jude (Letter), 65, 112
jurisdiction, power of, 166, 188, 197, 215, 217, 258, 290, 311, 328
jurisdiction, primacy of, 166, 188, 290–91
jurisdiction, universal, 219, 263, 329

kenosis ecclesiology, 352–53
Kievan Rus, 186, 228
kingdom of God (reign of God), 7–9, 13, 26, 34–36, 56, 67–68, 72, 80, 94, 334–35, 351, 384, 388
koinōnia, 53
Kulturkampf, 273

La civiltà cattolica, 280, 286
lapsi (the "fallen"), 140
Last Supper, 25–26, 32, 80, 87–88, 106, 385
Lateran Council IV (1215), 206–7
Lateran Council V (1512–17), 240, 255
Latin America, 344–47
Latin West, 101, 155–56, 162, 167, 174, 179
Laudato Si' (Pope Francis), 380
Law. *See* Torah
lay faithful, 166, 185, 201, 215, 254, 289, 299, 306, 333, 335, 339, 359, 363–64
lay observers (at Vatican II), 329
Lay People in the Church (Congar), 306
Lectures on the Hexaëmeron (Bonaventure), 207
Letter . . . Some Aspects of the Church as Communion (CDF), 360
liberation theology, 364–65
libertas, 190
Libri Carolini, 183
Life of Antony (Athanasius), 160
liturgical movement, 302–3
local church, 59, 90, 113, 121, 133, 140, 158, 166, 259, 272, 274, 292, 309, 328, 333, 336–37, 348–49, 352, 357–58, 360–62

Lollards, 217
Lord's Prayer, 10, 28, 41, 85, 119, 140, 142, 255
L'Osservatore Romano, 304, 361
Luke (Gospel), 8–11, 14–19, 23–25, 27, 32–34, 39, 41, 44, 57, 66, 74, 77, 81–88, 104, 108, 110, 112, 115, 158, 171, 369, 385
Lumen Gentium. See Second Vatican Council, documents: Dogmatic Constitution on the Church
Lyons I and II, Councils of, 212, 228

Magdeburg Centuries, 264
magisterium, 211, 261, 291, 331
Malachi, book of, 5, 114, 121, 135
Marana tha, 41
Marian piety, 282
Mark (Gospel), 8, 9, 11, 16, 18–19, 22–27, 32, 39, 41, 44, 57, 66–70, 71, 85, 87, 104, 109, 111, 190
martyria, 149
Mary Magdalene, 96
Mary, mother of the church, 202, 326
Mary, type of the church, 167, 368
Mass, 106, 129, 185, 204, 243, 252–53, 260, 270, 302
Matthew (Gospel), 16–18, 23–25, 27, 44, 51, 66, 70–81, 104, 108, 112, 125, 128, 140, 145, 156, 162, 165, 187–88, 221, 245, 338, 384–85, 388
Medellín, conference, 344–47
Mediator Dei (Pius XII), 303
medieval Christendom, 278, 280, 284
Méditations sur l'Eglise (de Lubac), 310
mendicant orders, 206, 211, 219, 258, 269

Messiah, 6, 22, 32, 34, 40, 42, 63, 78, 108, 114
Mind's Ascent to God (Bellarmine), 263
ministry as priestly service, 54
ministry in the church, 47, 54, 59, 60–61, 71, 76–79, 85, 87, 135–38, 141–42, 160, 164, 205, 216, 218, 249, 256, 259, 264, 266, 338–39, 346, 360, 371
missal, 123, 255, 259–60
Mission of the Redeemer (John Paul II), 365
missionary activity, 65, 112, 328–29, 337, 339, 373
Modern Roman Catholicism, 276–78, 285–86
modernism, 285, 301, 304, 313
modernity, 282, 291, 324, 376
monarchy (papal), 187, 189, 209, 211, 215–16, 265, 279
monasticism, 160–61, 237, 240
moon-symbolism of church fathers, 131, 374
Mozarabic Rite, 260
Mulieris Dignitatem (John Paul II), 371
Munich, congress at, 283
mystērion, 252
mystical body, 196–97, 208, 210, 218, 226, 258, 287–88, 302, 309–12, 318, 320
Mystici Corporis (Pius XII), 311

neo-Donatism, 217
neoscholasticism, 302, 304
New Testament, 18, 30, 38, 70, 92, 97, 101–3, 105–6, 113–14, 125–26, 134, 136–37, 139, 146, 150, 239, 264, 327, 383, 385, 390

Index of Subjects   407

New Testament images of church
   Colossians and Ephesians, 52,
     54–59
   First Letter of Peter, 102–4
   Hebrews, 104–7
   James, 62, 91–92
   Johannine Letters, 98–100
   John (Fourth Gospel), 91–98,
     100–101
   Letters of Paul, 38, 51–55, 59–62
   Luke-Acts, 33, 36, 38–39, 81–88,
     104, 108, 110, 112, 115
   Mark, 66–70, 71, 77, 104, 109,
     111
   Matthew, 23, 70–81, 104, 112
   Pastoral Letters, 88–91
   Revelation, 107–11
Nicaea, 152–54, 166
Nicaea, Second Council of, 178,
   183, 188
non-Christian religions, 310, 322,
   324, 326, 342
Non-Possessors, 233–34
North Africa, 123, 130, 140, 144,
   146, 152, 170–71, 180–81
notes of the church, 164, 213, 235,
   238, 245, 256, 268
nouvelle théologie, 304
nuptial imagery, 11, 57, 130, 168,
   198, 268, 368. *See also*
   bridegroom

oath against modernism, 285
oaths, 12–13, 28, 92
Old Testament, 4, 9, 11, 38, 52, 68,
   79, 83, 102, 107, 122, 125–27, 130,
   141, 156, 174, 202–4, 288, 335
"On Consulting the Faithful in
   Matters of Doctrine" (Newman),
   299

On the Councils and the Church
   (Luther), 245
On the Development of Peoples
   (Populorum Progressio;* Paul VI),
   345
On the Papacy in Rome (Luther), 244
On the Truth of Sacred Scripture
   (Wycliff), 217
On the Unity of the Catholic Church
   (Cyprian), 140–41, 145
ordination, 106, 170, 187, 197, 201,
   236, 325, 328, 338
ordo (order), 150–51
Orthodox Christians, 174, 177–78,
   225, 228, 230, 233–34, 305, 333,
   360, 381
other Christians, 174, 177–78, 225,
   228, 230, 233–34, 305, 333, 360, 381
other religions, 59, 320, 342, 349,
   365, 373

papal magisterium, 290–91
papal sovereignty, 213, 277, 279–80,
   291
Papal States, 281, 291
parables, 9, 14, 57, 67, 72–73, 75,
   85–86, 94
Paraclete-Spirit, 94, 96–97, 99, 101,
   112
paradise, 176
parishes, 149, 195, 347, 349
Passover, 25, 33, 40, 102, 135, 144–
   45
Pastoral Letters, 88–90, 125
Pastoral Rule (Gregory I), 159
patrimony of Peter, 181
patristic period, chaps. 3 and 4,
   115–16, 147, 157, 160, 174, 177,
   179, 197, 213, 217, 224, 239, 294,
   330, 374

Pentateuch, 48, 382
Pentecost, 33–34, 38, 83, 169, 361
people of God, 22, 50, 52, 103, 106, 117, 121, 126, 130, 135, 208, 288, 303, 309, 311, 318, 320, 331, 335–36, 339–40, 355, 357–58, 362, 368, 370, 379–81
perfect society, 272, 274, 282, 289, 315
Peri Pascha (Melito of Sardis), 135
persecution of Jews, 151, 207
Peter, Gospel of, 125
Petrine ministry, 76–77, 87, 380. *See also* pope *and* primacy
Pharisees, 21–22, 36–37, 48, 64, 76
Pisa, Council of, 219
plebs (people), 151
Politics (Aristotle), 221
Pontifical Biblical Commission, 285, 301, 383–86, 389
Poor Men of Lyons, 204
poor, concern for, 3, 39, 50, 85–86, 92, 112, 119, 160, 165, 205, 234, 268, 300, 318, 323, 345–47, 350, 352, 354, 356, 365, 378–79
pope, 191–95, 207, 213–14, 216–17, 219–24, 227, 231–32, 236–37, 242–44, 246, 250, 254–55, 257, 261, 263, 273, 277, 279–82, 284, 288, 290–91, 299, 307–8, 315, 321, 325, 328, 356, 363, 381. *See also* bishop of Rome
Possessors, 234
post-Jamnia Judaism, 98, 114
postmodernity, 366
poverty (of the church), 191, 217, 224, 233, 236, 318, 328, 378
power of orders, 258. *See also* ordination
prayer, 4, 10–11, 28, 35, 37, 41, 52, 56, 62, 82, 85, 87, 92, 98, 112, 120,
122–23, 131, 140, 151, 160, 183, 185, 229–30, 234, 245, 255, 267–68, 270, 308, 333, 350, 352, 386
preferential option for the poor, 346–47
Preliminary Explanatory Note (Vatican II), 325
presbyteros, 90
presbyter, 44, 84, 133, 136–38, 141, 144, 148–50, 338
priesthood (Christian), 78, 90, 103, 114, 137, 141–42, 150, 159, 169–70, 175, 183, 185, 187, 197, 201, 204, 212, 214–15, 217, 224, 236, 242–43, 249, 253, 258, 264, 270, 329, 338, 371, 385
priesthood (Jewish), 7, 21–23, 62, 103, 137, 141
priesthood of all believers, 249
priestly people, 102–3, 106, 109–10, 132, 166, 249, 258
primacy of honor, 155, 224
primacy (of the pope), 141, 145, 155, 157–59, 166, 214–15, 224–25, 227, 231, 280, 290–91, 322, 326, 358, 371, 374, 381, 384
prophet, priest, king, 298, 306, 338–39
proprietary church, 186, 188, 195
Protestants, 240, 251, 264, 295
Providentissimus Deus (Leo XIII), 383
Psalms of Solomon, 5
Psalter, 198
Puebla, conference, 346
purgatory, 217, 223, 242

Qahal Yahweh, 52
Quanta cura (Pius IX), 282
Quartodeciman, 144–45

Index of Subjects   409

Qumran, 17, 21, 36, 39, 44
Quod omnes tangit ab omnibus tractari debet, 381

Ratzinger Report, 353, 372
Ravenna, 176, 181
Redeemer of Man (John Paul II), 370
reform in head and members, 220, 254
reform of the church, 59, 108, 160, 180, 186–87, 190–93, 204–6, 215–16, 219–23, 226, 236, 238–42, 247, 249–54, 256, 258–59, 261, 267, 269, 272, 278, 305–7, 322, 330, 376
reign of God. *See* kingdom of God
religious liberty (freedom), 281, 313, 321–24, 329, 343, 376
religious orders, 218, 221, 317, 319
religious tolerance, 322–23
rescripts, 157, 162
respublica christiana, 272
ressourcement, 301, 303, 306–7, 313, 317, 319, 329, 333, 343
resurrection of Christ, 7, 11, 14–15, 17, 28–29, 31–35, 40, 42, 45, 63, 66, 70–71, 75, 77, 80, 88–89, 104, 145, 163, 168, 173, 385–86
Revelation, book of, 194, 107–12, 114
rhetoric of the fathers, 162, 320, 330
rhetoric of Vatican II, 319–20, 330
Roman Catholicism, 270–71, 277–79, 282–86
Roman Empire, 45, 64, 70, 113, 115, 136, 141, 147, 180–82. *See also* Eastern (Roman) Empire
Roman Missal (Pius V), 123, 259–60
Roman North Africa, 123, 140–43, 145, 152

Romanesque period, 184–85
Rome, bishop of, 133, 145, 152, 154–60, 162, 166, 181, 188, 218, 231–32, 246, 258, 261, 268, 273, 276, 290, 371, 380
Rome, church of, 60–62, 66, 104, 117, 122–23, 128–29, 136–37, 139, 141, 143–46, 155–57, 166, 170, 182–83, 189, 207, 224, 233, 259, 277, 280, 283, 348, 381
Rome, city of, 62–63, 82, 102, 108, 111, 119, 121, 144, 171–72, 180–81, 191, 218, 242, 260–61, 269, 291, 296, 304, 313
Rule of St. Benedict, 159, 161
Rules for Thinking with the Church, 265
Russian Orthodox Church, 228, 234

Sabbath, 12, 40, 79, 151, 208
sacrament, church as, 98, 210, 308, 332, 335, 339, 347, 353, 367, 373
sacraments, 14, 56, 69, 93, 95, 98, 130, 132, 146, 155, 161, 167–68, 170, 172, 175, 177–79, 183, 192, 195–97, 200–201, 204–5, 208, 210, 214, 217–18, 224, 227, 229–30, 232–33, 236, 242–47, 249, 250, 252–55, 257–58, 262–64, 266, 275, 297, 299, 308, 312, 320, 325, 332, 334, 336, 338, 356–57, 360, 379, 383–84
Sacred Heart, 282–83
Sadducees, 22, 36, 76
saints (early Christian designation), 35
salvation outside the church, 263
San Vitale, 176
sanctuary (of a church), 148, 177, 185, 203

410 The Church

Santo Domingo, conference, 347
Saulchoir, Le, 304
schema 13, 319, 323, 378
schism, 45, 99, 112, 140–41, 145, 152, 170, 177, 180, 191, 218–22, 224–25, 227, 230–31, 235–37, 254, 306
scholasticism, 199, 283, 296. *See also* neoscholasticism
SECAM (Symposium of Episcopal Conferences of Africa and Madagascar), 348
Second Temple Judaism, 4–6, 30, 36, 47, 62–63, 390
Second Vatican Council, documents
  Constitution on the Sacred Liturgy (*Sacrosanctum Concilium*), 332–34
  Declaration on Religious Liberty, 327, 329, 342
  Declaration on the Relation of the Church to Non-Christian Religions, 322, 324, 326, 342
  Decree on Ecumenism, 59, 322, 324, 326, 336
  Decree on the Apostolate of Lay People, 339, 358
  Decree on the Catholic Eastern Churches, 326
  Decree on the Church's Missionary Activity, 328–29, 337, 339
  Decree on the Ministry and Life of Priests, 329, 338
  Dogmatic Constitution on Divine Revelation (*Dei Verbum*), 331–32
  Dogmatic Constitution on the Church (*Lumen Gentium*), 320, 334–42, 361
  Pastoral Constitution on the Church in the Modern World

  (*Gaudium et Spes*), 319, 322–23, 326, 329, 339–40, 342, 346, 356
Second Vatican Council, history, 315–29
Second Vatican Council, theology of the church, 329–43
sect of the Nazarenes, 36
self-realization of the church, 362–63, 370
sensus ecclesiae, 125
Sensus Fidei in the Life of the Church (ITC; 2014), 363
sensus fidei, 363, 381
Sermon on the Mount, 72
Service Requesting Pardon (John Paul II; 2000), 371
Shekinah, 75
Shema Israel, 41
simony, 190–91
Slavorum Apostoli (John Paul II), 371
small Christian community (SCC), 348
social discipline, 253
socialism, 278, 283
Society of Jesus, 258, 265–66, 280, 303, 306, 307
Soli Deo Gloria, 249
Song of Songs, 127, 130, 143, 162, 198, 256, 267–68
Sources chrétiennes, 307
Sources of Renewal (Wojtyla), 370
Special Assembly for Asia of the Synod of Bishops, 351–52
Spiritual Exercises (Ignatius of Loyola), 265
Spiritual Franciscans, 208, 216
state churches, 272
subsists in, 336
Summa de Ecclesia (Torquemada), 227

Index of Subjects   411

Summa Theologiae (Aquinas), 210
Surnaturel (de Lubac), 309–10
Syllabus of Errors, 282–83, 324
Symbolik (Möhler), 294–95
synagogue, 4, 20, 41, 45–46, 48, 64–65, 79, 86, 99, 114, 121, 135, 151, 202
synaxis (Eucharist), 121
Synod of 1985, 353–57, 375, 378
Synod of Bishops, 327–28, 344, 346, 351, 356, 364, 372, 381
synodality, 381
Synoptics, 8, 23, 25, 27, 94, 111

temple of Jerusalem (Herod), 6–7, 12, 21–23, 30, 39, 41–43, 45, 49, 62–64, 79–80, 105, 113–14, 151, 385
temple of Solomon, 3–4
temple of the Spirit (church), 109, 300, 335, 340, 355, 362
temporal power (of the pope), 160, 181, 281, 291
That All May Be One (Ut Unum Sint; John Paul II), 336, 370
The Shepherd, 118–19, 131
theological method, 193, 199, 324, 232, 239
Théologie, 307
theology of the body, 371
Third Rome (Moscow), 233–34
Thirty Years' War, 278
"Those who call upon the name of the Lord" (early Christian designation), 35
three stages of gospel tradition, 18, 385–86
Torah (Law), chaps. 1 and 2 passim, 65, 70, 72, 77, 79, 81, 99, 125
Trent, Council of, 170, 239, 245, 251–55, 258–61, 264, 268, 271, 286, 290, 307, 317, 326, 333

Tübingen, 292–95, 298, 302, 305, 308, 311, 331
twelve tribes, 3, 17, 108
Twelve, the, 15–20, 27, 33, 42–43, 45–47, 67, 69, 82–84, 93–94, 108, 113, 118, 138, 141, 384, 389
typology, 127

Ultramontanism, 280
Unam Sanctam (Boniface VIII), 211–13, 235
Unam Sanctam (monographs), 304–5, 308
unity (of the church), 210, 235–36, 239, 256, 262
universities, 194, 199, 212, 218, 221, 284, 287
University of Louvain, 271, 319
University of Oxford, 222
University of Paris, 215, 218–19, 221, 236
University of Prague, 223

Vatican City State, 291
Vatican I. See First Vatican Council
Vatican II. See Second Vatican Council, documents
Vicar of Christ, 158, 209, 213, 244, 262, 265, 338
Vienna, Congress of, 275–76
Vienne, Council of, 212
virtue ecclesiology, 367
Vision of Innocent III (Giotto), 205
vita apostolica, 190–91, 204, 237
Vraie et fausse réforme (Congar), 305
Vulgate, 156, 185, 243, 252, 258, 271

Way (early Christian designation), 36, 68
wealth, 39, 86, 91–92, 165, 204, 224, 237

Westphalia, Peace of, 278
"What affects all must be dealt with by all," 221
whole Christ, the (*totus Christus*), 168, 311
women followers of Jesus, 16, 19–20, 27, 33
women in the church, 33, 58, 61–62, 91, 96, 112, 161, 166, 257, 262, 270–71, 339, 341, 352, 362, 371
world-church, 367

worship, 12, 21–22, 39, 41–43, 45, 54, 58, 76, 88, 104, 112, 114, 117, 121, 124, 130, 147–48, 150, 175–76, 178, 197, 202–4, 223, 234, 247–49, 252, 256, 274, 297–300, 302, 305, 331–33, 385

Year of Jubilee 2000, 321
Young Christian Workers, 286

Zealot party, 16

www.ingramcontent.com/pod-product-compliance
Lightning Source LLC
Chambersburg PA
CBHW051933290426
44110CB00015B/1958